MODERNIZATION AMONG PEASANTS

The Impact of Communication

MODERNIZATION AMONG PEASANTS

The Impact of Communication

Everett M. Rogers

in association with Lynne Svenning

Michigan State University

HOLT, RINEHART and WINSTON, INC.

New York   Chicago   San Francisco   Atlanta   Dallas
Montreal   Toronto   London   Sydney

To our respondents,
whose modernization provides
understanding of behavior change

The Natural History of an Investigation

During the first years of my academic career, my research was focused on communication and change among rural people in the United States. Since then, my interests have turned to what I consider a related, but much more important problem: investigation of the modernization of peasant villagers in less developed countries. This book is a report of such an investigation among Colombian villagers. Although the primary data come from Colombia, findings from similar settings allow for cross-cultural comparisons of our generalizations.

Researchers "go international" through a variety of random, unplanned routes, as well as through rational planning. In my case, it was in 1961 at the American Sociological Association in St. Louis, where I met Dr. Orlando Fals Borda, Decano of the Facultad de Sociología, Universidad Nacional de Colombia, Bogotá. Before I knew it, I had agreed to join his faculty as a Fulbright lecturer to teach and to conduct research. I began Spanish language preparation upon my return from St. Louis.

Several of my graduate students at The Ohio State University accompanied me to Colombia in 1963; chief among them were Johannes C. M. van Es and Ralph E. Neill. Twelve Colombian students in the Facultad de Sociología were employed in the present study; Alvarro Camacho, Elssy Bonilla de Ramos, and Eduardo Ramos were of special help in data gathering and analysis. The latter two investigators followed me to Michigan State University in 1964, and their theses research results are included in the present book.

A social scientist in an unfamiliar sociocultural setting must depend heavily upon both host country colleagues, such as the Ramoses, and upon institutional affiliation and support, such as that provided by the Facultad de Sociología and especially its Dean, Orlando Fals Borda. Although my initial sojourn in Colombia lasted only one year, it was vicariously lengthened through interaction with a former student and colleague, Eugene Havens, who preceded me by a year in his immersion in research among Colombian peasants.

Much of the Colombian data analysis and interpretation has been accomplished during the past several years while I was a faculty member of the Department of Communication at Michigan State University. One learns much from his colleagues, particularly those with a like-minded pursuit of the mysteries of communication and change in less developed countries. Chief among these osmotic intellectual influences were Frederick B. Waisanen, Hideya Kumata, John McNelly, and David K. Berlo.

Several graduate students at Michigan State University completed their theses on various aspects of the Colombian data. Testimony of their efforts appears in the chapters that follow. Chief among these students was J. David Stanfield, who assisted me in the data analysis at Michigan State and who, along with the Ramoses, conducted the follow-up data gathering in 1965 in three of the Colombian villages.

Two main sponsors had fiscal faith in the Colombian study: the Agricultural Development Council of New York and the Programa Interamericano de Información Popular (PIIP) of San José, Costa Rica.

Only a minority of the readers of this book will be interested solely in modernization in Colombia per se. Comparative data from India, Kenya, Brazil, and Turkey, and other countries have, therefore, been included in order to test generalizations of the present findings. Some of the data came from the U.S. Agency for International Development–sponsored project on Diffusion of Innovations in Rural Societies that is being conducted under my direction in Brazil, Nigeria, and India. Other data came from a UNESCO-sponsored investigation (for which I am a technical consultant) in eight Indian villages and fourteen Costa Rican villages; and from peasant respondents in two Indian and three Kenyan villages, who were interviewed by Dharam P. Yadav and Joseph Ascroft, respectively, two Ph.D. students at Michigan State University. Although there are certain hazards in comparing these data with our Colombian protocols, such danger is minimized through research designs that mimic and extend the central notions of the Colombia investigation.

Since my graduate student days, the lack of utility contained in the abstract, speculative, and prolific writings of the grand theorists on social change and economic development has been abhorrent to me, as the purely speculative nature of these works precludes empirical testing of their central notions in the foreseeable future. Our attempt in the present investigation is to demonstrate the advantage of "middle range analysis," where theories containing general concepts are tested with empirical data from the "real world." Two prototypes in this approach are intellectual leaders in the social sciences, Robert K. Merton and Daniel Lerner; both exerted strong influence on this work. An implicit theme is that middle range analysis offers the most direct route to a fruitful wedding of theory and data, with an immediate objective of testing generalizations about the role of communication in modernization.

The respondents whose behavior is analyzed are peasants, especially those living in five Colombian villages in the Andes Mountains. I feel that peasants are *the* crucial audience for programs of development and change in the world today. They constitute the majority of the population — sometimes up to 80 percent — in most less developed countries. In terms of occupation and life style, peasants are presently the largest single category of people in the world. They are also the most frustrating audience for international, national, and local programs of planned social change, evidenced by the widespread failure of many modernization programs. We fail, in part, because of our inadequate understanding of peasants and our inability to communicate effectively with them. Until there are some good books on this topic, written by peasants themselves, we must depend upon such linkages as this one. In this light, I must express thanks to the 255 Colombian peasant "coauthors" of this book (along with their counterparts in other nations) who, although their cooperation was unintended and at times reluctant, provided insight into their modernization.

East Lansing, Michigan   E.M.R.

January 1969

Contents

1

Social Change, Development, and Modernization*

Although peasantry is as old as civilization itself and constitutes the bulk of the population in the underdeveloped countries and in the world, we still have much to learn about peasants, their values, problems and aspirations, the intimate details of family living, the effects upon their lives of Western technology and culture and their potential for participation and leadership in the modern world.

(Oscar Lewis 1961: xxix)

The most difficult and complicated problem in the world today, next to the harmful effects of uncontrolled atomic energy, is modernization of the world's peasant millions. And the research devoted to modernization is not at all commensurate with its importance.

(An official in the U.S. Agency for International Development)

On the afternoon of November 22, 1963, I was in the Colombian village of Támesis, isolated deep in the Andes Mountains, where I was directing the communication research study on which this book is partly based. I was therefore in a novel position to observe the diffusion of news concerning the assassination of President Kennedy. Notice of his death first reached Támesis via radio and then was dispersed rapidly by word of mouth. Almost all the several thousand villagers knew of the fateful event within an hour or two after its occurrence in Dallas,[1] even though Támesis is five hours distant by bus from the nearest city.

The reactions were intense. By evening most village women were wearing black mourning clothes and veils, flags were draped from stores and homes, all the jukeboxes in the taverns were unplugged, and the school graduation (high point of the village's annual social season) was canceled. By the following morning a local storekeeper had obtained more than 400 signatures on a telegram of sympathy that was sent to the U.S. ambassador to Colombia.

---

*This chapter was written with assistance from John Winterton, Research Assistant, Department of Communication, Michigan State University.

[1] Greenberg and Parker (1965), after intensive search, were unable to locate a single investigation on news diffusion of the Kennedy assassination, or the reactions to it, conducted outside the United States. In fact, we have almost no research on the diffusion of news events of *any* kind outside the United States (one exception is found in Hamuy and others 1958), in spite of the fact that news diffusion has been one of the most popular topics in mass communication research during the past five years.

The rapid dissemination of news of this major event illustrates the high degree of mass media penetration, even in the remote villages of a less developed country.[2] Why was this news item spread so rapidly and why were the reactions so intense? In contrast to this instance of immediate communication, why have development agencies in these areas not been able to diffuse technological innovations with more success than the persistent failure that seems to meet their efforts?

Answers to these and related questions about the development and modernization of traditional peoples lie embedded in the interrelationships of a series of conceptual variables such as literacy, innovativeness, interpersonal and mass media communication, empathy, achievement motivation, cosmopoliteness, and fatalism. The present book attempts to increase our understanding of the theoretical relationships among such communication and modernization variables.

FOCUS OF THE PRESENT STUDY

The present volume is mainly an examination, through survey research methods, of modernization processes among 255 peasants. The place is Colombia, and the time under consideration is the mid-1960s. But our subject might well be some other Latin American, Asian, or African country, anytime between 1945 and 1975, where villagers are becoming dissatisfied with eating the cake of custom.

We shall probe the interrelationships of a number of social-psychological variables in order to determine the nature of the modernization process and the role of directed social change. The goal of the present work is to seek commonly occurring patterns of behavior among peasants that illuminate their paths toward modernization.

Another objective of the present undertaking is to demonstrate theoretical and methodological approaches to the study of modernization among peasants and, particularly, to determine the cross-cultural validity of the Colombian findings for such other less developed countries as India and Kenya. Hopefully, this book will raise provocative questions concerning modernization and will generate sufficient interest to initiate further search for answers.

Two purposes, then, guide the present survey of our field data: (1) to determine the interrelationships of modernization variables among peasants

---

[2] The convention adopted throughout this book is generally to use the term "less developed countries," rather than such current synonyms as underdeveloped, developing, traditional, or emerging. While such choice is in part arbitrary, we prefer to use "less developed" and "more developed" countries because such terminology implies a continuum of development.

in one less developed country, Colombia, and (2) to determine the cross-cultural validity of these findings for other less developed nations. In order to reach these objectives, one must first view modernization from the more general perspective of social change.

SOCIAL CHANGE

Man has long been interested in the process by which his social environment is changed. In recent years increased interest in social change has resulted in part from large-scale attempts by community, national, and international organizations to bring about directed social and economic change in the less developed countries of Asia, Africa, and Latin America.[3] Yet, in spite of this rapid pace of social change, there has been little attempt to explain the process in theoretically relevant and empirically verifiable terms. In short, no one has arrived at a theory of social change that provides a workable instrument for its systematic investigation.

WHAT IS SOCIAL CHANGE?

Social change is the process by which alteration occurs in the structure and function of a social system. National revolution, the founding of a village development council, creation of a government ministry, invention of a new industrial process — all these classify as social change. Alterations in both the structure and the function of a social system occur as a result of such actions. The structure of a social system is provided by the various individual and group *statuses* of which it is composed. The functioning element within this structure of statuses is a *role*, or the actual behavior of the individual in a given status. Status and role affect each other reciprocally. For example, the status of a minister of education determines how the individual holding that position will act, particularly in his official capacity. To the extent that he does not operate in the prescribed manner, his status may be changed. Likewise, social function and social structure are closely linked and affect each other. In the process of social change, as one is altered, so is the other.

The process of social change can be broken down into three steps: invention, diffusion, and consequence. *Invention* is the process by which new ideas are created or developed. *Diffusion* is the process by which these new ideas are

---

[3] It hardly seems necessary to emphasize the significance of this type of contemporary social change in less developed countries. The historian Black (1966:4), after surveying the entire range of human activities, singled out three great revolutionary transformations: (1) the evolution from prehuman to human life, (2) the progress from primitive to civilized societies, and (3) the modern era of change, which he termed "the most dynamic of the great revolutionary transformations in the conduct of human affairs."

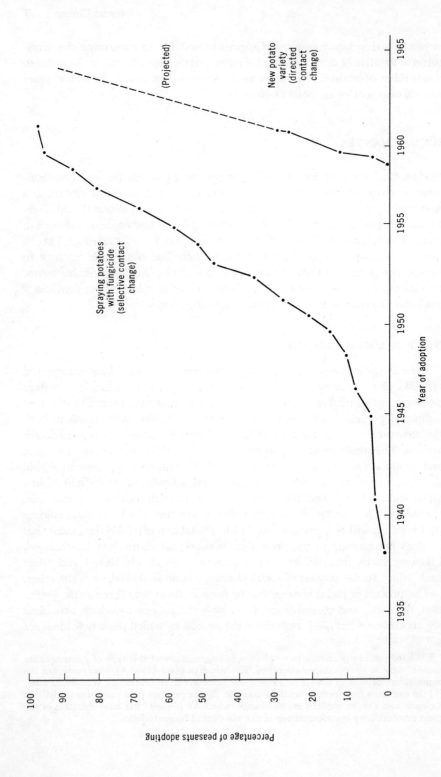

(Projected)

New potato variety (directed contact change)

Spraying potatoes with fungicide (selective contact change)

Percentage of peasants adopting

Year of adoption

communicated throughout a given social system. *Consequence* is change occurring within the system as a result of the adoption or rejection of the innovations. The new ideas must be created (either within or outside the social system under scrutiny) before they can affect the social structure or function. The innovations must then spread to all members of the system for change to occur. Through adoption (or rejection) of the new idea, the structure and function of the social system are altered.

IMMANENT AND CONTACT CHANGE: CATEGORIES OF SOCIAL CHANGE

Various classifications of social change have been developed. One of the more useful, for our purposes, is the dual categorization based on the source or instigator of the change: (1) immanent change and (2) contact change.

Immanent change occurs when invention takes place within a given social system with little or no external influence being exerted. The new idea is created by a member of the system and then is adopted by his peers. For example, climatic changes in an isolated community create the need for a new type of clothing, which in turn is recognized and met by a member of the village. Further illustration of immanent change is provided by the Colombian peasants who "perfected a carder in the form of a cross, set with thorny capsules from a local plant, to facilitate the combing of their *ruanas* [ponchos]" (Fals Borda 1960:10). Since the inspiration and initiative for development of this comb did not originate through contact with outsiders, an immanent social change took place.

Contact change is introduced from sources external to the social system under analysis.[4] It may be of two types: (1) selective or (2) directed.

1. *Selective contact change* occurs when outsiders unintentionally or spontaneously communicate a new idea to members of a social system, who in turn select those ideas they wish to adopt. The receptors of these innovative ideas choose, interpret, adopt, or reject the new ideas according to their distinct needs. There are many examples of selective contact change in Colombian villages, such as chicken raising, which was learned from the Spanish conquerors, or the wearing of trousers and other clothing items that were copied from urbanites. No one coerced or even made an effort to encourage villagers to adopt these items. The villagers, perceiving an advantage in these new

---

[4] Parsons (1961) uses the terms "endogenous" and "exogenous" sources of change in a manner somewhat similar to our concepts of immanent and contact change.

Figure 1–1. An Example of Selective Contact Change and Directed Contact Change in the Colombian Village of Saucío.

A much more rapid rate of adoption occurred for the new potato variety promoted by a change agent who began work in the village in about 1958, than the rate of adoption for potato spraying, an example of selective contact change.

SOURCE: Deutschmann and Fals Borda (1962a: 50). Reprinted with permission.

ways, adopted them of their own accord. A further illustration is provided by Fals Borda (1960:16–17), who reported that peasants in Saucío, an Andean village he studied, had experienced losses due to blight in their potato crop for several seasons. Then, some innovative farmers learned on their own initiative of fungicides and spray pumps (innovations developed outside their community), tried them, and were impressed by the results. From this limited adoption, their neighbors observed the advantages, which were visibly dramatized when potatoes in one field died from blight while those in an adjacent field survived because of the use of fungicide. The first sprayer was adopted in 1937, and by 1950 about 14 farmers were spraying their potatoes. By 1961, all 71 farmers in Saucío had adopted the practice, which had not been promoted by any external change agent (Fig. 1–1). Hence, this constitutes an example of the process of selective contact change.

2. Immanent and, perhaps, selective contact change were the most important types of change in the isolated peasant communities of the past. The present era is certainly one of *directed contact change*, caused by outsiders who, on their own or as representatives of programs of planned change, seek to introduce new ideas in order to achieve definite goals. An early example of directed contact change in Latin America was the introduction of Catholicism by the Spanish and Portuguese conquistadors. A more recent illustration occurred in the Colombian village of Saucío, where a change agent introduced a new potato variety (Deutschmann and Fals Borda 1962a). Figure 1–1 shows that, at least in this village, the directed change was adopted much more rapidly than was the selective contact change of spraying with fungicides.[5] In the case of directed contact change, the innovations, as well as

Table 1–1. Paradigm of Types of Social Change

Recognition of Need for Change	*Origin of the New Idea*	
	Internal to Social System	External to Social System
Internal: recognition is by members of the social system	I. Immanent change	II. Selective contact change
External: recognition may be by change agents outside the social system	III. Motivated immanent change[a]	IV. Directed contact change

[a]While this situation is highly improbable, it is not impossible. For example, a missionary enters a village and recognizes a need, brings it to the attention of the villagers, but does not offer suggestions on how to change the situation. Once the problem has been called to their attention, the villagers proceed to invent their own solution to the problem.

[5] Later observation in this community indicates, however, that after a rapid rate of adoption of the new potato variety, it was widely abandoned, partly because of its disease proneness (Deutschmann and Havens 1964).

recognition of the *need* for the change, *originate* outside the social system considered (Table 1–1). Change agents direct diffusion of new ideas by spreading information and by offering inducements for their adoption, thereby seeking to reduce the time span required for general use.

Economic development measures are a type of directed social change. New ideas are introduced into a social system in order to attain higher per capita incomes and levels of living through more modern production methods and improved social organization. The many government-sponsored development programs designed to introduce technological innovations in agriculture, health, education, and industry are contemporary examples of directed change.

Such development programs, begun largely since the close of World War II, resulted from government dissatisfaction with a rate of economic progress dependent solely upon immanent and spontaneous change. Increased external contact with more developed nations may be one of the major causes for this dissatisfaction. Today, governments of less developed countries invest substantial portions of their national budgets in large-scale attempts to direct change. High-level enthusiasm for development has not always met with overwhelming success in practical application. Millions of dollars have been spent on programs that resulted in colossal failure, where the initiatory desire for change exceeded scientific "know-how" in introducing and securing the adoption of appropriate innovations.

COMMUNICATION AND SOCIAL CHANGE

Communication, the process by which messages are transferred from a source to one or more receivers, is a vital aspect of social change. It is indeed the key that opens the door for change. Communication is inherent to both types of social change.

In the case of immanent change, the inventor must communicate his idea to his peers and persuade them to adopt it. In the case of contact change, the role of communication looms even larger, for it involves the process by which the potential adopter first hears of the new idea, learns more about the innovation, and decides to adopt it.

Communication is a part of the myriad decisions that, taken together, constitute social change: a peasant's decision to move cityward or to join an agrarian reform project, an industrialist's adoption of a new manufacturing technique, the decision of a husband and wife to limit the size of their family. Although communication and social change are closely related, care should be taken not to think of them as synonymous concepts. Social change is a more encompassing term in that it includes invention, diffusion of new ideas, and the consequences of these innovations. Whereas communication is central to diffusion, it is less a part of the invention process and is little involved in the consequence phase of social change.

Nevertheless, communication is an essential part of social change, and perhaps all analysis of social change must ultimately focus upon communication processes. The general theoretical viewpoint of the present book is that communication processes are integral, vital elements of modernization and development.[6]

INDIVIDUAL AND SOCIAL SYSTEM CHANGE: LEVELS AT WHICH CHANGE OCCURS

We have been discussing social change from the viewpoint of the processes involved. The nature of the *unit of analysis* provides yet another perspective from which to categorize social change.

1. Many changes occur at the *individual* level, where they are variously referred to as diffusion, adoption, modernization, acculturation, learning, socialization, or communication. Microanalytic in approach, research at the individual level of change attempts to explain individuals' change behavior. The focus of the present book is at the individual level.

2. Changes also occur at the *social system* level, where they are diversely termed development, differentiation, integration, or adaptation. Research on social change at the social system level is macroanalytic in that it concentrates on social systems as the units of analysis. An illustration is Cutright's (1963) study of the relationship between mass media development and political development; he constructed indexes for each of these variables for each nation from census and other data sources. His results show a high degree of correlation between a country's communication and its political development, but they tell us almost nothing about the behavior of individuals in these nations.

Of course, change at these two levels is closely interrelated. Social system changes (for example, the blockading of a nation's ports) may lead to many individual changes (such as decisions to grow new crops or make new products). Likewise, the aggregation of a multitude of individual changes may produce a system-level alteration. Farmers' decisions to adopt a more productive coffee variety in a Latin American country may eventually result in changes affecting the country's international balance of trade.

DEVELOPMENT: SOCIAL SYSTEM CHANGE

Development is a type of social change in which new ideas are introduced into a social system in order to produce higher per capita incomes and levels of living through more modern production methods and improved social

---

[6] Lerner (1967a:306) recognized the importance of communication as a stimulus for peasant modernization: "Rooted in their place and pride, traditional mankind lived by its constraints — unaware of them as constraints because no communications alerted them to alternatives."

organization.[7] The nations of the world are often divided into two camps on the basis of economic and social criteria: the less developed and the more developed, the traditional and the modern.

The United Nations classification of less developed countries includes all those of Latin America, Africa, and Asia, with the exception of Japan, South Africa, Australia, and New Zealand. Like all dualistic classifications, this leaves much to be desired.[8] For instance, it lumps both Haiti and Argentina in the less developed category, even though Argentina's per capita income is about seven times that of Haiti.

In spite of great heterogeneity among the less developed countries, they have certain common characteristics and problems. Less developed countries are generally typified by (1) a relatively low per capita income, (2) comparatively low productivity per person, (3) little commerce and high self-sufficiency, (4) a high rate of illiteracy, (5) limited transportation and mass media facilities, (6) inadequate nutrition, (7) little industry and few skilled technicians, (8) politically unstable governments, and (9) high birth and death rates and short life expectancy. These variables are, of course, strongly interrelated. Lack of industry and technicians is linked to illiteracy; lack of transportation and mass media facilities affects both. The image of a bundle of tangled string with many dangling ends comes to mind. One of the crucial problems for planned change programs in less developed countries is to know which end to pull first in order to achieve the goal of a more modern country.

A basic notion stemming from the functionalist point of view, prevalent in anthropology, sociology, and other social sciences, is that all the major social institutions in a society are interdependent. A change in one social institution will cause simultaneous changes in the others. For example, a change in the educational sphere may foster changes in the political (Lipset 1960; Cutright 1963). In another sense, this very interdependence of institutions acts as a barrier to directed social change. Static institutions can dampen or prevent the changes occurring in a dynamic sector of a nation.

Empirical investigations generally indicate that changes in the constituent parts of a society are closely interrelated. Perhaps, then, it is ideal for these changes to proceed in a manner that will not destroy the dynamic equilib-

---

[7] Thus we define development and economic development in essentially similar terms, although recognizing that there are types of development, such as political and social, which are not strictly economic. Our definition of development is generally congruent with that of Caplow and Finsterbusch (1964): "The process whereby a contemporary society improves its control of the environment by means of an increasingly competent technology applied by increasingly complex organizations."

[8] Similar classifications of social systems have been facilitated by the numerous social scientists who have coined pairs of contrasting ideal types to represent the extremes of a continuum of development. Examples of such ideal types are the *Gemeinschaft* and *Gesellschaft* of Töennies, Redfield's folk and urban, Becker's sacred and secular, and many others.

rium of the system.[9] For example, an increase in the literacy rate possibly should accompany similar increases in industrialization, urbanization, and public political participation. Similarly, greater urbanization leads to a greater need for literacy. Perhaps when these factors develop at vastly different rates, pressures are created to tip the balance toward return to a more stable equilibrium condition, thus dampening the rate of over-all development.

HISTORICAL SETTING OF CONTEMPORARY DEVELOPMENT

In order to understand the contemporary development situation, one should assess recent programs of planned change, for many of the problems encountered today can be traced to past development efforts. The three decades that are of major concern to us are the 1940s, 1950s, and 1960s.

THE MARSHALL PLAN AND EUROPEAN RECOVERY

Following the close of World War II, the late 1940s saw the beginnings of national and international development programs in the form of large-scale economic aid to Europe. Early optimism arose as a result of the Marshall Plan's rapid success in putting a war-torn Europe back on its feet. A massive infusion of capital led to reindustrialization, urbanization, and rising levels of living. In the wake of this dramatic improvement, it was somehow easy to forget that the European nations had been at high levels of development before the temporary setbacks of World War II, that the technical know-how and basic education for and the aspiration to higher levels of development were already present. In many instances, imprudent general analogies were made from the European recovery to development needs in Latin America, Asia, and Africa, areas where modernization efforts had to start from a colonial legacy of nearly zero. Our egregious error was in thinking that capital assistance and the resulting industrial development *alone* could raise levels of living and accomplish the other desired goals of development. The error was one of equating *re*development with development.

THE REVOLUTION OF RISING EXPECTATIONS IN THE 1950s

The 1950s might be considered the era of desire. Influential individuals and groups in most less developed countries began to concentrate on bringing about development in their nations. These eager candidates for moderniza-

---

[9] A dynamic equilibrium occurs in a system when change is occurring at a rate compatible with the system's ability to cope with the alterations, so that complete disorganization does not occur.

tion wanted to shed their biblical style of life for the ways of more developed countries. Their governments began to pursue development goals with an intensity that approached frenzy. During the 1950s the spread of the developmental desire to new states led some observers to characterize the era as a "revolution of rising expectations." A surge of expectancy was created by political leaders such as Nasser, Nehru, and Nkrumah. Most students of development welcomed this tide of rising aspirations; they agreed with Robert Browning's remark that "a man's reach should exceed his grasp." Such desires to shed the cocoon of custom were expected to provide the mass motivation for development and modernization. "The quiescent poor have become nervy seekers in the have-less-but-want-more process we call development" (Lerner 1967:104).

Development planners in the new nations saw their task as centering around industrial development. Perhaps the European model of recovery was uppermost in the policy-makers' minds. The less developed countries were mainly producers of agricultural commodities; the more developed countries were mainly industrial nations. Hence, the logic for less developed nations was seemingly self-evident: pursue a policy of industrial development, and sooner or later the societal spin-off from urban-industrial growth would reach all segments of the population, including the peasants. Late in the 1950s, however, certain nations began to realize that the problem was not as simple as it had seemed.

Let us take India as an illustration. In 1959, a team of Ford Foundation agricultural experts[10] predicted a dire food crisis for India in the 1960s (which in fact has occurred much as they expected). They saw an economy straining to speed its industrial growth, often at the expense of agricultural production. Hydroelectric dams and huge steel mills were constructed while food production lagged. The death rate dropped as a result of improved sanitation and health practices, while the birth rate remained high, creating a population explosion that meant millions of new mouths to feed each year. India was thus forced to spend large amounts of its precious foreign currency exchange for food imports, a policy that retarded national development even further. To make matters worse, a too rapid urban migration soon resulted in city slums filled with former peasants who were unemployed and unemployable.

The industrial development phase of the 1950s, of necessity, prompted the agricultural development of the 1960s.[11] Modernizing the peasant millions became a major goal. Emphasis was placed upon communicating such ideas as the use of fertilizer and other food-producing innovations, as well as family-planning ideas, and on securing their adoption. But a precious ten years

[10] Their report was appropriately titled *Report on India's Food Crisis and Steps to Meet It* (1959).

[11] Industrial development is still important in the 1960s, but the factories are more likely to service agricultural development by producing fertilizer rather than steel.

had been lost, a decade in which development problems had become much more serious.

While the exact timing of these changing development policies in India was not identical with that in other countries, the pattern was generally similar. An initial faith in the magic of factories as keys to development was followed by a realization of the importance of agricultural improvement. Even in Communist China, a parallel process[12] can be observed in the "great leap forward" of 1958-1960, which was an enthusiastic burst of industrialization. As an instrument of over-all development, it too failed.

FROM RISING EXPECTATIONS TO RISING FRUSTRATIONS

By the 1960s, it was readily apparent that "aspirations are more easily aroused than satisfied" (Lerner 1963:331). For example, in an investigation of two Indian villages, one traditional and the other rapidly modernizing, it was noted that the level of conflict and dissatisfaction was much higher in the developing village; their expectations were not being satisfied (Rao 1963).

Satisfaction is a ratio of "gets" to "wants," of achievements to aspirations.[13] And as actualities fell far short of aspirations, as the denominator in the gets/wants ratio increased faster than the numerator, Lerner[14] described the 1960s as a period typified by a "revolution of rising frustrations."[15] Political leaders in less developed countries came to realize that their speeches were often promissory notes on which they could not deliver. Government instability became prevalent in many African and some Asian and Latin American countries. Development analysts thus concluded that, while a certain level of aspiration for modernization was a good thing, too much led to a general frustration which could have deleterious consequences. Extreme discontent and revolution act to set back the rate of development rather than to speed it up.

Why do aspirations outrun actualities in many emerging nations? One reason lies with the use of mass media in less developed countries. As important heralds of the gospel of desires, the mass media have effectively put forth the message of wider horizons. Unfortunately, the mass media have not been

[12] Parallel except that the experience of Soviet Russia, rather than of postwar Europe, was the model for the industrial development policy in the late 1950s.

[13] This conception of satisfaction versus frustration with the rate of modernization is Lerner's (1963:333), whose "gets/wants ratio" is based on that of William James (1923:187). Both Davies (1962) and Gurr (1967) reflect similar notions that the causes of revolutions and civil disorder lie in *perceptions* of the situation rather than in the objective situation. "The necessary precondition for violent civil conflict is relative deprivation, defined as actors' perception of discrepancy between their value expectations and their environments' value capabilities" (Gurr 1967: 3).

[14] "The revolution of rising expectations has been a major casualty of the past decade. In its place has risen a potential revolution of rising frustrations" (Lerner 1963: 349).

[15] The Germans have coined an apt word for this English expression, *Entwicklungsmüdigkeit* — literally, "development weariness."

equally effective in showing their audiences how to achieve these new goals. For example, it is very likely more difficult to teach villagers how to read by way of radio instruction than it is to make city life appear desirable. Hence the need to utilize the mass media as tools for achieving development actualities (such as literacy) grows more important every day. When mass media audiences are encouraged to *want* more and not fully informed on how to *get* more (food production, higher incomes, better education for their children), the net result is frustration, not modernization.[16]

A second reason is that, in less developed nations, power often lies in the hands of oligarchs who dominate the national economic and political life. These latter-day Junkers, who often give public lip service to development goals, have proved generally reluctant to endorse programs that alter or upset the *status quo*. Rapid change usually brings with it a new corps of "influentials."[17] Thus, while espousing the gospel of a better life for all, a ruling elite hesitates to initiate *actual* major alterations in the social structure, which in turn could affect their positions of power.

For instance, in spite of strong pressures from the Alliance for Progress and other external influences, no Latin American nation has an effective legal-political means to correct a top-heavy system of land tenure that keeps most peasants in virtual serfdom.[18] The rigid social structure of less developed countries, coupled with the prodevelopment nature of their mass media messages, leads to the previously defined revolution of rising frustrations. Alternative communication and modernization policies are available. Such policies could, perhaps, maintain public aspiration at a healthy level of discontent, in order to prevent complete political and social disorganization.

A third reason for the rising tide of dissatisfaction lies with the developers. While there is a growing realization that development is a much more critical and difficult task than had been conceived by the early planners, the false optimism generated by the Marshall Plan's rapid success in Europe did

---

[16] However, Frey (1966: 185) concludes his study of Turkish peasants by stating that mass media exposure is not strongly associated with such generally unwanted changes as increased demands upon the government, augumented desire for political participation, excessive optimism, and a jaundiced view of village life in comparison to urban opportunities. Frey feels this is because media exposure mainly affects cognition rather than motivation. Taylor (1967) provides parallel evidence, using aggregate data with nations as the units of analysis, that mass media development is not associated with political instability.

[17] A basic notion of such varied writings as Plato's *Republic*, Pareto's speculations on the circulation of the elites, and Robert Penn Warren's novel *All the King's Men* is that these new elites, who rise when we throw the old rascals out, soon become firmly attached to the new *status quo*, which they in turn are reluctant to disturb.

[18] At least 16 of the 20 Latin American nations have enacted a legal basis for agrarian reform, largely since the advent of the Alliance for Progress. These laws, however, have acted as a detour rather than as a direct means of correcting land-tenure barriers to development, for once a land reform bill is passed by a Latin American legislature the large landowners (who generally control the national government) act to prevent adequate appropriations for land purchase by the government and otherwise block the effective functioning of the new legislation.

cause major problems and setbacks in programs of planned change in various less developed countries. Necessary changes in development policy were not fully realized until the 1960s, so that the actualities of such programs lagged far behind the expectations for rapid progress.

, Lest the reader conclude this review of planned development in recent decades with a totally pessimistic impression, he should be warned not to throw the baby out with the bathwater. The contemporary notion of large-scale development began a mere generation ago, armed with no body of knowledge or theoretical insight and few experienced personnel and in the less developed countries themselves no very clear idea of where the peoples involved wanted to go — much less how to get there. Today there are about 100,000 professionals involved in development activities; almost all less developed nations have short-range and long-term development plans; and a sizable body of social science knowledge about the modernization process has accumulated. The question posed for the next decade is whether our theories, knowledge, skills, and resources can be properly harnessed for the pull toward desired development goals, and whether these can be reached before a disastrous disequilibrium occurs as a result of racing human fertility, famine, and frustration.

MODERNIZATION: INDIVIDUAL SOCIAL CHANGE

Modernization at the individual level corresponds to development at the societal level. *Modernization* is the process by which individuals change from a traditional way of life to a more complex, technologically advanced, and rapidly changing style of life.[19] The root of the word modernization is from the Latin *modo*, meaning "just now."

The reader should be cautious of three common misconceptions about modernization.

1. Modernization has often been equated with Europeanization and/or Westernization. The authors' concept of modernization, instead, is synonymous with neither of these concepts. Branding the social change process as

---

[19] This definition shares certain elements with at least three previous attempts to clarify the meaning of modernization. Lerner (1958:89) defines this concept as " . . . a secular trend unilateral in direction — from traditional to participant lifeways." Riesman (1952) defines "tradition-direction" (an antonym of modernity) as the impossibility of conceiving alternatives to the specific ways in which people in a given culture act, think, and believe and as feeling that what exists, for his group at any rate, is all that can exist. Inkeles (1967b) describes modernity as a kind of mentality, less tied to time and place and things and more to a state of mind, such that the Greeks of Pericles might be called modern. Our definition is not identical with any of these but shares the implied meaning of modernization as an individual process by which one becomes psychologically nontraditional. Some authors use "modernization" to characterize a nation (that is, as a synonym for development at the social system level), but the authors prefer to limit its meaning to the individual level.

"Europeanization" or "Westernization" implies that the source or impetus for change necessarily comes from Europe or from the Western nations. It further implies that countries adopting ideas originating from the West become to a certain extent like the West. Such a view is much too limiting and in many ways inaccurate. As seen by the present writers, modernization is a *synthesis* of old and new ways and, as such, varies in different environments. The new element does not necessarily come from Europe or the West. Adoption of externally developed innovations need not make the receiving country into a replica of the source country, since most innovations require considerable adaptation to meet the differing conditions of the recipient countries.

2. It has often been implied that all modernization is "good." No such value judgment is intended in our definition. Modernization brings change, which may very well produce not only benefit but also conflict, pain, and relative disadvantage. Black (1966:27) warns us that "modernization must be thought of . . . as a process that is simultaneously creative and destructive, providing new opportunities and prospects at a high price in human dislocation and suffering."

AID participants from less developed countries, about to return to their homelands after a sojourn in the United States, often express their fear of the double-edged sword of modernization. While introducing the improved technology of agriculture and industry, they fear they will also set in motion destructive forces leading to the breakdown of the extended family group, a rise in crime and divorce rates, and many other aspects of American life they perceive as highly undesirable. Modernization means, therefore, adopting new ways of life, the consequences of which do not necessarily lead to a "better" life for all the individuals involved.

3. The modernization process is not unidimensional and therefore cannot be measured by a single criterion or index. One cannot assume that because an individual has a high level of living, he is necessarily modern or is becoming modern; he could, in fact, be quite traditional. Modernization should be viewed as a process involving the interaction of many factors, so that more than one aspect of an individual's behavior must be measured in order to determine his status on the modernization continuum. Variables such as level of living, aspirations, literacy and education, political participation, cosmopoliteness, and communication are all factors determining modernization. Therefore, one must take a multivariable approach to operationalization.[20]

Modernization, then, is a multidimensional concept which is not to be equated with Europeanization or Westernization and which implies no value judgment as to its desirability.

---

[20] This point and the major conceptual variables involved in the modernization process will be discussed in more detail in Chapter 3.

NEOTRADITIONALIZATION: REACTION TO MODERNIZATION

A Basuto tribal proverb warns that "If a man does away with his traditional way of living and throws away his good customs, he had better first make certain that he has something of value to replace them." In recent years, increasing numbers of the newly modern have heeded this theme. A latent counterreaction to modernization is noticeable in most less developed countries.

Neotraditionalization is the process by which individuals change from a modern way of life to a more traditional style of life.[21] One might also describe it as modernization in reverse. There are several possible motives for neotraditionalization.

1. The impetus may arise from a desire to conform or partially conform with more traditional ways as a means to reduce observed deviation from norms. This type of neotraditionalization sometimes occurs among individuals returning to less developed countries after education or travel abroad. An illustration is the "rebushing" attributed to Oxford-educated young Africans upon their return to Kenya. Such neotraditionalization may only be part of personal readjustment to the more traditional home environment; or it may be purposive, with a view to gaining credibility for the technological innovations in health, education, agriculture, or industry that the sojourner seeks to introduce upon his return.

2. Neotraditionalization may arise as a symbolic process through which the elites of newly independent countries demonstrate national identity. Examples are the ritualistic return to native dress and precolonial languages by Nigerian and Indian political leaders[22] following the independence of their countries. It is our observation that contemporary retraditionalization almost always occurs in symbolically important but functionally insignificant sectors of a culture. Those individuals who return to traditional dress, for instance, never suggest giving up railroads or radios. Thus modernization is especially technological, whereas neotraditionalization is mainly symbolic and nontechnological.

3. This notion further suggests that neotraditionalization is motivated by a desire to be modern in a traditional way, to obtain a syncretization of

---

[21] By no means does neotradltiunalization occur only in less developed nations. Perhaps the Black Muslims in the United States provide a case in point

[22] In these settings neotraditionalization has been called "Sanskritization" and Nigerian ization, depending upon the locale, but a concept that is not restricted to a particular place is preferable, since we argue for its universality. Sanskritization is a concept attributed to Srinivas (1952:30; 1962:42–62; 1966:1–45) and is utilized by anthropologists and sociologists in India, such as Sen and Roy (1966:51), Sen (1962), and Cohen (1959). Srinivas (1966) uses Sanskritization to mean the adoption of traditional ideas, especially those derived from the ancient Sanskrit culture of India. He argues that such neotraditionalization often is motivated by the desire of lower-caste individuals to appear more like the Brahmins or other upper castes.

older indigenous and modern ways,[23] to gain the best of two possible worlds. So neotraditionalization may be the result of a desire by nationals in less developed countries to retain certain of those cultural elements which are uniquely theirs, while at the same time adopting modern technology from external sources.

4. Neotraditionalization may be motivated by a disenchantment with the whole idea of modernization.[24] Since it is recognized that conflict and pain may accompany any change process, such retreat from the arena of modernization by some individuals is not unexpected.

While there is a trickle of neotraditionalization in comparison with a worldwide tide of modernization, one should not assume that modernization is entirely a facile downhill process. Certainly the reverse phenomenon deserves adequate empirical inquiry, which it has not received to date. The neotraditionalization process, as well as the reasons for its occurrence, must be better understood than it is at present.

SUMMARY

The purposes of the present study are, as stated earlier: (1) to examine the nature of modernization processes among peasants in one less developed country, Colombia, and (2) to determine the cross-cultural validity of these findings in other of the less developed nations. This chapter has dealt with key concepts that will be referred to in later chapters in order to dissect the modernization process.

Social change is the process by which alteration occurs in the structure and function of a social system. The three steps involved in social change are (1) *invention*, the process by which new ideas are originated or developed; (2) *diffusion*, the process by which these new ideas are communicated throughout a social system; and (3) *consequence*, the sum of the changes occurring within the system as a result of the adoption or rejection of innovations.

There are two categories or types of social change: (1) *immanent change*, which occurs when invention takes place within a given social system with little or no external influence; and (2) *contact change*, which is introduced from sources external to the social system under analysis. Further, there are two types of contact change: (1) *selective contact change*, which occurs when

---

[23] Sen and Roy (1966:52) utilize the word "renaissance" to describe the synthesis resulting from acceptance of modern ideas while still maintaining strong links with tradition.

[24] Professor Anthony Wallace has utilized the concept of "revitalization" for the construction of a new culture, often based closely on the revival of what once existed. Wallace argues that such revitalization is often motivated by the social disorganization of a society as a result of sudden change. As such, revitalization bears some close similarities to neotraditionalization.

outsiders unintentionally or spontaneously communicate a new idea to members of a social system, who in turn select those ideas they wish to adopt; and (2) *directed contact change*, which is caused by outsiders who, on their own or as representatives of programs of planned change, seek to introduce new ideas in order to achieve definite goals.

Social change and communication are not synonyms. *Communication* is the process by which messages are transferred from a source to one or many receivers. Social change is a broader concept, because it includes invention, the diffusion (that is, the communication) of innovations, and their consequences.

Development is a type of social change in which new ideas are introduced into a social system in order to produce higher per capita incomes and levels of living through more modern production methods and improved social organization. The 1960s are typified by a revolution of rising frustrations in less developed countries, which has replaced the revolution of rising expectations of the 1950s. This failure of many development programs emphasizes the need for a more adequate understanding and synthesis of development and modernization.

Modernization parallels at the individual level what development represents at the national level. Modernization is the process by which individuals change from a traditional way of life to a more complex, technologically advanced, and rapidly changing style of life. Modernization is not identical with Europeanization or Westernization; it is not necessarily always "good" for all members of less developed countries, nor should it be operationalized as a single variable or dimension.

Neotraditionalization is the process by which individuals change from a modern way of life to a more traditional style of life. It may be motivated by a desire to conform to traditional norms, to symbolize national identity, to synthesize modern with traditional ways, or it may result from disenchantment with modernization.

2

The Subculture of Peasantry*

We peasants are poor earthworms. We live with the animals, eat with them, talk to them, smell like them. Therefore, we are a great deal like them. How would you like to be a peasant?
[Italian peasant interviewed by Joseph Lopreato (1962)]

WHY STUDY PEASANTS?

"Peasants are the majority of mankind" (Shanin 1966), but in spite of their numbers, they are poorly understood. Marx and Engels (1933:159), writing over a century ago, described peasants as an "undecipherable hieroglyphic to the understanding of the civilized." Little wonder that the peasant is often portrayed as lazy, ignorant, resistant to change, and so on.[1] He remains an enigma to those who have not lived his life, and as a result he is often characterized in a negative light. Just as the peasant is charged with lack of empathy for modern life, so might his more "civilized" observers be charged with lack of empathy for the man with the hoe.

Limited understanding and insight cause many development failures, which lead to rising frustrations among development planners, who in turn develop a negative view of their "uncooperative" clients as a rationale for their failures. "Day by day the peasants make the economists sigh, the politicians sweat, and the strategists swear, defeating their plans and prophecies all over the world — Moscow and Washington, Peking and Delhi ... " (Shanin 1966).

Although clearly distinguishable as a unique category of individuals, peasants are an audience we know relatively little about in any reliable, generalizable, or scientific way.[2] The peasant audience must be reached in

* This chapter was written with assistance from John Winterton and H. Stuart Hawkins, Research Assistants in Communicaion, Michigan State University. It is based on a paper by Everett M. Rogers (1965a) presented at the Conference on Subsistence and Peasant Economics, University of Hawaii, Honolulu; this was later published in revised form (Rogers 1968) in Clifton R. Wharton, Jr. (ed.), *Subsistence Agriculture and Economic Development*, Honolulu, University of Hawaii, East-West Center Press.

[1] Foster (1967:14–15) argues that peasants have cognitive orientations conditioned by the past (when such attitudes and values were effective in daily living), that their cognitive orientations change more slowly than a rapidly modernizing world and are hence out-of-tune with reality. Therefore peasants behave in ways that seem irrational or ignorant to those more nearly attuned to reality, such as development planners and change agents.

[2] Frey (1966: 108) and Foster (1967:4) point to this lack of knowledge and understanding as sources of the negative picture of peasants.

order for a country to move forward on the development continuum; hence it becomes imperative that we understand the peasant life style. As Bailey (1966) puts it, "The modernizer cannot compel but must persuade: to do this he must know what values the people already hold; how they see the world and the society around them; in short, he must know their cognitive maps."

Drawing on the available theoretical, speculative, and empirical literature, we hope to create a composite picture of the peasant that will serve as a framework for our theories and data interpretation in later chapters of this book. The present chapter is thus a relatively qualitative, impressionistic synthesis of the peasant style of life; in the remainder of this book, we shall compare these salient characteristics of peasant life with the more rigorous data obtained from our Colombian respondents and from their counterparts in India, Kenya, and similar settings.

WHO ARE PEASANTS?

The common threads woven into most descriptions of mankind's majority include: subsistence agricultural producers and traditionally oriented rural villagers, who are seldom completely self-sufficient.[3] *Peasants* are farmers oriented largely (but not necessarily entirely) to subsistence production.[4] They consume the major portion of the food and other articles they produce. Peasant and *subsistence farmer* are, therefore, interchangeable terms.

[3] Wolf (1956) defines peasants as "Agricultural producers in effective control of land who carry on agriculture as a means of livelihood, not as a business for profit."

Firth (1956:87) states, "The term peasant has primarily an economic referent. By a peasant economy, one means a system of small scale producers, with a simple technology and equipment, often relying primarily for their subsistence on what they themselves produce. The primary means of livelihood of the peasant is cultivation of the soil."

Belshaw (1965:54) defines peasant societies as "ways of life which are traditionally oriented, linked with but separate from urban centers, combining market activity with subsistence production."

Kroeber (1948:248) describes peasants as "a class segment of a larger population which usually contains also urban centers. . . . They constitute part-societies with part-cultures."

Redfield (1956) describes peasants as "people in old civilizations, rural people who control and cultivate their land for subsistence and as part of a traditional way of life and who look to and are influenced by gentry or townspeople whose way of life is like theirs but in a more civilized form."

Foster (1962:46–47) also stresses that peasant societies are not self-sufficient units; the basic decisions affecting peasant villages are made from the outside. "Peasant communities exist in an intimate relationship with cities and towns."

If one accepts the viewpoint of Belshaw, Kroeber, Redfield, and Foster, that peasants differ from the pure folk society in that peasants depend, at least to some degree, upon cities, there must exist some "pre-peasants," who are not yet dependent upon cities. Undoubtedly, the difference between peasants and pre-peasants is a matter of degree in most less developed countries today, and here the authors do not feel it is particularly fruitful to distinguish between these two categories. Tribal peoples differ only from peasants in a matter of degree, and even such pre-peasants are beginning to feel some pressures toward modernization in most countries.

[4] Some authors extend their conception of peasants to include such nonfarmers as subsistence fishermen, who are indeed peasantlike in their life style.

What is subsistence? Wharton (1963) distinguishes between (1) subsistence production, characterized by a low degree of commercialization or monetization and (2) subsistence living, which refers to a living level that is a minimum for survival. Our discussion is limited to subsistence farm producers rather than to subsistence living (poverty) in general, although the two are often empirically related. Pure subsistence farming is defined by Wharton (1963) as "a self-contained and self-sufficient unit where all production is consumed and none is sold; correspondingly, no outside consumer or producer goods and services are purchased." Most peasants function in a largely subsistent manner; yet we cannot consider them "pure" subsistence types, since they are often at least partly market-oriented.

Even when the peasant sells part of his production, he seldom perceives agriculture as a business enterprise, in the way that the commercial farmer does. This point is emphasized by Wolf (1955): "The peasant aims at subsistence, not at reinvestment. . . . He sells cash crops to get money, but his money is used in turn to buy goods and services which he requires to subsist and to maintain his social status, rather than to enlarge his scale of operations."[5]

IMPORTANCE OF MODIFYING PEASANT ATTITUDES AND BEHAVIORS

Why are we interested in changing peasants?

(*1*) *Peasants Constitute a Major Portion of the Population in Less Developed Nations.* At least three-fourths of the population in most less developed countries are peasants. India alone has well over a half million peasant villages, and China has two-thirds of a million. Together, Asia, Africa, and Latin America have a total of no less than 1.75 billion peasants. As the basic and majority element in less developed nations, peasants are prime targets for change agencies. UNESCO, FAO, USAID, national governments, and other change agencies actively seek to speed the development process in modernizing nations. In order to accomplish their objectives, such development programs must reach and affect the peasant population. In order for a nation to move toward modernization, the majority of its population must change its life style.

(*2*) *The Food/People Imbalance.* The populations of Asia, Africa, and Latin America are now growing at the rates of 2.3, 2.4, and 3.0 percent a year, respectively. A growth rate of 2.3 percent a year doubles a population in 30 years, and a rate of 3.0 percent a year doubles the population in only 23 years. These rates of population increase are the highest in history and are still increasing.

The world food budget (USDA 1964:iii) suggests that present food deficits will become worse for at least five to ten years. There is a slightly

[5] A similar point is made by Thomas and Znaniecki (1918): "For the peasant, money property has not the character of capital . . . he does not at first even think of making money produce; he simply keeps it at home."

decreasing per capita food production each year. Total world population is increasing more rapidly than total world food production.

Throughout most of the world's history, the amount of cultivated land increased with population. Today in densely populated food-deficit countries, new lands for cultivation are no longer available (USDA 1964:iv). There is a dangerous[6] trend toward reliance on the more developed countries (especially the United States, Canada, Australia, and those of Western Europe) to provide an increasing share of the food needs of the less developed nations.

Obtaining a better food balance in terms of quantity will not erase all food deficit problems, for the food/people imbalance also results in nutritional deficiencies. Vitamins and protein are seriously lacking in most peasant diets.

There are solutions to the food-shortage problem, steps that can be taken toward ensuring a better-fed world. It is technically possible to rapidly double or even triple agricultural production (and increase nutritional quality of the food produced) in the less developed countries through widespread adoption of chemical fertilizers, improved seed varieties, agricultural machinery, and irrigation. Unfortunately, this new technology has not yet reached the majority of farmers. It is not only a problem of reaching these subsistence farmers with appropriate farm technology but also of persuading them of the advantages of the new ideas over their traditional ways. The small increases in national agricultural production that have occurred to date in these less developed countries can be attributed to a very small number of large commercial farmers. It is obvious that the subsistence farmers in less developed countries must become more agriculturally efficient in order to survive. To date, only faltering steps have been made in this direction. Smith (1956) notes that "probably more than half of all the people in Latin America today are gaining their livelihood through a system of agricultural techniques or a system of farming that is more primitive than that which the Egyptians were using at the dawn of history." For instance, the average yield of corn in Colombia is only 17 bushels per acre (compared with 60 in the United States), wheat yield is less than half that of the United States, and potato harvest per acre is only one-fourth that of Maine producers.

(3) Widening Gaps. Gaps in income and living levels (1) between less developed countries and more developed countries, (2) between rural and urban sectors within less developed countries, and (3) between peasants and commercial farmers in less developed countries appear to be growing. These widening gaps illustrate an obvious point: benefits of technological innova-

---

[6] "Dangerous" is applied in the sense that massive food imports have an adverse effect upon a less developed nation's international balance of payments unless there is a corresponding build-up of nonfood exports with which to buy food products. India in the mid-1960s is an illustration of this undesirable situation.

tions, such as increased productivity and higher incomes, accrue first to the most responsive sectors of a social system. The rich get richer, and the poor get hungrier.

If we visualize all the countries of the world as beads moving along a string (representing the continuum of development), the distance between the various beads increases as time wears on. Galbraith (1962:18) explains that "development becomes easier the farther it proceeds. This is because each step in this [development] process invariably makes the next one easier. . . . It would be well were we all to realize that if the pace of less favorably suited countries is slow, it is necessarily because their task is so much greater."

The expanding socioeconomic gaps today constitute a challenge for programs of directed social change. These programs are asked not only to bring about greater development but also to raise levels of living where they are now lowest, that is, among peasants.

World peace and progress are in part dependent on narrowing the gaps between the haves and have-nots. We cannot afford to allow these gaps to continue widening.

(4) *Revolution and Political Instability.* The political stability of national governments in less developed countries depends in part upon the public opinion of their peasantry.[7] Lewis (1964a: xxx) notes that "It has commonly been held that peasants are essentially a stabilizing and conservative force in human history. The events of our own century, however, throw some doubt on this comfortable stereotype." Peasants have played an important, if not crucial, part in at least four major revolutions: the Mexican revolution of 1910, the Russian revolution of 1917, the Chinese Communist revolution, and the Cuban revolution under Fidel Castro.

Attempts to control guerilla warfare emphasize the crucial role of peasant public opinion in determining the success of guerilla activity. This is as true of South Vietnam as it was in the case of "La Violencia" in Colombia, where police and army control of political and bandit killings were largely ineffectual until Andean peasants were convinced to cooperate with government forces rather than with the guerillas.[8]

Peasant attitudes toward government must change in order for the national governments of less developed countries to attain a relative degree of political stability. Only when a government feels relatively secure can it turn its full attention to development plans.

Many of the present-day world problems could be alleviated to some extent if meaningful communication and collaboration could be established with

---

[7] And it is undoubtedly significant that many of the postwar international crises have occurred in less developed areas: Cuba, Algeria, the Congo, Goa, the Dominican Republic, Vietnam, and the Middle East.

[8] For a description of the recent guerilla warfare in Colombia, see Guzman *et al.* (1962, 1964).

the peasant millions. As the majority audience in less developed countries, they represent the key element in overcoming food and population problems. The more developed countries possess technical knowledge that could bring about wide-scale improvement in peasant levels of living. But in order to persuade peasants, one must know them. In the following discussion, the authors have attempted to synthesize what is known about mankind's majority.

THE SUBCULTURE OF PEASANTRY

If a book were dropped from an airplane in three different parts of New Guinea, an observer would probably note three different reactions due to varying cultural beliefs. One tribe might attempt to read it, one might worship it, and the third would eat it. Although it is known that village life varies tremendously even within countries,[9] the great diversity among peasant peoples does not preclude identifying certain features common to most peasant cultures. In fact, the central assumption of this chapter is that meaningful generalizations about peasants can be made which will hold true in most national settings. This is not to say that there are not many exceptions to our generalizations. There *are* important differences, for instance, between Colombian peasants and Indian villagers in language, food, dress, and religion; yet, in spite of this cultural variation in specifics, there are many basic common attitudes and beliefs.

One of the dangers in attempting to *generalize* about peasant life in this chapter is the possibility that significant idiosyncratic features may be masked or obliterated. There is much cultural variation in peasant life styles both (1) *among* less developed countries and (2) *within* each such nation (for example, inhabitants of South India are markedly different from those of North India, Kurds are little like other Turks, and Andean peasants in Colombia can be distinguished from their coastal counterparts).[10] Nonetheless, the intent here is to seek general patterns in peasant life styles rather than focus upon their differences.

The notion of a peasant subculture has been suggested by others but has not been systematically synthesized in terms of its central elements. For

[9] A typical statement of this "principle of diversity" was made by Tax (1963: ix): "Each continent and each region has its own kinds of peasant communities, and in the end, of course, every one is unique." Taken to a ridiculous extreme, the principle of diversity would argue that every peasant is somehow different from every other peasant, which is true with respect to individuality but not very helpful.

[10] One of the major differences between less developed and more developed countries is that the latter are characterized by much greater cultural homogeneity. Of course, there are differing subcultures within a more developed nation such as the United States, but the degree of such difference is relatively less than is found in Colombia, India, or Kenya. This fact poses special problems for the proper conduct of survey research, as will be seen in Chapter 16.

instance, Foster (1962:45) argues for the universality of a peasant subculture: "The similarities in peasant life in the world around are so marked . . . "; as does Redfield (1956:25): "Peasant society and culture has something generic about it. It is a kind of arrangement of humanity with some similarities all over the world."

In delineating the central elements in a culture of *poverty*, the anthropologist Oscar Lewis (1964b) paved the way for a parallel delineation of the subculture of peasanty. Lewis's culture of poverty includes such universal elements as a provincial orientation, a lack of integration into national institutions, low formal participation, and a constant struggle for survival. He stresses the functional interrelatedness of these elements and points out that the total configuration of poverty is more than the sum of its parts. Lewis (1961: xxvi–xxvii) notes some of the specific psychological and ecological aspects of living in a poverty culture thus: "crowded quarters, . . . a high incidence of alcoholism, . . . early initiation into sex, . . . a strong disposition to authoritarianism, and a greater emphasis upon family solidarity, . . . a strong present time orientation with relatively little ability to defer gratification and plan for the future, a sense of resignation and fatalism."

Somewhat similarly, in this book, there will be described a subculture of *peasantry* whose elements are functionally interrelated. Although some of the elements of peasantry are similar to Lewis's poverty traits, others differ because (1) all peasants are not necessarily in the poverty class,[11] and (2) the culture of poverty is meant to apply to urban poor as well as the poorer subsistence farmers. The descriptions of the two subcultures also differ in method of construction: Lewis seems to have induced his culture of poverty primarily from observations of Mexican poor, whereas this author's subculture of peasantry is abstracted from a variety of analyses of subsistence farmers in diverse national settings.

A *subculture* contains many elements of the broader culture[12] of which it is a part but can be characterized by particulars that set it apart from other sectors of the general culture. Colombian peasants are Colombians, and therefore they share many national characteristics with other Colombians. However, as subsistence farmers, they possess certain traits that make them members of a "peasant culture" which transcends national boundaries.

Central elements in this subculture of peasantry are: (1) mutual distrust in interpersonal relations; (2) perceived limited good; (3) dependence on and hostility toward government authority; (4) familism; (5) lack of innovativeness; (6) fatalism; (7) limited aspiration; (8) lack of deferred gratification; (9) limited view of the world; (10) low empathy.

---

[11] A fact that Lewis (1964b:150) recognizes: "The culture of poverty would apply only to those people who are at the very bottom of the socioeconomic scale, the poorest workers, the poorest peasants. . . . "

[12] A *culture* consists of both material and nonmaterial aspects of a way of life, as shared and tramsitted among the members of a society.

These elements seem to appear repeatedly in observational descriptions and empirical investigations of peasant villages by anthropologists and sociologists. Hillery (1961) points out that these descriptions of peasant villages "are in reality sources of data, sources which have greater value if they are taken in concert rather than if examined singly." While the description of one village in a less developed country provides few guidelines for national change programs, generalizations that appear to hold true for numerous village descriptions in several less developed countries can be of significant value. Supporting evidence from the world's major "peasant continents"[13] will be furnished for each of the elements in our subculture of peasantry. A rather consistent picture emerges from our synthesis of the varied descriptions of peasants — péons, fellahs, muzhiks, *fazendeiros*, *contadini*, and *campesinos*.

MUTUAL DISTRUST IN INTERPERSONAL RELATIONS

Peasant communities are characterized by a mentality of mutual distrust, suspiciousness, and evasiveness in interpersonal relations.[14] Lewis' (1951: 428–429) findings in a small Mexican village emphasize "the underlying individualism of Tepoztecan institutions and character, the lack of cooperation, the tensions between villages within the *municipio*, the schisms within the village, and the pervading quality of fear, envy, and distrust in interpersonal relations." Lewis (1960b) describes the typical peasant as an individualist, withdrawn, self-reliant, and reluctant to seek or give economic aid or to cooperate with others. Foster (1967:91) determined that among the Mexican peasants he observed, "So deep is the suspicion and mistrust of others, it is difficult for people to believe that no hidden meaning underlies even the most casual acts."

Lopreato (1962:21–24) concluded that his data from a farm village in South Italy provided support for the view of the peasant as suspicious and noncooperative in his interpersonal relations with peers. Friedmann (1960: 33) stated that the Italian peasant "is suspicious of everyone's motives and stays on the defensive in an almost pathological way."

Similarly, Reichel-Dolmatoff and Reichel-Dolmatoff (1961:xvii) found that the people in Aritama, a Colombian peasant community they studied, were "controlled and taciturn, evasive and monosyllabic. They are always afraid of giving themselves away somehow, of being ridiculed because of the

---

[13] Unfortunately, many more descriptions of Latin American peasants are available than of their African, Asian, or Middle Eastern counterparts. Wagley (1964:22) states, "The peasants of Latin America are perhaps the best studied segment of the population."

[14] As is perhaps illustrated by C. M. de Jesus' (1963:19) vivid comment about her neighbor women in a Brazilian slum: "They want to know everything. Their tongues are like chicken feet. Scratching at everything. . . . "

things they say or do, or of being taken advantage of by persons of authority."

An identical pattern of interpersonal relations was found in India by Carstairs (1958). His Hindu peasants were characterized by paranoid reactions of mutual distrust, displays of goodwill and flattery followed by dubious afterthoughts, and an apparent lack of empathy regarding others' feelings. The motives of their fellows always seemed arbitrary, inscrutable, and suspect. Bailey (1966), also observing Indian peasant behavior, notes the significance of the distrust syndrome: "Any peasant who adopts new ways and becomes rich, must have cheated, must have exploited his fellows. . . . "

The nature of interpersonal relations among peasants serves as a powerful block to cooperatives and to most community development programs, which are based on the notion that people can cooperate (perhaps with the help of some professional technical advice) to solve their social and economic problems Hickey (1964:279–280) analyzed the career of an unsuccessful credit cooperative in a South Vietnamese peasant community[15] and concluded: "The trust and cooperation needed to make a success of the organization clearly was lacking."

This lack of concern with community affairs was explained by Banfield (1958) in terms of the rule by which Italian peasants seem to play their game of life: maximize the material, short-run advantages for oneself and assume that all others will do likewise. From this basic rule flow various consequences for the peasant:

1. The claim of any person to be inspired by public interest should be regarded as fraudulent.

2. Since a peasant wants to prevent others from getting ahead, he "will vote against measures which help the community without helping him because, even though his position is unchanged in absolute terms, he considers himself worse off if his neighbors' position changes for the better" (Banfield 1958:101).

Banfield regarded his respondents as prisoners of their own social ethic. Their inability to act concertedly for the common good was a fundamental impediment to their economic progress.

A popular peasant fable illustrates the mutual distrust that peasants perceive in human relationships. It seems there was a monkey and a scorpion on the bank of a flood-swollen river. The two formed a pact to solve their transportation problem. If the monkey would swim the river, the scorpion agreed to perch on his head and give directions. In midstream the scorpion stung the monkey, and they both drowned.[16]

[15] The economist Hendry (1964:244) concludes from his study of the same village: "Community activities in Khanh Hau do not seem to go very far."

[16] In fact, this fable is related to children in many Middle Eastern and Asian countries by parents in order to imprint on the minds of the younger generation the necessity of being distrustful.

This fable is not thoroughly representative of the peasant mentality of mutual distrust. Were the monkey and the scroption true peasants, they would never have agreed to cooperate to mutual advantage in the first place; both would still be waiting to "cross the river" to economic development.

PERCEIVED LIMITED GOOD

A closely related facet of peasant mentality, which may in part account for this interpersonal distrust, is the tendency for peasants to view the world as having only an absolute quantity of that which is *good*. Foster (1965a, 1965b; 1967:122–152) terms this perceptual framework "the image of limited Good." He contends that peasants commonly hold to the notion that all desirables in life (including land, wealth, health, love, power, and safety) exist in finite quantity, are always in short supply, and cannot be increased in quantity by any means within the peasant's power.[17] If good exists in limited amounts in the village, and if the system is relatively closed (as are most peasant villages because of isolation and other factors), it follows logically that one can improve his position only at the expense of others. Oriented to a philosophy that the pie is limited by an unexpandable pie tin, the peasant is suspicious of his always-hungry neighbors. If one man tries to eat a larger slice, the division for his peers is upset. Thus, perceptions of limited good lead to unbridled individualism in which each peasant "sees himself in a perpetual and unrelenting struggle with his fellows . . . for possession . . . of scarce values" (Foster 1967: 134). Specific consequences of the image of limited good include a refusal by Mexican villagers to give blood transfusions and a belief in hoarding their (perceived) limited supply of semen (Foster 1962), as well as the failure of cooperatives, which are seen as personal threats rather than devices for community improvement (Foster 1967:136).

Since the basic notion of perceived limited good has been noted in locales other than the Mexican village studied by Foster,[18] there is reason to believe that many peasants give credence to this notion. Mandelbaum (1963:x) states that Indian villagers hold "the idea that the good things of the village are forever fixed in amount, and each person must manipulate constantly to garner a larger slice for his own." It is easy to see how the image of limited good might account for mutual distrust in peasants' interpersonal relations.

While there may also be a parallel image of limited bad,[19] no student of

---

[17] This conception of the image of limited good by Foster set off an exchange of critical remarks by anthropologists (Kaplan and Saler 1966; Bennett 1966; Piker 1966; Kennedy 1966) and a retort by Foster (1966).

[18] Leslie (1960:71), who investigated another Mexican village, states that his peasants "assumed that one man's gains were another man's losses."

[19] Professor Foster, who called the image of limited good to scientific attention, relates an illustration of limited bad encountered in a Navaho village with a high incidence of congenital hip disorders. The villagers believed that if a child had the disorder he was to be envied, because he had received his share of bad and would be blessed with good fortune for the rest of his life.

peasant life has reported that his respondents hold such a belief. Nor would such an image of limited bad seem to cause as many problems for programs of planned change.

DEPENDENCE ON AND HOSTILITY TOWARD GOVERNMENT AUTHORITY

The interpersonal distrust of peasants carries over into their attitudes toward government. Numerous investigators have commented upon the peasants' distrust of government leaders. For example, Dube (1958:82) notes that "the relations between the common village people and government officials are characterized by considerable distance, reserve, and distrust," and Foster (1962:48) points out that "the villager has been victimized by persons more knowledgeable than he since the beginning of time."

Of Italian peasants, Levi (1947: 76) said: "The State is more distant than heaven and far more of a scourge, because it is always against them. . . . Their only defense . . . is resignation, the same gloomy resignation, alleviated by no hope of paradise, that bows their shoulders under the scourges of nature."
In his account of Indian peasant attitudes and beliefs, Bailey (1966) reports: "One justifies cheating government agencies by saying that the officials concerned are cheating you. This perception is often so firm that even behavior which is patently not exploitative, but benevolent, is interpreted as a hypocritical cover for some as yet undisclosed interest: by definition, all horses are Trojan."

A long history of exploitation at the hands of outsiders has conditioned the villager to this hostile view. In villages in the process of modernizing, where peasants' subsistence-style independence is gradually giving way to increasing control by town merchants and government officials, it is not surprising that villagers view these authorities with hostility and apprehension.

Confounding this hostile attitude is the seeming dependence of peasants on local and national governments for the solution of village problems beyond their ken. Rao (1963:60) observes that, because the perception of the possibility of self-help is low, dependence upon the government is high. A national sample of Turkish peasants widely recognized the importance of such village problems as inadequate roads and the lack of water for irrigation (MIT Center for International Studies 1964:9), but, "Villagers tend to regard most village improvements as the job of the government rather than their own."[20] The "help-me" philosophy is more firmly imbedded in peasant minds than is the self-help approach.

This dependence on government authority may in some cases lead to overreliance of peasants upon suggestions from such official sources. Deutschmann and Fals Borda (1962a) found that the predominant pattern for peas-

[20] Similarly, in a recent inquiry among about 1,200 Brazilian peasants, we asked what was the most important problem facing their village and how it could be solved. Almost every peasant replied that only the government could solve these village problems.

ants in a Colombian village was to adopt farm innovations on a 100 percent basis without first trying them on a limited scale.[21] In comparison, American farmers almost always pass through a partial trial stage en route to full use. The difference in behavior can perhaps be attributed to the greater receptivity of Colombian peasants to authoritarian influences, such as extension change agents. Perhaps it is worth noting that in Saucío, the Colombian village investigated, there was a high degree of subsequent disuse of certain innovations, such as a new potato variety, in the years following their "forced" adoption by change agents. The peasants had implemented the new practice "by the numbers," without a thorough understanding of how to use it correctly. The eventual result was a delayed failure, brought about by a potato disease that the peasants did not know how to combat.

A more common result of peasant dependence on government authority, however, has been a frustrated wait for the arrival of development help, which seldom comes.

FAMILISM

The subordination of individual goals to those of the family, *familism*, is another related element in the subculture of peasantry. It could be argued that mutual distrust of one's peasant associates leads to greater dependence on the members of one's own family; or perhaps strong kinship ties help the family to stand together against others outside the extended family group. Whatever the basis, the family plays a central role in almost all peasant societies. Mead (1955:153) observes that to be a Latin American villager is, by definition, to belong to a *familia*. The considerable importance of the family as a reference group for peasants was emphasized by Lewis (1960b: 54) in his observations of Tepoztlan, a Mexican village: "Cooperation within the immediate family is essential, for without a family, the individual stands unprotected and isolated, a prey to every form of aggression, exploitation, and humiliation known in Tepoztlan." Barzini (1964:195) states, "The Italian family is a stronghold in a hostile land."

Individualism among peasants, although a strong force in their personality, is secondary to conformity and submission to the needs of the family. The phenomenon of individualism coexisting with strong family ties is also characteristic of Greek peasants. "Individualism is prized and rampant, yet there is no atomization. Self-esteem is paramount, and rests on freedom and self-dependence; yet Greeks do not seek freedom from the family" (Mead 1955:57). The subordination of the individual to the family is reflected by the words of a typical Indian peasant, as reported by Wiser and Wiser (1963:

[21] Similar results were reported by Rahim (1961) in Pakistan. One possible reason that peasants do not adopt on the installment plan may be that their fields are so small, often only a fraction of an acre, that it would be impractical to try a new idea partially, because of the inconvenience of planting, cultivating, and harvesting on such a diminutive scale.

122): "Each of us is not thinking of his own self. No villager thinks of himself apart from his family. He rises or falls with it. . . . Our families are our insurance."

In many peasant villages, family and kinship ties provide the basic structure for most social and political units within the community.

LACK OF INNOVATIVENESS

Peasants generally do not react to new ideas with a positive attitude. To say that peasants are tradition-oriented is to state a truism, not to offer an explanation of their behavior. The tendency for villagers to follow the prescribed ways of their ancestors may be attributed to their lack of knowledge about available alternatives. However, even when innovations in agricultural production, health, and marketing are presented to subsistence farmers, their record of adoption has seldom been enthusiastic.

Why aren't peasants more innovative? First of all, his life pattern inclines the peasant to follow those ways he knows will produce positive, even though small-scale, results rather than to try a new idea that might end in failure and thereby endanger his existence. Strassman (1964:161) notes a favorite peasant watchword: "Sharks are only dangerous to those who go swimming." This unfavorable disposition toward change is a result, in part, of generations of negative cultural conditioning — an accumulation which discourages adoption of innovations.

It is often said that the lack of peasant innovativeness is a function of scarce economic resources or of technology inappropriate for village settings.[22] Peasants are poor, and a lack of ready capital undoubtedly serves to discourage the adoption of those new ideas which require cash outlay. Peasants are also poor in technological resources and know-how. For example, since most agricultural research is conducted in temperate climates, the innovations resulting from this experimentation are generally more appropriate for the United States and Western Europe rather than for Asia, Africa, or Latin America. Many agricultural innovations from temperate climates have been introduced in tropical settings without adequate adaptation to the new conditions.[23] The result has been failure, and further negative conditioning of peasants' attitudes toward innovation.

Available evidence seems to indicate that peasant behavior is far from fully oriented toward rational and economic considerations. Undoubtedly, however, the degree to which peasants are efficiency-minded and economi-

[22] Schultz (1964) argues strongly that peasants make highly rational decisions regarding agricultural innovations within the bounds of their economic and knowledge restrictions. This position is opposed by much empirical evidence, as will be discussed in Chapter 13.
[23] The potential of agricultural research in producing culturally and climatically adapted innovations, thereby contributing to agricultural development, is pointed out by Mosher (1966) and Schultz (1964).

cally rational depends in large part on their level of modernization. It does not seem justified to assume that subsistence farmers will be promptly motivated to adopt agricultural innovations merely if the pecuniary advantages of such acceptance are pointed out.[24]

In summary, most peasants have negative attitudes toward change as a result of generations of unfavorable conditioning toward new ideas. Inherited norms against innovativeness are firmly enforced by various means of social control on the part of the villagers.[25] Deviation from these established norms will gradually be encouraged as village isolation breaks down and peasants gain new reference groups outside their village. One consequence will be a gradually more favorable reception of technological innovations by villagers,[26] but such change may be some years in coming.

FATALISM

Fatalism is the degree to which an individual recognizes a lack of ability to control his future. Fatalistic attitudes are widely reported as characteristic of peasant peoples. For example, Banfield (1958:109) found that 90 percent of the TAT (thematic apperception test) stories told by his Italian respondents had themes of calamity and misfortune; only 2 or 3 of a total of 320 protocols were happy in tone. Levi (1947:77) characterizes his peasant respondents as possessed by "passive brotherliness" and "fatalistic, comradely, old-age patience." Carstairs (1958:106) observes that the fatalistic orientation of his respondents was reflected in their pervasive uncertainty, a feeling that "nothing and nobody can be relied on, not even one's own self."

Fals Borda (1955:245) reported his Colombian peasants had "an ethos of passivity — that quality of moving only when acted upon by an outside force, or of receiving and enduring with little or no reaction." The religious beliefs of his respondents were typified by complete resignation: "The Lord giveth and the Lord taketh away." These spiritually fatalistic peasants were "anesthetized by religion" to be content with their relative distress.

---

[24] Schultz (1964:164), however, claims as follows: "Since differences in profitability are a strong explanatory variable, it is not necessary to appeal to differences in personality, education, and social environment."

[25] Foster (1967:142–143) poignantly described village social control over a typical Mexican peasant who "spends his life walking a psychological tightrope, on which a single misstep . . . will spell disaster. On the one side lie the ever-present dangers of gossip, criticism, character assassination, and perhaps witchcraft and physical attack. Too much ambition, too much aggressive action, too much improvement in one's way of living . . . will invoke them."

[26] "The notion that all farmers are handcuffed by tradition, making it impossible for them to modernize agriculture, belongs to the realm of myth" (Schultz 1964:162). If the definition of "farmers" is peasants in less developed nations, the authors would disagree with the foregoing assertion of Schultz.

Other analysts, such as Lewis (1960b:77), feel that peasant fatalism derives from an authoritarian family structure, which tends to produce passive and dependent children. Levi (1947:78) credits his respondents' strong fatalism to their ignorance of cause-effect relationships; all happenings were explained as the outcome of adverse fate. Somewhat similarly, Reichel-Dolmatoff and Reichel-Dolmatoff (1961:259) assert: "The villager's fatalistic outlook on life results in failure to see a relationship between work and one's economic condition. Having enough is thought to be almost entirely due to luck (*suerte*) and is never believed to be brought about or furthered by personal initiative."

Just as an omnipresent Fate is blamed for misfortune by peasants, so is it credited for success. Sariola (1965) found that "luck" was the response most frequently provided by Colombian peasants when they were asked the reasons for success in farming. A subsistence farmer has always found it difficult, through his struggles with nature, to raise his level of living. When he or one of his neighbors achieves progress, therefore, it is reasonable for him to credit this success to supernatural intervention. Examples are the often-encountered Latin American myths of a successful individual's "pact with the Devil," his finding buried treasure (Foster 1965; Carstairs 1958), or some other fatalistic explanation.

Peasant fatalism has dysfunctional consequences for programs of directed social change. How can change agents convince peasants of the efficacy of self-help efforts when the clients believe that the determinant of their potential well-being is a supernatural Fate? While the fatalistic orientation of peasants historically may have arisen as a rationalization for their relatively deprived state, once imbued this fatalism serves dysfunctionally to discourage efforts at progress through self-help. Rao (1963:58) aptly observes that a "fatalistic tendency prevents people from being in a state of healthy discontent." If one sees himself in control of his life situation, he can be motivated to improve his existence, but if he resigns himself to the hands of Fate, he cannot be induced to seek a higher standard of living.

LIMITED ASPIRATIONS

Aspirations are desired future states of being, such as living level, social status, education, and occupation. A common observation by most students of peasantry is that their respondents have relatively low levels of aspiration.[27]

Evidence of low aspirational levels in one Latin American village was reported by a sociologist who found the villagers had no commonly used word for "future." A sense of fatalism, the image of limited good, and the reality of blocked opportunities have conditioned peasants to low aspirations

[27] That is, in comparison with commercial farmers or urbanites. The level of aspiration can only be judged as "too high" or "too low" in terms of the relative level of actualities, as pointed out in the discussion on the revolution of rising frustrations in the preceding chapter.

for advancement. Imagine the frustration of the well-meaning Mexican plantation owner who doubled his employees' salaries, only to find they then reported to work every second day (Klineberg 1966:78).

Niehoff (1964:110) has emphasized lack of opportunity as one reason for low aspirations in Southeast Asian countries. "The Lao, Thai, Burmese and Cambodian peasant has been exploited and used by authoritarian rulers for so long, in conditions where true economic expansion was next to impossible, that he has developed an attitude of resignation and acceptance."

Achievement Motivation

When levels of aspiration remain low and fatalism is strong, the need to achieve becomes a rare mental commodity among peasants. For example, Lewis (1960:90) notes that "The majority of Tepoztecans [Mexican villagers] seem to lack strong drive or ambition for self-achievement. They tend to be satisfied if they have enough food and clothing from harvest to harvest." Foster (1965b: 307) points out: "The Anglo-Saxon virtues of hard work and thrift seen as leading to economic success are meaningless in peasant society. Horatio Alger not only is not praiseworthy, but he emerges as a positive fool, a clod who not knowing the score, labors blindly against hopeless conditions."

A peasant's life situation, with its limited resources, authoritarian child-rearing, and long history of exploitation by others, tends to produce individuals with low levels of *achievement motivation*, a social value that emphasizes a desire for excellence in order for an individual to develop a sense of personal accomplishment. Limited aspiration, a lack of achievement motivation, and a sense of fatalism may be functional for peasants whose opportunities have historically been severely limited, especially by pressures upon their major resource, land.

Inconspicuous Consumption

Even when a peasant achieves a higher level of living than that of his peers, he consumes his material gains in a non-Veblen style. Wiser and Wiser (1963:157) emphasize this tendency in the title of their book, *Behind Mud Walls*. One of their respondents said, "Our walls . . . [are] of earth so that they might be inconspicuous . . . Old walls tell no tales." Similar evidence of the "mud walls complex" is reported by scholars in several other locales; for example, Foster (1967:138) states that his Mexican respondents "wear less good clothing than they can afford, they are reluctant to reveal well-being by improving their homes, they try to eat unobserved so the quality and quantity of their food will go unnoticed, and they build high walls around their patios so envious neighbors cannot see in."

The image of perceived limited good may be related to the notion of inconspicuous consumption. Peasants who reap more than their share are thought to be "grabbing" that which does not belong to them, and thus will be ostracized. Rather than face the negative sanctions of the village, they hide their success.

The net effect of this inconspicuous consumption on one's fellow peasants is that it limits their own aspirations to material possessions.[28] How can one keep up with the Joneses when their new consumer products are hidden behind mud walls?

LACK OF DEFERRED GRATIFICATION

Functionally related to low aspirations and fatalism is a lack of *deferred gratification*, the postponement of immediate satisfaction in anticipation of future rewards (Schneider and Lysgaard 1953). Peasants are typified by impulse gratification rather than by the deferred-gratification pattern. For example, they opt for spending versus saving money. Foster (1967:115) notes this characteristic among the Mexican villagers he studied: "When people have money, they spend it; when they have nothing, they hope to borrow."

The proportionately high percentage of peasant incomes that goes for alcohol is sometimes cited as evidence of impulse gratification.[29] Undoubtedly, specific levels of alcohol consumption are strongly influenced by cultural factors, and high levels of consumption are not universal among all peasants (Hindu farmers rarely, if ever, indulge). Nevertheless, where found, this behavior signifies a lack of capital saving, from which one might infer a lack of deferred gratification.

The immediacy of the subsistence living pattern argues for concern with the here-and-now necessities of life. Banfield (1958:98) suggests that Italian peasants will not use the ballot for their long-run interest if their voting affects their short-run material advantage. The deferred-gratification pattern may well be a way of life that only those with more-than-adequate resources can afford to follow.[30] If deferring means going hungry now, one can hardly expect peasants to put much aside for the future.

For whatever reason, deferred gratification is not characteristic of peasants. In Aesop's terms, subsistence farmers behave more like the grasshopper than the ant. This lack of deferred gratification tends to perpetuate their position as hungry grasshoppers rather than as well-provisioned ants. Upward social

[28] Rostow (1964:132–144) proposed a U.S. State Department policy to create "national markets" in developing nations, whereby household consumer goods would be distributed to villagers, thus leading to higher aspirations for consumer goods, which might in turn be satisfied by higher farm production.

[29] Fals Borda (1955:145–146) reported that 20 percent of his Colombian respondents' expenditures went for drinks and tobacco (rising to 40 percent during fiestas), in comparison with 40 percent for food, 20 percent for clothing, and 10 percent for farm inputs.

[30] A notion supported by Chu's (1967) findings that Taiwanese banana growers exhibited little deferred gratification until they attained at least the minimum living standard.

mobility certainly depends in part on ability to postpone immediate gratification for the sake of long-range ends — a motivation at least in part inspired by a high level of aspiration.

LIMITED VIEW OF THE WORLD

The peasant's view of the world is shaped by the present tense and by a
restricted social environment.

Limited Time Perspective

"Greeks 'pass' the time: they do not save or accumulate or use it" (Mead
1955:70). Most peasants lack the degree of time-consciousness possessed by
urbanites or commercial farmers. Punctuality and precision are largely
foreign to village life, and, in fact, were probably not characteristic aspects
of existence in the purely traditional village. Peasants "are bewildered and
overwhelmed by our pace. To them life is not to be ticked off by seconds,
minutes, and hours. They go by the sun and the moon, by the seasons, and by
long, seemingly endless years" (Tannous 1956).

Pierce (1964:12) describes a typical instance of time-related behavior
in a Turkish village. An old man was requested to deliver some logs to the
construction site of a house. He was always "on time," but being on time
meant something quite different to him from what it meant to urban Turks.
When the old man said he would deliver the logs in the morning, he might
appear shortly after sunrise or just before noon, for he measured time in
terms of the four segments of the day between the five prayers of a good
Moslem.

Peasants generally operate in unrefined time periods, which lack the
precision[31] felt to be important by their clock-watching urban cousins. "It
is distasteful to Greeks to organize their activities according to external
limits; they are therefore either early or late, if a time is set at all" (Mead
1955:71). Subsistence farmers attach less importance to the time dimension.
In their nature-oriented, fatalistic, and localistic style of life, concern with 9
o'clock appointments, May 1 planting dates, and five-year development plans
is neither necessary nor particularly functional.

Not only are peasant perceptions of time imprecise and unimportant, but
their thinking is also less future-oriented. "The truth is that the [Egyptian
peasant] does not think outside the immediate present; he is fettered to the
moment. . . . Life is a succession of todays" (Ayrout 1963). This tendency to
think more in terms of the past and present tenses than of the future is related
to such other elements in the subculture of peasantry as fatalism and lack of
deferred gratification.

---

[31] A Filippino peasant respondent, when asked how far it was to the center of his village,
replied "One cigarette" (Feliciano 1964). He meant that he could reach the center in the
time required to smoke one cigarette. His answer implies the commonly encountered
peasant disdain for standardized quantification of time.

Localiteness

The rural and urban sectors of developing countries still coexist as separate worlds largely unknown to each other. *Localiteness* is the degree to which individuals are oriented within, rather than external to, their social system. A localistic perspective is the norm in most peasant communities. Cosmopoliteness, an orientation to the world beyond the immediate social system, is generally much less characteristic of peasants than of urbanites or elite farmers. The localiteness of peasant villagers, which indicates a lack of urban orientation and of awareness of modern possibilities, may stem from a lack of physical mobility.

(1) GEOGRAPHIC MOBILITY

The composite picture one gains of the peasant is of an individual severely circumscribed by his physical surroundings. The isolation of Colombian peasants is described thus by Reichel-Dolmatoff and Reichel-Dolmatoff (1961:26): "Year after year they use only a certain trail and when asked about trails in another direction they are often ignorant or uncertain of them . . . A man who owns a field on the slopes west of the village does not necessarily know how the slopes to the east of it can be reached. And there is little interest in knowing."

The exact degree of geographical localiteness obviously varies according to the availability of roads and means of transportation, nearness to cities, and other factors. Results from a national sampling of Turkish peasants show that "the median Turkish villager lives in a village which is about nine kilometers [six miles] from the nearest road over which regular highway transport passes" (MIT Center for International Studies 1964:9). Furthermore, nearly half of the peasants live more than three hours' travel (by usual means) from the nearest small town, and almost half live in a village totally isolated by the weather for four months of every year. Only 55 percent have ever been to the nearest city. In fact, 77 percent have no family members living outside their village and, hence, are unlikely to receive letters or visits from outsiders. "The world outside of the [peasant's] familiar circle of observations has an overall vagueness' (Bequiraj 1966:93).

(2) MASS MEDIA EXPOSURE

While mass media should to some extent compensate for the physical remoteness of peasant villages, many villagers have very little exposure to the outside world via the mass media. Such exposure to mass media on the part of peasants leads them down the road of modernization. Exposure to newspapers, magazines, films, radio, and television therefore spreads the ethic of modernity. Attendance to the mass media is a broadener of horizons, an informer, and a persuader for change.

However, mass media exposure among peasants is generally very limited.

For instance, Frey (1964) found that only about one-third of the Turkish villagers he surveyed read a newpaper once a month and about 43 percent listened to the radio once a week.

Whereas mass media exposure *could* help overcome the localiteness of peasants caused by their physical isolation, the generally low degree of media exposure among villagers at present suggests it is not doing so very substantially.

LOW EMPATHY

Empathy is the ability of an individual to project himself into the role of another person. Many villagers find it difficult to picture themselves as anything other than they are. When asked what he would do if he were president, a low-empathy Turkish peasant declared: "My God! How can you ask such a thing? How can I . . . I cannot . . . President of Turkey . . . master of the whole world?" (Lerner 1958:3). Low empathy has been cited as characteristic of peasants in Turkey (Lerner 1958; MIT Center for International Studies 1964), in Pakistan (Eister 1962), and in India (Rao 1963).

Limited exposure to other ways of life and extreme sociopsychological distance between peasants and elite urbanites make it difficult for villagers to imagine themselves in roles such as president of their country. Yet there is reason to believe that until peasants can empathize with more modern roles, such as those depicted in the mass media, they will have difficulty assuming a more modern approach to life.

The development of empathy probably results from meaningful interaction with persons in different roles. It is not enough for the peasant to realize that different roles exist; he must somehow experience what it feels to be in these roles. For example, personal ties between a villager and a schoolteacher from outside the village might serve to develop further the peasant's capacity for empathy.

Exposure of nonempathic individuals to mass media (or even trips to cities) is unlikely to have much modernizing impact. The lack of empathy among peasants acts as a sort of "mental insulator," which immunizes the villager against cosmopolite influences.

Geographical localiteness, limited mass media exposure, and an inherent lack of empathy combine to act as a barrier between modern ideas and the villager.

FUNCTIONAL INTERRELATIONSHIP OF ELEMENTS IN THE SUBCULTURE OF PEASANTRY

The preceding discussion of ten main elements in the subculture of peasantry implies a functional interdependence. In fact, to separate the subculture — in reality, a harmonious whole of mutually reinforcing parts —

into ten such components is to perform a heuristic violation that can only be allowed in an analytical sense.

Actually, there is little available empirical evidence of the interrelationship of these elements of peasant subculture although high correlation must surely be the case. For instance, Bose (1962) found six peasant values (including innovativeness and familism) in India to be interrelated about as one would expect.

The strong interrelationship of these subcultural elements suggests the difficulty of finding a "handle" with which to prime the pump of planned change, for to alter one peasant value is to affect the others. Many of the complex connections that seem to exist among the elements in the subculture of peasantry remind one of a series of locked boxes, with each box containing the key to the next box. Later chapters of this book will furnish suggestions of where it is most fruitful to pry first.

THE SUBCULTURE OF TRADITION

There is a high degree of correspondence between the subculture of peasantry, as it has been described here, and the style of life of urban poor in the United States and elsewhere. That is, a striking parallel exists between the urban poor of more developed countries and the peasants of less developed countries.[32] Much evidence of this similarity is provided by Gans' (1962) analysis of Boston slum dwellers. In fact, he entitled his book *The Urban Villagers*, suggesting that his Italian second- and third-generation respondents were still Sicilian peasants in their attitudes and style of life, even though they were living in the center of a major American city. "These data suggest strongly that the society and culture of the West Enders are quite similar to those of the Southern Italians, past and present" (Gans 1962:200). The slum dweller who is not yet integrated into American society faces a process of modernization[33] similar to the traditional villager in countries such as Colombia. In fact, the subculture of peasantry defined here may be essentially a *subculture of tradition* typifying all types of traditional individuals: urban poor, hillbillies, and many ethnic minorities, as well as peasants. These ten elements characterizing traditional persons thus serve as a benchmark for analysis of the modernization process in this book.

---

[32] And also of more developed countries. For example, Ford (1965) summarizes what is known about the value orientation of Southern Appalachian residents in the United States in terms of their familism, fatalism, impulse gratification, limited aspirations, and mutual distrust. Similarly, Donohew and Singh (1967) found the characteristics of poor Appalachian farmers to be very similar to our ten elements in the subculture of peasantry, as did Spain (1962) in West Virginia..

[33] "At present, then, lower-class cultures breed men who find it increasingly difficult to survive in modern society" (Gans 1962:268).

SUMMARY

Peasants are farmers oriented largely (but not necessarily entirely) to subsistence production. They themselves consume a large portion of their production. A subsistence economy is one in which a producer is not characterized by commercialization and monetization. Peasants, or subsistence farmers, are important subjects of study by social scientists because they constitute a majority of the population of most less developed nations. They are the largest single occupational category in today's world. There is a worsening world food/people imbalance, and disparities in per capita income and level of living are becoming greater between peasants and nonpeasants. The political stability of national governments in less developed countries often depends, in part, upon the public opinion of their peasantry.

A worldwide subculture of peasantry has been described in this chapter; it is characterized by ten functionally interrelated elements. A *subculture* contains many elements of the broader culture of which it is a part, yet can be identified by particulars that set it apart from other parts of the culture. The central elements in the subculture of peasantry defined here are: (1) mutual distrust in interpersonal relations; (2) perceived limited good; (3)dependence on and hostility toward government authority; (4) familism; (5) lack of innovativeness; (6) fatalism; (7) limited aspiration; (8) lack of deferred gratification; (9) limited view of the world; (10) low empathy.

Peasant communities are characterized by *mutual distrust*, suspicion, and evasiveness in interpersonal relations. Peasants tend to believe in the notion of *limited good* (that all desirables in life are in fixed supply) and in the related idea that one man's gain is another's loss. Government officials are viewed with both dependence and hostility. Villagers are *familistic*—that is, they subordinate their individual goals to those of the family. Peasants generally *lack innovativeness* and have an unfavorable attitude toward change.

Fatalism is the degree to which an individual perceives a lack of ability to conrol his future. Fatalistic attitudes are widely reported as characteristic of peasants. Social *aspirations* involve desired future states of being, such as living standards, social status, and occupation. A common observation in most studies of peasantry is that the respondents have relatively limited aspiration. They also lack *deferred gratification*, the postponement of immediate satisfaction in anticipation of future rewards. Peasants are also characterized by a limited view of the world. They are localistic in geographic mobility and in their exposure to mass media and have a limited time perspective. *Localiteness* is the degree to which individuals are oriented within, rather than external to, their social system. Peasants are distinguished by relatively low *empathy*, defined as the ability of an individual to project himself into the role of another.

This description of the subculture of peasantry summarizes and synthesizes what is presently known about peasants. The exact degree to which the sub-culture may be generalized is unknown, since the supporting data have come largely from case studies of single villages and observational techniques have been used mainly. The need now is to know less about more; that is, what are needed are less intensive studies of a greater number of villages in countries throughout the world.[34] How generalizable is this subculture of peasantry in various communities within the same country, and to all the less developed nations of the world? The discussion in this chapter suggests that much of the peasant subculture may be valid cross-culturally, and that it may even be valid to describe most types of traditional peoples, whether they be peasants or not. The subculture of peasantry outlined here represents a synthesis of what is known. It suggests that the peasant style of life contains many social-psychological barriers to modernization and change. The diverse elements in this subculture will be subjected to empirical analysis in forthcoming chapters.

[34] In addition to our Colombia investigation, several such studies have become available in recent years. Such peasant surveys will be cited in later chapters, and they generally provide empirical support for our concept of a subculture of peasantry, even though they were not designed explicitly to do so. Examples include Frey (1966) in Turkey, Sen and Roy (1966) in India, Bonilla and Michelena (1967: 128) in Venezuela, Smith and Inkeles (1966) in several less developed countries, and Kahl (1968) in Brazil and Mexico.

3

Middle-Range Analysis of Modernization: Closing the Gap between Grand Theory and Raw Empiricism

History teaches little else so clearly as that humanity has assumed much and learned little about the nature of social change.

(Alfred McClung Lee 1965:7)

It is futile to attempt to treat this interaction between communication and economic development as a causal relationship and isolate the chicken from the egg. The interaction is constant and cummulative.

(Y.V. Lakshmana Rao 1963)

   While a Fulbright Professor in sociology at the National University of Colombia, this writer offered a course on methods of theory construction at 9 A.M. each day and a course on social change at the following hour. In the first-mentioned class the process of conceptualizing and developing theories was examined, then how one goes about testing these formulations with empirical data. As the semester wore on, it became apparent that many of the tenets of scientific methodology taught at 9 A.M. were violated by the "grand" theories of social change considered at 10 A.M. Magniloquent and speculative in nature, many of the proferred theories appear mere intellectual baubles when one attempts to test them. It became evident that if the comprehensive theories were to be useful in guiding empirical investigation, the breach between theory and research would have to be closed.

   In an attempt to bridge this gap, middle-range analysis was chosen as our approach to the modernization process, in the belief that it would ultimately provide theoretical bases applicable to empirical investigation.

   The purposes of this chapter are to lay the foundation for a theory of modernization, to define the key concepts utilized as analytical tools in this investigation, and to describe the general methodology adopted in the chapters that follow. The primary theme to be developed is: *modernization is essentially a communication process.* Therefore, concepts and methods utilized in communication research can provide insights and instruments for a scientific dissection of the modernization process.

MIDDLE-RANGE ANALYSIS

GRAND THEORY VERSUS RAW EMPIRICISM

A great deal has been written about the related topics of social change, development, and modernization. These words have flowed from two quite different kinds of pens. On the one hand, there have been the abstract speculations of the grand theorists of social change. Their approach has been general, their concepts fuzzy; their concern has been with nation, society, or social system as the unit of analysis; and the resulting theories have seldom been translatable into empirically testable hypotheses.[1] While such theorists have undoubtedly contributed something by sensitizing us to the change process, detailed scientific understanding of this process has been advanced little.

One critic of the grand theorists, C. Wright Mills, took a lengthy passage from one of the noted works in this vein and then succinctly expressed the same propositions in a few words of "plain English," scoring the grand theorists for their verbosity: "Grand theorists are so deeply involved in [unintelligibility] that I fear we really must ask: Is grand theory merely a confused verbiage or is there, after all, also something there?" (Mills 1959: p. 27). His general conclusion seems to be: not much. "There is no 'grand theory,' no one universal scheme in terms of which we can understand the unity of social structure . . . " (Mills 1959: pp. 46–47).

Writings from the grand theory school are indeed hard to read and difficult to comprehend[2]; however, we feel that there is "something there." That "something" is a useful set of concepts and typologies, as well as some rather exiguous propositions relating these concepts.[3] What is missing in the intellectual exercises of the grand theorists is a consistent system of interrelated propositions about human behavior and how it changes, formulated at a

---

[1] Furthermore, these grand theories seldom pay explicit attention to *time*, an important variable in any change process. This neglect of the time dimension in almost all social science theory and research, except investigations dealing with the diffusion of innovations, was pointed out by Carlson (1965).

[2] This is particularly regrettable because, as Mills (1959:218) states, "Such lack of ready intelligibility, I believe, usually has little or nothing to do with the complexity of subject matter, and nothing at all with profundity of thought."

[3] Merton (1957:9) notes the tendency to create concepts, but not to relate them, in the products of the grand theorists: "A large part of what is now called sociological theory consists of *general orientations toward data, suggesting types of variables which need somehow to be taken into account,* rather than clear, verifiable statements of relationships between specified variables."

level of generalization that facilitates testing.[4] Therefore, the major short-coming of grand theory is neither unintelligibility nor lack of potentially useful content, but its *grand level*.

In stark contrast is the approach of the raw empiricists, who scurry about the world gathering data concerning the minutiae of change without generalizing their results beyond the particular peasants or village studied. Consider the enormous number of anthropological and sociological descriptions of peasant villages. There are more than 500 such published accounts of Indian villages alone. While these researchers are to be commended for their energy, they have contributed little to our ability to see village life in a *general* perspective. Just as narrow in scope as the ethnological studies of single villages are the numerous current investigations relating to the diffusion of innovations, particularly those reporting results from less developed countries. Some 1290 publications dealing with diffusion are available, and although these are less descriptive and somewhat more analytical than the village ethnologies, they suffer from a similar lack of conceptual orientation.[5] Whatever its nature, empirical investigation without theoretical basis inevitably becomes bogged down in masses of irrelevant data, and, at the same time, ignores potentially fruitful objectives.

LERNER'S MODEL OF MODERNIZATION

In this book, the authors hope to build a bridge between the writings of the grand theorists and the findings of the raw empiricists. Lerner's (1958) classic study of modernization in the Middle East has great influence on our approach. His work is commendable in several respects: he utilized certain theoretical concepts to guide his empirical investigation, and he attempted to generalize beyond the single village (and perhaps implicitly to even broader targets than the six countries he studied), thereby representing the "middle range" of analysis,[6] at once in touch with both general concepts and empirical data.

The Colombia investigation herein reported was designed to profit from

---

[4] The move away from the classical theories of social change in recent years, according to Etzioni and Etzioni (1964:7), is because "though they supplied valuable insights, when veiwed in their entirety, they turned out to be either untestable, and hence scientifically unacceptable, or only partly true at best." The more recent writings by such contemporary grand theorists as Talcott Parsons have not corrected this shortcoming. "The grand theorists gave inadequate guidance for sociological research, but no modern theory of social change has replaced them" (Etzioni and Etzioni 1964: 75).

[5] Mills (1959:55) categorically castigates members of the empirical school: "Abstracted empiricism is not characterized by any substantive propositions or theories."

[6] This notion comes from Merton (1957:9), who asks for "theories of the middle range," that is, postulated relationships which are testable but which deal only with a rather limited, particular type of behavior. These middle-range theories may eventually be consolidated into more general conceptual schemes. The authors prefer to speak of middle-range *analysis*, which is the formation and testing of theories of the middle range.

Lerner's approach. Though his study is masterful in scope and level and has proved quite influential, it suffers from at least one shortcoming. Lerner's analysis was obviously circumscribed by the fact that his data were gathered some eight years before his conceptual framework was finalized. The inadequacy of this "research-in-reverse" is not so serious as might be expected,[7] because of the ingenious way in which Lerner constructed indices (like his empathy scale, for example) to measure concepts that had not been explicitly anticipated when his data-gathering instruments were developed almost a decade earlier. Nevertheless, one cannot help but conjecture that Lerner would have wished that his conceptualization could have preceded his instrumentation, for his operations might then have shown more perfect correspondence with his concepts.

For Lerner (1958:50), the crucial variable intervening between mass media exposure and modernization effects is *empathy*, also defined by him as the capacity to place oneself in the roles of others. A traditional individual without the ability to empathize with the roles of others (as might be represented in the mass media, for example) would perhaps be entertained, but his attitudes would not be changed, by radio, film, or newspapers. Lerner found that, among the some 300 individuals he interviewed in each of six Middle Eastern countries, those who rated high in empathy were aslo more likely to be literate, urban, mass media users, and generally nontraditional in their orientations. He stated, "The acquisition and diffusion of psychic mobility [empathy] may well be the greatest characterological transformation in modern history. . . . It is in any case the most fundamental human factor that must be comprehended by all those who plan rapid economic growth by means of rapid social change" (Lerner 1963:332).

Lerner's (1958:46) model of modernization also brings concepts other than empathy into focus: "Everywhere . . . increasing urbanization has tended to raise literacy; rising literacy has tended to increase (mass) media exposure; increasing media exposure has 'gone with' wider economic participation (per capita income) and political participation (voting). . . . The same basic model reappears in virtually all modernizing societies on all continents of the world." In symbolic notation, Lerner's model may be represented as:

Urbanization → Literacy → Mass media exposure → Income and voting

In addition to several other relevant concepts, Lerner's central variables of empathy, literacy, mass media exposure, urban contact (cosmopoliteness),

---

[7] In fact, Lerner (1953) says that, although "the interview schedule was designed on a 'soup-to-nuts' basis, covering some 60 pages with questions that ranged over a dozen large categories and took over 3–4 hours to administer, the richness of the data produced . . . is a strong argument for what has been called a 'fishing expedition' approach to areas of which the investigator is ignorant, rather than more precise 'hypothesis-test' research designs."

[8] Causal inferences supporting this sequential model are provided by McCrone and Cnudde (1967), using the method of "path analysis" with aggregate correlational data.

and political participation have been utilized in the present investigation.[9] Whereas Lerner primarily studied the relationships between two variables at a time (for instance, literacy and empathy), this investigation takes advantage of the additional information that can be gleaned from multivariate analysis, which would seem to be an improvement in that multivariate analysis allows one to examine the nature of intervening relationships. For example, the relationship between literacy and empathy might be (affected by) another variable such as mass media exposure, which is related to both literacy and empathy. Multivariate analysis allows us to test the effects of a third (or fourth or more) variable on the relationship between two other variables.

RELATING THEORY AND RESEARCH: THE MIDDLE RANGE

The authors prefer to operate in the middle range, an area relating theory to research and research to theory.[10] The theoretical basis for this must be specific enough to be empirically testable, or else it is useless. Conversely, the specific data must test theoretical hypotheses, or else they become irrelevant. Such interplay between theoretical concepts and empirical data, though complex in nature, may perhaps be demonstrated with the following illustration of the essential steps in middle-range analysis.

Concepts are dimensions stated in their most basic terms. An example is empathy, defined previously as the ability of an individual to project himself into the role of another person. Stated conceptually in such general terms, empathy could be studied in a number of different situations: the theater, counseling, employer-employee relations, or any other facet of communication behavior. Relationships posited between empathy and other concepts are examples of *theories* or *theoretic hypotheses*.[11] Application of one theory deal-

---

[9] Also adopted is Lerner's implicit assumption that modernization can occur among *adults*, in addition to children (as a result of socialization experiences). Most other social-psychological theories of modernization, like those of McClelland and Hagen, are based upon alterations in values and attitudes of children (see Chapter 11).

[10] Our approach is an illustration of the viewpoint prescribed by Glaser and Straus (1967: vii–viii), which they term "grounded theory." Attempts to close the gap between theory and research in the past have concentrated mainly on the improvement of methods for testing theory, and efforts to close the gap from the theory side have not been very successful. Glaser and Straus seek middle-range theories that are grounded in social research itself, to generate these theories from data. While there is utility in the grounded-theory approach, the authors also wish to draw upon available theories as guidance for directing empirical research. That is, the intent here is to use deduction as well as induction in middle-range analysis.

[11] A theory or a theoretic hypothesis is defined as a postulated relationship between two or more concepts. Merton (1957: 89) states, "It is only when . . . concepts are interrelated in the form of a scheme that a theory begins to emerge. Concepts, then, constitute the definitions (or prescriptions) of what is to be observed; they are the variables between which empirical relationships are to be sought. When propositions are logically interrelated, a theory has been instituted."

ing with empathy may be expressly limited to the modernization process. This should not prevent, but rather encourage, the postulation of similar relationships dealing with other types of behavior. Middle-range analysis can offer one route toward more general theories; but middle-range hypotheses deal only with a rather specific type of behavior.

In order to test a theoretic hypothesis, such as, "literacy is positively related to empathy," we must operationalize or measure each of the two concepts. These empirical measures of concepts, called *operations*, may be attitude scales, indexes, observations, or answers to direct questions. Empathy can be operationalized by an empathy scale, and literacy by a functional literacy test. An *epistemic relationship* is the correspondence between a concept and its operation. The degree to which isomorphism is present between concept and operation is always of great importance in any type of scientific research, but this type of epistemic validity cannot be definitely determined except on intuitive grounds. It is impossible to compute a measure of association, like a correlation coefficient, between concept and operation because the concept exists at the theoretical rather than at the empirical level.

An *empirical hypothesis* corresponds to the theoretic hypothesis, but it expresses the postulated relationship between two or more operations, for example, that functional literacy scores are positively related to empathy scores. Statistical methods are often, but not necessarily, utilized to provide a basis to accept or reject empirical hypotheses. They provide sufficient, but not necessary, tools for testing hypotheses. If an empirical hypothesis is accepted, we are provided with some positive evidence for the accompanying theoretic hypothesis. Suppose that a correlation of .56 is found between functional literacy scores and empathy scores — a relationship significantly different from zero. The empirical hypothesis and the theoretic hypothesis that literacy is positively related to empathy are therefore accepted.

Thus, propositions at the theoretical and empirical levels are related by the joint processes of *deduction* (proceeding from theoretic to empirical hypotheses) and *induction* (from empirical results to the conceptual level). The eventual goal of middle-range analysis is the development of an interrelated, integrated series of concepts, linked in a set of theories. As additional findings become available, further truth claims for these theoretic relationships accumulate in a consistent and meaningful manner, and the eventual goal, a set of principles or perhaps even laws[12] of human behavior, may be realized.

In the chapters that follow the authors hope to demonstrate this middle-range approach to inquiry. However, the empirical hypothesis will seldom be stated, since it is fairly self-evident from the theoretic hypothesis and often is quite repetitious in its wording.

---

[12] We shall use the terminology sequence of "theories," "generalizations," "principles," and "laws" throughout, as one proceeds from low to high probability along the continuum of claims to truth.

A summary of the essentials in middle-range analysis is provided schematically in Fig. 3-1.

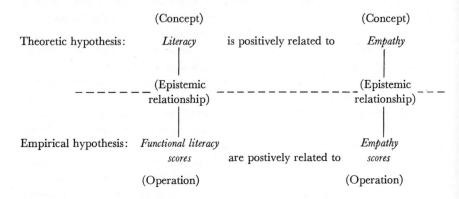

THE COMMUNICATION APPROACH TO STUDY OF MODERNIZATION

Modernization has been defined earlier as the process by which individuals change from a traditional way of life to a more complex, technologically advanced, and rapidly changing style of life. Change from the traditional to the more modern necessarily involves the communication and acceptance of new ideas. Examining this process at the village level, one can see that programs of change in villages are usually initiated by sources external to the social system. Communication thus becomes a vital factor in implementing and securing change. If the communication approach[13] is taken as the basic point of view, the authors are in general agreement with Pye (1938:38), except for his choice of verb tense, that "It was the pressure of communications which brought about the downfall of traditional societies." Since invention within a closed system like a peasant village is a rare event, until there is communication of ideas from sources external to the village, little change can occur in peasant knowledge, attitudes, and behavior. Communication is therefore central to modernization in such circumstances.

Not only is communication the essential link through which externally oriented ideas *enter* the village, it is also a central force for facilitating further dissemination *within* the village. Modernization can therefore be advantageously viewed as a communication process.

Communication, the process by which messages are transferred from a source to a receiver, is the central and vital concept explaining human behavior. Usually some external stimulus, perceived by an individual, provides impetus

---

[13] The communication approach can naturally be utilized by social scientists in a number of disciplines such as sociology, social psychology, anthropology, political science, and economics. The viewpoint is essentially interdisciplinary and multidisciplinary but is perhaps expressed in its most integrated aspects by communication researchers in the modest number of departments and institutes of communication that have sprung up, largely since the end of World War II, in American and other universities.

for behavior alteration. In terms of the oversimplified but useful model of the communication process called S-M-C-R-E[14]: a *source* (S) sends a *message* (M) via certain *channels* (C) to the *receiving* individual (R), who responds or reacts to this stimulus with an *effect* (E). Much present-day communication research focuses on the effects of the source, message, or channel on change in knowledge, attitudes, and overt behavior of the receiver.[15]

Modernization, as has been stressed, is largely a communication process,[16] in which the receivers are generally the people of less developed nations. Modernization messages may be technological, economic, political, or social, but all are concerned with new methods for societal functioning. The information sources are scientists, government planners, change agents, and other originators of new ideas from both the homeland and abroad. A variety of communication channels are utilized, ranging from nationwide radio broadcasts to personal discussions taking place between two villagers on a rural path. The basic elements of the communication process are thus involved in all the myriad decisions that together constitute modernization. The fruitful utilization of communication as a focus for observing and analyzing the modernization process will, hopefully, become apparent in the course of the present study.

ANTECEDENT, INTERVENING, AND CONSEQUENT VARIABLES

When analyzing a process such as modernization, which occurs over time, it is methodologically useful to classify one's variables as antecedent, intervening, and consequent. *Antecedent variables* are those which precede the others in order of time and which theoretically are expected to lead to or be followed by certain other variables. *Consequent variables* follow the antecedents in time.[17]

[14] Postulated by Berlo (1960) as S-M-C-R.

[15] A number of useful propositions have emerged from communication research dealing with S-E relationships. For example, numerous experimental investigations suggest that highly credible sources (that is, message origins perceived by receivers as relatively more trustworthy) cause more attitude change than sources with low credibility.

[16] "The basic process of political modernization and national development can be advantageously conceived as problems in communication" (Pye 1963:8). Unfortunately, there is no evidence that government officials in charge of development programs recognize this fact. Until they do, this statement that modernization is a communication process is intellectually true but is irrelevant in a policy sense.

[17] Antecedents do not necessarily *cause* consequences. For X to cause Y, it must (1) precede Y in time, but (2) X must also have a "forcing quality" on Y. A folk tale illustrating the complexity of determining causality (which some argue cannot be done definitively with empirical research procedures, but only on a theoretical basis) concerns a hungry peasant who purchased a huge roll and ate it. But he was still hungry, so he bought another roll and ate it; and similarly, a third roll. When the three rolls failed to satisfy his hunger, he bought some pretzels. After eating one pretzel, he no longer felt hungry. Suddenly he clapped his hand to his head and cried, "What a fool I am! Why did I waste all those rolls? I should have eaten a pretzel in the first place" (Tolstoy 1962). Because of the complexities of ascertaining causal relationships, this book shall deal only with antecedents and consequences of modernization, not with causes and effects.

Intervening variables affect the relationship between antecedent and consequent variables. In an illustration already cited, it was suggested that mass media exposure may function as an intervening variable between the antecedent of literacy and the consequent of empathy. Chapters 4 and 5 will present empirical tests of whether a conception of media exposure as intervening (that is, literacy → mass media exposure → empathy) is more valid than a view of literacy as being directly related to empathy. In other chapters, similar multivariate methods of analysis will be employed to determine whether empathy and fatalism intervene between certain antecedent and consequent variables. Here, literacy, mass media exposure, and cosmopoliteness (and change agent contact, in Chapter 8) will generally be utilized as the major antecedent variables, although in certain chapters, media exposure and cosmopoliteness may be tested as intervening variables. Innovativeness, political knowledge, and educational and occupational aspirations are conceptualized only as consequent variables. In certain chapters, and especially in two-variable hypotheses (where there is only an antecedent and a consequent), other concepts such as empathy and mass media exposure occasionally may be regarded as consequences.

The general classification of the central concepts in the present inquiry into antecedent, intervening, and consequent groups is shown in Fig. 3-2. Various, more specific versions of this type of paradigm will be presented in the chapters that follow. A basic notion conveyed in the diagram in Fig. 3-2 is that

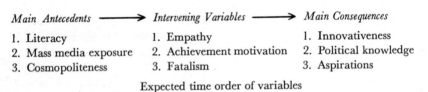

Main Antecedents ⟶ Intervening Variables ⟶ Main Consequences

1. Literacy
2. Mass media exposure
3. Cosmopoliteness

1. Empathy
2. Achievement motivation
3. Fatalism

1. Innovativeness
2. Political knowledge
3. Aspirations

Expected time order of variables

Figure 3-2. Paradigm of Antecedent, Intervening, and Consequent Variables in Modernization.

modernization is mainly directed or brought about by factors external to the social system. A peasant village is ordinarily in a state of dynamic equilibrium[18]; that is, change occurs at a rate compatible with the system's capability to absorb it in an orderly fashion, without causing complete disorganization or disruption of the system. Innovations, usually technological, are communicated to the village, generally from an external source. Introduction of such an innovation temporarily disturbs the equilibrium of the social system, and social change (alteration in social structure and functioning) occurs. Such alterations help to bring the system back to a state of equilibrium.

[18] It is not implied that no change is occurring in a social system which is in a state of dynamic equilibrium, but only that the rate of change in such a system is manageable by the system.

Each of the three antecedent variables in our paradigm are concerned with external channels by which technological innovations reach peasant villages: (1) literacy is a necessary prerequisite to most print media exposure[19]; (2) mass media exposure indicates use of one type of communication channels by which modernization messages may reach large peasant audiences; and (3) cosmopoliteness is an indicator of exposure to phenomena external to the immediate social system.

The consequent variables listed in Fig. 3-2 are certain conditions that are to be brought about as a result of directed change programs in less developed countries. For example, it is hoped that innovations will be adopted as a result of directed change.

CONCEPTS: THE BUILDING BLOCKS OF THEORY

A concept, as previously defined, is a dimension stated in its most basic terms. For each of the nine main concepts [20,21] examined in our study, we shall now present (1) a definition derived from past definitions as well as from conceptual considerations, and (2) the measure or measures utilized to operationalize the concept. Further detail on both the meaning of each concept and its measure are then provided in later chapters.

LITERACY

Literacy is the degree to which an individual possesses mastery over symbols in their written form. This concept was measured in Colombia with a functional literacy test. Each respondent was handed a small card during the interview and was asked to read a sentence that was printed on it (in Spanish). His functional literacy score equaled the number of the six key words in the sentence he could read correctly.[22]

[19] Someone in the village, if not all, must be literate before a newspaper can have impact, for example.

[20] At this point, one might ask how the nine main concepts of this investigation were selected and on what basis additional concepts were excluded. Our general focus, as has already been pointed out, is upon a communication approach to development; thus, economic variables are not much emphasized here. (Such concepts as per capita income and production per acre proved extremely difficult to operationalize among our Colombian subsistence respondents.) There is a close correspondence between the nine main concepts in this study and the ten elements in the subculture of peasantry as outlined in Chapter 2, but this is not a one-to-one relation, because adequate measures could not be devised in Colombia for some of the subculture elements (deferred gratification, for instance).

[21] Some confirming evidence of the importance of these nine concepts was provided by Smith and Inkeles (1966) after the present analysis was largely completed. They analyzed data from 5500 men in six developing countries and found fourteen items (out of 119) most central to modernization. Seven of our nine main concepts are clearly represented among their fourteen variables; the exceptions are literacy and achievement motivation.

[22] This functional literacy test is described in some detail by Mendez and Waisanen (1964), as well as in the following chapter.

Literacy is certainly one of the key antecedent concepts from which numerous modernization consequences flow. "The impact of literacy cannot be underestimated" (Powdermaker 1962: 280). Literacy enables a villager to gain direct exposure to the print media. Literacy also seems to unlock certain mental abilities (such as symbol manipulation and the capacity to think counterfactually) that may, in turn, lead to modernization. Further, literacy allows the receiver (1) to control his rate of message inputs and (2) to retrieve past messages from print media.

MASS MEDIA EXPOSURE

Mass communication channels include newpapers, magazines, films, radio, and television, all of which enable a source of one or several individuals to transfer messages to an audience of many. Exposures to each of these five media were combined into a composite mass media exposure score for each of our Colombian respondents. The indicator of degree of exposure to each medium was in terms of the number of radio shows listened to per week, newspapers read per week, films seen per year, and so on.

The mass media in less developed countries like Colombia carry mainly prodevelopment messages (McNelly 1966). Thus, we expect exposure to these messages to be positively related to innovativeness, political knowledge, and other consequent variables. These and other hypotheses about the role of mass media exposure in modernization will be tested in Chapter 5 with data from Colombia, India, and Kenya. The different roles of mass media and interpersonal communication channels in diffusing innovations and how they may be combined in media forums to maximize their modernization effects are discussed in Chapter 6.

COSMOPOLITENESS

Cosmopoliteness is the degree to which an individual is oriented outside his social system. In general, it is expected that cosmopolite villagers will be leaders in the modernization process, and serve as links with the larger society. The cosmopolite is partially freed from the pressures of social control that demand conformity to traditional village norms. He has other reference groups in the market town or the city. As Thoreau remarked, "If a man does not keep pace with his companions, perhaps it is because he hears a different drummer. Let him step to the music which he hears, however measured or far away." The cosmopolite marches to a more distant tune.

Basically, cosmopoliteness is viewed as bringing about other modernization variables; however, the arrows of time order may actually point in the other direction. It is possible that a higher degree of innovativeness (and other modernization indicators) may lead the peasant to seek escape from village norms by travel to the city, by contact with change agents, and by other types of cosmopolite behavior.

The main indicator of cosmopoliteness in the present investigation (see Chapter 7) is the number of trips made by villagers to urban centers; but it is not necessary to travel outside the village to be cosmopolite. Other indicators of this concept are contact with such external change agents as extension workers, school teachers, and salesmen of farm products (Chapter 8). External communication can even be gained via interpersonal contact with fellow villagers who are cosmopolites; this multistep flow of communication will be discussed in Chapter 10.

EMPATHY

Empathy has been variously described by Lerner as: (1) "the capacity for identification with new aspects of [the respondent's] environment" (1958: 49); (2) "the capacity to see oneself in the other fellow's situation" (1958: 50); (3) "the capacity for rearranging the self-system on short notice" (1958:51); (4) "mobile sensibility" (1958:49); and (5) "psychic mobility" (1958:51). Throughout all these statements there is a central theme: empathy is the individual's ability to identify with others' roles, especially with those who are different from oneself. In defining empathy as the ability of an individual to project himself into the role of another, we assume that if he understands this other's feelings he will take them into account when dealing with him.

Lerner operationally measured empathy as the ability to identify with certain others' roles, particularly those who were more modern than the respondent. His empathy scale included items in which the respondent was asked to put himself in such roles as a radio station director and the president of the country. Other recent measures of empathy have focused on public roles of varying psychological distance from the respondent, but always those more modern and of higher status than that of the respondent.[23] In Colombia our investigators measured empathy with five such items. A typical question was: "If you were president of the village development committee, what would you do next year?" Judges scored each item on a three-point scale in order to measure the respondent's empathic ability. Further detail on the construction of our measure of empathy is presented in Chapter 9.

The ability to put oneself in others' roles is seen here as one result of communication with the world outside the village. Lack of empathy comes about from personality socialization in a restricted environment, such as an isolated peasant village, where the number of different roles being played is severely circumscribed. The resulting lack of role-taking ability later leads to a psychological rejection of unfamiliar roles when these are encountered (as in the mass media or when a peasant travels to the city) and a distrust of people who are cast in these novel roles (Stewart and Hoult 1959). Lack of empathy

[23] Examples are Eister (1962), Rao (1963), and Lerner (1964a).

serves to insulate the traditional individual from the very cosmopolite communication messages that could develop higher empathy in him. Low empathic ability also dampens the effects of such cosmopolite communication exposure upon innovativeness and other possible consequences. The non-empathic receiver is thus psychologically waterproofed against modernizing influences.

ACHIEVEMENT MOTIVATION

There is seldom a perfect balance between what an individaul *wants* and what he *gets*. These states of unfilled desires or motivations are predictive of much future human behavior. The present study deals mainly with two kinds of motivational variables: (1) occupational achievement motivation; (2) aspirations, both educational and occupational.

A definition of achievement motivation that is both precise and widely accepted is to some extent wanting. McClelland (1961:76) stated that achievement motivation "is the desire to do well not so much for the sake of social recognition or prestige, but to attain an inner feeling of personal accomplishment." In our study, *achievement motivation* is defined as a social value that emphasizes a desire for excellence in order for an individual to attain a sense of personal accomplishment. Undoubtedly, achievement motivation could be expressed in sports, love, and many other activities, but our interest is mainly in its *occupational* expression. There is much theoretical justification for expecting that villagers with high levels of occupational achievement motivation should be more innovative in adopting new ideas and, generally, should be more modern in their outlook.

Achievement motivation was measured in past studies by thematic apperception tests (TAT) and by sentence-completion quizzes. Illustrative of the sentence-completion items utilized to measure achievement motivation among our Colombian peasants is the following: "In the next 10 years I am going to. . . ." The judges coded the responses in five levels of achievement motivation, and the scores on individual items were summed for the total score. Results of a detailed scale analysis, described in Chapter 11, show that the achievement motivation scale met acceptable levels of reliability, internal consistency, and scoring agreement.

ASPIRATIONS

As previously defined, aspirations are desired future states of being. *Educational aspirations* are the level of formal education desired by parents for their children. In the Colombian inquiry the respondents were asked how many years of formal schooling they desired for their oldest son. The question was put hypothetically, in order to apply equally to respondents with and without sons.

Similarly, *occupational aspirations* are defined as a level of occupational prestige that parents desire for their children. In the present investigation, villagers were asked what occupation they wished for an eldest son. Their responses were coded in terms of five levels of occupational prestige, ranging from manual labor to the professions.

Because it is probable that both educational and occupational aspirations are generally raised as a result of increased contact with the world outside the village, these are regarded mainly as consequent variables[24] in later chapters.

FATALISM

Fatalism is the degree to which an individual perceives a lack of ability to control his future. Following the lead of Niehoff and Anderson (1966), this author developed a nine-item scale to measure three subdimensions of fatalism: (1) supernatural influence, including belief in theological and magical explanations of human behavior; (2) situational fatalism, which is a belief (often realistic) in limited opportunities for improvement of conditions; and (3) project negativism or apathy toward development activity because of past failures. Typical items in this scale are:

1. When man is born, his life is predetermined and he cannot modify it.
2. New techniques and machines work better than good weather in assuring good crops.[25]

A factor analysis of responses to items in the nine-item scale indicated that they seemed to measure a total dimension, which appeared to be fatalism, and that the three subdimensions seemed to be represented within the total scale about as expected. Thus, responses to each of the nine items were summed to make a total fatalism score.

What is the role of fatalism in the modernization process? We conceive of it as an intervening variable, following such antecedent variables as literacy, mass media exposure, and empathy (because communication with a less fatalistic world outside the village ideally should decrease fatalism), and in turn as being related (negatively) to such consequent variables as innovativeness, achievement motivation, and aspirations. In Chapter 12 an alternative conception of fatalism — that it is a *post hoc* rationalization by peasants for failure, rather than an intervening variable between modernization antecedents and consequences — will be explored.

---

[24] It was pointed out earlier that, when aspirations increase more rapidly than actualities, the result is rising frustration, which in extreme cases may be expressed in terms of political revolution or social disorganization. No data are available from our respondents in this study, however, about these more radical consequences of unfulfilled aspiration, although we have a measure of satisfaction with their level of living (Chapter 16).

[25] Agreement with this scale item indicates a low degree of fatalism, so that its scoring is reversed from that of the other items.

INNOVATIVENESS

Innovativeness denotes the degree to which an individual is earlier than others in his social system to adopt new ideas (Rogers 1962:159). Two different operational scales of innovativeness were constructed: (1) an agricultural innovativeness scale including the composite time-of-adoption of sixteen new farm practices, such as use of fertilizers, new crop varieties, insecticides, and machinery; and (2) a home innovativeness scale (constructed similarly), in which more points are awarded for earlier adoption of seven home innovations, such as installation of latrines and medicine cabinets.

Adopting new technological ideas is certainly the heart of the modernization process. Hence, innovativeness is utilized as a consequent variable throughout most of the chapters that follow. A detailed discussion of predicting innovativness will appear in Chapter 13.

POLITICAL KNOWLEDGE

Modernization and economic development of a country is accompanied by an expansion of government services, as well as a greater importance of the political institution in daily life. Citizen participation in political affairs must accordingly be emphasized if a developing country is to function properly.

Lerner (1958) found that greater political participation was associated with empathy, literacy, and mass media exposure among his Middle Eastern respondents. Largely as a result of interview rapport difficulties in determining the degree of respondents' political participation (such as voting in national elections), political knowledge is more often utilized as a measure of their political modernization.[26] *Political knowledge*, then, is the degree to which an individual comprehends facts essential to his functioning as an active and effective citizen. Such information might be gained from formal education, mass media exposure, trips to urban centers, or via interpersonal communication with others more knowledgeable than himself in these matters. Such political awareness probably indicates active information-seeking, a distinct feeling of being a part of a nation's citizenry, and at least a minimal degree of political modernization.

Our measure of political knowledge is a five-item scale including questions referring to such information as the name of the local representative to the national legislature. In the chapters that follow, political knowledge will be utilized as a consequent variable.

MULTIVARIATE CORRELATION ANALYSIS

After this review of some of the key concepts in the present inquiry, let us consider the research methods that will be utilized to analyze the empirical relationships among these concepts. We shall seek to untangle the threads of

---

[26] An illustration is Deutschmann's (1963) study conducted in a Colombian peasant village.

modernization among the Colombian peasants studied by determining the degree of correlation between pairs of variables, sometimes controlling or removing the effect of third, fourth, and additional variables. Therefore, this type of inquiry can be classified as *correlational* rather than experimental. The basic measure of association utilized is the Pearsonian coefficient of correlation r, which ranges from $+1$ (a "perfect" positive relationship) to 0 (no relationship) to -1 (a "perfect" negative association). It should be remembered that correlation coefficients measure only *linear* relationships among variables. In the chapters that follow, there is little reason to anticipate curvilinear relations among variables; and in fact, such relationships are not encountered when the variables are checked empirically.

Our approach to the study of modernization is essentially multivariate. Undoubtdly, many of the concepts previously discussed in this chapter are highly interrelated, and several may covary almost completely. This is an appropriate situation in which to use multivariate statistical procedures to consider relationships among more than two variables at one time. The three chief multivariate statistical methods to be utilized are the following.

1. *Partial correlation* is a measure of association that mathematically removes the effect of other variables from the relationship between a pair of variables. Partial correlation techniques are often used to determine whether a variable intervenes in the relationship between two other variables. An example of this occurs in Chapter 5 when the effect of literacy upon selected modernization consequences (like innovativeness) is determined, with control on mass media exposure. In our illustration, using data gathered from the peasants in Pueblo Viejo, we shall compute a zero-order correlation r_{12} (that is, a relationship between a pair of variables without controling on any others) of .437 between literacy scores and empathy scores. In other words, about 19 percent (r_{12}^2 or $.437^2$) of the variance in literacy and empathy scores occurs in common. Next, partial correlation techniques are used to remove the effect of mass media exposure from the relationship of literacy and empathy. The first-order partial correlation of literacy and empathy, with a control on mass media exposure, is .345. The zero-order correlation r_{12} and the partial correlation $r_{12.3}$ are diagrammed as shown below to demonstrate that the literacy-empathy correlation is lowered when the effect of mass media

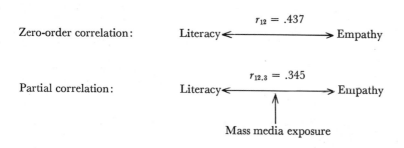

Zero-order correlation: Literacy $\xleftrightarrow{\quad r_{12} = .437 \quad}$ Empathy

Partial correlation: Literacy $\xleftrightarrow{\quad r_{12.3} = .345 \quad}$ Empathy

Mass media exposure

exposure is removed.[27] Hence mass media exposure does tend to act somewhat as an intervening variable.

2. *Multiple correlation* is a statistical method in which two or more independent (or antecedent) variables are used to predict or explain the variance in a dependent (or consequent) variable. An example of the use of multiple correlation occurs in Chapter 11, where we seek to predict the variance in achievement motivation scores with a battery of three antecedent variables[28] — literacy, cosmopoliteness, and empathy. With data from Pueblo Viejo, the following results were obtained:

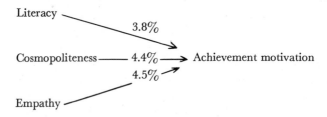

In this illustration, the results of the multiple correlation analysis show that a total of 12.7 percent of the variance in achievement motivation scores is explained by the three antecedent variables of (1) literacy, which explains 3.8 percent of the variance in achievement motivation exclusive of that explained by cosmopoliteness or empathy; (2) cosmopoliteness, which contributes 4.4 percent; and (3) empathy, which explains 4.5 percent of the variance.

This example shows how multiple correlation methods of data analysis give the share of the variance in the consequent variable that is explained by each of the antecedent variables, independent of that part explained by all the other antecedent variables.

3. *Factor analysis* is a statistical procedure in which a common factor[29] (or factors) is abstracted from the interrelationships among a number of variables. Factor analysis is used as a means of determining the number of subdimensions present in a series of scale items, as in our fatalism scale (Chapter 12).

[27] In certain of the chapters that follow we shall use the z test for difference between two correlations to determine whether the zero-order correlation and the corresponding partial correlation differ significantly. Some critics point out that this procedure is appropriate only when the two correlations are independent, that is, when they are drawn from different samples. Our experience indicates that violation of this assumption is not very important. For example, when we divide the total sample randomly into two independent subsamples and compute the zero-order correlation from one of these and the partial correlation from the other, the result obtained is almost always the same as when the total sample is not divided in this way.

[28] Three additional independent variables (formal education, social status, and mass media exposure), are included in this multiple correlation analysis in Chapter 11 but, for the sake of simplicity, are not shown in the present example.

[29] A *factor* is a general and abstract dimension that is found to recur in a number of empirical variables which share common variance and which therefore reflect a single dimension "causing" the set of variables to associate with each other.

Factor analysis is also used to select a minimum set of variables that indicate the general dimension of modernization (see Chapter 14). This procedure recognizes that all the variables are correlated to some degree, as will be seen in the next ten chapters, and seeks to determine the web of interrelationships among these modernization factors.

Thus, the statistical methods of data analysis utilized in this investigation are described as correlational and multivariate.

SHORTCOMINGS OF THE PRESENT APPROACH

There are several procedural limitations in the conceptual approach proposed in this chapter:

1. Our modernization model greatly oversimplifies reality.
2. The classification of variables as antecedent, intervening, and consequent is rather arbitrary.
3. Dangers of nonequivalence in cross-cultural comparison of findings (those from Colombia with data from India, Kenya, and other countries) arise from such sources as cultural and language differences in measurement of concepts.

CONCEPTUAL OVERSIMPLIFICATION

One problem with the antecedent-intervening-consequent variables paradigm presented earlier in this chapter is its deceptive neatness and simplicity, for the categorization of our variables into these three types is at best arbitrary and at worst a misconception. In reality, the concepts represented in our modernization model are probably connected in a mosaic of interrelationships rather than as antonomous antecedents, intervening variables, and consequents. Because of this functional interconnectedness, a change in any one of these variables brings about alterations in all the others. This notion is implicit in Lerner's (1958:78) remark that individuals and their environments change together or else little modernization occurs.[30] When we study two-variable relationships (such as the hypothesis that literacy is positively related to empathy) or even three-variable "chains" of relationships, we should not forget that we are, thereby, artificially and heuristically chopping up reality into conceptual "morsels." While such processing may aid ingestion, it also adds an ersatz flavor.

ARBITRARY TIME-ORDER CLASSIFICATION OF VARIABLES

A further problem with our paradigm is the questionable validity of the implied time-order. An antecedent variable ideally should precede a consequent variable, in the real world as well as in our model. Although the

---

[30] Also in Lerner (1963:329): "Modernity is an interactive behavioral system. It is a 'style of life' whose components are interactive in the sense that the efficient functioning of any one of them requires the efficient functioning of all the others."

time order of our concepts seems more-or-less logical, it is difficult or even impossible to prove, for many of the relationships are probably interdependent.[31] Zetterberg (1965:70) describes an interdependent relationship as one in which "A small increment in one variable results in a small increment in a second variable; then, the increment in the second variable makes possible a further increment in the first variable, which in turn affects the second one, and so this process goes on until no more increments are possible." For example, literacy may cause a small increase in empathy, which in turn leads to an increment in literacy, which leads to a further increase in empathy, and so on. Who is to say whether literacy or empathy is the antecedent variable in this relationship? Each is, and yet neither is. Hence our time-order classification of variables as antecedents and consequences is empirically arbitrary, even though perhaps logically correct.

CROSS-CULTURAL EQUIVALENCE

The third problem is that of cross-cultural comparison and generalization of results from Colombia to other less developed countries like India and Kenya. Even though the importance of cross-culturally valid generalizations from modernization research is obvious, we must also be properly cautious. Kluckhohn and Strodtbeck (1961: 82) warn that "anyone who has attempted cross-cultural testing, using the medium of language, is well aware of the deep and as yet bridgeless chasms which separate the linguistically ordered thought-ways of the peoples of varying cultural traditions. . . ." One can never be certain that what is measured by the functional literacy test in Colombia (in Spanish) is identical with what one measures with a seemingly similar measure in India (in Hindi).[32] Obviously one must resort to the level of *conceptual equivalence* in cross-cultural comparative inquiry, rather than pursue the goal of *operational equivalence*, which would seem an impossible objective. But even conceptual equality is difficult to attain perfectly, and its assessment must be made on logical rather than directly on empirical grounds.

The three-pronged problem of conceptual oversimplification, the arbitrary time-order categorization of variables in our modernization model, and the perils of cross-cultural comparison will continue to plague us throughout this work. We shall return to a discussion of its seriousness and its possible amelioration in the last chapter.

---

[31] As Lerner (1958:58) realized when he stated, "Once the modernizing process is started, chicken and egg in fact 'cause' each other to develop."

[32] This problem of linguistic equivalence is as serious in comparative research as in international relations and diplomacy, where a number of famous misunderstandings have occurred. For instance, the off-quoted Khrushchev remark, "We will bury you," has usually been interpreted in English in its active sense to mean "We will destroy you." Actually the translation as "We will bury you" is literally correct, but only in the sense that "We will still be alive when you are dead" (Klineberg 1966:153).

GATHERING THE DATA

Peasant life represents the traditional base line against which the modernization process is observed and measured. Our research design for the present study purposely required a number of peasant villages *to represent a range in the degree to which modernizing influences had penetrated.*[33] What were wanted were one or more villages that were very traditional and others that were relatively more modern.

The main focus here is on the progress of peasants in Colombian villages as they proceed along the continuum from traditional to modern styles of life. Peasants around the world exhibit certain common attitudes, behavioral patterns, and life styles; deciphering the common relationships among these variables should lead to some cross-culturally valid generalizations about the modernization process. After describing the data gathering in Colombia for our study, we shall explain how comparable data were obtained in India and Kenya.

TRADITIONAL AND MODERN VILLAGES IN COLOMBIA

Colombia was selected as the main site for this study because it offered a first-hand research opportunity for examining the process of modernization in a less developed nation. This investigation is primarily concerned with five Colombian villages and 255 villagers, although in one section of this book (Chapter 11) data from a sixth village, Támesis (Fig. 3-3), is included. Four villages (Támesis, Pueblo Viejo,[34] San Rafael, Cuatro Esquinas) are relatively more modern than the other two (La Cañada, Nazate). The most progressive community in the study was Támesis, about 120 miles from Bogotá; the most traditional was La Cañada, an isolated village in the southernmost mountains of Colombia near Ecuador. San Rafael, Cuatro Esquinas, and Pueblo Viejo are all located close to the major city of Bogotá, whereas Nazate and La Cañada are relatively isolated from external influence because of their remote geographic location and inadequate transportation. Greater detail on the nature of these Colombian villages and villagers is provided in the appendix of this book.

These villages range in the degree of penetration of mass media, change agents, and technological innovations in health and agriculture (as shown in Table 17-1 of the Appendix). Peasants in the more modern villages are

[33] An alternative research design, used by Smith and Inkeles (1966), compares peasants (1) with urban nonindustrial workers and (2) with urban industrial workers. We prefer to study individuals who have the same occupation and who do not reside in urban centers, but who live in villages that vary in their degree of modernization.

[34] It is indeed an ironic historical accident that one of the most modern villages here is named Pueblo Viejo, meaning "old village" in Spanish.

characterized by more formal education, a higher rate of literacy, and larger-sized farms. When compared with the two more traditional villages, the modern social systems are typified by the following elements:

1. Active programs of directed contact change: Change agents from the

Figure 3–3. The Six Villages of Study in Colombia.

National Agricultural Extension Service spend one day per week in each of the more modern villages. In contrast, no such change program exists in the two traditional villages, and attempts by extension workers to introduce new ideas were largely unsuccessful in the past.

2. More active formal education programs: Elementary schools offering two years of education are located in each of the more modern communities, but in only one of the traditional villages.

3. More recent examples of community development activities: Two of the three modern villages have recently initiated farm cooperatives, but the traditional communities have none. A new water aqueduct and an impoved road system are also found in the modern villages.

4. Improved transportation and decreased social isolation: Three of the modern communities are but an hour's bus ride from Bogotá, a city of a million people, and 91 percent of the respondents from these villages have traveled there at least once in the past year. In contrast, the traditional villages are located at a much greater distance from an urban center and along much poorer roads; travel to the cities by these peasants is much less frequent.[35]

5. Higher levels of health and sanitation: Families in one of the traditional villages, La Cañada, are afflicted with intestinal parasites, venereal disease, and nutritional deficiencies. In part, this is because of a lack of preventive medicine and lack of contact with a doctor, even though one is available nearby.

Támesis, Pueblo Viejo, San Rafael, and Cuatro Esquinas appear to be more modern than are Nazate and La Cañada.

DATA GATHERING IN COLOMBIA

Less developed countries are internally heterogeneous,[36] and the wide subcultural differences among the village study areas in Colombia led us to utilize somewhat different sampling procecures in each area.[37] However, standard criteria for inclusion of a household in the sample were used within each community. All respondents were both (1) the head of the family and (2) the most influential family member in making farm innovation decisions. These criteria excluded family heads who were employed only in nonfarm work or who worked only as farm laborers. Both farm owners and renters

---

[35] Peasants in the two traditional villages averaged 2.7 trips per year to an urban center, whereas the corresponding figure in the modern villages was 14.9.

[36] As evidenced by such expressions as "the many Colombias," "the world of Brazil," and the "diversity within unity" of India.

[37] In all six villages, except Támesis, we sought a complete census of heads of farm households, to facilitate the analysis of sociometric data about opinion leadership and innovation diffusion. In Támesis, interviews were conducted with a more random, but representative, sample of heads of farm households.

were included. Most respondents were males, but a few widows were included in the sample because they were family heads who made the farm decisions.

A somewhat different interview schedule was utilized in each study area, but a similar list of concepts was measured. For instance, innovativeness was measured by the relative time required for adoption of various new farm ideas in each village. The agricultural innovations studied were somewhat different in each community, but the general concept measured was the same in each area.[38]

The interview schedule was given extensive preliminary testing in each village, and appropriate adaptations were made. The interviewers went to the homes of the respondents by auto, on horseback, or on foot, depending on local transportation facilities. Instructed to introduce themselves as students from the Facultad de Sociología at the Universidad Nacional de Colombia, these interviewers were selected from among students enrolled in third- and fourth-year research methodology classes at the University.

Two types of interviewing methods were used in this investigation: (1) most of the data were gathered from personal interviews using a prepared schedule, and (2) these data were partially supplemented by less structured interviews using a tape recorder. In carrying out the research, 302 personal interviews were completed, as well as 23 tape-recorded interviews. Table 17-2 (see Appendix) indicates that 90 percent of the eligible subjects were interviewed: 47 in Támesis, 67 in Pueblo Viejo, 36 in San Rafael, 57 in Cuatro Esquinas, 41 in Nazate, and 54 in La Cañada. Interviewing was conducted during late 1963 and early 1964. The responses were then coded, punched onto IBM cards, and subjected to various kinds of hand and computer analyses[39] in Colombia and at Michigan State University.

In addition to these original interviews in 1963–1964 some 135 of the 160 peasants in Pueblo Viejo, San Rafael, and Cuatro Esquinas were also interviewed in September, 1965.[40] The purpose of the reinterviews was to obtain data on additional modernization variables that had not been previously measured and to trace the spread of certain farm innovations then diffusing in the three villages.

---

[38] Thus we sought concept equivalence, rather than item or operational equivalence, in the Colombian villages. Obviously, the same quest for concept equivalence guided our design of the data-gathering instruments in India, Kenya, and the other countries from which comparative data will be drawn in later chapters.

[39] Several of these analyses appeared as papers, theses, reports, and articles. For example: Bonilla (1964, 1966); Chou (1966); Kuo (1968); Portocarrero (1966); Ramos (1966); Rogers (1964a, 1964b, 1965a, 1965b, 1966); Rogers and Bonilla (1965); Rogers and Herzog (1966); Rogers and Meyen (1965); Rogers and Neill (1966); Rogers et al. (1964); Rogers and van Es (1964); Stickley (1964); Stickley et al. and van Es (1964).

[40] Similar procedures were followed in the 1965 reinterviewing as had been used in the 1963–1964 data gathering. The 25 peasants who were not reinterviewed either were deceased, had migrated from the villages, or else could not be contacted after several visits to their homes by interviewers.

DATA GATHERING IN INDIA AND KENYA

In several chapters of this book, the Colombian findings will be compared cross-culturally with similar data from India and Kenya. A brief description of the major studies that will be drawn upon for comparative purposes follows.

India UNESCO Study

India data were gathered from 702 peasants in eight villages in Uttar Pradesh, in North Central India near the city of Lucknow. This study was conducted by the National Institute of Community Development (NICD), Hyderabad. The data are made available through the generosity of Dr. Prodipto Roy, Director of Sociology at NICD, and the UNESCO Division of Applied Social Sciences, cosponsor of the project.

Personal interviews were conducted by research interviewers on the NICD staff in 1964. The respondents comprised all the heads of farm households in the eight villages. The interview schedule was similar to that used in the Colombian villages, but the questions were appropriately adapted to Indian conditions. The author of this book (in his role as consultant to the UNESCO investigation) aided in the planning of the inquiry, construction of the interview schedule, and analysis of the data, which was largely completed under his direction at Michigan State University. The India UNESCO data will be used for comparative purposes in subsequent chapters on literacy, mass media exposure, cosmopoliteness, change agent contact, empathy, achievement motivation, and innovativeness.

Kenya Survey

In certain chapters (those dealing with mass media exposure and the factor analysis of modernization variables), we shall draw on Kenya data gathered in 1965 from 624 villagers in three locations, Samia, Kabondo, and Bomet,[41] each located about 300 miles from Nairobi. The respondents were all heads of farm households and represented a random sample of those residing in the three villages. The investigation was cosponsored by the government of Kenya and the U.S. Agency for International Development mission to Kenya. Data gathering was conducted by trained interviewers from Marco Surveys, Ltd., of Nairobi (under the direction of Joseph Ascroft, formerly Technical Manager of Marco Surveys and at present Research Assistant in Communication at Michigan State University). The Kenya interview schedule was partly based on that used in the Colombian villages, and the author participated in its design. The data were analyzed, in part, at Michigan State University under the direction of Joseph Ascroft and the author.

---

[41] These three locations were sampled from the Luhya, Luo, and Kipsigis tribal groups, respectively, each of which represents a basic language division: the Nilo-Hamitic, Nilotic, and Bantu.

India Punjab Study

In the chapter on mass media exposure, we shall also utilize data from personal interviews with all heads of farm households in two villages in the state of Punjab in northern India. In 1964 interviews were conducted with 54 peasants in a very modern village and with 30 respondents in a more traditional village. The research method was based on the interview schedule used in the Colombian villages.[42] The interviewing was conducted by Dharam P. Yadav, who was at that time Research Officer, Package Programme Evaluation Research Unit, in Ludiana (Punjab). The data were later analyzed at Michigan State University by the same interviewer, then Research Assistant in Communication, and by the author.

It is evident that similar types of peasant respondents, interview schedules, and data analysis (that is, to those for the Colombian villages) were involved in these other three surveys, two in India and one in Kenya. All the villages studied were subject in varying degree to programs of directed social change, such as agricultural extension services, public health campaigns, and community development programs. All were moving in the direction of modernization at the time of their study, some rapidly and others much more slowly. This focus upon "villages-on-the-move" provides certain advantages for our analysis of modernization, but one must also remember that these peasant settings were not selected solely as being typical of village life in each country.[43]

SUMMARY

In this book modernization is viewed as essentially a communication process; modernizing messages must reach the peasant via such communication channels as the mass media, change agents, or the villager's trips to cities. These concepts, plus literacy (which facilitates media exposure), are considered the major antecedent variables in our model of modernization. The main consequent variables are innovativeness, political knowledge, and aspirations. In the chapters that follow, empathy, achievement motivation, and fatalism will be used as possibly intervening variables between antecedents and consequences. There are three possible shortcomings of our modernization model and our method: conceptual oversimplification, arbitrary time-

[42] Further methodological detail on this study is provided by Yadav (1967).

[43] For this reason some question might be raised as to the use of statistical tests of significance in the chapters that follow, a procedure based on the assumption that we have data from a random sample of a larger population. We test our coefficients of correlation in order to determine whether they are significantly different from zero. This would seem preferable to ignoring tests of significance, but the reader should be cautioned that the assumption of random sampling is violated in the sense that our villages were purposively, rather than randomly, selected.

order categorization of concepts (as antecedent, intervening, and consequent), and the dangers of cross-cultural equivalence.

The methodological approach to theory construction in the present work is *middle-range analysis*, a procedure that would appear to aid in closing the gap between grand theory and raw empiricism. A *theory* is a postulated relationship between two or more concepts, which are defined as dimensions stated in their most basic terms. An *empirical hypothesis* expresses the postulated relationship between two or more operations. An *operation* is an empirical measure of a concept. The correspondence between a concept and its operation is called an *epistemic relationship*. In middle-range analysis one may proceed from the theoretical to the empirical level (deduction), or from the empirical to the theoretical (induction).

Data were gathered from peasants in six Colombian villages varying in degree of modernization; comparable data-gathering procedures and measures were used in two studies in India and one in Kenya in order to provide cross-cultural tests of generalization.

4

Literacy*

Mass illiteracy is India's sin and shame and must be liquidated. But the literacy campaign must not end with a knowledge of the alphabet. It must go hand in hand with the spread of useful knowledge.

(Mohandas Karamchand Gandhi)

George Gundger can spell and read and write his own name; beyond that he is helpless . . . he thinks it is unlikely that he will ever manage to get the figures and letters to stick in his head . . . these intellects died before they were born; they hang behind their eyes like fetuses in alcohol.

(James Agee and Walker Evans 1939:277)

As soon as one undertakes research on international development, it becomes apparent that literacy is an important variable in less developed countries. This is in contrast to the rural peoples of more developed countries like the United States, where virtually all adults have attained a minimum educational threshold of literacy.[1] The majority (probably about 70 to 80 percent) of the peasants in less developed countries are functionally illiterate. Nearly half of the world's adult population, or some 700 million persons, can neither read nor write. World illiteracy has grown by at least *200 million* in the last six years! In less developed countries 70 percent of the children are not in school today, so that in another generation there will be millions more of adult illiterates. Many experts view literacy instruction as the best possible means for an underdeveloped nation to break the vicious cycle of low incomes, high birth rates, and slow development, and make progress along the path toward modernization.

During the time I lived in Colombia, my interest in and understanding of the meaning of literacy was brought into sharper focus by Emma, a house maid. Although born of peasant stock in a village near Bogotá, she had lived in an urban setting for several years before coming to work for me.

---

* This chapter is an expanded version of an article by Rogers and Herzog (1966), which is used with permission of the University of Chicago Press. Certain of the ideas contained herein are described in greater detail in a Ph.D. dissertation by Herzog (1967a).

[1] Only 2.5 percent of the adult population of the United States is illiterate in the eyes of the U.S. Census Bureau, which uses six years of schooling as its measure of literacy. However, some observers estimate that there are 11 to 40 million *functional illiterates* in the United States (Olsen 1965).

Unable either to write her name or to read a newspaper, Emma skillfully performed an amazing number of tasks for which one might suppose that reading ability would be necessary. For example, when sent to a nearby supermarket to purchase a specified brand of soap, she would return with the correct brand, evidently identified by color and other visual configurations. Illiterates compensate in various ingenious ways for their inability to read, including rote memorization of vast quantities of information. Had Emma been able to read "Oxydol soap," she would not have had to memorize the "Gestalt" of the Oxydol package.

With literacy, change occurs in a number of mental abilities, such as a loss of eidetic ability,[2] which becomes unnecessary. Doob (1966) argues that eidetic imagery (a "photographic" ability to remember stimuli) "must reflect a human ability which has survived from some earlier evolutionary state and which has become virtually functionless in modern (literate) adults." Education and literacy are also accompanied by expansion of a number of mental abilities. For example, literates seem better able to manipulate symbols and to think abstractly. One therefore expects literacy to have instrumental relevance in explaining peasant modernization. Perhaps if Emma had been literate, her transformation from peasant to urbanite would have been easier and more complete. Literacy must be appreciated as an important facilitator of modernization, a process that requires the absorption and comprehension of a vastly increased amount of complex information. The individual who becomes literate has learned to learn for himself (Burnet 1965:14).

In spite of widespread consensus that literacy is a key to national development and individual modernization, there are only a few studies[3] in which the literacy rate of a *nation* was used as an explanatory variable in economic development, and there are even a smaller number of investigations[4] that focus on *individual* literacy in relation to such consequent variables as innovativeness. Many publications are available on how to *teach* literacy, but there is a dearth of reported research on how to measure literacy, its antecedents, and its consequences in the modernization of peasants.

[2] The early research of Doob (1964b) among Africans suggested that illiterates have higher eidetic ability than literates. It is reasoned that, because the eidetic ability of children seems to decrease at the onset of literacy, such might also be the case among adult illiterates. However, Doob's more recent investigations (1965a, 1966) do not clearly support this proposition.

[3] Among these studies are those of Lerner (1958), Golden (1955), Cutright (1963), Lipset (1960), Simpson (1964), Banks and Textor (1963), Almond and Coleman (1960), and Caplow and Finsterbusch (1964).

[4] For example, Lerner (1958, 1964), Deutschmann (1963), Wright et al. (1967), Herzog (1967a), and Schuman et al. (1967).

LITERACY AND ITS MEASUREMENT

MORE THAN READING SKILL

There is little empirical research dealing with the social psychological changes that accompany the acquiring of the ability to read and write; however, speculations from quite diverse sources imply that it represents more than just a simple skill. Lerner (1963:341) states: "Literacy is indeed the basic personal skill that underlies the whole modernizing sequence. . . . The very act of achieving distance and control over a formal language gives people access to the world of vicarious experience."

Why is literacy an important element in the modernization process? There are several reasons:

1. Perhaps the most obvious is that as the individual gains reading skill, he is able to extend the scope of his experience through the *print mass media.*[5] Since messages in the print media tend largely to promote or favor change, the peasant who can read is exposed to a generally favorable attitude toward new ideas, as well as to specific technical information that he may consider and adopt. One might, therefore, expect those peasants with high media exposure to have favorable attitudes toward change, as well as greater technical know-how gained from such exposure. Literacy, then, becomes a catalyst of modernization by giving an individual access to certain mass media communication. The following paradigm illustrates this relationship of literacy to modernization variables through the intervening variable of mass media exposure.[6]

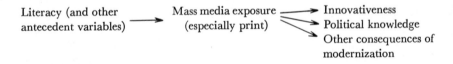

Literacy (and other antecedent variables) → Mass media exposure (especially print) → Innovativeness, Political knowledge, Other consequences of modernization

2. Print media exposure also permits the individual *receiver to control the rate of message input,* rather than the sender, as is the case with interpersonal communication and, even more so, with electronic mass media (Herzog 1967a). With literacy, thus, comes opportunity for the receiver to determine

[5] This view of literacy as a means of widening experience via the print media is illustrated by Powdermaker (1962:228), who studied South Africans: "Literacy is not just learning how to read but is concerned with comprehending a form of reality beyond immediate experience." Mendez and Waisanen (1964) state, "Mastery over symbols, with literacy as the requisite skill, puts the boundaries of human experience beyond the visible horizon and thus *extends social space.*"

[6] This model and an alternative conception of the direct relationship of literacy to other modernization variables (with literacy not acting through mass media exposure) will be empirically tested in this and the following chapter.

the rate at which he receives and decodes communication symbols. He can interrupt the communication process, when reading, in order to examine more thoroughly the symbols involved; he can specify and vary the input rate according to his own comprehension and intellectual ability. The ability to control the rate of absorbing written messages is of special import to the newly literate, who may at first lack many of the associated mental skills for rapid comprehension of print media content.

3. Literates not only are able to control the rate of print message input, but they can also *store and retrieve print information for delayed use.*[7] For certain technical information, such as that dealing with agricultural innovations, this retrieval ability may be quite important. The illiterate must be able to remember the entire message (gained orally), whereas the literate need only remember *where* the print message may be found. You might try to recall a speech you heard a year ago. How many of its details can you remember? Probably only a few. If, however, you are literate and have access to a printed copy, the information contained in the speech will not have been lost.

4. As suggested earlier, literacy seems to be a key for unlocking *more complex mental abilities.* Whereas the illiterate is largely dependent on memorization of details, the literate individual is able to manipulate symbols, which allows counterfactual thinking. The ability to generalize through symbolization, the faculty of restructuring reality via the manipulation of symbols, and the ability to empathize with strange roles are all mental capacities that facilitate one's effective functioning in a complex, rapidly changing urban-industrial world.[8] These skills are less necessary for a satisfactory life style in a purely traditional village, where knowledge is more or less routine and roles are simple and well-defined.[9] Thus, one might view literacy as development of the fundamental skills of reading and writing, which leads to or is accompanied by growth of a set of mental abilities that are necessary to modernization.

Support for this view of literacy is provided by Carothers' (1959) psychiatric research among African tribesmen. Illiterates seem to ascribe a special magic power to the spoken word. When words are expressed in written form, however, illiterates perceive them in a passive state because of the separation of symbol from referent.[10] The effect of literacy is to reduce this magic efficacy of the word, to make words represent thought symbols, and

[7] "Print provided a vast new memory for past writings that made a personal memory inadequate" (McLuhan 1964: 174).

[8] "Where the social setting itself is changing, the more literate man will be quicker to perceive the change and will find it easier to redefine his beliefs in ways that fit his new needs and interests" (Schuman et al., 1967).

[9] The illiterate in an urban environment has the need for reading brought home to him more forcefully. "A city is itself a book" (Burnet 1965), with its signs, pricetags, labels, and instructions.

[10] Carothers (1959) states, "It is clearly far more easy for words, when written, to be seen for what they are — symbols, without existence in their own right."

thus to create a mental distinction between symbol and reality. This distinction enables literates to think in terms of symbols.[11] Building on Carothers' work, McLuhan (1962) claims that when use of one of the senses predominates, as does the aural among illiterates, the other senses become to some degree anesthetized. With literacy comes an arousal of the visual sense, thereby attuning the individual to both the audio and the visual messages being transmitted. Indeed, McLuhan's (1964:7–21) main thesis that "the medium is the message" implies that the psychological impact or meaning of a message depends on the channel by which it is transmitted.

There is little empirical data to substantiate the notions of Carothers or McLuhan. However, their theories lend support to our position that literacy is more than just the mechanical ability to read and write, that it opens the way for more complex mental activity.[12]

Literacy, therefore, contributes to the modernization process by (1) providing the means for print media exposure, (2) allowing the receiver to control the rate of message input, (3) facilitating the retrieval of print messages for delayed use, and (4) unlocking more complex mental abilities.

DEFINITION

Literacy is defined as the degree to which an individual possesses mastery over symbols in their written form, or is able to encode and decode written messages — to write and to read. Even though operational measures of literacy may consist only of an evaluation of the individual's reading and writing ability, our conceptual definition also implies manipulative ability with printed symbols. Naturally, literacy is not the only means whereby one acquires the ability to manipulate symbols.[13] Nevertheless, such ability *is* attained in conjunction with acquiring literacy.

PROBLEMS IN MEASURING LITERACY

Lack of uniformity in measuring devices makes it difficult to compare literacy rates cross-culturally. Wide variance in degree of competence in reading and writing is assumed by the diverse empirical definitions of literacy. These differences make it difficult to arrive at operational equivalences among nations. In the U.S. census, literacy is defined as equivalent to having

[11] This notion that literacy leads to a greater distinction between symbol and reality has an interesting parallel in Jean Paul Piaget's research on the early stages of child development.

[12] Schuman et al. (1967) conclude, on the basis of their analysis of data from Pakistani villagers and industrial workers, that literacy is especially important in leading to those dimensions of modernization "where vicarious and abstract experience" is involved. This evidence supports our notion that literacy unlocks more complex mental abilities, such as symbol manipulation. Schuman and his collaborators found some rather indirect evidence that literates had higher intelligence (measured orally) than illiterates.

[13] A course in logic, for example, might teach symbol manipulation.

completed six grades of schooling.[14] In the Colombia census, however, literacy is measured on the basis of an individual's ability to write his name. Other national censuses determine literacy by asking individuals if they can read a newspaper and write a letter.

The United Nations Economic and Social Council (1963:39) reports two definitions offered by committees concerned with the problem of measuring literacy. In 1951, a committee of experts on the standardization of educational statistics suggested the following criterion: "A person is literate who can with understanding both read and write a short, simple statement on his everyday life." A meeting of experts on literacy convened by UNESCO in 1962 went somewhat beyond this definition to propose that an individual is literate when he has "acquired the essential knowledge and skills which enable him to engage in all those activities in which literacy is required for effective functioning in his group and community, and whose attainments in reading, writing and arithmetic make it possible for him to continue to use these skills."

The usual census-type, self-defined measure of literacy depends both on the honesty of the respondent and on his ability to assess accurately his own competence in reading and writing. In situations where individuals think that it is not socially acceptable to be illiterate (such as in urban areas),[15] or where they have little opportunity to maintain a former competence in reading and writing (as in peasant communities),[16] self-defined literacy is likely to be a relatively less accurate measure.

We also find wide disparity in the age groups included in national rates of literacy. Indonesia, for example, calculates its literacy rate for persons between 13 and 45 years of age; Cuba and Malaysia report literacy rates for those 10 years of age and over, whereas Bulgaria includes only people who are more than 15 years old.

FUNCTIONAL LITERACY

Because of the inherent weaknesses of self-defined literacy measures, this chapter will be concerned primarily with *functional literacy*, which is measured as the ability to read and write written symbols at a level of competence

---

[14] However, until the 1940 decennial census in the United States, literacy was determined by asking adults whether they could read and write.

[15] Burnet (1965:11) and Freeman and Kassenbaum (1956) point out this tendency for concealment by illiterates who are in environments where literacy rates are high.

[16] It must be emphasized that literacy is a skill which, if not used continuously, may atrophy. An illustration comes from Turkey, where army recruits are brought to a basic level of literacy. However, upon their discharge and return to their home villages, where there is little to read and their fellow villagers regard their new-found ability to read as pretentious, a high proportion of the exservicemen soon revert to illiteracy. Another instance comes from a major Latin American nation, where the total number of adult literates (reportedly) created in the past ten years is greater than the nation's total population of illiterates, suggesting that great numbers of the newly literate evidently regress to their former state (or else, that literacy rates and the number of newly literate are rather incorrectly reported).

adequate for carrying out the functions of the individual's role in his customary social system.[17] This type of measure[18] implies that (1) literacy is a process, and therefore, should be regarded as a continuous variable (although for some analytic purposes, it may be useful to treat it dichotomously (2) functional literacy is different for different roles (for example, the peasant in rural Colombia can probably function adequately with a lesser ability to read and write than is necessary to his urban counterpart); and (3) the requirements of functional literacy may change as the individual or his circumstances change (for instance, if the peasant migrates to the city, then his level of literacy must rise in order for him to function with the same comparative efficiency in his new urban role as he had in his village).

A number of investigators have attempted to fabricate an empirical measure of functional literacy. Goldsen and Ralis (1957) asked Thai villagers if they could write a letter. Those who responded affirmatively were then asked to demonstrate their ability by writing something on the interview schedule. Spector et al. (1963) developed an ingenious means of measuring functional literacy among their Ecuadorean respondents. At the close of each interview, the subject was asked if he were able to read a card which stated (in Spanish), "This concludes the interview; many thanks for your cooperation." De Young and Hunt (1962) measured functional literacy among Filipino villagers by asking them, in the course of personal interviews, to read a short written selection and then answer prepared questions about it.

The present study employed a measure of functional literacy originally developed by Waisanen and his associates in the Programa Interamericano de Información Popular, a Latin American communication research program. This standard, first used in a 1963 study in Guatemala and Costa Rica, has since been used in Mexico, Chile, and India. A Spanish sentence was developed around six words of varying difficulty.[19] The sentence, printed

---

[17] This definition is essentially similar to that used by Wright and others (1967:2), who state that an individual was functionally literate "if he could comprehend the written materials which deal with his problems of daily living; i.e., those of health, nutrition, and personal-social economics." Functional literacy shall be regarded here as one type of operational measure of literacy.

[18] There are numerous difficulties with the notion of functional literacy, most of which center around the empirical problem of determining just what written symbols are adequate for carrying out a given respondent's comprehension of a sample of words at various levels of common usage as determined from word lists (which exist for most major languages). For example, one might select certain words for the functional literacy test from the 1000 most commonly used words, certain others from the next most common 1000 words, and so on. Nor is this approach without its shortcomings; for instance, most word lists are based on school children's responses rather than on those of peasants.

[19] "El hombre movió su mano rapidamente en un ademán de respeto" ("The man moved his hand rapidly in a gesture of respect"). A Guttman scale analysis of the measure, using data from the five Colombian villages, indicated a concentration of error-free responses at the extremes of (1) all words answered correctly (31 percent of the respondents) and (2) all words answered incorrectly (47 percent of the respondents). The coefficient of reproducibility is 95.5 percent, although this is inflated by the large proportion of respondents who were fully literate or completely illiterate. A detailed discussion of the development of the present functional literacy measure and its correlates is found in Mendez and Waisanen (1964).

on a card, is handed to the respondent during the interview. His functional literacy score reflects the number of words he is able to read.[20] In order to utilize the rather small degree of sensitivity present,[21] literacy was viewed as a continuous variable rather than a dichotomous variable (of literacy and illiteracy). When used dichotomously, functional literates were regarded as those who read all six words correctly.

While the results obtained with this measure of functional literacy were encouraging, there were also indications of a need for its revision and improvement.[22]

FUNCTIONAL VERSUS SELF-DEFINED LITERACY

To what extent is a respondent's self-defined literacy related to an objective test of that ability? Some indication of this relationship is provided by the Colombian data in Table 4-1, where functional literacy scores are cross-tabulated with the self-defined ability to read a newspaper. The close agreement of these two measures of literacy (functional and self-defined) provides some evidence that the usual census-type literacy measure (self-defined) may be fairly accurate, at least for rural Colombia.[23] Nevertheless, 12 percent of those who could not read one word correctly *said* they were able to read a

Table 4–1. Relationship of Self-defined Ability to Read a Newspaper to Functional Literacy Scores (Data from Five Colombian Villages)

Self-defined Ability to Read a Newspaper	Scores on Functional Literacy Measure, percent		
	No Words Correct (N = 120)	1–5 Words Correct (N = 57)	All 6 Words Correct (N = 78)
Able (literate)	12	89	91
Not able (illiterate)	88	11	9
Total	100	100	100

[20] Our present test should thus be regarded as only a partial measure of functional literacy, which at least calls for the respondent to *demonstrate* his ability to read, rather than relies completely on his self-reported ability to do so.

[21] We have recently learned of a resourceful measure of functional literacy that provides a greater range of sensitivity. It was developed by Joseph Ascroft, while he was Technical Manager of Marco Surveys in Nairobi. The respondent is handed, *upside down*, a card containing a short question. If he indicates that he knows which side is "up" by turning the card right-side up, the respondent thus categorizes himslf in a more nearly literate level of nonliteracy than if he does not turn the card. A further degree of functional literacy is indicated if the respondent is able to read and to reply to the question on the card, thus indicating some comprehension of what is read.

[22] A detailed discussion of needed research on functional literacy measures appears later in this chapter.

[23] This relationship may be lower where the norms of a community frown upon illiterates and the respondent is aware of these norms, as in urban areas.

newspaper, and 9 percent of the peasants who read the entire test sentence correctly said they could *not* read a newspaper. Hence, although there is general agreement between functional literacy and self-reported literacy measures, the correlation is less than perfect.[24]

Further support for the validity of the functional literacy test is given by the correlations presented in Table 4-2. Comparison of the peasant's evaluation of his ability (1) to write a letter and (2) to read a newspaper and (3) his years

Table 4–2.   Correlation of Functional Literacy with Other Indicators of Literacy in Five Columbian Villages

	Correlations with Funtional Literacy in Five Columbian Villages					
	Modern Villages			Traditional Villages		All Five Villages (Aggregate)
Other Indicators of Literacy	*Pueblo Viejo*	*San Rafael*	*Cuatro Esquinas*	*Nazate*	*La Cañada*	
1. Ability to write a letter	.746[b]	.782	.658	.683	.648	.711
2. Ability to read a Newspaper[a]	.809	.782	.734	.756	.666	.784
3. Years of formal education	.540	.661	.467	.687	.625	.575

   [a] The two self-defined measures of literacy, ability to write a letter and ability to read a newspaper, are highly interrelated. Intercorrelations are .835, 1.000, .919, .900, and .819, respectively, for the five villages. All five correlations are significantly different from zero at the 1 percent level of probability.

   [b] All correlation values shown within the table are significantly different from zero at the 1 percent level of probability.

of formal education, with his functional literacy score indicates that all the measures are positively correlated, yet are far from unity. For example, in Pueblo Viejo the self-defined ability to write a letter and functional literacy are correlated at .746. This means that about 55 percent of the variance in these two variables overlaps, while 45 percent does not.

FUNCTIONAL LITERACY AND FORMAL EDUCATION

According to UNESCO standards, a minimum of four years of schooling is required for the typical individual to reach and maintain functional literacy (Gray 1956).[25] In Table 4-3 is shown the relation between years of schooling

   [24] Generally similar evidence is provided by De Young and Hunt (1962), who found that 80.8 percent of 2688 Filipino villagers who claimed to be literate could read, by Goldsen and Ralis (1957) in Thailand, by Spector et al. (1963) in Ecuador, and by Schuman et al. (1967) in East Pakistan.

   [25] This fourth-grade level is roughly in terms of the U.S. equivalent and obviously varies widely from country to country, since the curriculum content of these four years of schooling is not at all standardized.

and rates of functional literacy for respondents in the five Colombian villages of the survey. Only one of the respondents, with a functional literacy score of zero had more than four years of education.[26] However, numerous respondents

Table 4–3. Relation of Functional Literacy to Years of Formal Education in Five Colombian Villages

Scores on Functional Literacy Measure	Years of Formal Education[a] Received by Peasants						
	None (N=114)	1 (N=43)	2 (N=39)	3 (N=29)	4 (N=9)	5 (N=10)	6 or more (N=11)
No words correct, percent	79	32	23	21	0	0	9
1–5 words correct, percent	10	42	26	34	44	30	0
All 6 words correct, percent	10	26	51	45	56	70	91
Total, percent	99[b]	100	100	100	100	100	100

[a]The dashed line dividing the table shows the level of formal education (four years) considered minimum by UNESCO to maintain functional literacy.

[b]This column does not total 100 percent because of rounding.

with all six words correct had less than four years of formal schooling,[27] although only twelve of these individuals had *no* formal schooling. Evidently, functional literacy can be attained and maintained by peasants with less than the UNESCO standard of four years of education.[28] Some of the discrepancy between years of formal education and literacy may be a result of adult literacy

[26] Bostian and Oliveira (1965) found that, among a sample of Brazilian peasants, 18 percent who had four years of education *said* they could not read or write.

[27] Lerner's (1964a) study of Turkish villagers disclosed that only about half of the peasants who said they were able to write a letter had completed four years of schooling.

[28] Ascroft (1966a) suggests a solution to the problem which results from the fact that the functional literacy test does not adequately differentiate among peasants above a minimum level of education. He developed a combined measure of functional literacy and formal education, which is somewhat more sensitive than either functional literacy or education alone. The Ascroft measure uses functional literacy scores up to the level where all words on the test are read correctly, and then utilizes years of formal education to further differentiate among the respondents who are functionally literate. This combined operation appears to be superior to either literacy or education in predicting other modernization variables, especially with data from villagers with generally high levels of literacy and considerable education. In the present case, Table 4-3 shows that 78 of the 255 Colombian peasants were functionally literate (that is, could read all 6 words correctly), and only 17 of these had had more than 4 years of formal education. However, when, the Ascroft measure of literacy-education was computed (changing only the scores of these 17 peasants) and correlated with other variables, some improvement resulted in the prediction of the other modernization variables.

programs such as Radio Sutatenza.[29] Although data is lacking on this point from the present investigation, it is reasonable to assume that some of the peasants with no, or with only one or two years of, education learned to read from such adult literacy programs. Just as we cannot assume that all individuals having no formal education will be illiterate, neither can we assume that four years of formal education is an absolute guarantee of the ability to read. Generally, however, one finds a positive relationship between functional literacy and formal schooling.

AN EDUCATIONAL THRESHOLD TO MODERNIZATION TAKE-OFF

Some interesting data gathered from residents of Santiago, Chile, suggest there is a point of "modernization take-off" in such attitudinal variables as aspirations when the individual has more than five years of schooling — in other words, at about the point at which functional literacy occurs (Briones and Waisanen 1966). Respondents with two or three years of schooling are not much different in attitudes from those with no education; however, with further education, indicators of modernization also rise proportionately.[30]

Why might we expect a modernization take-off with the completion of about four years of schooling?

1. As has already been suggested, about four years of education marks the point at which functional literacy is achieved by most individuals. Once having attained a literate state, the individual is able to continue learning from printed sources throughout his life. Those who stop short of this literacy watershed (that is, with only three or less years of schooling) have little likelihood of becoming modernized through self-directed information seeking in later years.

2. Usually postprimary education[31] begins in the fourth or fifth year of schooling. The modernization take-off effect may coincide with the beginning of postprimary education because (1) *course content* in postprimary classes is likely to reflect knowledge of a more modern sort; (2) the *location* of the post-

---

[29] Radio Sutatenza is the original and most famous radiophonics school. Peasants regularly listen in small "classes" on a transistor radio to literacy instruction, which they then pursue with the help of an untrained teacher. Initiated by the Roman Catholic Church, Radio Sutatenza has since been reproduced in numerous Latin American countries in a manner generally similar to the Colombian prototype. For details on literacy courses in these radiophonics schools, see ACPO (1965), Torres and Corredor (1961), or Chapter 6.

[30] There is confirmation of the notion of an educational threshold in Puerto Rico. Tumin and Feldman (1956) found that "it would appear that while education up to four years of school may matter, and though its effects may be cumulative, once the fourth year is passed, a new vista of life possibilities seems to be opened." Needless to say, the exact educational level at which the modernization take-off occurs will vary with such factors as the quality of schooling and individual differences in intelligence.

[31] Postprimary education is often called "secondary education" in less developed countries. Secondary education as such should not be confused with the meaning of the term in the United States, where it is synonomous with high school education.

primary school is usually a town or city (rather than the local village), and the new environment is likely to have an urbanizing influence on the student; and (3) *teachers* in postprimary schools are better trained and more modern[32] and, hence, provide their students with a personal model of more neoteric behavior.

The Colombia data do not permit us to determine which of these possible reasons might explain the modernization take-off. In fact, the relatively small number of our peasant respondents with more than four years of education (only about 8 percent) makes it difficult to assess whether such a modernization take-off clearly occurs.[33] Each of four modernization variables (agricultural innovativeness, achievement motivation, empathy, and educational aspirations) were plotted against years of formal education. Only in the case of educational aspirations[34] (Fig. 4-1) could a very marked take-off point be detected.[35]

If an education threshold occurs among individuals in most less developed nations at about four or five years of schooling, then a wise strategy for development planners is to concentrate educational opportunities only upon those children who can be carried through postprimary education to a lasting literacy. At present, an opposite policy is generally followed in most less developed countries, perhaps due to political pressures to allocate a "little education" to almost everyone, rather than to concentrate educational efforts where they might have a major impact. Evidence of this policy is apparent in the following data: for Brazilians who enter school, the average number of years of education completed is only 2.6; for Venezuelans, it is 2.6; and for Panamanians, 3.6. Only 8.4 percent of Brazilian school children ever reach grade four.

Literacy and the formal schooling that leads to it are human resources which are in short supply in less developed countries. The data that have just been reviewed suggest that the limited educational opportunities available in these nations are poorly allocated from the viewpoint of optimizing their effects on modernization.

---

[32] This difference in the training level of teachers in primary and postprimary schools in Colombia is especially marked. About 78 percent of the rural primary school teachers in Colombia in 1961 possessed *only* a primary school education themselves!

[33] This problem was not encountered by Briones and Waisanen (1966) or Tumin and Feldman (1956) because they used data from nonpeasant subjects with higher average levels of formal education. We sought to detect modernization take-offs in the India UNESCO data, described later in this chapter, but in these there were an insufficient number of peasants with more than four years of schooling.

[34] Educational aspirations also seemed to reveal one of the strongest take-offs in the case of the Chilean data of Briones and Waisanen (1966) and the Puerto Rican data of Tumin and Feldman (1956). Other modernization indicators demonstrated less striking take-offs.

[35] The more-or-less linear relationships for agricultural innovativeness, achievement motivation, and empathy, respectively, compared with years of schooling, provide some reassurance for the use of Pearsonian correlation in the present study, a measure of association which assumes linear relations. This assumption was discussed in Chapter 3.

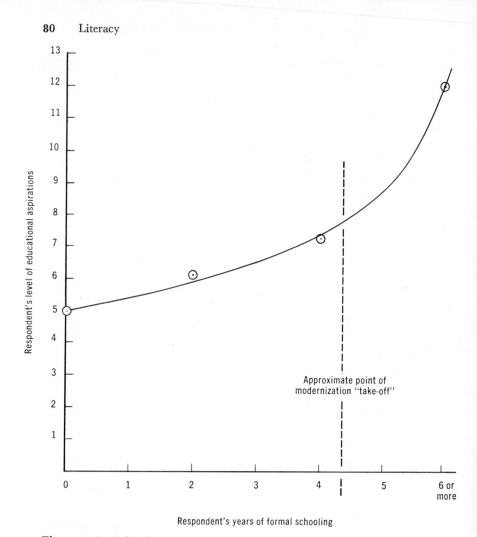

Figure 4–1.   A Modernization Takeoff in Educational Aspirations Occurs at about Four Years of Formal Schooling.

The data plotted here are from the 255 Colombian peasants living in 5 villages. The reader should note the caveat that only a small portion of these respondents had more than 4 years of education, and so our finding of a takeoff in educational aspirations at this point should be viewed with proper caution, in that the part of the aspiration curve that rises sharply has an inadequate data base.

LITERACY AND MODERNIZATION

Literacy probably has an interdependent relationship with other modernization variables. Literacy is necessary for modernization; but modernization, as it develops, also impels literacy forward. The arrows expressing this relationship are reciprocal, as seen in the diagam below. A small increase in one variable probably leads to a minute increment in the other, which in turn leads to change in the first variable, and so forth.

Literacy   Modernization

Some authors imply that literacy must precede in time certain other dimensions of modernization. Perhaps literacy does *cause* modernization consequences in mass media exposure, empathy, and innovativeness. This position, however, is contrary to our general view of the interdependence among modernization variables. Whether the nature of this relationship is interdependent or causal (and if so, the time-order of the variables) cannot be adequately tested with data from the present investigation, which deals with correlational rather than experimental data analysis.[36]

What do our data reveal about the relationships between functional literacy and (1) mass media exposure,[37] (2) empathy, (3) innovativeness, (4) achievement motivation, (5) social status, (6) cosmopoliteness, (7) political knowledge, and (8) opinion leadership? (A general picture can be obtained from Fig. 4-2).

MASS MEDIA EXPOSURE

Numerous past investigations have found a *positive association between literacy and mass media exposure* both (1) at the aggregate level of analysis[38] and (2) when individuals were used as the units of analysis.[39]

The Colombian data support the findings of these previous studies (Table 4-4) and, further, lead to the conclusion that *literacy is more highly related to*

[36] Herzog (1967a), however, has attempted to determine the time-order of the literacy-modernization relationship in a field experiment in Brazil, where adult villagers were studied before, during, and after their participation in a literacy course. He found that there were no significant changes in empathy, mass media exposure, achievement motivation, or political knowledge after adult illiterates gained the ability to read and write. However, he argues that this might be the result of the short time elapsed since the onset of literacy.

In a field experiment in Guatemala, Wright et al. (1967: iii) concluded that "the bright, highly motivated illiterate peasant will avail himself of the opportunity to become literate" and that "literacy classes are a screening device for these brighter individuals." The recruits to the Guatemala adult literacy classes were more empathic and achievement-motivated than were the peasants in the same villages who did not enroll. The Guatemala inquiry, unfortunately, has not progressed to the point where changes in modernization variables can be traced to the fact of becoming literate.

[37] As was pointed out earlier in this chapter, mass media exposure may be an intervening variable between literacy and other modernization consequences. Partial correlation techniques will be used in the following chapter to determine empirically whether the most appropriate time-order model is (1) literacy →mass media exposure and other modernization consequences or (2) literacy → mass media exposure → modernization consequences.

[38] Examples are Lerner (1958:58) and UNESCO (1961:17).

[39] Illustrations are Lerner (1958, 1964a), Rahim (1961), and Deutschmann (1963).

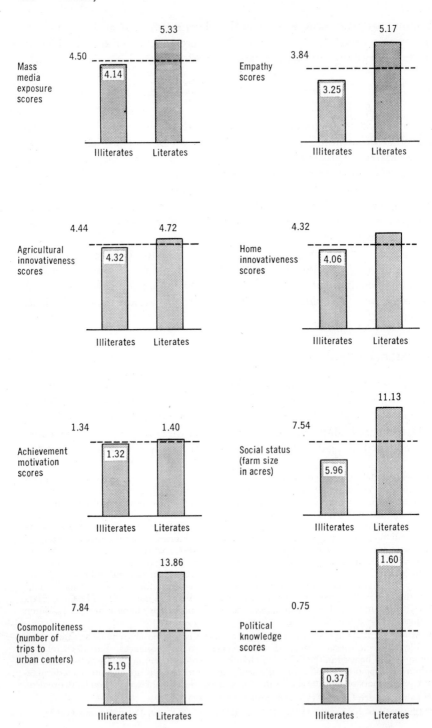

Table 4–4. Relationship of Functional Literacy to Mass Media Exposure in Five Colombian Villages

Mass Media Exposure Variables	Correlations with Functional Literacy in Five Colombian Villages					
	Pueblo Viejo	San Rafael	Cuatro Esquinas	Nazate	La Cañada	All Five Villages (Aggregate)
1. Mass media exposure index	.374[a]	.559[a]	.355[a]	.439[a]	.421[a]	.422[a]
2. Number of radio shows listened to in past week	.370[a]	.398[b]	.335[b]	[.142]	.388[a]	.336[a]
3. Number of newspapers read (or read to) in past week	.365[a]	.616[a]	.360[a]	.476[a]	.396[a]	.430[a]
4. Number of magazines read (or read to) in past month	[.138]	.562[a]	[−.104]	[c]	[.148]	.207[a]
5. Number of movies seen in past year	.314[b]	.471[a]	[.160]	[c]	[.105]	.254[a]
6. Number of TV shows seen in past year	[.197]	.422[b]	[.114]	[c]	[c]	.216[a]

[a]Significantly different from zero at the 1 percent level of probability.

[b]Significantly different from zero at the 5 percent level of probability.

[c]In Nazate, none of the respondents had read a magazine (or been read to) in the month before the interview, had seen a movie in the past year, or had seen a TV show in the past year. It was impossible for a respondent to have seen a TV show in either Nazate or La Cañada because both were outside the range of TV reception.

newspaper exposure than to nonprint media expousure. Literacy is also related to radio exposure (although less so to TV and movie exposure), which suggests the presence of the *centripetal effect*.[40]

While the relationships between functional literacy and print media exposure are significant, one may wonder why they are not higher (Table 4-4). There are two possible explanations: (1) perhaps exposure to the print media by literates is limited to some degree by cost, lack of accessibility, or other

[40] A clear statement of this concept may be found in Lerner (1963:341; 1964a). He defines the centripetal effect as the tendency for an individual exposed to one mass medium also to be exposed to other media.

Figure 4–2. Functional Literates (N = 78) Have Higher Average Scores on Each of Eight Modernization Indicators than the Functional Illiterates (N = 177) in the Five Colombian Villages.

factors; and (2) there is a strong possibility that illiterates gain exposure to the print media through literate family members or friends.[41] Deutschmann (1963) reasons in this vein in order to explain his finding that some Colombian peasant illiterates did have print media exposure (for example, 48 percent purchased newspapers). Deutschmann's data, however, did not allow the testing of this hunch. Our Colombian data indicate that 19 percent of the illiterates had newspapers and 6 percent had magazines *read to them*. Oral readings thus provide one route around the barrier of illiteracy. The interview data indicate that many of those who read aloud to others are children, who generally have higher literacy rates than their parents (Table 4-5). In fact, the percentage of all households (where the head of the house-

Table 4–5.   Levels of Literacy (as Reported by Household Head) of Various Family Members in Five Columbian Villages

	Percentage of Family Members Literate in Five Columbian Villages				
Type of Family Members	Pueblo Viejo	San Rafael	Cuatro Esquinas	Nazate	La Cañada
Farm operators[a]	57	53	65	37	45
Wives[b]	34	58	67	3	32
Children[b] (aged 9 to 19)	90	73	83	56	45

[a]These are self-defined literacy rates and hence are somewhat different from the rates of functional literacy reported previously for the five villages.

[b]These data are reported by the household head for all family members, and it is necessary to assume that the household head could accurately assess and report the literacy status of his household members. In any event, this is the usual census measure, where one household member is asked to report the literacy status of all other members.

hold was illiterate) containing at least one literate family member was 52 percent in Pueblo Viejo, 59 percent in San Rafael, 84 percent in Cuatro Esquinas, 76 percent in Nazate, and 85 percent in La Cañada. *The number of households that did not contain at least one literate family member was fairly low.* Only about one-fourth of the households did not have at least one literate member. An implication of this finding is that one should think more often of *family literacy* than of individual literacy, at least insofar as the literacy of one family member enables other family members to be exposed to print media.

EMPATHY

To reiterate, empathy is the ability of an individual to project himself into the role of another person. An important step in an individual's transformation from traditional to modern is the ability to conceive of himself per-

---

[41] Thus obscuring the correlation between functional literacy and print media exposure.

forming a role apart from his normal mode of behavior. Lerner (1958:64) regards literacy as a major force in unlocking this empathic process: "With literacy people acquire more than the simple skill of reading. ... [It] trains them to use the complicated mechanism of empathy which is needed to cope with this world." The empathic individual is better able to imagine himself in different roles, including more modern ones. Lerner found a strong relationship between literacy and his measure of empathy in both Syria (1958) and Turkey (1964a).[42]

The measure of empathy used in the present study is a five-item scale that determines the respondent's ability to imagine himself in such roles as president of the village development council, a local extension agent, mayor of the nearby market town, the national minister of education, and the President of Colombia. Correlations of empathy scores with functional literacy scores for the various villages are shown in Table 4-6. All the corre-

Table 4–6. Relationship of Functional Literacy to Various Modernization Variables in Five Colombian Villages

	Correlations with Functional Literacy in Five Colombian Villages					
Variables	Pueblo Viejo	San Rafael	Cuatro Esquinas	Nazate	La Cañada	All Five Villages (Aggregate)
1. Empathy	.437[a]	.568[a]	[.143]	.420[a]	.411[a]	.390[a]
2. Agricultural innovativeness	.377[a]	[.292]	[.140]	.485[a]	[.196]	.316[a]
3. Home innovativeness	.397[a]	.537[a]	[.257]	[.243]	.485[a]	.432[a]
4. Achievement motivation	[.219]	[.285]	.294[b]	.436[a]	.353[b]	.316[a]
5. Social status (farm size in acres)	.265[b]	.426[b]	[.177]	.447[a]	.279[b]	.304[a]
6. Cosmopoliteness number of trips to urban centers)	.269[b]	.530[a]	[.193]	[.123]	[.255]	.322[a]
7. Political knowledge	.480[a]	.595[a]	.341[b]	[.292]	.492[a]	.444[a]
8. Sociometric opinion leadership	[.189]	.422[b]	[.221]	[.273]	.353[b]	.291[a]

[a] Significantly different from zero at the 1 percent level of probability.
[b] Significantly different from zero at the 5 percent level of probability.

[42] Lerner's measure of empathy in both investigations consisted of asking respondents to imagine themselves in the role of persons more modern than themselves.

lations are positive, and only one is not significantly different from zero. As was expected, *literacy is positively related to empathy*. One must remember, however, that the strength of correlations between these two dimensions is not very great. Even in the case of the highest correlation, namely, .568 in San Rafael, only about 32 percent of the variance in the literacy and empathy measures occurs in common. Other variables must explain the remaining 68 percent of the variance in literacy and in empathy.

INNOVATIVENESS

Innovativeness has been defined as the degree to which an individual adopts new ideas relatively sooner than his peers.[43] This trait is usually indexed (as in the Colombian study) by asking respondents when they adopted certain recently introduced ideas. The time required for a respondent to adopt these new practices, as compared with that for other respondents in the same village, is a measure of his innovativeness.

Lerner (1964a) found that literate Turkish peasants were more likely to perceive themselves as innovators in their village. Goldsen and Ralis (1957) reported that literate Thai villagers were more innovative than illiterates. Rahim (1961) found that literacy was positively related to adoption of farm innovations in Pakistan. Wright et al. (1967:17) found literate Guatemalan peasants were more innovative than illiterates.

The Colombian data (Table 4-6) indicate positive correlations between literacy and both agricultural and home innovativeness in all five villages, although only half of these relationships are significant. Therefore, one can conclude only tentatively that *literacy and innovativeness are positively related* (Fig. 4-2). Literates are able to learn about innovations sooner than their illiterate neighbors (although it will be seen in a later chapter that mass media are only rarely reported as having importance in informing villagers about technical innovations) as a result of their higher print media exposure. The literates' ability to manipulate abstract symbols may also lead them to relatively earlier adoption of new ideas. An innovator, by being the first to adopt, cannot rely on the more direct stimulus of observing the new idea on his neighbor's farm. He must be able to conceptualize the nature of the innovation, and its likely consequences, from more abstract communication messages.

ACHIEVEMENT MOTIVATION

Achievement motivation is a social value that emphasizes a desire for excellence in order for an individual to attain a sense of personal accomplishment. McClelland (1961) claims that achievement motivation is a cause of

---

[43] The adoption of new ideas is one important indication of an individual's willingness to break with tradition.

national economic development and modernization. One might expect achievement motivation to be related to literacy, since literacy allows and facilitates print media exposure. The injection of such promodern messages could lead to the development of achievement motivation.

In the present study, achievement motivation scores[44] are correlated with functional literacy scores (Table 4-6). All the correlations are positive, and three of the five are significant. *A positive association between literacy and achievement motivation is evident*, indicating that literates have a stronger desire for occupational excellence than do illiterates (Fig. 4-2).

SOCIAL STATUS

Size of farm is commonly regarded as an important measure of socioeconomic status in peasant societies. Deutschmann and Fals Borda (1962) found a low positive relationship between literacy and farm size. The present data show positive — and significant in four of the five communities — correlations between functional literacy and farm size (Table 4-6), which lead to the conclusion that *literacy is positively related to social status*. Perhaps farm size, income, and other factors in socioeconomic status facilitate school attendance, which then leads to literacy among adults.

COSMOPOLITENESS

Cosmopoliteness, defined as the degree to which an individual is oriented outside his social system, is indexed in the Colombia study by the number of trips to urban centers made per year by the respondents. There are several reasons why one would expect literacy to be positively related to cosmopoliteness. The analyses by Lerner (1958) and Golden (1955) of aggregate data (where countries were the units of analysis) suggest that the relationships they found between literacy and urbanization may be due to the greater functional utility of literacy in the city. Urban orientations among villagers may lead to the acquiring of literacy skills, so that they can participate more fully in urban life. On the other hand, literacy may encourage a peasant to travel to cities because the literate villager has greater awareness of the business, recreational, and other services available only in urban centers in countries like Colombia. Literates are better able to function in the urban ambience. As Lerner (1964b: 230) points out,

Only cities require a largely literate population to function properly — for the organization of urban life assumes enough literacy to read labels, sign checks, ride subways. A population of illiterates might learn that they are not to smoke and spit in the subway, or that express trains run on the local tracks between 5 and 7 A.M.; but trial-and-error can be a wasteful societal procedure.

[44] Details on the measurement of occupational achievement motivation are provided in Chapter 11 of this book and in Rogers and Neill (1966).

Whether as cause or effect, literacy is expected to go hand-in-hand with cosmopoliteness.[45]

The Colombian data (Table 4-6) show that functional literacy is positively related to the number of trips to urban centers in all five Colombian villages. While this relationship is significant in only two of the villages, it can be concluded provisionally that *there is a positive association between literacy and cosmopoliteness.*

POLITICAL KNOWLEDGE

In developing nations, political knowledge is transmitted largely through the mass media, particularly the print media. However, Deutschmann (1963) found no relationship between literacy and political knowledge in the Colombian village that he studied.

The present measure of political knowledge is a five-item scale of awareness of Colombian political affairs. Table 4-6 shows that there are positive correlations of political knowledge with functional literacy in all five communities; these relationships are significant in four of the five communities. Perhaps literate individuals through their higher mass media exposure, learn more about political issues and personalities; or maybe they possess a general attitudinal bent toward the new and modern, and interest in political events is part of this *Gestalt*. In any event, one may conclude that *literacy is positively related to political knowledge.*

OPINION LEADERSHIP

Opinion leadership is the ability to influence informally other individuals' attitudes in a desired way and with relatively high frequency. Stycos (1952) found that opinion leaders in a Greek village were often literate priests and schoolteachers who received messages (that is, knowledge) from the print media, which they in turn passed along to their illiterate followers.

Opinion leaders in each of the five Colombian villages were identified through sociometric measures. The villagers were asked whom they would seek out for advice about agriculture, new farm ideas, health problems, marketing, and local politics.[46] Table 4-6 shows the positive correlations with literacy that were obtained in the five villages; in two communities, the correlations are significant, providing some evidence for the conclusion that

[45] Positive associations between literacy and cosmopoliteness are reported among peasants in Turkey (Lerner 1964a), in Guatemala (Wright et al. 1967:17), and in Pakistan (Schuman et al. 1967).

[46] Four sociometric questions were utilized in the two traditional communities, and six queries were used in the three modern communities. Responses to the various sociometric questions were combined into a single score because of the high correlation found among the responses to each equestion. For further detail, see Rogers and van Es (1964) or Chapter 10.

literacy and opinion leadership are positively related. Further detail is shown in Fig. 4-3, where the functional literacy of opinion leaders and followers in both modern and traditional villages is compared. In both types of villages, opinion leaders (the 10 percent of respondents in each village receiving the most sociometric choices) are more likely to be literate than followers; however, the opinion leaders are far from 100 percent literate. Opinion leaders are sought for information and advice by their peers, so that one would expect them to be more competent regarding the topics discussed. Literates are more likely typified by such competence because of their greater access to print media and their ability to think in and manipulate symbols.

CROSS-CULTURAL COMPARISON OF FINDINGS IN INDIA

In order to provide a cross-cultural test of the validity of the present findings, data have been analyzed from 702 peasants living in eight villages in North Central India.[47] The respondents were interviewed personally in 1964, by interviewers with a research instrument similar to that used in Colombia, but with proper cultural adaptation.

MEASURING FUNCTIONAL LITERACY IN INDIA

The measure of functional literacy was a seven-word Hindi sentence, "Samai par kam karna achchhi adat hai" (translated literally,"A regular work time is a good habit"). This sentence was handed to the respondent on a card during the interview.

The correspondence of functional literacy and self-defined ability to read a newspaper was much closer than was evident in the Colombian study at lower levels of literacy.[48] Less than 1 percent of the Indian respondents who claimed to be literate were not able to read any words in the functional literacy test, whereas the corresponding figure for Colombian peasants was 12 percent. However, there was a greater discrepancy in India between the two measures of literacy among those peasants who read all words correctly. Of the Indian villagers who read all seven words correctly, 13 percent (as opposed to only 9 percent in Colombia) *said* they could not read a newspaper. This difference between the two countries may have resulted from the different nature of the sentence utilized in the functional literacy test. In India, the seven words

---

[47] These data were gathered by the National Institute of Community Development, Hyderabad, and were analyzed in the Department of Communication at Michigan State University by N. C. Jain, Research Assistant.

[48] But across the entire range of the two variables, the correspondences were slightly closer in Colombia than in India. The correlation between functional literacy scores and self-defined ability to read a newspaper was .784 for the Colombian villagers and .740 for the Indian peasants.

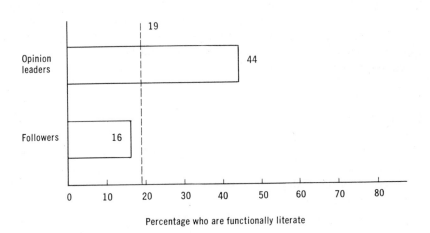

Figure 4–3.   Functional Literacy by Opinion Leadership for Colombian Villages with Traditional and Modern Norms.

In both the traditional and the modern villages, opinion leaders are more likely to be functionally literate than are their followers. However, in the modern villages, where the percentage of all peasants who are functionally literate is twice that of the traditional villages (38 as opposed to 19 percent), we observe a wider leader-follower difference in literacy (71–34 or 37 percent). Even in the modern villages, however, the opinion leaders are far from 100 percent literate.

used may have been less difficult than the reading level needed for newspaper comprehension.

In the Colombian study the correlation between functional literacy scores and self-reported ability to write a letter ranged from .746 to .648 among the five villages, with an average of .711. The corresponding correlation for Indian peasants was only .207. However, the correlation between functional literacy scores and years of formal schooling was higher for Indian peasants ($r = .736$) than for the Colombian peasants ($r = .575$). In fact, it was found that *all* the Indian peasants with more than the UNESCO minimum of four years of education were functionally literate. Only about 4 percent of the Indian villagers with no formal schooling were able to read any words correctly on the functional test, as compared with 20 percent in Colombia.

Thus, when one compares the various measures of literacy in India with those in Colombia, the following conclusions are formed:

1. *There are generally similar relationships between functional literacy scores and self-reported ability to read and write.*

2. *Formal educational attainment and functional literacy are more strongly related in India*, where the UNESCO standard of four years of education seems to approximate more closely the watershed in functional literacy.

In an overall estimate, however, the cross-cultural similarities outweigh the differences in these relationships of functional literacy to other literacy-education measures in India and Colombia.

LITERACY AND MODERNIZATION

In general, *functional literacy was found to be related to other modernization variables in India much as in Colombia.* For example, functional literacy is positively (and significantly) related to total mass media exposure scores ($r = .384$) in India, to newspaper and magazine readership[49] ($r = .468$), and to radio listening ($r = .367$). It is apparent that literacy is more highly related to print media exposure than to electronic media exposure. (Literacy is related to movie exposure by a correlation of only .163, which is not significantly different from zero.)

In India functional literacy scores are positively related to these variables with the following correlation values:[50]

1. Empathy ($r = .350$)
2. Agricultural ($r = .315$) and home ($r = .374$) innovativeness
3. Achievement motivation ($r = .215$)
4. Social status ($r = .253$ with farm size in land units)
5. Cosmopoliteness ($r = .111$ with number of trips to cities)
6. Political knowledge ($r = .343$)
7. Opinion leadership ($r = .178$)

---

[49] Magazine and newspaper exposure were combined in a composite score in India.

These relationships are quite similar in both direction and strength to their counterparts in Colombia, thus providing some evidence of the cross-cultural generalizabiliy of our findings.

SUMMARY OF THE FINDINGS

Functional literacy was measured among the Colombian peasants by asking each respondent to read a six-word sentence in Spanish. Although this functional literacy test proved fairly satisfactory, it should be lengthened for greater sensitivity, in order to better distinguish degrees of literacy and to improve its reliability. Functional literacy is the ability to read and write word symbols at a level of competence adequate for carrying out the individual's functions in his social system. For present purposes, functional literacy was regarded as one type of operational measure for literacy, defined as the degree to which an individual possesses mastery over symbols in written form.

Highly positive relationships were obtained between functional literacy scores and (1) self-defined literacy and (2) years of formal education. However, some individuals who said they could read a newspaper could not read the six-word functional literacy test, and vice versa. Whereas numerous functional literates had less than the UNESCO standard of four years of education, only one of the functional illiterates had four years of education or more. Evidently there has been substantial acquisition of literacy outside the classroom among our respondents.

The consequences of literacy found in the present study generally emphasize the importance of this variable in individual modernization in less developed nations. Functional literacy is related to mass media exposure (and even more strongly related to newspaper than to electronic media exposure); is more characteristic of children than adults; is associated with empathy, agricultural and home innovativeness, achievement motivation, farm size, trips to urban centers, political knowledge, and sociometric opinion leadership. All these Colombian findings have been confirmed with data from a sample of 702 Indian peasants, whose responses lend cross-cultural credence to our conclusions.

The village-to-village differences in Tables 4-2, 4-4, 4-5, and 4-6 emphasize the importance of studying several communities in a country such as Colombia, where wide subcultural differences are encountered. Evidently the patterns of relationship of functional literacy to its correlates, although generally in a similar direction (either positive or negative), are subject to rather wide intercommunity variation. This point is an argument also, of

---

⁵⁰ All these correlations are significantly different from zero.

course, for the priority of extensive replication of the present study in other less developed nations (as was done in India) before its conclusions can be considered definitive. Nevertheless, the present work clearly indicates the importance of literacy as a variable in explaining many facets of modernization. One gains the general impression, from this analysis of Colombia and India data, that literacy is of considerable importance in relation to other modernization variables.[51]

In comparing the findings of this chapter with those in later chapters of this book, one is again reminded that modernization is a complex process. The variables related to literacy also are related to each other. The more innovative individual is typically more literate, empathic, and cosmopolite. He rates higher in achievement motivation and has greater political knowledge. It would appear, however, that these are not simple, additive relationships. The contribution of one variable in explaining the variance in another, as well as the nature of possible interactions, particularly in peasant societies. is poorly understood. Therefore, while the scope of inquiry in the present chapter was largely limited to a study of zero-order (that is, two-variable) relations in later sections of this book, the authors intend to probe further into the nature of these reationships by means of multivariate techniques.

FUTURE RESEARCH

The present investigation is but a modest attempt to determine the correlates of and, in one sense, the "meaning" of literacy. Future study is needed on the following:

1. *Improved measures of functional literacy.* Several ways in which our survey instrument could be improved became apparent during the course of the investigation. For example, greater reliabiliy and sensitivity could be obtained by lengthening the functional literacy measure. Preliminary testing of a functional literacy instrument in a number of linguistically common countries among both urban and rural respondents would help determine the breadth of its applicability. Further, comprehension and writing aspects of functional literacy should be incorporated with the test of reading ability. It is undoubtedly possible that some respondents were able to read the sentence aloud but did not understand its meaning. In East Pakistan, many villagers can "read" the Koran, but few are able to *comprehend* even a sentence. Lastly, an improved operation of functional literacy should consider the syntactic position of the words (which can affect the degree of difficulty). For example, "thee" is uncommon in modern-day English; yet it is not diffi-

---

[51] Further evidence of this point comes from aggregate analysis, in which nations are the unit of analysis. National literacy rates are strongly correlated with indicators of economic, political, and social development (Chapter 14).

cult to identify when presented to a respondent at the end of a sentence such as "My country tis of. . . . "

While our attempt to measure functional literacy, rather than to rely on self-reporting measures, may represent a step forward, a great deal of work on functional literacy measures is still needed.

2. *The newly literate adult and how his attitudes and behavior are changed when he attains the ability to read and write.*[52] What does it *mean* to become literate? This type of investigation calls for a before-after experimental pattern in which the levels of modernization (on such variables as empathy, achievement motivation, cosmopoliteness, and mass media exposure) are measured among a sample of villagers both before and after they enroll in an adult literacy course. Such research would enable us to make more accurate time-order statements about the relationship of literacy to other modernization variables. At least two such investigations (Herzog 1967a; Wright et al. 1967) have been completed or are now underway.

3. *Cultural and ecological settings as they affect the functions of literacy.* There is a great difference between being illiterate in a rural village and being illiterate in a city, where literacy is more or less demanded of the inhabitant.[53] Golden (1952) stated: "Though not essential to traditional agriculture and its related crafts, literacy is required for urban-industrial occupations. . . . Since neither business documents nor accounts need be kept [by peasants], and since the work requires no blueprints, reading and writing are not essential to everyday life." To determine the functions of literacy in the city, one might study how recent illiterate immigrants adjust to the new setting.

4. *Motivations for the adoption of literacy,* itself an innovation for illiterate villagers, are important. Wright (1965:43) has identified some of the factors that drew villagers to adult literacy training in Guatemala; most important was a general motivation for modernization, perhaps typified by one peasant who said he enrolled "to come from darkness into light."[54] Almost half of the Turkish villagers who were illiterate said they would like to learn to read and write (MIT Center for International Studies 1964). This interest in becoming literate was inversely related to age; as one grows older, he seems to lose some of the desire to learn. The traits and attitudes of villagers drawn to literacy training should be studied closely. Perhaps the positive relationships between literacy and other modernization variables are due simply to the fact that more modern peasants (1) enroll in literacy classes[55]

---

[52] Perhaps becoming literate as an *adult* does not lead to so much change in accompanying social psychological variables (such as symbol manipulation) as when one becomes literate in childhood.

[53] Herzog (1967a) found that no significant changes occurred in such modernization variables as empathy, political knowledge, and mass media exposure when adult Brazilian peasants were taught to read and write. He reasoned that when there is no accompanying change in occupation or in environment, as might occur with urban migration, the modernization consequences due to the onset of literacy are comparatively minimal, at least in the short range.

and (2) remain enrolled until they become literate. Among the Hausa in Nigeria, Doob (1961:178) has pointed out, "It is also probable that the more alert people of the community responded to the opportunity to attend the literacy classes. Or perhaps both sequences occurred: the initially more alert became literate and then, having become literate, they could become still more alert."

5. How we can *circumvent the barriers of literacy?* Radio, movies, television, oral communication systems such as animation and leader training, or pictorial, nonverbal print media are all "illiteracy-jumping" methods requiring further investigation. The importance of children reading aloud to illiterate parents has been underlined in this study. At least in the short range (within one generation), primary school education and adult literacy courses are not nearly effective enough to create world-wide literacy. For a considerable number of adult illiterates, ways must be found for effective, rapid communication that does not depend upon reading skill.

6. How does becoming literate alter the relative *credibility*[56] that a peasant places in the print media as opposed to other communication channels? Some recent evidence from an investigation of the effects of radiophonics schools in Honduras and El Salvador indicates that the newly literate tend to regard *everything* seen in print as absolute truth (Rhoads and Piper 1963: 50). This Central American radiophonics literacy campaign was sponsored by the Roman Catholic Church, and Biblical materials were used by the new readers. The religious sponsorship may have lent extra credence to the print materials; however, it is likely that print media generally have high credibility among the newly literate. This hypothesis should furnish the subject for future research.

Certain of these six research leads are currently under investigation by the authors in a UNESCO-sponsored field experiment in Costa Rica and India and in a U.S. AID-sponsored investigation in Brazil, Nigeria, and India.

[54] More specific reasons for participation were also mentioned, such as to earn higher wages, to write to girlfriends, to be able to sign one's name on documents, and so on.

[55] Wright et al. (1967:iii) indeed found that this was so in Guatemalan villages, but Herzog (1967a) reported contrary evidence among Brazilian peasants.

[56] This term is here defined as the trustworthiness and competence that an individual attributes to a communication source or channel.

5

Mass Media Exposure:
The Magic Multiplier*

It was the pressure of communications which brought about the the downfall of traditional societies.

(Lucien W. Pye 1963: 3)

In the oral, traditional society the provisions for wide-horizon communication are inefficient: the traveler and ballad singer come too seldom and know too little. A modernizing of society requires mass media . . . .

(Wilbur Schramm 1963:38)

Several years ago, I made my first trip to an Indian village, which was located about thirty miles outside of Delhi. The mud huts, cow dung cakes drying in the sun, and the small horde of curious children were typical of many Indian villages I have visited since. The villagers were extremely poor, the monsoon rains had come late, and food was in short supply. In spite of their proximity to the capital, only a few of the villagers had ever traveled there. The only literate adults were the village teacher and a large landowner, and they did not subscribe to any newspapers or magazines. The only radio in the village, owned by the president of the village council, was tuned to music rather than to news of the outside world.

As we were about to leave, the village headman proudly invited us to tour the village school. The building was a mud hut, like the villagers' homes, without door or windows. Once inside, and after my eyes had adjusted to the darkness, I saw the last thing in the world that I expected to find in this village. There, in a corner of the schoolroom, was a 24-inch television set!

I later learned that the TV set was part of a foundation-sponsored investigation of the use of television in teaching village children. Perhaps this experience illustrates the degree to which mass media have now penetrated even to villages of less developed countries like India. Some alarmists point out that unless studies of the effects of mass media exposure on modernization

---

* Parts of this chapter have appeared in an earlier version (Rogers 1965b) and as a chapter in *Mass Communication and the Development of Nations* (Rogers 1966b). The data appearing toward the end of the chapter come from Keith and others (1966a) and from Rogers (1966b).

are launched now, it soon will be difficult to find virginal settings from which to obtain comparative data.

While this problem is not yet crucial,[1] the general question of the effect[2] of mass media communication in modernization deserves considerable attention. Exposure to the mass media can undoubtedly be an important variable in bringing about large-scale directed social change and modernization in less developed countries. Yet a search of the literature indicates only four research studies[3] on mass media exposure of peasants in less developed nations and only six investigations of urbanites' media exposure in these settings.[4] It appears that our state of knowledge about mass media exposure and modernization in the underdeveloped nations is still relatively underdeveloped in itself.

Our Colombian investigation has several advantages over those previously completed in that (1) the data from the five Colombian peasant villages exhibit considerable disparity in mass media penetration, as well as differences in the relative modernity-traditionalism of their norms; (2) improved measures of mass media exposure, of antecedent and consequent variables, are used; and (3) multivariate statistical methods are utilized to determine the interrelationships of these variables, while a control is placed on the effects of others. The basic Colombian data are supplemented by data from two recent investigations in other cultural settings, India and Kenya, which provide evidence for generalizing the mass media exposure and modernization findings across cultures.

Before moving to a discussion of the empirical findings, however, let us look more generally at the nature of the mass media in countries like Colombia and at the role of mass media in modernization.

NATURE OF THE MASS MEDIA IN LESS DEVELOPED COUNTRIES

Important differences in the nature and function of the mass media institutions in less developed countries are apparent when these are compared with their counterparts in more developed nations.

[1] At least for some time to come. UNESCO presently estimates that none of the less developed nations comes up to the minimum standard of mass media availability of 10 copies of daily newspapers, 5 radio receivers, 2 movie seats, and 2 television receivers per 100 inhabitants (Davison 1965:130).

[2] The most common topic in all communication research is the study of *effects* (resulting from variations in source credibility, communication channels, message design, and so on) upon knowledge, attitudes, and overt behavior of the receivers. Determination of mass media's role in modernization is quite consistent with, and is but a special case of, the objective of most communication research.

[3] These investigations were completed in six Middle Eastern countries (Lerner 1958), Colombia (Deutschmann and Fals Borda 1962a, 1962b; Deutschmann, 1963), Turkey (Frey 1964, 1966), and Ecuador (Spector et al. 1963).

[4] In addition to these studies in which the individual is the unit of analysis, there are a number of aggregate-type investigations in which the nation is the unit of analysis. Farace (1966) and Chapter 14 provide a summary of these aggregate studies.

1. *The mass media in less developed countries reach much smaller audiences than those in more developed countries.* Examine, for instance, the availability of the mass media (on a per capita basis) in Colombia as compared with the United States (Table 5-1).[5]

Table 5–1. Availability of Mass Media in Columbia and the United States

Media, per 100 population	Colombia	United States
Radio receivers	15.3	100.0
Newspapers	5.6	32.6
Cinema seats	3.9	5.6
Television receivers	1.4	33.2

2. The figures on media availability mask the differences in exposure between rural peasants and elite urbanites in Colombia, which are very wide. There is evidence that *certain elite audiences (such as university students and middle class urbanites) in less developed countries have mass media exposure levels which are just as high as those for similar elites in more developed nations.*[6] This means that mass media exposure is especially low among rural villagers in less developed countries.

3. *Audiences for the electronic mass media, especially radio and film, are larger than for print mass media such as newspapers and magazines in less developed countries.* This differential in the size of media audiences is less characteristic of more developed countries, perhaps due to higher literacy rates, which permit more widespread reception of the print media, as well as to other factors.

4. *Mass media messages in less developed countries are of low interest and relevancy to villagers because of the strong urban orientation of the mass media.* The mass media institutions are usually located in the capital city, or at least in the larger cities, and their content features national and international news that does not elicit much interest from a peasant audience characterized by a limited view of the world. In the more developed countries, there are often specialized media (such as farm magazines) for rural audiences.

5. *There is a greater degree of government control over the mass media, especially the electronic media, in less developed countries than in more developed countries.* National governments in less developed countries are very active promoters of development activities; the higher degree of government control may be one reason why mass media messages in less developed countries have such a

---

[5] Compiled in the early 1960s, these data may be slightly out-of-date.
[6] Studies illustrating this generalization are reviewed by McNelly (1966).

strong prodevelopment content.[7] In fact, most national governments in countries like Colombia view the mass media as integral tools in their development campaigns.

Although the mass media in modernizing nations *could* carry messages in favor of change to millions of villagers each day, the actual proportion of the populace reached by such content is relatively small. Who is in the audience and who is not? What is known of the effects of mass media messages on modernization? What content does get through to peasants?

MASS MEDIA: THEIR RELEVANCE TO MODERNIZATION[8]

Students of development would seem increasingly convinced that mass communication is a catalytic agent in the modernization process. *Mass communication* denotes message transfer via such mass media as newspapers, magazines, film, radio, and television, which enables a source of one (or several individuals) to reach an audience of many.[9] In comparison with interpersonal face-to-face communication, mass media communication is generally distinguished by the following elements: (1) the larger potential size of the simultaneous audience that can be reached; (2) interposed mode of communication between source and receiver; (3) the possibility of delay in reception; (4) the difficulty of obtaining feedback from receivers; (5) absence of mutual source-receiver surveillance (that is, neither source nor receiver has much direct control over the other).

A small but growing body of research in less developed nations (which will be reviewed shortly) indicates the crucial, integral role of mass media in modernization. National development planners have, however, tended to neglect the potential of the mass media, even though these communication channels may well be one of the sharpest tools in the developer's kit. Few (noncommunist) developing countries have given much emphasis to mass communication in the past decade. Pool (1963:235) has pointed out that mass media development is seldom regarded as significant in priority compared with steel mills, power dams, and other conspicuous indicators of development. India

[7] McNelly (1966) emphasizes the promodernization theme of the mass media in less developed countries: "Much of the content in all of the media, including advertising, is informational, educational, or propagandistic in nature, designed to inform or persuade people about various kinds of modernization." However, a content analysis of these themes in comparable mass media in less developed and in more developed nations has not been made. Nevertheless, any North American visitor to Colombia who picks up a copy of *El Tiempo*, one of Bogotá's leading newspapers, is immediately struck by the very large proportion of front-page space devoted to development activities.

[8] Certain of the ideas contained in this section have appeared in Bebermeyer and Rogers (1966).

[9] Some authors distinguish between mass *media* communication and mass communication. The second term includes not only communication via mass media channels but also the interpersonal communication linked with these media channels. Further detail on the interfaces of mass and interpersonal channels is found in Chapters 6 and 10.

where there are only two radios per 1000 persons, is perhaps typical. In the 1950s, only 0.2 percent of India's national development budget was allocated to radio broadcasting, and only about half of this amount was actually spent. And in the 1960s, India's development planners cut this broadcasting budget in half.[10]

Only in less developed communist nations such as mainland China and Cuba have national planners viewed mass media development as a central factor in propelling their country forward. These countries utilize the mass media, often in combination with interpersonal communication among small discussion groups of workers and peasants, to enlist mass audiences in various governmental development campaigns.

What is the argument for mass media development? Stripped to barest essentials, it can be outlined as follows:

1. Interpersonal communication channels alone are inadequate for reaching the huge peasant audiences of the less developed countries, even when these channels are primed at the village level by government change agents. The cost and effort necessary to train sufficient numbers of local development workers for every village would be colossal. Imagine the immense task of training and maintaining one village-level worker for each of India's 500,000 villages! Even if they could be provided in sufficient numbers, local change agents might not be judged credible by villagers who have a deep distrust of all government officials.

2. In recent years, advances in mass media techniques[11] have made it economically practical for national governments to provide radios, films, and other mass media facilities to villages, thereby enabling officials to reach mass audiences with rapid, standardized, and accurate messages about development. By improving mass media facilities, such as radio and television stations, news-gathering services, and newspaper printing plants, the governments of less developed countries could reach larger audiences through these media channels. "The required amount of information and learning is so vast that only by making effective use of the great information multipliers, the mass media, can the developing countries hope to provide information at the rates their timetables for development demand" (Schramm 1964: 246–247).

3. Larger mass media audiences, accompanied by high levels of mass

[10] In spite of a recommendation to the contrary by the Ford Foundation Mass Communication Study Team (1963): "Radio should be permitted to open up the whole outside world to the villagers. No other medium can do so as inexpensively and to such good effect as radio."

[11] Probably one of the most significant contemporary examples of improved mass media technology is the transistor radio, an innovation now found in increasing numbers of villages because it is within the price range of many peasants. The ubiquitous nature of the transistor radio was brought home to the author by a recent incident in Colombia. A peasant boy mounted on a burro loaded with firewood was approaching along a mountain trail. The scene was the popular stereotype of the barefoot Latin American peasant, complete with sombrero; but that romantic picture was shattered when the boy came closer and the wire from his transistor was seen inserted into his ear.

media exposure per capita, can be expected to lead those exposed to more favorable attitudes toward change and development,[12] to greater awareness of political events,[13] and to more knowledge of technical information. Mass media have the potential of multiplying efforts to modernize traditional peoples, especially when the media are combined with interpersonal communication in small discussion groups.[14] Next, let us look more specifically at a model of exposure to the mass media and its modernization effects.

A MODEL OF MASS MEDIA EXPOSURE AND MODERNIZATION

It should be stressed that the main variable in the following analyses is mass media *exposure*. At best, this factor is a gross indicator of individual mass media "inputs." Not taken into consideration here, for example, is the degree to which messages *originating* in the mass media later disseminate through the community via more informal communication channels.[15] Nor does our measure of exposure consider the specific nature of the messages received from the mass media — whether musical, news, or technical content. It should be remembered that *exposure*, not influence or *internalization*, of mass media messages is what is being dealt with here.

In spite of this crude measure, our analysis of mass media exposure can yield answers to questions such as the following:

1. *What antecedents determine the extent of villagers' exposure to mass media?* Among those of apparent interest are social status, literacy, education, age, and cosmopoliteness.

2. *What modernization consequences are associated with mass media exposure?* A basic proposition of this chapter is that exposure to mass media on the part of peasants leads them down the road to modernization.[16] Specific meaures

[12] A distinction must be made here between two different types of attitudes: (1) a psychological "climate for modernization" (McNelly 1966) that is essentially a *general* attitude toward change; and (2) *specific* attitudes toward innovations. It seems that mass media are able to create a generally favorable mental set toward change but are seldom able to change specific attitudes toward new ideas, a task better accomplished by interpersonal communication channels.

[13] And hence, perhaps to enable the mass audience in less developed countries to exercise somewhat greater surveillance over the ruling elites. The great potential of the mass media in conveying political news is underlined by the high priority that revolutionists give to gaining control of mass media institutions, which are usually one of their first targets.

[14] A detailed discussion of the effects of combining mass media and interpersonal communication channels in media forums can be found in the following chapter.

[15] We do credit our respondents, however, with exposure to print media via family or friends who read to them.

[16] There is much support for this general notion in the writings of Pye (1963) and Schramm (1964). A typical statement about the modernizing effects of media exposure is Powdermaker's (1962:228): "The mass media introduced to Africans another form of reality — a world and peoples beyond their experience." Similarly, Lerner (1967b:122–123) states, "Increasingly, in the villages and hamlets of the world, the mass media are bringing 'strange new worlds' into the traditional environment of rural people."

of modernization consequences to be correlated with mass media exposure include empathy, innovativeness, political knowledge, achievement motivation, and aspirations.

A paradigm of the theoretical model underlying the present investigation is shown in Fig. 5-1. This model is based, to a large extent, on the models and

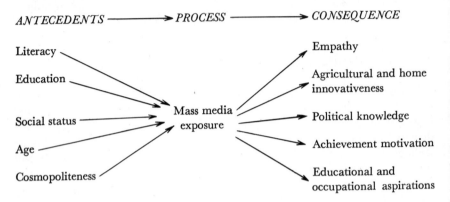

Figure 5-1. Paradigm of the Role of Mass Media Exposure in Modernization.

findings of Lerner (1958) and Deutschmann (1963). On the left-hand side of the paradigm are possible variables that may act to determine whether an individual will be in the mass media audience or not. These variables include literacy and formal education, which are expected to be associated with media exposure. Other likely determinants of exposure are social status (at least one indicator of the economic ability to afford the mass media), age, and cosmopoliteness, which furnishes an alternative avenue (to mass media exposure) for contact with modern urban life.

The role given to mass media exposure in this model is a central one. It is viewed as the indicator of contact with mass media messages, ideas that should lead to greater empathy with the roles portrayed in the media, to adoption of new ideas, to wider political knowledge, and to stronger aspirations to a better life.

MEASURING MASS MEDIA EXPOSURE

Past research in the United States, Chile (Carter and Sepulveda 1964), and Turkey (Lerner 1964a; Frey 1966) indicates a general pattern of overlapping audiences for the mass media.[17] That is, exposure to one medium is positively related to exposure to other media. This "centripetal effect,"[18]

[17] In Quito, Ecuador, McLeod and other (1967) found a similar overlapping pattern among exposure to radio, newspapers, and so on, although the correlations among these items were not very high.

[18] Which was named by Lerner (1963:341).

expressed as high correlations among exposure to the five mass media (newspapers, magazines, films, radio, and TV), is also found in the five Colombian villages.[19] This centripetal clustering of media exposure has both desirable and undesirable consequences for modernization (Frey 1966: 182). On the one hand, multiple media exposure probably increases media influence in producing effects in the audience, for each mass medium tends to reinforce the others. On the other hand, peasants who are not directly reached by one mass medium tend not to be reached by others either, a fact that leads to two categories of peasants: (1) those who are in the audience for all the mass media and (2) the "unreachables."

In any event, the presence of the centripetal effect in media exposure among our respondents, coupled with a desire to utilize a *general* measure of mass media exposure rather than separate measures of exposure for each of the five media, led to the construction of a composite mass media exposure index. The respondents' indications of degree of exposure to each medium, in terms of number of radio shows listened to per week, and so on, were combined into a mass media exposure index by use of a standard score called the "sten score."[20] The advantage of transforming the data in this manner is that exposure to each medium is thus accorded equal weight for its contribution to the total index.[21]

This mass media exposure index was subjected to a Guttman scalogram analysis to determine the degree to which the items measured a single dimension. The coefficient of reproducibility for the data from the three modern communities is 91 percent, and from the two traditional communities it is 97 percent. This result provides some evidence for the unidimensionality of the present index and is similar to the results with peasant respondents of Deutschmann (1963) in Colombia and Frey (1964) in Turkey,[22] but contrary to those of Carter and Sepulveda (1964) among urbanites in Santiago, Chile. Our data indicate that exposure to the five mass media, when summed, form a single dimension of mass media exposure.

Different degrees of penetration of the various media exist for the modern

[19] The thirty-seven correlations among degree of exposure to the five media in the five Colombian villages (with no magazine, film, or television exposure in Nazate and no television exposure in La Cañada, meaningful correlations could not be computed in these locales) ranged from .243 to .869. All the correlations were significantly different from zero.

[20] Sten scores, originally described by Canfield (1951), are a type of "relative" scores (in this respect, somewhat like percentile scores) that normalize any set of data into a distribution with a standard mean and variance.

[21] The present method is an improvement over that used by Lerner (1958:95) for the construction of his mass media exposure index, in that (1) our index contains data on magazine and TV exposure, as well as on newspaper, radio, and film exposure, and (2) a more nearly equal weight is given to each medium, based on actual frequency of exposure rather than on an arbitrary assignment of "equal weights" to each medium.

[22] A coefficient of reproducibility of 88.3 percent was calculated by the present author from data provided by Frey (1964).

Colombian communities (where films reach the most peasants), as compared with the traditional communities (where radio gets through to the largest audience). Part of this difference is explained by the fact that, in the three modern communities, extension service agents had shown free public films several times during the year preceding the data gathering. However, neither type of village displays a pattern of media exposure identical to that found in Saucío, a Colombian community studied by Deutschmann (1963), where newspapers reached a wider audience than either radio or films. Frey's (1964) Turkish villager data are similar to those of the two traditional Colombian communities, where radio reached the largest audience.[23] In fact, in most less developed countries, radio seems to reach more villagers than any of the other mass media.[24]

ANTECEDENTS OF MASS MEDIA EXPOSURE

LITERACY

Until peasants become literate, they cannot have print mass media exposure, except through an oral reader. Even though radio, films, and TV are media that have the potential for penetration to illiterates, there is evidence from Deutschmann's (1963) study that literate Colombian peasants are much more likely than illiterates to appear in the radio audience; about twice as many literate farmers listened to radio as did illiterates.

In the present study (Table 4-4) functional literacy is most highly related to newspaper readership (correlations are .430 for all five villages in the aggregate; .365, .616, and .360 in the three modern communities; and .476 and .396 in the two traditional villages), somewhat less so to radio listening (.336; .370, .398, .335; .142 and .388, respectively and magazine readership (.207; .138, .562, −.104; and .148), and least to film (.254; .314, .471, −.160; and .105) and TV watching (.216; .197, .422, .144). These findings show that literacy is more highly related to newspaper exposure than to nonprint media exposure. It might be considered surprising that literacy does not explain more of the variation in mass media exposure, especially print media exposure. Literacy, at least as presently measured, offers far from a complete explanation of mass media exposure.[25]

[23] Similar results are also available from a national sample of 7224 villagers in India; Sen and Roy (1966: 32) found that radio reached 58 percent, films reached 53 percent, and newspapers 22 percent.

[24] Although, as modernization proceeds in a country to a point where a majority of its villagers are literate, one might expect that the print media audience could eventually exceed the radio audience.

[25] In fact, even in the case of the highest of the twenty-five correlations (r = .616), functional literacy explains only 38 percent of the variation in newspaper exposure in one village. Possible reasons that these correlations are not higher were discussed in Chapter 4.

A clearer insight into this relationship is provided in Fig. 5-2, where the functional literacy measure is dichotomized into (1) literates, who could correctly read all six words in the functional literacy test, and (2) illiterates, who could not. Each indicator of mass media exposure was also divided into (1) at least some exposure (for example, readership of newspapers at least once per week) and (2) no exposure. Furthermore, exposure to both newspapers and magazines was classified according to whether (1) the respondent himself read these media or (2) others read these media to the respondent.

Figure 5-2 indicates that in most instances *literates have more mass media exposure, both print and electronic, than do illiterates.*[26] An exception is provided by exposure to newspapers and magazines through others. In the modern communities[27] illiterates have more exposure via oral readers than do literates, as one would expect.[28] *There is considerable exposure of illiterates to newspapers and magazines through oral readers,* a finding hypothesized by Deutschmann (1963). For the electronic media exposure indices, radio, film and TV exposure are higher for literates than for illiterates. This finding may partially reflect the interrelationship between literacy and economic level, since many illiterates are too poor to own radio or TV sets.

EDUCATION

A factor closely allied with functional literacy is years of formal education, since formal schooling would seem to facilitate and encourage media exposure. The Colombian data indicate that the correlation between formal education and mass media exposure is even higher than the correlation between functional literacy and media exposure. *A positive relationship between education and mass media exposure* is indicated by a correlation coefficient of .508.[29]

COSMOPOLITENESS

A positive relationship between mass media exposure and cosmopoliteness is strongly supported.[30] Both media exposure and trips to urban centers are means by

[26] Correlations of literacy with total mass media exposure are .422 for all five villages pooled; .374, .359, and .355 in the modern villages; and .439 and .421 in the traditional villages. All correlations are significantly different from zero at the 1 percent level of probability.

[27] There was almost no exposure to magazines through others in the traditional villages.

[28] However, remember that literates have the highest incidence of newspaper and magazine reading.

[29] This figure represents the aggregate of the five villages; .531, .745, and .449 are the correlations in the modern villages; .283 and .511, in the traditional villages.

[30] The correlation for all five villages is .551. Correlations for the modern villages are .427, .657, and .664; for the traditional villages, correlations are .324 and .617.

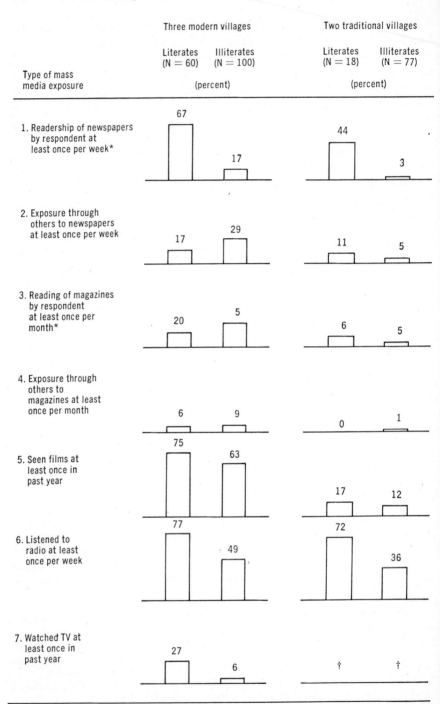

	Three modern villages		Two traditional villages	
Type of mass media exposure	Literates (N = 60)	Illiterates (N = 100)	Literates (N = 18)	Illiterates (N = 77)
	(percent)		(percent)	

1. Readership of newspapers by respondent at least once per week* — 67 / 17 / 44 / 3

2. Exposure through others to newspapers at least once per week — 17 / 29 / 11 / 5

3. Reading of magazines by respondent at least once per month* — 20 / 5 / 6 / 5

4. Exposure through others to magazines at least once per month — 6 / 9 / 0 / 1

5. Seen films at least once in past year — 75 / 63 / 17 / 12

6. Listened to radio at least once per week — 77 / 49 / 72 / 36

7. Watched TV at least once in past year — 27 / 6 / † / †

which villagers put themselves in touch with the world beyond their village. A peasant who makes the effort to travel to an urban center is also likely to keep in touch with happenings in urban centers through the mass media.

SOCIAL STATUS

The more socially elite[31] among our peasant respondents have higher media exposure. They are economically able to afford media facilities such as radio and TV sets, which are in themselves status symbols. The correlation[32] of .500 between social status and mass media exposure is evidence that *social status is positively related to mass media exposure.*

AGE

Older peasants, who are likely to have relatively low levels of formal education and lower social status, seem to attend less to the mass media.[33] Older villagers are probably less neoteric in their attitudes and values, so that selectively they expose themselves less to the mass media (saturated with modernizing content) then do younger peasants. It was also found that age was negatively correlated with literacy in the two most traditional villages,[34] so that the negative age-exposure relationship may occur because of the intervening variable of literacy.

In sum, our peasant respondents do not have equal exposure to the mass media. Literacy, formal education, cosmopoliteness, social status, and age all bear influence on who will be in the mass media audience in a country like Colombia.

[31] Social status was measured by interviewers' ratings of the respondent at the conclusion of the research interview.

[32] For all five villages taken together; correlations by village are .513, .578, and .610 for modern ones, and .183 and .534 for the traditional ones.

[33] Support for this assertion comes from the consistently negative correlations with age in all five villages (−.306, −.180, −.183; −.287, and −.022). Only one of these correlations is significantly different from zero; but after pooling, the correlation of −.197 is significantly different from zero. The tentative conclusion is that *there is a negative relationship between age and mass media exposure.*

[34] Age is related .308, .443, .215; −.278, and −.107 with functional literacy in the three modern and the two traditional villages, respectively.

Figure 5–2. Mass Media Exposure by Functional Literacy in Three Modern and Two Traditional Colombian Villages.

*That some illiterates claimed to have read newspapers and magazines may not be surprising because a number of those classified here as "illiterates" were able to read one or more words on the functional literacy measure (but less than all six words).

†Nazate and La Cañada are not within the range of television transmission, so no TV exposure was possible.

CONSEQUENCES OF MEDIA EXPOSURE

There is much theoretic exploration to suggest that a general consequence of mass media exposure among peasants is the development of more modern attitudes, the adoption of new ideas (both technological and aspirational), greater political knowledge and more empathy.[35] The limited empirical investigation to date tends to support this conceptual notion.

EMPATHY

Empathy has been defined as the degree to which an individual is able to project himself into the role of another person. The measure of empathy for the research reported here determined the concept as the ability of peasants

Table 5–2. Correlation of Mass Media Exposure Scores with Various Consequent Variables in Five Colombian Villages

	Correlation with Mass Media Exposure Scores					
	Modern Villages			Traditional Villages		All Five Villages (Aggregate)
Consequences of Mass Media Exposure	Pueblo Viejo	San Rafael	Cuatro Esquinas	Nazate	La Cañada	
1. Empathy scores	.378[a]	.500[a]	.395[a]	.609[a]	.376[a]	.446[a]
2. Agricultural innovativeness scores	.407[a]	.398[b]	.426[a]	.329[b]	.510[a]	.422[a]
3. Home innovativeness scores	.489[a]	.819[a]	.349[a]	.317[b]	.540[a]	.515[a]
4. Political knowledge scores	.530[a]	.745[a]	.691[a]	.368[b]	.460[a]	.572[a]
5. Achievement motivation scores	[.169]	.373[b]	[.181]	.511[a]	.457[a]	.318[a]
6. Educational aspirations for children	.245[b]	.754[a]	.564[a]	.401[b]	.612[a]	.508[a]
7. Occupational aspirations for children	[.083]	.642[a]	[.255]	[.215]	.407[a]	.300[a]

[a] Significantly different from zero at the 1 percent level.
[b] Significantly different from zero at the 5 percent level.

[35] A recent statement of this viewpoint is found in Schramm (1964).

to assume (imaginatively) the roles of a village leader, an extension agent, a district official, the national Minister of Education, and the President of Colombia. In support of the findings of Lerner (1958) and Frey (1966) in the Middle East, the present results (Table 5-2) indicate positive, significant relationships between media exposure and empathy. Mass media exposure may provide peasants with knowledge of new roles, prompting them vicariously to put themselves in the shoes of persons depicted in mass media messages. Or, it may be that those villagers who already possess higher levels of empathy seek the stimulation of messages presented in the print and electronic media. Whatever the exact nature or direction of the causal arrows, *mass media exposure and empathy are positively associated.*[36]

INNOVATIVENESS

Innovativeness, as has been noted, is the degree to which an individual decides earlier than others in his social system to adopt new ideas. Table 5-2 indicates a positive and significant relationship between media exposure and both measures of innovativeness (agricultural and home) in all five villages. Mass media exposure is generally more strongly associated with innovativeness than with almost any other of the consequent variables in Table 5-2. The correlations range from .819 for home innovativeness in San Rafael (67 percent of the variance in media exposure and innovativeness occurs together) to .317 for home innovativeness in Nazate (10 percent covariance). The evidence indicates that *mass media exposure is positively related to innovativeness.*[37]

In spite of this relationship, in the following chapter on communication channels it will be seen that our peasant respondents did not mention *any* mass communication medium at any stage in their adoption of one farm innovation, namely, 2,4-D weed spray. Similar evidence of the relative lack of importance of mass media channels in providing specific information about agricultural innovations also has been reported in Pakistan, Mexico, and Colombia.[38] This seeming inconsistency in the two types of findings, on the one hand, a high correlation between mass media exposure and innovative-

[36] Empathy scores were correlated with each of the five types of mass media exposure in each of the five villages, in order to see whether some are more highly related to empathy than others. In the three more modern villages, empathy scores are most highly related to film exposure, somewhat less so to radio and newspaper, and least with television and magazine exposure. In Nazate and La Cañada, empathy scores are most highly related with newspaper exposure, and much less so with exposure to the other media.

[37] Similar evidence for this generalization was reported by Deutschmann (1963) in a Colombian village and by Waisanen and Durlak (1966) for a national sample of Costa Ricans.

[38] By Rahim (1961), Myren (1962), and Deutschmann and Fals Borda (1962a), respectively.

ness,[39] and, on the other, the near absence of mass media channels in leading to the adoption of a specific innovation, suggests one possible conclusion: *the mass media's role in modernizing peasants of a less developed country may be mainly to form a generally favorable attitude toward new ideas, the so-called "climate for modernization", rather than to provide the specific details needed for adoption of these innovations.*

This is not to say, however, that the mass media *could not* effectively transmit technical details about innovations to villagers in less developed countries. The experience with radio farm forums in India (Neurath 1960, 1962) clearly indicates an important *potential role* for the mass media in diffusing innovations, especially when utilized in combination with organized interpersonal discussion. Similar evidence of the strong potential for electronic mass media in transmitting innovations to peasants comes from two field experiments in which the villagers listened in informal groups (but not in forums specifically organized for that purpose by change agents):

1. In selected Ecuadorian villages, Spector and others (1963) gave a transistor radio to each family. This almost guaranteed high exposure. Furthermore, the content of the radio programs was localized and focused on such peasant interests as weather, agricultural practices, and market information. Radio was named afterward by the villagers as the most important and influential communication channel in their decisions to adopt agricultural and home innovations.[40]

2. A television set was placed in each of two villages on the island of Taiwan, and samples of the residents were interrogated before and after this mass medium was introduced (Chu 1966). The sets were placed in the homes of the village headman, and most TV watching occurred in group fashion. Often, as many as seventy persons came to watch such varied programs as "I Love Lucy," "Lassie," and "77 Sunset Strip," as well as Taiwanese drama and musical shows. Only a very small portion of the programs dealt with farm innovations; nevertheless, some of the TV watchers adopted new fertilizers, implements, and other agricultural innovations, as well as became interested in birth control techniques. However, innovations less compatible with the peasants' values, such as latrines and other sanitation ideas, were not adopted as a result of TV viewing.

So what can one surmise about mass media exposure and innovativeness? Such exposure is positively related to innovativeness, but under usual con-

[39] This relationship might simply arise from the fact that mass media exposure is itself an innovation among our villagers, and so its "adoption" is positively associated with agricultural and home innovativeness. However, among the present respondents there is reason to believe that the media (1) were fairly customary aspects of the peasant's style of life and (2) had been present in the five villages for many years (except for TV in Nazate and La Cañada, where it could not be received and, hence, does not affect the correlation of media exposure to innovativeness).

[40] Of course, we do not know, but strongly suspect, that much of the radio's short-term effect might have been the product of its novelty among these Ecuadorian peasants.

ditions in less developed countries this relationship may result from the creation of a generally favorably mental set toward change rather than from the transmission of specific details about innovations. When the mass media are coupled with group discussion among villagers, however, and when the mass media content is relevant,[41] it appears they may be able effectively to transmit technical knowledge about innovations to peasants. Hence, the mass media have an important potential role in furthering innovativeness, but one that is seldom fulfilled in most less developed countries today.

POLITICAL KNOWLEDGE

In less developed nations like Colombia, the mass media are major transmitters of political news and events. One anticipates, therefore, that media exposure would be associated with political knowledge. Table 5-2 shows that these two variables *are* positively and significantly related in all five of the villages. Deutschmann in Colombia (1963), Frey in Turkey (1966), and McLeod et al. (1967) in Ecuador found corraborating evidence. Field experiments (1) in Taiwan, where TV was introduced into two villages by Chu (1966), and (2) in India, where Menefee and Menefee (1965, 1967) introduced mimeographed newspapers and radios in three villages, have demonstrated increases in political knowledge as a result of mass media exposure.

Mass media exposure is positively related to political knowledge. Government leaders in less developed countries feel that the mass media are powerful transmitters of political news, creators of meaningful citizen interest and participation in politics, and developers of nationalistic spirit. Present findings suggest that this belief in the role of the mass media in political modernization may well be justified.[42]

ACHIEVEMENT MOTIVATION

Achievement motivation, defined as a social value which emphasizes a desire for excellence in order for an individual to attain a sense of personal accomplishment in his occupation (agriculture in the present case), was measured by a sentence-completion test in Colombia.[43] McClelland (1961) argues that achievement motivation is a cause of national economic develop-

---

[41] By providing feedback to the mass media source, media forums may increase the relevancy of the program content. Another means of increasing the media's relevancy for peasant audiences, Frey (1966) suggests, is to achieve greater peasant participation in the programs through peasant interviews, request programs, and roving rural reporters.

[42] But only, of course, among individuals who have at least some media exposure. UNESCO estimates that about two-thirds of the world's population still lack the barest means of being informed about domestic — let alone foreign - - news (Davidson 1965:13).

[43] Further details about this measure are contained in Chapter 11.

ment and individual modernization. If the mass media in a developing country convey a favorable view of more developed countries and of modern urban life, peasants with higher exposure should have higher levels of achievement motivation through a process of invidious comparison. The data here (Table 5-2) support this hypothesis, especially in the two traditional communities. The correlations are not especially high, but they indicate a *positive relationship between mass media exposure and achievement motivation*. In Chapter 11 it will be seen that a number of other variables are more important than media exposure in explaining achievement motivation.

EDUCATIONAL AND OCCUPATIONAL ASPIRATIONS

Theoretically, it would seem that peasants with higher media exposure should have higher educational and occupational aspirations for their children. Until peasants in relatively isolated and traditional villages are connected with the "outside world" of opportunities, they are largely unaware of the status levels which their children might achieve.[44] Awareness of higher levels of living gained through mass media exposure, should lead to higher aspirations.

Levels of aspiration were measured in the present investigation by asking respondents (1) the number of years of education and (2) the occupation (which was coded in terms of levels of occupational prestige) that they wished their eldest child to have. *Both types of aspirations are positively correlated with media exposure*[45] (Table 5-2), but educational aspirations are correlated most strongly. Greater contact with the larger society via the media seems to be associated with higher aspirations. Some development theorists postulate that creating a broad need for higher aspirations is an important early step in peasant modernization. Although the precise cause-effect nature of the relationship is not known, our Colombian data suggest that one road to higher aspirations is mass media exposure.[46]

MASS MEDIA EXPOSURE AS AN INTERVENING VARIABLE IN MODERNIZATION

The model presented earlier in this chapter shows mass media exposure intervening between antecedents and consequences of exposure. It has been demonstrated that mass media exposure is related, much as was expected, to both the antecedent and the consequent variables. Yet these findings do not indicate that media exposure is necessarily an *intervening* variable between the

[44] As Lerner (1958) has pointed out.

[45] Waisanen and Durlak (1966) provide similar evidence for a national sample of Costa Ricans.

[46] Schramm (1964:127-144) argues that the mass media can raise aspirations in less developed countries, even though they cannot directly alter strongly held attitudes.

Table 5–3. Zero-Order Correlations and First-Order Partial Correlations (with Control on Mass Media Exposure) of Functional Literacy with Five Selected Consequent Variables[a]

Type of Correlation	Modern Villages			Traditional Villages		All Five Villages (Aggregate)
	Pueblo Viejo	San Rafael	Cuatro Esquinas	Nazate	La Cañada	
I. Zero-order correlations (r_{12}) of functional literacy with:						
1. Empathy scores	.437	.568	.143	.420	.411	.388
2. Agricultural innovativeness scores	.377	.292	.140	.485	.196	.291
3. Political knowledge scores	.480	.595	.341	.292	.492	.446
4. Educational aspirations for children	.403	.440	.180	−.344	.388	.345
II. First-order partial correlations $(r_{12.3})$ of functional literacy, controlling on mass media exposure,[b] with:						
1. Empathy scores	.345	.401	.003	.215	.301	.245
2. Agricultural innovativeness scores	.266	.092	−.013	.402	.027	.264
3. Political knowledge scores	.357	.323	.142	.160	.371	.282
4. Educational aspirations for children	.347	.035	−.026	−.631	.182	.254

[a] Purpose of this table is to facilitate comparison of the zero-order correlations with the first-order partial correlations. For example, the zero-order correlation of functional literacy with empathy in Pueblo Viejo is .437, but the first-order partial correlation of functional literacy with empathy (when controlling on the effect of mass media exposure) is .345. Thus, in this case one may conclude that mass media exposure is an intervening variable between functional literacy and empathy. By removing the effect of mass media exposure, the correlation of functional literacy and empathy is lowered from .437 to .345. However, this difference is not significant.

[b] The effect of controlling on mass media exposure was tested for statistical significance by the z test for difference between the zero-order correlation and the first-order partial correlation, which is underlined once in the table if significant at the 5 percent level and twice if at the 1 percent level.

antecedent and consequent variables. For example, literacy is known to be related to media exposure, and media exposure to agricultural innovativeness. However, there may be a direct relationship between literacy and innovativeness, rather than a relationship interposed by mass media exposure.

Whether mass media exposure is indeed an intervening variable can be tested with the method of partial correlation. This procedure determines the difference between r_{12} and $r_{12.3}$, where

r_{12} = the zero-order correlation between an antecedent variable X_1 and a consequent variable X_2.

$r_{12.3}$ = the first-order partial correlation between an antecedent variable and a consequent variable while controlling (or mathematically removing) the effect of a possible intervening variable X_3, which in the present case is mass media exposure.

If $r_{12.3}$ is different from r_{12}, some evidence is available that mass media exposure intervenes between the antecedent and consequent variables. Results of this analysis are shown in Table 5-3. Only functional literacy (from among the five antecedent variables) was tested in the partial correlations, because of literacy's theoretical and practical relevance and the strength of its relationships with mass media exposure. On the basis of similar criteria, empathy, agricultural innovativeness, political knowledge, and educational aspirations for children, were selected for testing from among the seven consequent variables analyzed previously (Table 5-2).

The results shown in Table 5-3 provide consistent support for our hypothesis that mass media exposure is an intervening variable between functional literacy and the four consequent variables (empathy, agricultural innovativeness, political knowledge, and educational aspirations for children) in all five Colombian villages. All nineteen positive zero-order correlations shown in the upper half of Table 5-3 are lower (two of them become slightly negative) when the effect of mass media exposure is removed from the relation between functional literacy and the consequent variables by partial correlation. These first-order partial correlations are shown in the lower half of Table 5-3.[47] The one negative zero-order correlation shown in Table 5-3 between functional literacy and educational aspirations in Nazate (in itself rather difficult to explain) becomes much stronger and remains negative when the intervening effect of mass media exposure is removed.

The analysis presented in Table 5-3 consistently shows that *part of the effect of functional literacy on various indices of modernization occurs through mass media exposure.* This is tentative support of the earlier model (Fig. 5-1), which showed that mass media exposure intervenes between literacy and various

---

[47] The z test for difference between each pair of zero-order and first-order correlations in Table 5-3 showed that nine of the twenty pairs were significantly different at either the 5 percent or the 1 percent level.

modernization consequences.[48] Functional literacy enables peasants in a less developed nation to attend to the mass media; this exposure, in turn, leads to various modernization consequences such as innovativeness, empathy, political knowledge, and higher educational aspirations for children. There also is evidence in the first-order partial correlations (Table 5-3) that *the full effect of functional literacy, in its relationship to the selected consequent variables, is something more than just that of facilitating mass media exposure.* Many of the first-order partial correlations remain fairly strong (at least they do not become negative) even when the intervening effect of mass media exposure is removed. Speculation is thus invited on the meaning of literacy; as was stated in the preceding chapter, it is more than merely a facilitator of mass media exposure. Evidently, functional literacy leads to different mental abilities, such as a capacity to deal with abstract symbols, to an interest in cosmopolitan events outside the peasant's village, and to a general motivation to modernize, all of which are evidently partially independent of mass media exposure per se.

SUMMARY OF THE COLOMBIAN FINDINGS

When one compares the mass media in less developed countries with their counterparts in more developed nations, it is seen that the former reach much smaller audiences. However, certain elite audiences (such as university students or middle class urbanites) in less developed countries have mass media exposure levels that are just as high as those for similar elites in more developed countries. Audiences for the electronic mass media, especially radio and film, are larger than for the print mass media, such as newspapers and magazines, in less developed countries. The messages carried by the mass media in less developed nations are of low interest and relevancy to villagers because of the strong urban orientation of the media. Government control over the mass media, especially the electronic media, is greater in less developed countries.

[48] Some confirmatory evidence, though of a quite different nature, is provided by Chu's (1966) field experiment in introducing TV sets in Taiwan villages. Television exposure had its greatest modernizing effects among the literate peasants, which Chu attributed to the fact that media reception among villagers above a minimum threshold of education and literacy will have greater modernizing effects in terms of innovativeness and political knowledge. The reasoning is similar to that presented by Briones and Waisanen (1966), which was reviewed in the preceding chapter. However, conflicting evidence to Chu's results were obtained by Neurath (1960), who found that illiterates gained more agricultural knowledge than literates in Indian radio farm forums (Chapter 6).

Further supporting evidence for the Colombian conclusion that mass media exposure intervenes between modernization antecedents and consequences is provided by Keith et al. (1966). Their correlational analyses of India and Kenya data, patterned methodologically after our results in Table 5-3, show that twenty-three of twenty-five antecedent-consequent correlations are lowered by removing the effect of media exposure.

Mass communication is message transfer via such mass media as newspapers, magazines, film, radio, and television, which enable a source of one or a few individuals to reach an audience of many. Mass media communication is more important in changing cognitions (that is, in increasing knowledge of ideas), whereas interpersonal communication is more likely to cause attitude change. This complementary role of mass media and interpersonal communication channels is maximized in such media "forum" communication systems as India radio forums, communist Chinese study groups, and Latin American radiophonics schools. It appears that the modernization effects of mass media communication among peasants in less developed countries are greater when these media are coupled with interpersonal communication.

Mass media exposure among 255 Colombian peasants was measured by an index composed of exposure to newspapers, magazines, films, radio, and TV. Cosmopoliteness (measured by the number of trips to urban centers), years of formal schooling, and functional literacy were most strongly related (of five antecedent variables studied) to mass media exposure, although social status consistently was positively related to mass media exposure in all five villages, whereas age consistently was negatively related. Substantial exposure by illiterates to newspapers and magazines through others who read aloud to them was observed.

Among the consequent variables, empathy, agricultural innovativeness, home innovativeness, political knowledge, and educational aspirations for children were those most strongly related to the mass media. The conclusion is that the mass media's role may be mainly to achieve a *climate for modernization* rather than to provide specific details needed for adoption of innovations. To this extent the mass media *are* "magic multipliers" of the modernization ethic among peasants but are much less potent in diffusing technological innovations and securing changes in overt behavior. Achievement motivation and occupational aspirations for children, also, were consistently positively (but not always significantly) related to media exposure in the five villages. Thus, mass media exposure is seen to be related to certain modernization consequences, much as was expected.

Both the antecedent and consequent correlates of media exposure are generally similar in both modern and traditional villages. The differences that exist in these correlates do not seem to show a consistent distinction on the basis of type of community norms. Nevertheless, there is justification for having studied five different villages in a country such as Colombia and treating these five sets of data as replications. In fact, the consistency of the present results is all the more compelling when viewed in the light of the wide subcultural variation within Colombia.

A partial correlation analysis indicated the general utility of regarding mass media exposure as an intervening variable between literacy and various measures of modernization. However, one should also remember that the full effect of literacy on modernization consequences is something more than simply the facilitating of mass media exposure.

Now, let us investigate the degree to which the relationships found in Colombia also hold true in Kenya, India, and Brazil.

TOWARD CROSS-CULTURAL GENERALIZATIONS: COMPARATIVE DATA FROM INDIA, KENYA, AND BRAZIL

In the present section data from four other investigations are compared with the Colombian data, which are treated in two categories: the three modern villages and the two traditional villages.

1. Data are utilized from an Indian study conducted in two villages, Ghungrali and Majara, both in the state of Punjab.[49] Interviews were conducted in 1964 with all household heads, 54 in Ghungrali, a very modern village, and 30 in Majara.

2. Data for the Indian UNESCO study were collected via personal interviews with 702 heads of households in eight villages in Uttar Pradesh in 1964.

3. The Kenya data were gathered in 1965 from 624 villagers in three locations, Samia, Kabondo, and Bomet, which are approximately 300 miles from Nairobi.[50]

4. Personal interviews were conducted in 1966 with 1307 farm household heads in twenty villages in the state of Minas Gerais, Brazil (Herzog 1967b).

LEVELS OF MEDIA EXPOSURE

Table 5-4 shows the levels of exposure to each of the mass media in seven different field surveys of villagers (the Turkish and Indian national sample data are included here because of their comparability). While much variability is apparent from country to country, it is seen in general that:

1. *Radio reaches the largest (or at least one of the largest) audiences in each country.*
2. *The electronic mass media generally reach larger audiences than the print media.*
3. *Of the print mass media, newspapers reach larger audiences than magazines.*
4. *Television has not reached any of these peasants except in the Colombian villages near Bogotá.*[51] TV may, however, have great potential as a modernizer once it reaches wider village audiences than at present. In spite of its relatively high

---

[49] These Indian data were gathered by Dharam P. Yadav, Research Assistant in the Department of Communication, Michigan State University, while he was a research officer in the Package Programme Evaluation Research Unit, Ludhiana.

[50] The sponsors of the Kenya study were the government of Kenya and the U.S. AID Mission to Kenya. Data gathering was conducted by Marco Surveys, Ltd., Nairobi.

[51] And probably none of these peasants owned their own TV set but viewed it in stores and urban homes.

Table 5–4. Comparative Levels of Mass Media Exposure among Peasants in Colombia, India, Kenya, and Turkey

Type of Mass Media Exposure	Percentage of Total Sample with at Least Some Exposure						
	Colombia Modern (N = 160)	Colombia Traditional (N = 95)	India Punjab (N = 84)	India UNESCO (N = 702)	India National Sample[a] (N = 7224)	Kenya (N = 624)	Turkey National Sample[b] (N = 6436)
1. Newspaper	60	20	34	8[c]	22	17	48
2. Magazine	18	6	13	8[c]	–	17	–
3. Radio	60	44	76	34	58	66	64
4. Television	13	–	–	–	–	–	–
5. Film	68	11	56	38	53	38	44

[a] From Sen and Roy (1966:32).
[b] From Frey (1966:51).
[c] Newspaper and magazine exposure were combined as one question in the India UNESCO Study.

cost, the government of India is now constructing television transmitters in five areas in order to reach its vast peasant audiences with modernization messages.

ANTECEDENTS

Table 5–5 shows a considerable consistency in the antecedent correlates of mass media exposure across the six different samples of villagers. Of the five antecedent variables, functional literacy, cosmopoliteness, and formal education are most strongly related to mass media exposure.[52] Social status and age are related (positively and negatively, respectively) to mass media exposure, although generally not so closely as education, literacy, and cosmopoliteness.

CONSEQUENCES

Table 5–6 shows the relation of mass media exposure scores to seven indicators of modernization. Again the results are quite similar to those obtained in the Colombia villages. One exception is the correlation of media exposure to agricultural innovativeness ($r = .035$) in Kenya; this might proceed from the rather poor measure of innovativeness utilized in that investigation. Another exception occurs in the case of educational and occupational aspirations in Brazil. However, it appears that the Colombian generalizations discussed previously, regarding antecedents and consequences of mass media exposure, are generally supported by data from India, Kenya, and Brazil.

MULTIVARIATE ANALYSES

The results of two types of multivariate analysis of the cross-cultural data from Colombia, India, and Kenya indicate that:

1. Functional literacy, formal education, and cosmopoliteness are the prime predictors (in a multiple-correlation analysis) of media exposure in all three countries.

2. Mass media exposure was combined with nine other predictor variables in a multiple-correlation analysis to predict each of four modernization variables: agricultural innovativeness, home innovativeness, achievement motivation, and educational aspirations for children. The results show that mass media exposure and formal education are the two most consistent predictors of agricultural and home innovativeness and achievement motivation (but not of educational aspirations). Mass media exposure and education

[52] One exception is the correlation between cosmopoliteness and mass media exposure in Kenya, which might be attributed to an inadequate measure of cosmopoliteness in the Kenya study. Cosmopoliteness was measured in terms of the size of villages, towns, and cities (both within and outside Kenya) that the respondents could recall having visited during their lifetime.

Table 5–5. Correlation of Antecedent Variables with Mass Media Exposure Scores in Colombia, India, Kenya and Brazil

Antecedents Of Mass Media Exposure	Correlation with Mass Media Exposure Scores					
	Colombia Modern (N = 160)	Colombia Traditional (N = 95)	India Punjab (N = 84)	India UNESCO (N = 702)	Kenya (N = 624)	Brazil (N = 1307)
1. Functional literacy	.422[a]	.438[a]	.348[a]	.384[a]	.397[a]	.087[a]
2. Cosmopoliteness	.553[a]	.494[a]	.506[a]	.122[a]	[.055]	.277[a]
3. Formal education	.566[a]	.373[a]	.487[a]	.379[a]	.310[a]	–[d]
4. Social status	.537[a]	.400[a]	.224[b,c]	.143[a]	.332[a,c]	–[d]
5. Age	−.214[a]	[−.156]	−.242[b]	−.132[a]	−.150[a]	–[d]

[a] Significantly different from zero at the 1 percent level.
[b] Significantly different from zero at the 5 percent level.
[c] Level of living scores were used as a measure of social status in the Punjab and the Kenya investigations.
[d] Measures of these antecedent variables are not available.

Table 5–6. Correlation of Mass Media Exposure Scores with Various Consequent Variables in Colombia, India, Kenya, and Brazil

Consequences of Mass Media Exposure	Correlation with Mass Media Exposure Scores					
	Colombia Modern (N = 160)	Colombia Traditional (N = 95)	India Punjab (N = 84)	India UNESCO (N = 702)	Kenya (N = 624)	Brazil (N = 1307)
1. Empathy scores	.418[a]	.509[a]	.405[a]	.334[a]	–[c]	.162[a]
2. Agricultural innovativeness scores	.412[a]	.394[a]	.519[a]	.294[a]	[.035]	–[c]
3. Home innovativeness scores	.511[a]	.399[a]	.482[a]	.293[a]	.291[a]	–[c]
4. Political knowledge scores	.633[a]	.369[a]	–[c]	.283[a]	–[c]	.201[a]
5. Achievement motivation scores	.220[a]	.485[a]	.463[a]	.174[a]	.196[a]	.144[a]
6. Educational aspirations for children	.495[a]	.486[a]	[.114]	.233[a]	.097[b]	–.132[a]
7. Occupational aspirations for children	.300[a]	.307[a]	.313[a]	.121[a]	–[c]	[.001]

[a] Significantly different from zero at the 1 percent level.
[b] Significantly different from zero at the 5 percent level.
[c] The consequent variables were not measured in these investigations.

account for proportionately more variance in the dependent variables than do the eight other independent variables.

The cross-cultural data thus show that: (1) the Colombian findings regarding correlates of media exposure, are largely supported in India, Kenya, and Brazil; (2) the best predictors of mass media exposure are functional literacy, formal education, and cosmopoliteness; and (3) media exposure is one of the strongest predictors (when included along with nine other variables) of such modernization consequences as innovativeness, achievement motivation, and educational aspirations. The data lend some credence to our model of mass media exposure as intervening between certain antecedents and consequences of modernization.

FUTURE RESEARCH

An implicit assumption running throughout this chapter is that the contents of the mass media in less developed countries are pro-development. Such a notion could be tested by utilizing the method of content analysis. Especially useful would be cross-cultural assessments of the nature of mass media messages. Are these messages particularly in favor of change in less developed countries? Are there differences in message content between print and electronic media?

Most of the findings in this chapter were based on correlational analyses, which indicate the strength of associations between variables but which do not shed much light on the time-order nature of these relationships. Certainly, a step with high priority in future research on mass media exposure and modernization is *field experimentation*. In these inquiries, one would introduce a new mass medium in a peasant village, as in the experiments of Chu (1966), Spector and others (1963), and Menefee and Menefee (1965 and 1967), or he might utilize a new or an existing mass medium in a novel way, as in the Neurath (1960) study of radio farm forums in India. Then, the impact of a communication treatment would be assessed over a period of time.

Future work is also needed to determine how credibility, defined as the degree to which a communication source or channel is perceived by a receiver to be trustworthy and competent, intervenes between the antecedents and consequents of mass media exposure. Both Herzog (1967) and McLeod et al. (1967) extended our paradigm of this chapter (antecedents → mass media exposure → consequents) to include mass media credibility.[53] The model they tested is as follows:

| Antecedents (such as literacy) | → | Mass media exposure | → | Mass media credibility | → | Consequents (such as political knowledge) |

---

[53] Herzog (1967) measured mass media credibility among Brazilian peasants with a forced-choice, paired-comparison technique, as did Ramos (1967). McLeod et al. (1967) asked their Ecuadorian respondents a direct question about their degree of "confidence" in each mass media channel.

These investigators argue that exposure to the mass media will have little effect on peasants if they mistrust these channels. However, evidence both from Brazilian peasants (Herzog 1967) and from Quito urbanites (McLeod et al. 1967) indicates that credibility is an unnecessary appendage to the antecedents → exposure → consequents model. Credibility shows only low relationships with either exposure or modernization consequents. Further, the Brazilian and Quito studies suggest that mass media credibility is not a unidimensional concept, for individuals who have high credibility in one medium such as radio may have low credibility in another.

By no means do these early and tentative research results dictate that we should ignore the concept of media credibility in future investigations. Needed are inquiries (1) to establish more definitively the degree of unidimensionality of mass media credibility, (2) to determine the characteristics of villagers with high and low credibility, and (3) to probe the mental process by which credibility in mass media and other channels is created and developed.

Eventually, our goal in mass communication and modernization is to understand and be able to predict the effects of a specific mass medium or combination of media on a certain audience when the messages deal with a particular kind of idea. As yet, we are far from this objective.

6

Interpersonal and Mass Media Communication Channels*

The process of development is less dependent upon increased investment in the modernized, urbanized mass media system than it is upon the adjusting of the informal, rural systems to each other and to the mass media systems.

(Lucien W. Pye 1963:7)

Imagine for the moment that you are a change agent whose primary task is to secure the adoption of a new weed spray by peasants in a less developed country like Colombia. This innovation has just been released by a research station where it has proven to be a highly successful method of weed control and one that is quite profitable if used correctly. There are two basic communication channels through which you can convey messages about the weed spray to your audience: mass media and interpersonal channels. You know from many research studies conducted in the United States that these channels play different roles for earlier adopters than for later adopters, and in creating knowledge as opposed to persuading. To what extent would you be willing to plan your national communication campaign in Colombia around these generalizations from another culture?

Data to be presented in this chapter suggest that you would be very unwise to do so, for it appears that the role of mass media and interpersonal channels is quite different in countries like Colombia.

CHANNEL CATEGORIZATION

Communication, as it has previously been defined, is the transfer of ideas from source to receiver. Of the four elements in a communicative act (source, message, channel, and receiver), channels play a central role. An important strategy for any communicator is to determine what channel to use in order to affect the receiver's knowledge, attitudes, and behavior in desired ways. *Channels* consist of means through which the source conveys a message to the receiver. It is often difficult to distinguish between source and channel; from

* Parts of this chapter originally appeared in Rogers and Meynen (1965). Rudy N. Salcedo, Research Assistant in Communication, Michigan State University, assisted in preparing this chapter.

the standpoint of the receiver, the channel is often mistaken for the source (the origin of the message). For example, if a change agent (the source) wants to communicate with his clients, he may use either interpersonal or mass media channels to reach them. In either case, the source is the originator of the message, and the channel is the medium used to convey the message to the audience. In an interpersonal communication situation, the receiver may be in direct contact with the source (another person), who thus may act as both source and channel.

We find it useful to categorize communication channels as either interpersonal or mass media in nature and as originating from either *localite* or *cosmopolite* sources.

INTERPERSONAL VERSUS MASS MEDIA CHANNELS

Word-of-mouth communication from family members, neighbors and friends, storeowners and salespeople, schoolteachers, extension agents, and others[1] is classified as *interpersonal*. All types of print and electronic channels are considered *mass media*.

Some of the more important distinguishing characteristics of interpersonal and mass media channels are:

Communication Characteristic	Interpersonal Channels	Mass Media Channels
1. Direction of message flow	Two-way	One-way
2. Speed to a large audience	Slow	Rapid
3. Message accuracy to a large audience	Low[2]	High
4. Ability to select receiver	High	Low
5. Ability to overcome selectivity processes	High	Low
6. Amount of feedback	High	Low
7. Possible effect	Attitude change	Increase knowledge

[1] It is difficult to categorize "self" (with the above classification system) — a response that probably indicates the respondent obtained the message from his own past experience, that is, from some previous communication act he can no longer recall. We rather arbitrarily classified these "self" responses from our Colombian peasant respondents as interpersonal and localite, which seemed preferable to categorizing them as mass media and cosmopolite.

[2] The low message accuracy sometimes encountered with interpersonal communication channels is illustrated by the fact that oral exchange is usually regarded as an identifying characteristic of *rumors*, defined as false or at least unverified messages (Shibutani 1966: 3–4). Rumors are particularly common when innovations are introduced among peasants, as Niehoff (1967) illustrates.

The frequency of rumor mongering under these conditions might be accounted for by the fact that rumors occur most often (1) when there is great anxiety but inadequate knowledge about an idea (as usually occurs in the case of innovations), and (2) when mass media fail to carry the message load (a common happening among peasants where media exposure is low). Niehoff (1967) cites an example of a rumor among Peruvian Indians that blamed American change agents, who were introducing improved potatoes, for intending to fatten the local residents so that they could be boiled down for oil for American machinery.

It is obvious that the two types of channels function (efficiently) in different ways. Interpersonal channels provide for two-way interaction and feedback, which make them more effective when the goal is persuasion; whereas mass media channels provide a potent means of spreading information quickly. There is much evidence in the United States, and corroborative support from research in less developed countries, that widespread mass media exposure *alone* is unlikely to effect substantial changes in human behavior. Communication research shows that the "hypodermic needle" model of mass media effects — the mass media considered as furnishing the stimulus that causes direct and immediate response — is largely a false conception. Research results suggest that *mass media communication is more important in changing cognitions (that is, in increasing knowledge of ideas), whereas interpersonal communication is more likely to cause attitude change.*[3] When the object is persuasion, therefore, word-of-mouth channels would seem preferable to the mass media.

It is also known that the mass media are usually perceived and used in a very selective manner. Only messages that reinforce prevailing attitudes and beliefs are likely to "get through," while conflicting messages are shut out by the individual's mental screens of selective exposure and selective perception[4]. For example, peasants often give more attention to music and other entertainment programming on radio[5] than to such prodevelopment messages as news and technical information, which may not agree with their traditional beliefs.

Although the communication channels used by peasants are largely interpersonal in nature,[6] increased literacy and other forms of modernization pave the way for a gradual increase in the utilization of mass media channels.

Why not combine mass media with interpersonal communication channels in order to obtain the wide audience potential[7] (and other advantages) of the mass media with the ability to "get through" that characterizes interpersonal communication? Used in complementary roles, mass media and interper-

---

[3] One type of evidence for this statement comes from research on the role of mass and interpersonal communication channels in the diffusion of innovations, both in the United States and abroad (Rogers 1962).

[4] *Selective exposure* is the tendency to attend to communication messages that are consistent with one's existing attitudes and beliefs; *selective perception* is the tendency to interpret communication messages in terms of one's existing attitudes and beliefs.

[5] Doob (1961:288–289) suggests that when traditional peoples are first exposed to mass media they use them mainly for entertainment. With further experience, the media may also be utilized for instrumental purposes. Wright et al. (1967:17) found that illiterates in Guatemalan villages listened mainly to music and entertainment programs on radio, whereas the literates were more interested in news and information programs.

[6] "At the early stages of transition, mouths may be more common than newspapers or radio" (Pool 1967:247).

[7] "The mass media are clearly the primary resource for developing societies-in-a-hurry. They reach the most people fastest and cheapest with their message" (Lerner 1967:316).

sonal channels could prove an unbeatable force in the modernization process. In fact, this combination of mass media with group discussion is utilized in radio listening forums in several countries, in study groups in Communist China, and in radiophonics schools in Latin America.[8] These experiences suggest that the modernization effects of mass media communication among peasants in less developed countries are greater when these media are coupled with interpersonal communication channels in media forums. A detailed consideration of media forums follows the discussion of our Colombia findings on communication channels.

LOCALITE VERSUS COSMOPOLITE CHANNELS

Channels may also be categorized as either localite or cosmopolite, depending on the point of origin. Localite channels originate within the social system of the receiver, and cosmopolite channels have their origins outside his immediate social system. For example, word-of-mouth channels may be either cosmopolite or localite, depending on whether or not the source is inside or outside the social system of the receiver. A neighbor is a localite channel, whereas an extension agent who has come from elsewhere is a cosmopolite channel; yet both represent interpersonal communication. Mass media channels are almost always cosmopolite.

CROSS-CATEGORIZATION OF CHANNELS

The categories just outlined become most useful when used conjunctively, for channels can be categorized both according to whether they are interpersonal or mass media and according to whether they are localite or cosmopolite in origin. For example, a message from a change agent travels through an interpersonal cosmopolite channel to reach a peasant receiver. The paradigm in Table 6-1 illustrates some possible communication channels in peasant villages.

[8] In addition to these formal, planned types of group listening to the mass media, there is also a considerable amount of group receiving of a less structured nature, where the group members gather informally in a coffee house, tavern, or in a home, perhaps on a regular basis, but not in groups created by a change agent. This type of informal group reception of the mass media occurs more often in less developed countries than in more developed countries, and among villagers (more often than among urbanites in less developed countries), where the number of electronic media receivers is in shorter supply. As an illustration of the extent of group receiving, Frey (1966:180) reports that about 25 percent of Turkish peasants listen to radio in a public place, such as a coffee house, and about 40 percent ordinarily listen at another villager's home. Generally similar findings have been reported in three Thai villages (Jacobs et al. 1964: 13–14).

Table 6–1. Categorization of Illustrative Channels as Localite/Cosmopolite and Interpersonal/Mass Media

Nature of Channel	Point of Origin	
	Localite	Cosmopolite
Interpersonal	Neighbor[a] Village council Relative	Extension agent Wandering storytellers Salesman
Mass media	Village newspaper Wall posters	Radio Television Cinema City newspaper

[a] There are instances when a neighbor could be a cosmopolite interpersonal channel if he learned of a new idea from travel outside the village.

USE OF COMMUNICATION CHANNELS IN COLOMBIA

The usual method of obtaining data about channels in the diffusion of an innovation is to question adopters concerning what channel they had utilized at each stage of their decision process.[9] In Colombia, our peasant respondents were queried as follows:

1. *Awareness stage:* Where or from whom did you first receive information about [the innovation]?
2. *Interest stage:* Where or from whom did you receive further information about [the innovation] when you were interested?
3. *Persuasion stage:* Who or what convinced you to use [the innovation] on your own farm?
4. *Trial stage:* Where or from whom did you receive information about how to use [the innovation] on your farm?

Only the channel that was most important for a respondent at each stage was recorded and categorized as mass media/interpersonal or localite/cosmopolite. Data about channel use in the adoption of 2,4-D weed spray

[9] Research evidence suggests that individuals usually pass through several stages in the innovation decision process, from (1) *awareness* that the innovation exists, (2) to *interest* in it, usually indicated by seeking further information about it, (3) to *persuasion*, where the individual becomes convinced that the innovation is advantageous, (4) to *trial*, when the new idea is adopted on a small-scale basis (5) to *decision*, when the individual chooses to adopt or reject the innovation (Rogers with Shoemaker 1968). This general focus on the psychological aspects of individuals' decisions to adopt new ideas was first emphasized by Barnett (1953), although he did not propose separate stages in the innovation decision process.

(called in Spanish *matamaleza*, or literally *"weed killer"*) were gathered in the three modern Colombian villages of Pueblo Viejo, San Rafael, and Cuatro Esquinas.

INTERPERSONAL VERSUS MASS MEDIA CHANNELS IN THE INNOVATION DECISION PROCESS

Since our peasant respondents made no mention of any mass media channels at any stage in the innovation decision process, one concludes that *interpersonal channels are of prime importance at every stage in the innovation decision process* (Table 6–2). Obviously then, *mass media channels are no more important*

Table 6–2. Communication Channels by Stage in the Innovation Decision Process for 2,4-D Weed Spray in Three Modern Colombian Villages

Communication Channels	Percentage of Respondents Utilizing Each Communication Channel by Stage[a] in the Innovation Decision Process			
	Awareness Stage	Interest Stage	Persuasion Stage	Trial Stage
1. Mass media	0	0	0	0
2. Interpersonal cosmopolite:	44.1	34.1	14.7	49.5
Extension workers	(7.5)	(6.9)	(3.1)	(8.3)
Farm store personnel	(36.6)	(27.2)	(11.6)	(41.2)
3. Interpersonal localite:	55.9	65.9	85.3	50.5
Neighbors and friends	(40.8)	(46.6)	(24.6)	(35.7)
Haciendados[b]	(10.0)	(7.4)	(5.7)	(6.6)
Family	(3.3)	(1.0)	(5.5)	(3.1)
Self	(1.8)	(10.9)	(49.5)	(5.1)
Total	100.0	100.0	100.0	100.0

[a] The number of respondents decreases somewhat from the awareness stage to the trial stage: 5 of the respondents were not yet at the interest stage, 27 were not yet at the persuasion stage or the trial stage, and 56 had not yet adopted.

[b] *Haciendados* are a few large farmers in each village who hire some of their neighbors to work for them on a daily wage basis during peak work periods, such as at planting and harvest times.

than interpersonal channels (1) in creating knowledge of innovations or (2) for relatively earlier adopters of innovations than for later adopters.

These findings support Myren's (1962) conclusion,[10] "The hypothesis

---

[10] And also agree with the findings of Deutschmann and Fals Borda (1962a) in a Colombian village, where mass media channels were almost never reported by peasants at any stage in the innovation decision process. Both Myren (1962) and Deutschmann and Fals Borda (1962a) found, however, that the few times when peasants reported having used mass media channels were mainly at the awareness stage.

about the impact of the mass media can be applied only in areas where media circulate widely, and where, equally important, they command attention and deal with questions of interest to farmers in comprehensible terms." In settings such as these Colombian villages, reception of the mass media is much lower than in more developed countries. For example, only 18 percent of our peasant respondents read magazines once a month, whereas in the Iowa farm community[11] studied by Rogers and Beal (1958) 95 percent of the farmers read farm magazines. Furthermore, the content of the Colombian mass media is seldom of an agricultural nature, and those few programs involving such content emphasize farm innovations infrequently.

Figure 6–1 provides a comparison of the relative importance of the various categories of communication channels for the same innovation (2,4-D weed spray) among (1) Iowa farmers and (2) the Colombian peasants of our study. It is evident that mass media channels are frequently mentioned, especially at the awareness stage, by the Iowa farmers, but not even by *one* of the Colombian peasants.

Frey (1966) has pointed out a possible reason for the tendency of peasant respondents to cite interpersonal rather than mass media channels. He suggests that individuals are "probably biased toward the more proximate and specific stimuli and slight the temporally more remote or more general stimuli. The mass media would probably fall into the latter class." In other words, when asked what prompted the adoption of 2,4-D weed spray, peasants are more likely to recall a recent conversation with a neighbor than a radio program heard several months ago. However, this caveat about the possible underreporting of mass media channels seems unlikely to change our major conclusions about the relative importance of interpersonal channels, particularly when the evidence is so overwhelming.

LOCALITE VERSUS COSMOPOLITE CHANNELS

Figure 6–1 and Table 6–2 indicate that for these Colombian peasants, *interpersonal localite channels are generally more important than interpersonal cosmopolite channels at each stage in the innovation decision process.*[12] Conversations with neighbors and friends are the prime channels for awareness, interest, and persuasion. Figure 6–1 also shows that interpersonal localite channels are more frequently reported by Colombian peasants than by Iowa farmers at both the awareness and persuasion stages.[13]

[11] These Iowa respondents are all the farm operators in one highly commercialized, prosperous rural community, who were interviewed by Rogers and Beal (1958) in 1955.

[12] Only at the trial stage did interpersonal cosmopolite channels appear to be almost as important as interpersonal localite channels.

[13] Part of the importance of interpersonal localite channels at the persuasion stage in Colombia is due to the inclusion of "self." Almost 50 percent of the peasant respondents mentioned self at this stage, whereas the corresponding figure in the Rogers and Beal (1958) study in Iowa was 13 percent.

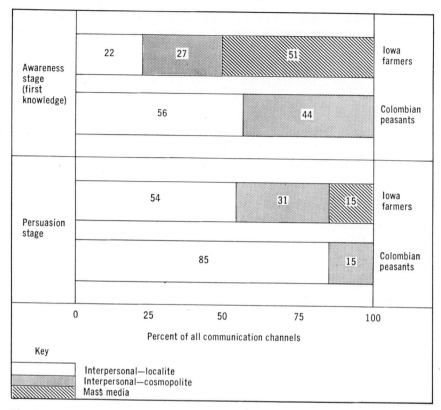

Figure 6–1. Communication Channels by Stages in the Innovation-Decision Process for Iowa Farmers and Colombian Peasants.

In comparison to Iowa farmers, the Colombian respondents are (1) unlikely to mention mass media at either the awareness or persuasion stage, (2) more likely to report interpersonal localite channels at both stages, and (3) more likely to use interpersonal-cosmopolite channels at the awareness stage. Both samples of respondents utilize interpersonal-localite channels relatively more at the persuasion stage than at the awareness stage.

SOURCE: Rogers and Beal (1958) and Rogers and Meynen (1965). Reprinted by permission.

While interpersonal localite channels are generally more important than interpersonal cosmopolite channels, Fig. 6–1 and Table 6–2 make clear the importance of interpersonal cosmopolite channels at the awareness and the trial stages. About 44 percent reported interpersonal cosmopolite channels (especially farm store personnel) at the awareness stage, but only 15 percent at the persuasion stage.[14] However, about 50 percent of our respondents reported use of interpersonal cosmopolite channels at the trial stage. This phenomenon is largely the result of the important role of commercial personnel (such as farm store dealers and salesmen) in providing "how-to" information when a peasant is about to use the new spray in a small-scale trial. *Interpersonal cosmopolite channels are more important in creating technical knowledge about an innovation than in forming favorable attitudes toward the new idea.*[15]

Table 6–3 shows that *cosmopolite communication channels are more important at each stage in the innovation decision process for earlier than for later adopters of 2,4-D*

Table 6–3. Cosmopolite Communication Channels Were More Important at Each Stage in the Innovation Decision Process for Earlier than for Later Adopters of 2,4-D Weed Spray in Colombia

Adopter Category	Percentage of Respondents Utilizing Cosmopolite Communication Channels[a] by Stage[b] in the Innovation Decision Process			
	Awareness Stage	Interest Stage	Persuasion Stage	Trial Stage
1. Innovators	60.0	c	20.0	60.0
2. Early adopters	50.0	76.4	12.5	50.0
3. Early majority	50.0	35.4	8.1	46.2
4. Late majority	42.1	25.7	19.5	54.2
5. Nonadopters	28.6	22.2	c	0
Percentage of all respondents utilizing cosmopolite channels	44.1	34.1	14.7	49.5

[a] Cosmopolite communication channels include both interpersonal cosmopolite and mass media channels.

[b] The number of respondents decreases somewhat from the awareness stage to the trial stage: 5 of the respondents were not yet at the interest stage, 27 were not yet at the persuasion stage or the trial stage, and 56 had not yet adopted (as shown previously in Table 6-2).

[c] Insufficient cases for computation of a meaningful percentage.

[14] The low citation of commercial change agents at the persuasion stage may be because of their relatively low credibility among Colombian peasants (channel credibility should be more important as a factor in persuasion than in creating awareness of a new idea). Ramos (1966) found that the relative positions of various communication channels on a continuum of credibility in diffusing agricultural innovations (ranging from least to most credibility) are: newspaper, commercial salesman, neighbor, radio, schoolteacher, and extension agent (Chapter 8). Herzog (1967b) reported similar channel credibility ratings by Brazilian villagers.

[15] We also found confirmatory evidence among our Colombian respondents in the case of another innovation, a new bean variety. However, Sawhney (1966) found just the opposite result among farmers in India.

weed spray in Colombia.[16] Perhaps this is because, at the time the innovators adopt a new idea, there is no one else in the village who has experience with the innovation. The later adopters need not rely so much on cosmopolite channels because of the "bank" of localite experience that has accumulated in the village by the time they decide to adopt.

Our researchers performed one further type of data analysis, designed to determine the *characteristics* of the Colombian peasants who had reported using cosmopolite channels in the adoption of 2,4-D weed spray. Generally, cosmopolite channel use was positively related to education, empathy, opinion leadership, and (general) agricultural innovativeness and was negatively related to fatalism.[17] Thus, it can be concluded that those villagers who use cosmopolite communication channels are typified by a modern rather than a traditional mentality.

CONCLUSIONS

A general conclusion of the present anlysis is that only some of the generalizations about the role of communication channels in the diffusion of innovations, which were largely developed in the United States, have cross-cultural validity. Among the Colombian peasants of this study, hypotheses about the role of mass media channels were not supported, because no media channels were reported by any of the Colombian respondents in their adoption of the new weed spray. In general, extension agents and farm-supply store personnel have a role in first introducing the innovation in the village and also in explaining how to use it at the trial stage, but interpersonal communication among fellow farmers is of greatest importance at each stage except the trial stage.

Cosmopolite channels play a more important role (1) in informing than in persuading peasants to adopt a new idea and (2) for earlier, rather than later, adopters of the innovation. Whereas the interpersonal/mass media classification of channels seems to have limited utility in predicting channel usage in the innovation decision process (because the media are so rarely utilized), the cosmopolite/localite categorization seems to be more serviceable in explaining channel usage (and in a manner similar to that found previously in the United States). In other words, our results suggest that perhaps the cosmopolite/localite channel classification has greater cross-cultural utility in explaining diffusion than does the interpersonal/mass media categorization.

[16] The respondents were classified into five categories (shown in Table 6-3) on the basis of their relative time-of-adoption of 2,4-D weed spray (Chapter 13).

[17] We were able to explain from 13 to 21 percent of the variance in cosmopolite/localite channel usage by innovation decision process using these five variables (education, empathy, and so on), plus seven others, in a multiple-correlation approach.

COMBINING INTERPERSONAL AND MASS COMMUNICATION CHANNELS IN MEDIA FORUMS[18]

In the introduction to this chapter we posed the hypothetical question of what you would do if you were a change agent responsible for introducing a technological innovation to Colombian peasants. The most common method utilized in such nations involves the training and guidance of a large corps of change agents, each of whom are assigned the task of conveying the new technology via interpersonal channels in one or a few villages. This, however, is a discouragingly long-range approach. Let us take India as an illustration. After twenty years of intensive and costly efforts, it is estimated that the total number of village-level change agents is about 35,000. But the peasant audience in India constitutes a forbidding 560,000 villages! Translated to the individual level, this means that each change agent must try to somehow reach about 10,000 villagers — clearly an impossible task. And in other nations (Colombia, for instance), the ratio of clients to change agent is even less favorable.

The approach advocated here is the combination of mass media and interpersonal channels. It is our belief that by incorporating the advantages of each type of channel into a single propelling force, more peasants can be reached with new ideas and a greater percentage of those reached can be persuaded to utilize these innovations.

MEDIA FORUMS AND MODERNIZATION

Media forums are organized, small groups of individuals who meet regularly to receive a mass media program and discuss its contents. The mass medium linked to the forum may be a radio, as in India radio farm forums and the radiophonics schools of Latin America, or the medium may be print, as is usually the case in Communist Chinese study groups.

Our advocacy of media forums is based on the following logic:

1. As was previously pointed out, the ratio of change agents to clients in less developed countries is impossibly out-of-balance. The recruitment and training of change agents is a costly and lengthy process that alone cannot meet the communication needs of peasant villagers. To rely solely on interpersonal communication from change agents to reach the millions of peasants is folly.

2. Although some breakdown in the localiteness of peasant villages can be brought about through improved roads and public transportation, the mass media seem to provide a quicker means of overcoming the isolation barrier. There are just too many villagers and too many villages in the less developed world, and the rate of road building is too slow, to concentrate solely on this

---

[18] Parts of this section originally appeared in Bebermeyer and Rogers (1966).

method to reach peasants. The mass media are more effective tools for prying open the "locked box" of localiteness.

3. We know, however, that the mass media, though very effective in creating knowledge of new ideas, are relatively ineffective (compared with interpersonal communication) in changing attitudes[19] and stimulating action (Klapper 1960). A radio or TV message usually leads only to passive listening, rather than to attitude or behavior change. One must conclude that there are certain modernization tasks the mass media can do and others they cannot do (Schramm 1964:127–144). The introduction of technological innovations among peasants in less developed nations on a *mass* basis would seem to be most effectively brought about by mass media channels coupled with interpersonal communication.[20]

4. Further, the notion of media forums squares closely with the existing pattern of values, attitudes, and social organization of peasant life. Informal discussion groups are very much a part of the daily culture of every peasant village; witness the palaver groups of African communities, the evening discussions under the Banyan tree in Indian villages, the teashop sessions of Southeast Asia, and the *tienda* discussions of Latin American peasants. Group exposure to the mass media (especially radio listening, but also to newspaper or magazine reading) is a customary part of village living. Hence, even though the formation of a media forum is a "contrived" effort by the forum organizer, the forum seems to be perceived by most villagers as "natural."[21]

5. Media forums are more directly attuned to the needs of peasants than are the mass media alone. Feedback from the regular meetings in the form of direct peasant response and forum secretarial reports (which usually include the conclusions reached and the questions left unanswered) provides a method for adapting media programming to peasant interests. All too often the mass media in less developed countries are beamed primarily at an urban elite audience. Feedback from forums can result in program content and levels appropriate for the peasant audience.

6. Evidence from empirical research strongly supports the great potential of media forums as effective means of reaching peasant audiences with modernizing messages. Although sketchy and of uneven quality, this re-

---

[19] As Frey (1966) points out, however, the mass media may be more effective in *forming* peasant attitudes than in *changing* them.

[20] However, we do not negate the possibility of direct mass media effects on knowledge and attitudes among peasants. Our position sees mass media communication neither as a simple hypodermic injection of a virulent message in an audience nor as a necessarily neat, two-step flow from media to opinion leaders to general audience, but rather as a highly complex multistage, multidirectional process with possibilities for both direct and indirect effects of mass media messages (McNelly 1966).

[21] In fact, some analyses of media forums in less developed countries report the spontaneous formation of media forums without the assistance of a professional organizer (Neurath 1960; Abell 1965).

search shows that such an approach to communication and modernization holds much promise.

Media forums, therefore, seem to offer several advantages over purely interpersonal or mass media communication campaigns. In the approach advocated here, mass media channels are to be used in place of the scarce and costly interpersonal channels constituted by change agents, in order to promote knowledge and interest. Instead of acting as the sole channel through which technological messages must pass, the change agent can function as an organizer and servicer of media forums,[22] a task which allows him adequately to serve 50 to 100 peasant villages rather than 3 or 4. Group participation by peasants encourages involvement and offers support for innovation utilization, thereby increasing the rate of adoption. The media forum approach offers one route to reach development and modernization goals as quickly as possible under the rather difficult logistical/administrative conditions of less developed countries.

TYPES OF MEDIA FORUMS

Various combinations of mass media and interpersonal channels are utilized effectively in several varieties of media forums in less developed countries today.

Radio Forums

The notion of adult education through group listening to a mass medium perhaps began[23] in Great Britain in 1928, when radio was first introduced for such purposes (Cassirer 1959). During a twenty-year period, about 4000 of these radio listening groups were organized to discuss public affairs. Eventually interest waned, and these groups died of apathy in 1948.

Radio farm forums are probably the best-known type of media discussion group. The basic idea was launched first in Canada in 1939, during the depression days of agricultural protest (Nicol et al. 1954), and has since been widely copied in Japan (1952), in India (1957), in Pakistan and Mali (1961), in Nigeria (1962), and in Ghana, Madagascar, and Jordan (1964). Radio forums have also been tried in Costa Rica, Brazil, Togo, Malawi, and Niger.[24]

The basic elements of the Canadian forums (and most other radio forum programs) were as follows: organizers who established forums and helped service them; written discussion guides containing information and dis-

---

[22] Of course, this alteration in the nature of the change agent's task involves a change in the requirements of the position. Rather than needing technical competence in the subject matter dealing with the innovations he is spreading, he would need to be able to organize and encourage villagers to attend media forums.

[23] It must be pointed out that the general notion of *discussion groups* had existed for many years in a variety of forms, such as the Danish folk schools.

[24] Schramm et al. (1967a:60–61).

cussion questions, which were distributed to forum leaders; regularly scheduled radio programs beamed at forum members gathered in homes or public places to hear the broadcasts, followed by group discussion; and regular feedback reports of decisions and questions of clarification to the broadcast programmers. The motto of the Canadian forums was "Listen, discuss, act," and emphasis was placed not only on creating knowledge of rural problems but on doing something about them. In their heyday, the Canadian forums numbered over 1600, but these broadcasts ended officially in 1965 after ten relatively prosperous years for agriculture because, it seemed, the need they filled no longer existed.[25]

Undoubtedly, the largest and the most thoroughly researched media forum program today is India's, representing "a degree of experience with the radio rural forum unequalled in the world" (Schramm et al. 1967:107). This communication system was launched on a national basis in 1959, as a result of a UNESCO-sponsored investigation directed by Dr. Paul Neurath. Details of his results on forum effectiveness will be discussed later in this chapter.

How do Indian forums work? They meet twice weekly to listen to a half-hour radio program beamed from a station of All-India Radio, the government network. Discussion usually lasts for about another half-hour after the radio is turned off. A chairman leads the discussion, and a secretary keeps a written record of decisions and unanswered questions, which are mailed regularly to the radio station. Attendance at the average twenty-member forum is likely to be about sixteen or seventeen. Of these, there are usually three or four lively participants in the discussion, eight or ten occasional participants, and five or six nonparticipants.

Television Forums

Following a pattern similar to that used in the radio forums, several organizations have used television as the mass media channel for their forums. In 1954, UNESCO sponsored an experimental "teleclub" program among French farmers (Cassirer 1959; Dumazedier 1956; Louis and Rovan 1955). Apparently the teleclub program was organized without provision for feedback; however, the experiment did use peasant performers, a technique that proved popular with the forum listeners. UNESCO, long active in efforts to promote media forums in less developed countries, also helped to launch about 10,000 television viewing groups in southern Italy in 1958. The groups met in customary gathering places such as cafes and bars — a wise approach in Italy, "where the most popular [TV] shows are seen by 30 million people on only 1 million sets." The rather disappointing results from the Italian television clubs were attributed to lack of group participation and to passive viewing (Cassirer 1959).

[25] And possibly, Nicol et al. (1954) suggest, because the agricultural change agencies in Canada never became fully involved in forum planning or execution.

The Italian *telescuola* ("school by TV") experience in basic education, however, is usually considered highly successful (Schramm 1967a:7). These broadcasts showed adults, very like the audience, being taught by expert teachers who wove humor into their presentation. Printed supplementary materials were provided for the learners in the media forums. The television students were encouraged to participate by submitting questions and lessons for correction.

Recently, India has undertaken an experimenal television farm forum in villages surrounding New Delhi.

Radiophonics Schools in Latin America

Like the Italian *telescuola*, the fundamental purpose of the "radio schools" in Latin America is basic education. Initiated in Colombia by Jesuit Father José Joaquin Salcedo in 1947, their aim is to reduce illiteracy in remote rural areas. For the equivalent of $19, adults can buy a one-band radio on which to receive instruction at 6 A.M. and 3:30 P.M. from Radio Sutatenza, named for Father Salcedo's village. Between class hours, the station presents news, agricultural programs, religious instruction, and classical and popular music.

The radio "schools," often simply a group of peasants who pool their funds to buy a radio receiver, are organized by local parish priests and other church workers. Each school group is led by a trained monitor who helps the "students" learn and encourages them to listen regularly. Radio Sutatenza is financially supported by the Roman Catholic Church and by the national government of Colombia. The program claims to have about 16,000 radio schools (that is, forums) with some 130,000 students, 90 percent of whom are from the rural areas. Over 60 percent of those enrolled in the schools are illiterate. Radio Sutatenza claims that of all illiterates enrolled, 64 percent can read and write after a one-year course.[26]

Radiophonics school programs similar to Radio Sutatenza have been organized in many other Latin American countries in the past decade. All are under the control of the Catholic Church (partly justified as a means to guarantee freedom of program content from partisan political control), and all aim to carry modernization messages to peasants. Unfortunately, solid empirical evidence about the effectiveness of the radio forums is extremely limited.

One available study is the investigation of radio schools in El Salvador and Honduras by Rhoads and Piper (1963), who found that:

1. Fifteen percent of the participants in the radio schools said they had learned to read as a result of the radiophonic programs.

2. Four-fifths of the respondents reported they had received more out of the

---

[26] There is apparently some difference in interpretation of the effects of Radio Sutatenza, however; a less enthusiastic conclusion about audience size and program effectiveness is provided by Martin (1951).

radio schools than expected, with an added element of satisfaction stemming mainly from learning about agricultural innovations. Almost two-thirds of the radio school members put some of the information learned into practice. In fact, most of these enrolled in the radio literacy classes reported that they perceived the meetings mainly as radio forums about agricultural topics, rather than as literacy *classes*.[27]

3. Those who learned to read in the radiophonic schools reported they *believed everything they read*. This high print media credibility is perhaps the effect of novelty and the religious content (such as the Bible) of the material used.

Some of the adult literacy "schools" have grown to tremendous size. Cruzada ABC (literally, "crusade for literacy") centered at Recife, Brazil, is an example. This program, which presently has over 200,000 adults enrolled each weekday night, aims to create 5 million new adult literates over the next five years. Although it uses CARE packages and surplus food from the United States as an incentive to regular attendance in some areas, Cruzada ABC reports that 90 percent of those enrolled have perfect attendance even in areas where no food is distributed. The program uses mainly print materials as the media link with its thousands of "schools," but is experimenting with a partial substitution of radio and television.

Chinese Communist Study Groups

The Chinese Communist Party has employed magazine and newspaper discussion groups as a means of indoctrination and learning among their party cadres and recruits for fifty years. More recently, since the Communist takeover of mainland China in 1949, and especially during the "Great Leap Forward" campaign in 1958 the Chinese Communists used study groups as a means of securing political loyalty and promoting increased development effort among their masses of citizens.[28] Such study groups usually are organized about and meet in the work unit, that is, in factories and offices in urban areas or in peasant communes. Approximately 60 percent of the adult Chinese population regularly participates in study groups where print material is read and discussed (Hiniker 1966). Literates and illiterates, men and women, urbanites and peasants are all organized into these study groups.[29]

---

[27] Perhaps this is a face-saving misperception by village adults who hesitate to indicate that they are actually learning to become literate in classes, which they may consider a task appropriate only for children. In any event, their misperception emphasizes the great importance of lesson content (for example, agriculture) to learners as a motivation for participation in adult literacy classes.

[28] The notion of study groups seems to have been adopted from Russia's experience with "agitation meetings."

[29] However, literates, urbanites, and individuals of higher social status seem more likely to participate in study groups. Hiniker (1966) reports the following degree of such participation by occupation: farmers, 56 percent; skilled workers, 75 percent; white-collar workers, 91 percent; and intelligentsia, 81 percent.

Radio discussion groups existed but were of more importance during the early days of the Communist regime than now.

The typical Chinese study group consists of a Communist leader who reads or directs the reading of print materials to a small (5 to 30 members) group of personally acquainted coworkers. The cadre leader maintains strict control of discussion and forces each member to take a position on the issue and voice his opinion to the group. The effects of such study groups can only be estimated indirectly,[30] but their great importance is suggested by their central position in the communication strategy of the Chinese Communist government.[31] Study groups are considered essential elements in the special communication campaigns launched to achieve such varied goals as fly killing, river swimming, antispitting, family planning, and farm communization.

EFFECTS OF MEDIA FORUMS

Although there are important country-to-country and program-to-program differences in the four types of media forum systems that have just been reviewed, they possess certain elements in common. All utilize a mass medium (radio, television, or print) to carry the major load of disseminating messages about technical innovations to the discussion forums. All feature small-sized groups that are regularly exposed to the mass media channel and then participate in discussion of the message. All the media forum programs *seem* to be generally effective in diffusing knowledge, in forming and changing attitudes, and in catalyzing behavioral change. Adequate scientific evidence of these media forum effects is rare; an exception is the Neurath (1960) study of India radio forums.

The Neurath experiment was set in a single language area of 100 by 300 miles in the State of Bombay, where cooperating Government of India agencies organized forums in 150 villages. Experienced change agents, on loan to the project from the Ministries of Education and Community Development, organized the forums. During the experiment they visited each forum every few weeks for observation and maintenance.

The broadcasts focused on specific agricultural, health, and community improvement innovations. In treatment, they ranged from "old-style religious plays, through folk songs, sketches, panel discussions, and talks with peasants, to plain lectures" (Neurath 1962:277). Five minutes of each broadcast was

[30] Hiniker (1965) conducted an experiment with Chinese refugees in Hong Kong to test one aspect of the study groups, the effect on persuasion of voicing counterstatements. Contrary to American findings, the Chinese did not exhibit a significant amount of attitude change as a result of this process; the Oriental mechanism of "seeming compliance" was cited as one reason for the absence of such attitude change.

[31] Perhaps one reason for the pervasive success of the Chinese Communist campaigns rests on the totalitarian political rule that governs the mass media, so that they speak with one voice.

reserved for a "listeners' corner" to answer questions from the previous forum discussion. There were twenty programs broadcast over ten weeks.

Professor Neurath designed his field experiment so that comparisons could be made in knowledge of innovations among peasants who lived in three types of villages: (1) those in which he established radio forums; (2) those in which radios were already present, but no forums were organized; and (3) those with neither a radio nor a forum. Figure 6–2 shows that the forum villages had much greater gains in knowledge of innovations[32] than did the control

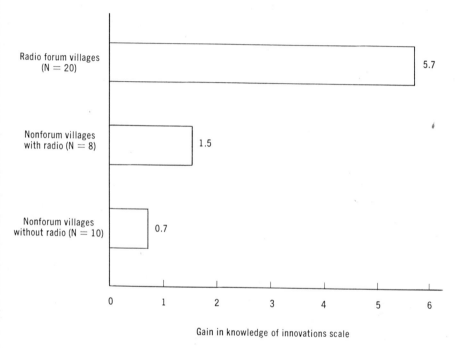

Gain in knowledge of innovations scale

Figure 6–2. India Radio Forums Resulted in a Gain in Knowledge of Innovations among Villagers.

The greater knowledge gain in the India radio forums is either due to the effects of group discussion per se or perhaps to such other variables as (1) enforced regular attendance at the forums (which is not the case with nonforum mass media exposure), or (2) the composition of the forum's membership, which may be drawn from quite untypical portions of the community (such as its leadership), which will result in greater or in less media effects.

SOURCE: Neurath (1960: 136).

[32] To measure knowledge, each respondent was queried about six topics that were included in the forum broadcasts, both before and after the twenty forum broadcasts. A series of questions dealing with one of these topics might be: "What damage do rats do? Do rats carry disease? What do you do against rats?" Knowledge level was categorized in one of three levels for each respondent for each of the innovations, so that total scores ranged from 0 to 18 (Neurath 1960:127).

villages. In fact, the nonforum villages with a radio did not gain much in knowledge level; this emphasizes that *the modernization effects of mass media communication channels among peasants in less developed countries are greater when these media are coupled with interpersonal communication channels in media forums.*[33]

Neurath (1960:196) notes that the forum members showed "an impressive gain in knowledge" and that "this gain is equally impressive for many different groups in the forums, such as: illiterates and literates, agriculturalists and nonagriculturalists, village leaders and others," despite different pretreatment knowledge levels for these categories. Figure 6–3 depicts this

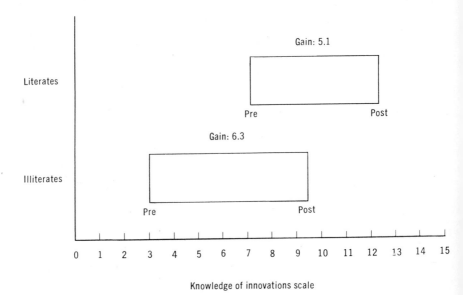

Figure 6–3. Illiterate Forum Members Gained More Knowledge of Innovations Than Literate Members, Even Though Their Pre-forum Level Was Much Lower. SOURCE: Neurath (1960: p. 155).

"pooling" or "leveling" effect among Neurath's peasant respondents; the illiterates gained as much knowledge as (actually, slightly more than) the literate forum members.[34] The *pooling effect* occurs in media forums when those individuals who begin at lower levels of knowledge, persuasion, or adoption of innovations gain more in these factors than do forum members who begin at higher levels.

[33] Evidence for this generalization is also provided by Menefee and Menefee (1967), who found much greater effects (on political knowledge) of a community weekly newspaper in Indian villages when the newspapers were read and discussed in forums.

[34] Additional support for the pooling effect in India radio forums is reported by the Planning Research and Action Institute (1962).

Not only did knowledge result from the forums, but changes in group process were also noted. Observers reported that the forums "functioned on the whole very well" (Neurath 1962:179). A systematic trend was noted over successive forum sessions toward a decrease in the tendency of certain members to dominate the discussion and, also, toward gradual involvement of those who spoke up very little at first. "The group method of discussion brought with it a learning process both in meeting and discussing things together and in decision making" (Neurath 1960:197). It was also noted that "the group method of discussion tends to bring out into the open a good deal of knowledge that is present in a latent form in the villages."

Why do peasants learn more when they are members of media forums?

1. Attendance is usually more regular (because of group pressures to participate) than with individual listening or viewing. Concentration on the program's topic may also be encouraged by group pressures.

2. Attitude change appears to be more readily achieved when individuals are in groups. Research studies of small groups support this generalization (Lewin 1958; Coch and French 1948; Levine and Butler 1952; Giffin and Ehrlich 1963). Further, several of these experiments indicate that group decisions are more likely to be accepted by the individual if he participates in making the decision, as usually occurs in the radio forums.

Indian radio farm forums have been steadily increasing in number; in 1965 there were about 12,000 forums, enrolling a quarter of a million villagers in the twice-weekly meetings (Schramm and others 1967a:53). Official evaluations by Indian government inspectors usually have confessed some disappointment, however, that the forum program is not going so well as it should, and certainly not so well as the Neurath experiment seemed to promise. "The trouble is not with the forum pattern itself, but with the way it is being operated" (Schramm et al. 1967b:123–124). The forums require continuing care from professional organizers, the forum members drop out, the radios break down or their batteries are exhausted. Radio forums[35] will not in most cases run themselves (Schramm and others 1967b:132–133); in fact, perhaps a forum that has continued for about two years may have accomplished the maximum results possible for its village.

It appears that the effectiveness of these mass media *cum* interpersonal communication forums depends on:

1. Program *content* relevant to peasant problems (usually new farm or

[35] Radio forums should not be thought of as a completely inexpensive operation, although this opinion is sometimes expressed by those who do not see the partially hidden costs of "free" radio time and forum organization, which are often absorbed by other budgets. If all expenditures are included, Schramm et al. (1967b:130–131) estimate that the total cost per forum per year is about $72. This is the equivalent of $3.46 per forum member per year, or 9 cents per listener hour. While it is very difficult to estimate returns, Schramm and others (1967a:151) appraise the cost of motivating each community action project (like planting trees or building a well) by a forum at about $40.

health ideas) beamed at an appropriate audience level.[36] Visual aids, such as charts and blackboards, can add to learning effectiveness in the forum.

2. The postprogram *discussion*, which emphasizes local application of the ideas presented.

3. *Feedback* from the audience in terms of their reactions, interests, and questions of clarification to the mass media communicator.

4. Including village *opinion leaders* in forum membership, to ensure the spread of information to villagers who are not forum members.

5. Careful *organization, operation, and maintenance procedures*.

In essence media forums intervene in the "normal" diffusion process. Villagers are organized in forums to bring them in regular contact with a mass medium for exposure to a specific message. The stage is set for discussions immediately following the broadcast, and feedback channels are provided (to serve a control function in a cybernetic sense). Forum members are encouraged to discuss the forum topics with other villagers. Essentially this intervention in normal communication behavior serves to increase the impact of the modernization messages carried by the mass media.

The authors strongly advocate the use of media forums. However, no program of media forums should be undertaken without incorporating evaluation mechanisms to determine audience effects and to suggest where improvements should be made.

NECESSARY RESEARCH

Much more must be learned about the potential and operation of media forums in the modernization process:

1. We need to ascertain whether the knowledge gains found by Neurath in the India radio forums were partly a function of the short-term novelty effect of the forums or whether they are indeed widely reproducible. Certainly, ten weeks is hardly time enough to become anesthetized to the media forums; two or three years may be quite another matter.

2. Does persuasion and actual adoption of innovations accompany the knowledge gains that occur in media forums? The answer can be secured from field experiments that run over a longer time period.

3. How important is the make-up of the forum membership in terms of its homogeneity-heterogeneity in age, literacy, social status, and so on?

[36] When the message content is irrelevant to villagers' interests, the media forums are no more effective than any other type of communication system. An example comes from an Indian village that I once visited, where a forum session was composed almost entirely of Brahmin villagers, a high caste. Unfortunately, the forum program that evening was concerned with chicken raising. Brahmins have strong religious convictions against tending chickens; their lack of interest in the forum topic was evident in their polite inattention to the radio broadcast and their refusal to discuss its contents.

4. What effect does the forum have on nonmembers who live in the same village?

5. To what extent are forum effects upon nonforum members (who live in the same village) affected by the opinion leadership and other characteristics of the forum members?

6. What is an optimum concentration of forums per village, and what is an ideal life span for them?

7. How important is feedback from the forums to the mass media institution that produces the messages?

SUMMARY

Communication *channels* consist of means through which a source conveys a message to the receiver. Mass media and interpersonal channels were analyzed in this chapter in terms of their role in the diffusion of innovations. Mass media communication is more important in changing cognitions (that is, in increasing knowledge of ideas), whereas interpersonal communication is more likely to cause attitude change. Thus, mass and interpersonal communication channels can be complementary rather than competitive in diffusing innovations.

None of our Colombian peasants reported any mass media channels at any stage in the innovation decision process for 2,4-D weed spray. Interpersonal channels are of prime importance at every stage in the innovation decision process. Mass media channels are no more important than interpersonal channels (1) in creating knowledge of innovations or (2) for relatively earlier adopters of innovations than for later adopters. Interpersonal localite channels are generally more important than interpersonal cosmopolite channels at each stage in the innovation decision process. Interpersonal cosmopolite channels are more important in creating knowledge about an innovation than in forming favorable attitudes toward the new idea. Cosmopolite communication channels are more important at each stage in the innovation decision process for earlier than for later adopters of 2,4-D weed spray in Colombia.

Media forums are organized small groups of individuals who meet regularly to receive a mass media program and discuss its contents. Examples are India radio forums, the radiophonics schools of Latin America, and study groups in Communist China. The modernization effects of mass media communication channels among peasants in less developed countries are greater when these media are coupled with interpersonal communication channels in media forums. Further, there appears to be a *"pooling effect"* in media forums, by which those members who begin at lower levels of knowledge, persuasion, or adoption gain more in these respects than do forum members who begin at higher levels.

7
Cosmopoliteness

To innovate, to discover, to awake for an instant . . . the individual must escape, for the time being, from his social surroundings. Such unusual audacity makes him super-social rather than social.
(Gabriel Tarde 1903:87–88)

If a man does not keep pace with his companions, perhaps it is because he hears a different drummer. Let him step to the music which he hears, however measured or far away.
(Henry David Thoreau)

The cosmopolite peasant, with one foot in the village and the other in a wider sphere is a vital link in the modernization process. Lerner's (1958: 19–42) parable of the grocer and the chief in the Turkish village of Balgat illustrates the importance of cosmopoliteness in less developed nations. The cosmopolite grocer was characterized by his frequent trips to Ankara, his modern dress, and his imaginative longings for a better way of life. Whereas the localite chief was traditional, autocratic; he accepted life as it was. The grocer encountered difficulty in conveying his feelings and ideas meaningfully to his peers in the village. "I am not like the others here. They don't know any better. And when I tell them, they are angry and they say that I am ungrateful for what Allah has given me" (Lerner 1958:24). Eventually however, the cosmopolite grocer prevailed over the traditional admonitions of the localite chief. The grocer was described with admiration after his death by a Balgat villager, who said: "Ah, he was the cleverest of us all. We did not know it then, but he saw better than all what lay in the path ahead. We have none like this among us now. He was a prophet" (Lerner 1958:41).

In this case the cosmopolite villager, who was in contact with urban life, provided a communication linkage between the traditional village and the fast-changing external world. From the vantage point of his wider perspective, the grocer predicted changes that were to effect his fellow villagers.

Whether such cosmopolites are referred to as "marginal men" (Park 1928, Stonequist 1937) "strangers" (Georg Simmel in Wolff 1950), "gatekeepers" (Lewin 1958, Stycos 1952), "cultural brokers" (Pye 1963), or "urbanites" (Foley 1952),[1] they remain a relatively unstudied breed. As Wagley (1964)

[1] Each of these concepts share much commonality with cosmopoliteness, but none is the exact equivalent.

points out, most studies of peasant communities have focused on the local community structure, rather than on the relationships of the peasant village to the larger society. The study of modernization requires a focus on the interfaces between traditional villages and modern cities in less developed nations. A vital interpersonal communication link between the village and larger society is the cosmopolite peasant.

WHAT IS COSMOPOLITENESS?

Cosmopoliteness is the degree to which an individual is oriented outside his immediate social system. Individuals who confine their interests to their immediate environment, with little interest in the world beyond, are called *localites*, whereas those who consider themselves an integral part of the larger

---

1. The *marginal man* is described by Park (1936) as a "personality type that arises at a time and place where, out of the conflict of races and cultures, new societies, new peoples and cultures are coming into existence. The fate which condemns him to live at the same time, in two worlds is the same which compels him to assume, in relation to the worlds in which he lives, the role of the cosmopolitan, and a stranger. Inevitably he becomes, relative to his culture milieu, the individual with the wider horizons, the keener intelligence, the more detached and rational viewpoint. The marginal man is always relatively the more civilized human being." Both Park and Stonequist perceive the two societies that the marginal man transcends as not only different, but also antagonistic. To the extent that the peasant village and the urban center hold opposing norms, the cosmopolite peasant will also be a marginal man.

2. Simmel characterizes the *stranger* as "the potential wanderer: although he has not moved on, he has not overcome the freedom of coming and going. He is fixed within a particular special group. . . . But his position in the group is determined, essentially, by the fact that he has not belonged to it from the beginning, that he imparts qualities into it, which do not and cannot stem from the group itself. . . . He is freer, practically and theoretically; his criteria for them are more general and objective ideals; he is not tied down in his action by habit, piety, and precedent" (Wolff 1950:402–404). Simmel introduces the aspect of migration in his concept. The stranger is by definition not born a member of a given social system. If the cosmopolite peasant is a "settler" in a community, it is likely that he will maintain his interests outside the village. Since many peasant villages are relatively closed social systems, the peasant who comes to the village as a stranger is likely to remain a stranger, and thus in some ways he is forced to assume a cosmopolite orientation.

3. *Gatekeepers* and *cultural brokers* are concepts used to describe individuals who function in a mediating role between the source and receiver in a communication system. Cosmopolite peasants who serve as a sieve through which information flows, are gatekeepers. Very often the peasant who owns a radio can serve a gatekeeping function in a village by "editing" the information he feeds to his fellow villagers. The cosmopolite peasant who brings new cultural ideas from urban centers to his village is serving a broker function, negotiating messages between modern and traditional systems.

4. *Urbanites* are individuals who have emancipated themselves "from any marked dependence on or identification with a local neighborhood," whereas neighbors organize their living much more completely around the facilities and the friendships of a residential system (Foley 1952). The peasant is not likely to achieve a complete urbanite status; even if he maintains a cosmopolite orientation, it is unlikely that he is able to emancipate himself from any marked dependence on, or identification with the peasant village.

world are *cosmopolites*.[2] For the most part, peasants are at the localite end of the continuum, representing what Lerner and Riesman (1955) describe as "rooted individuals."

The isolation of peasant communities has, over the years, conditioned the peasant to be concerned only with his immediate environment. Road construction and mass media development are relatively recent activites in less developed nations, and have yet to crumble the crust of localistic conditioning.

To explain the localite behavior of peasants, one must turn to the societal environment that produces them. The village is a localistic or *gemeinschaft* society, whereas the city is by nature a cosmopolitan or *gesellschaft* society.[3] *Gemeinschaft* (localite) and *gesellschaft* (cosmopolite) societies tend to produce two basically different modes of mentality and behavior.[4] The *gemeinschaft* village promotes behavior that is traditional, spontaneous, uncritical, non-examining and nonreflective because the traditional fund of knowledge handed down through kin and neighbors is considered conclusive and final. The traditional ethic stands against new ideas and the expansion of knowledge. The modern *gesellschaft* environment encourages the development of reflective, rational, and critical behavior, which is based on "secular rather than sacred considerations. It embraces the spirit of enlightenment" (Pye 1963:19).

The individual's degree of cosmopoliteness is relative to the other members of his social system;[5] therefore in each of the societal environments we find both localites and cosmopolites (Table 7-1).

The cosmopolite in a traditional system is much more deviant from pre-

[2] Merton (1957:393) describes a typical localite in Rovere (a New Jersey suburban community) thusly, "The localite largely confines his interests to this community. Rovere is essentially his world . . . . He is strictly speaking, a parochial." In contrast, Merton (1957:394) describes a typical cosmopolite: "He resides in Rovere but lives in the Great Society." The cosmopolitan is essentially ecumenical.

[3] Writing in 1887, Toennies developed these polar categories to conceptualize the differences between what he considered to be the two main stages of societal development. Similar concepts were used in the writings of Confucius, Plato, Aristotle, Cicero, St. Augustine, St. Thomas Acquinas, and Ibn Khaldun, as well as in Redfield's folk-urban categories, Becker's sacred-secular concepts, Sorokin's familistic-contractual classification, and our traditional-modern categories. Each set of these polar categories represents an attempt to characterize essentially the same societal phenomena. For example, Redfield (1941) describes the folk society as an isolated, nonliterate, homogeneous grouping of peoples with a strong sense of solidarity, and Becker (1957) describes the sacred society as isolated vicinally, socially and mentally, where traditional and ritual play a large part in the life of the individual.

DeS. Brunner (1942) questions the fundamentality and functional usefulness of Toennies' concepts; he argues that in addition to being descriptive, adequate theories must be functionally useful in explaining change.

[4] Of course, a different time-order sequence could be argued; two different modes of mentality and behavior produce two different societal types. For example, pockets of urban villagers tend to produce a localite society within the cosmopolite, urban environment.

[5] And, of course, the cosmopoliteness of the system is also a relative matter.

Table 7–1.   Illustrations[a] of Types of Localites and Cosmopolites in Traditional and Modern Systems

| Individual's Degree of Cosmopoliteness | *Nature of the Social System* | |
	Traditional (*Gemeinschaft* or Localite)	Modern (*Gesellshaft* or Cosmopolite)
Localite	1. Majority of peasant villagers 2. Old Order Amish (U.S.)	1. Urban poor in more developed nations 2. Members in ethnic neighborhoods in urban cities
Cosmopolite	1. Peasants who travel to cities 2. Traders	1. National and international travelers 2. Urban upper-middle class

[a] These examples are intended to be illustrative, rather than absolute; that is, many urban poor are localites, but certainly not all.

vailing patterns than the cosmopolite in a modern system where norms favor a wider perspective. The cosmopolite peasant is likely to be a unique individual in that he is motivated to look beyond his environment, when most others are content to maintain a localistic frame of reference. He is, in turn, made to feel more unique if his cosmopoliteness leads to modernization, while the others in his system maintain their traditional point of view.

COSMOPOLITENESS AND MODERNIZATION

How, when, and why do peasants develop cosmopolite interests? What leads individuals to turn away from the norms of the peasant village to those of the larger society? What happens to the peasant as a result of his cosmopoliteness? These are some of the questions that will be dealt with in discussing the significance of cosmopoliteness in the total modernization picture. Cosmopoliteness undoubtedly is interdependently related to other modernization variables.[6] Cosmopoliteness promotes other forms of modernization, which in turn likely increase the degree of cosmopoliteness. The time-order arrows of this relationship are mutual and reciprocal. The first impact of contact with the external world produces a small increment in moderniza-

[6] The nature of cosmopoliteness-modernization relationships, whether causal or interdependent, cannot be adequately tested with data from the present investigation, where we are dealing with correlational, rather than experimental, data.

tion, which in turn is likely to lead to more contact with the external world, and so forth. Therefore . . .

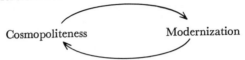

Cosmopoliteness   Modernization

We believe that *cosmopoliteness plays a central role in the modernization process*.[7] Certainly, contact with the external world must be viewed as an initiator of the drive towards a more modern life. In turn, cosmopolite communication enables the peasant to maintain and increase his interest in modernizing ideas. So cosmopoliteness can be considered an indicator of modernization, as well as a possible initiator of the process (Figure 7–1).

Although cosmopoliteness is conceptualized as an antecedent in the modernization process, certain factors may precede initial contact with the world external to the village.

ANTECEDENTS OF COSMOPOLITENESS

Cosmopoliteness requires a view of the larger society. This awareness of the outside world is possible only when certain conditions are met, then other factors serve to facilitate further interest in the broader sphere.

Necessary Conditions

The peasant must be *connected* with the outside world in some manner before he can become a cosmopolite. The connection can be *actual* or *vicarious*. Physical transportation facilities such as roads and public bus service provide the possibility for actual peasant contact with the world outside of his village,[8] whereas "mental transportation" facilities such as the mass media provide vicarious connections.

In less developed nations these necessary connections are often non-existent, or at best not in very good working order. Bisbee (1951), for ex-

[7] Evidence for the great importance of cosmopoliteness in modernization is indicated (1) by the very strong correlations of cosmopoliteness with modernization variables, which will be reported later; (2) by its ability to predict and explain variance in innovativeness (Chapter 13); (3) by the salience of cosmopoliteness in the factor analysis of the Colombia data (Chapter 15); and (4) by the factor analysis of data from poor Kentucky farmers (Donohew and Singh 1967), which indicates that urban contact is the most important single variable distinguishing modern and traditional respondents.

[8] Occasionally one encounters almost humorous examples of peasant desire for wider travel and urban contact once transportation facilities are provided. One is reminded of the typical rural bus encountered on the roads of most less developed nations; in Colombia such conveyances are usually packed with people, potatoes, and chickens on their way to an urban market. Another example is the sight of the occasional tractor, whose fenders and drawbar are covered with city-bound peasants. Somewhat of a record for tractor-powered cosmopoliteness must have been established by a Turkish villager who trekked some 2000 miles with his family to Berlin (Karpat 1960).

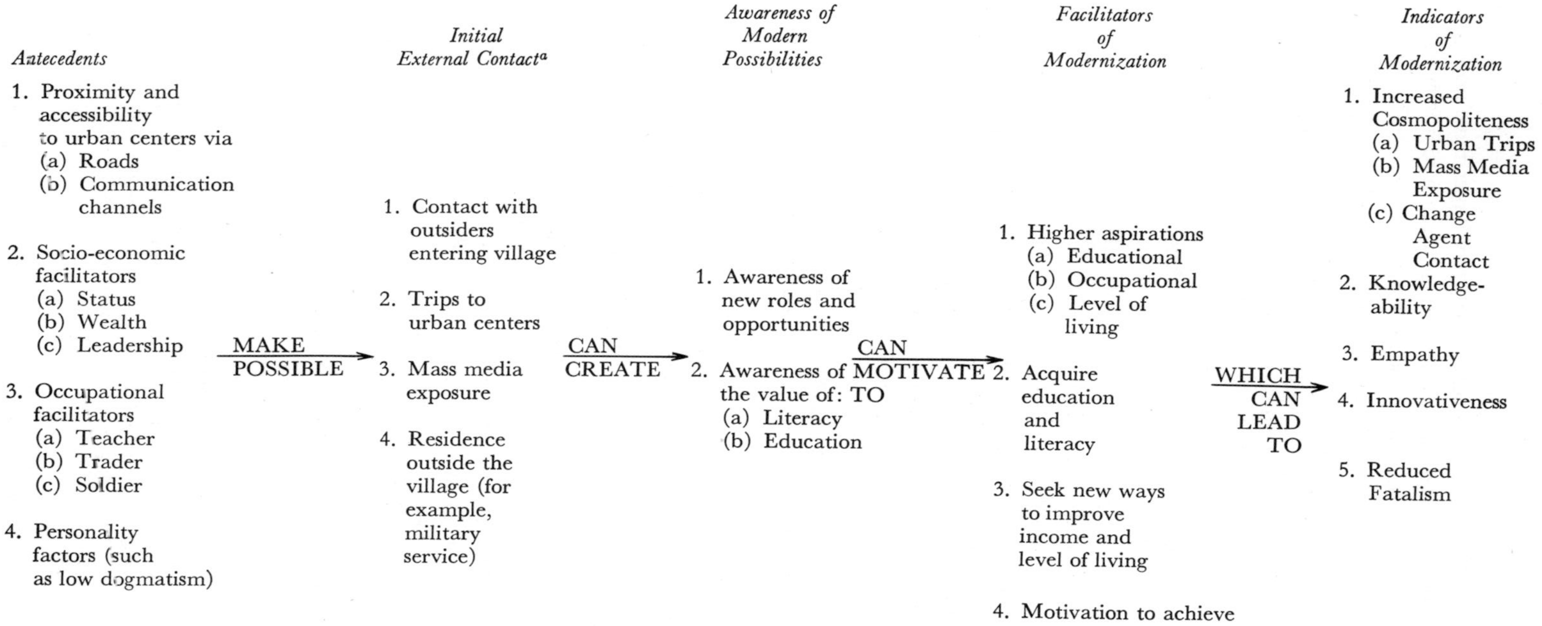

Antecedents	*Initial External Contact*[a]	*Awareness of Modern Possibilities*	*Facilitators of Modernization*	*Indicators of Modernization*
1. Proximity and accessibility to urban centers via (a) Roads (b) Communication channels	1. Contact with outsiders entering village	1. Awareness of new roles and opportunities	1. Higher aspirations (a) Educational (b) Occupational (c) Level of living	1. Increased Cosmopoliteness (a) Urban Trips (b) Mass Media Exposure (c) Change Agent Contact
2. Socio-economic facilitators (a) Status (b) Wealth (c) Leadership	2. Trips to urban centers	2. Awareness of the value of: (a) Literacy (b) Education	2. Acquire education and literacy	2. Knowledgeability
3. Occupational facilitators (a) Teacher (b) Trader (c) Soldier	3. Mass media exposure		3. Seek new ways to improve income and level of living	3. Empathy
4. Personality factors (such as low dogmatism)	4. Residence outside the village (for example, military service)		4. Motivation to achieve	4. Innovativeness
				5. Reduced Fatalism

Arrows between columns: **MAKE POSSIBLE** → **CAN CREATE** → **CAN MOTIVATE** → **WHICH CAN LEAD TO**

Figure 7-1. Paradigm of the Hypothesized Sequential Role of Cosmopoliteness in the Modernization Process[b]

[a] This initial contact may lead to further cosmopoliteness (as indicated, in the paradigm) or cause a negative reaction to modernization.

[b] This is a hypothetical model which represents one way of looking at the modernization process, when the focus is upon cosmopoliteness. Within the limitations of our research methodology, we can offer only speculations about the time-order sequence of the variables involved in modernization. While we cannot *prove* the vadility of the notions implied in our cosmopoliteness paradigm, we can support our contentions with logical reasoning and evidence from correlational research, as well as data from observational studies. The relationships we hypothesize are possible and probable, but represent only one arbitrary view of the concepts that are discussed.

ample, describes village isolation in Turkey: "Many villages have no better connection with the nearest town or another village than a footpath which even a donkey cannot travel in any but good weather." A peasant in such an isolated setting has little chance of becoming a cosmopolite; the requisite means of access are not yet developed.

Roads and transportation facilities physically enable peasants to transcend the boundaries of the local village. Transportation facilities open the peasant to the centripetal pull of the city (Fals Borda 1955). Rao (1963) concludes that the key difference between a very modern and a very traditional Indian village that he studied, was the existence of a *road* linking the more modern community to a nearby urban center.

Roads also provide the possibility that outsiders will enter the village. In his description of this "outside-in" influence on the Colombian community of Saucío, Fals Borda (1955) delineates the role of a nearby dam construction on peasant modernization: The dam brought many outsiders into contact with the villagers (including truck drivers who willingly ferried peasants to the city), who challenged the *gemeinshaftlichen* characteristics of Saucío.

The isolation barrier can also be broken by the mass media, which gives the peasant a vicarious connection with the larger society. The rapid development of Japan, especially the modernization of her traditional peasants following World War II, illustrates the role that the mass media *can* play in breaking the barrier of isolation and in promoting cosmopolite interests among rural people.

. . . Even the most isolated mountain or island community is in touch with the rest of the nation and shares its changing culture. . . . Thoroughly developed mass media of communication and a great network of public trains and buses keep all parts of the nation in touch with each other (Norbeck 1965:12).

Unfortunately, Japan represents the exception, not the rule, for developing nations. In most less developed countries, villages remain physically isolated and have yet to be thoroughly penetrated by the mass media (Chapter 5). Frey (1966) found that one in every eight Turkish villagers lives in an isolated community where there is no direct access to radio — the medium reaching the widest peasant audience.

Proximity of the village to the city, or to more modern communities, increases the likelihood of access both through transportation and the mass media.[9] For example, the closer the village to the city, the more likely the road will be in good shape, thus facilitating travel both to and from the vil-

---

[9] Frey (1966) found the *less* physically isolated Turkish villages had *more* mass media exposure. We encounter a somewhat similar evidence of the complementarity of urban travel and mass media exposure among our Colombian respondents. In a multiple correlation analysis, we find trips to cities highly related to achievement motivation in modern villages, and mass media exposure highly related to achievement motivation in traditional, isolated villages (Chapter 11).

lage. The further removed the community is from the city, the less likelihood that either roads or mass media will bring peasants into contact with modern life. The Colombian data illustrate the effect of urban proximity on peasant travel. Pueblo Viejo, San Rafael, and Cuatro Esquinas are all located relatively close to Bogotá. Peasants in these communities average about 18, 31, and 26 trips, respectively, per year to Bogotá. Peasants in the more isolated communities of Nazate and La Cañada average only 1.4 and 4.4 trips respectively, per year to urban centers. Poor road conditions and long distance combine to limit the number of urban trips.

Access, facilitated by proximity, is a *necessary*, but not a sufficient, condition for cosmopoliteness.

Facilitating Factors

If the necessary conditions prevail, other factors increase or decrease the probability of a given peasant becoming cosmopolite. One might think in terms of a facilitating-inhibiting continuum. For example, economic resources can be a facilitating factor if they are plentiful, but an inhibiting factor if they are scarce. Certain personality characteristics may facilitate the development of cosmopolite interests, whereas other personality configurations may insulate the peasant from the larger society. The following are factors that may make initial contact with the outside world more *probable*.[10]

(1) SOCIOECONOMIC FACTORS

Socioeconomic factors can affect the probability of a given peasant establishing outer-village contacts in several ways. First, social status, which is usually accompanied by economic wherewithal in peasant villages, is a primary consideration for change agents in choosing village contact points. An outsider entering a village is most likely to seek contact with the village influentials. Missionaries usually seek out the chief as the principal target for conversion, because persuading him almost certainly ensures the recruitment of many of his followers. Failure to consult individuals in positions of authority and high status can undermine attempts to establish development activities in a village. So a peasant's status and authority facilitate his contact with outsiders coming into a village. Social status and leadership characteristics are also likely to affect the probability of peasants travelling out of the village;[11] for example, many youths sent abroad to study are sons of village leaders.

Economic resources further facilitates development of cosmopolite orienta-

[10] For our purposes, a look at the positive forces encouraging cosmopoliteness is most useful, so we shall focus on the facilitating aspects and leave the reader to draw inferences about the opposite (inhibiting) forces.

[11] Although the evidence from less developed countries is rather meager at this point, several studies completed in the United States point out that cosmopolites tend to have higher socioeconomic status; examples are MacLean and others (1959) and Dye (1963).

tions. Whatever the cost — maintaining a donkey, riding a bus or truck, or losing a day's work — the peasant must be able to afford a trip to the city. The more affluent he is, the more often he *can* travel. Availability of economic resources also makes it easier to afford the radio, magazine, or newspaper necessary to maintain cosmopolite interests.

(2) OCCUPATIONAL ROLES

Villagers who engage in such occupations as trading and teaching are more likely to be cosmopolites, than are people who earn their living from the land. Through military service, greater numbers of village boys become acquainted with city life and the larger society.[12] Peasants who must travel beyond village borders to pursue a livelihood establish contacts with the outside world, and take the first step toward developing cosmopolite interests.

(3) PERSONALITY FACTORS

All other factors being equal, an individual's personality configuration further affects the probability of his becoming cosmopolite. Social-psychological studies of peasant personality are relatively few, so one can only speculate about which of these variables affect cosmopoliteness.[13] Dogmatism[14] appears to be negatively related to cosmopoliteness because a peasant raised in a localistic social structure must have an open value system to be vulnerable to the wider perspective available through travel, change agent contact, and so forth. Personality variables like dogmatism, intelligence, flexibility, independence, and self-reliance will probably either facilitate or inhibit the development of cosmopoliteness.

INITIAL EXTERNAL CONTACT[15]

Peasants come into contact with the world beyond the village through a variety of channels. These initial contacts set off a series of interacting factors that cause *some* peasants to become more cosmopolite and more modern. Initial contact with the external world occurs in the following ways:

---

[12] We are reminded of a very innovative young cultivator in a Punjabi village who was a veteran of the Indian army. While in military service this individual played on a championship soccer team, which traveled throughout India and Europe. He kept careful notes on the agricultural practices that he observed, and after his discharge, returned to his home village to put them into use. However, it is also true that many veterans do not return to the village.

[13] Other than achievement motivation and empathy, which are variables included in the present study (Chapters 11 and 9, respectively).

[14] Dogmatism refers to the strength with which beliefs are held (Rokeach 1960).

[15] We hesitate to label the initial contact that the peasant has with the external world as cosmopoliteness. Initial contact *can* lead to cosmopoliteness (orientation to the larger society), but it can also reinforce localiteness. In describing the nature of initial contacts, we only point out the ways in which the peasant can be made *aware* of the external world. Of course these same variables are involved once the peasant's initial interest is stimulated.

Outsiders Entering the Village

Awareness of the world beyond is often created by outsiders permeating the village. Throughout history, the itinerant trader or wandering minstrel was about the only communication link between isolated villages. Such individuals brought news and goods from other villages and cities, often stirring the imaginations of their listeners and promoting interest in places beyond the village. Missionaries are another example of the outsider who brings new ideas to the village.[16] Today, it is often the extension agent, teacher, or visiting relative who brings ideas from the outside world to the village, establishing a vital linkage between the modern and traditional worlds. Occasionally, migrants will settle in the village, bringing with them "outside" ways and interests.

Villagers' travel

Trips by villagers are another way in which contact is established with the larger society.[17] Whether he travels to the next village or to the largest city in the nation, a peripatetic peasant gains a wider perspective from which to view village life. Extended travel, involving *residence in cities and other countries*, is a more recent phenomenon.[18] Villagers who take up temporary residence in cities to earn money for land purchase and so on, return home with new ideas from their urban stay.[19] Military service is another way in which some villagers gain initial access to the larger world.

Contact Through Mass Media

The mass media may also serve as sources of initial cosmopolite contact. Villagers become aware of the world beyond the village primarily through radio and cinema[20] channels, which do not require literacy.

Once contact is made with the urban and more modern world, the villager becomes aware of a way of life different from his own. He may view this different world as an attractive and desirable horizon or he may reject it altogether. The peasant who is attracted to the big society has taken the first step to becoming a cosmopolite.

[16] In some of Latin American and African countries, these missionaries were the first contact villagers had with anyone beyond their own system.

[17] It is possible that actual exposure to the more modern life of the city is more likely to serve as a motivator to become more modern than vicarious exposure through outsiders.

[18] Although it is not usually an initial contact, some educated individuals from less developed countries participate in training or education programs in more developed countries, and return to their traditional environments with new ideas and cosmopolite interests.

[19] This form of travel is probably not a likely type of initial contact, although Mexican *braceros* are an illustration.

[20] For example, Frey's date (1966) show that 43 percent of the Turkish peasants were frequent radio listeners, whereas only 20 percent had frequent newspaper exposure.

AWARENESS OF MODERN POSSIBILITIES

Urban contact can, but does not necessarily, serve to increase peasant awareness of (1) new roles, occupations, and opportunities; (2) the value of education and literacy; and (3) happenings and developments in the larger society. Although it cannot be proved that increased contact with the world beyond the village develops modern peasants, we agree with Stirling (1965: 291) who states: "The very great increase in communication with the outside world is at the root of the change." Awareness can in turn raise the level of aspirations, and motivate the peasant to take steps to achieve the desired aspects of modern life.

MODERNIZATION FACILITATORS

Once the motivations of the peasant are aroused they can lead him down several different avenues of aspiration and aquisition. He may be motivated to migrate to the urban center, and satisfy his desire for modernness by becoming part of it. More likely, however, he will be motivated to take smaller steps in changing his way of life.

Higher Aspirations

The peasant who is intrigued with the opportunities of modern life is likely to develop aspirations for a better education, a different occupation, or a higher level of living. These aspirations may be reflected in desires for himself or for his children.

Education and Literacy

Villagers may be motivated to acquire the educational and literacy skills necessary for a more modern life.

Seeking Information about New Ideas

Awareness that alternatives for better living and farming exist may motivate the peasant to *begin to seek* information for improving his lot. This seeking process is likely to cause an increment in the cosmopoliteness of the peasant, as he usually will find these new ideas outside his village.

EMERGENCE OF MORE MODERN INDIVIDUALS[21]

Through the interaction of all the previous variables discussed (and possibly through others not yet considered), one is likely to see the emergence

[21] The interacting nature of the variables that combine to produce modern peasants make it difficult to specify their time-order as pointed out previously. For example, cosmopoliteness may be a consequent, rather than an antecedent, of innovativeness; that is, the peasant who is already innovative may be forced to develop a cosmopolite orientation in order to satisfy his drive for new ideas, or to escape censure of his peers, who regard him as a deviant from traditional village norms.

of more modern attitudes and behaviors. A modern peasant is likely to be characterized[22] by the following.

Increased Cosmopoliteness[23]

For the peasant interested in new ideas, the urban world is a more meaningful referent point than the local village: therefore, he may increase the number of *trips* he takes to the city. He also may become more exposed to the *mass media* eminating from urban centers. Frey (1966) reports a positive relationship between geographic mobility[24] and mass media exposure. A desire for better farming may lead the peasant into more *contact with change agents*. Once attracted, the peasant is increasingly likely to turn toward the urban center, as did Lerner's grocer. Redfield (1941) concluded from his data that an increase in cosmopolite contacts constitutes one sufficient cause of secularization (modernization) and individualization.

Increased Knowledgeability

Increased exposure to the world beyond the village is likely to be reflected in increased political and social knowledge. The peasant who travels to the city, reads newspapers, and listens to the radio, is likely to be knowledgeable about governmental matters, especially those related to development activities.

Increased Empathy

As more modern ways of life become less strange to the villager, he is better able to empathize with modern roles. Exposure and understanding make for greater cognitive flexibility, which in turn increases the peasant's capacity to empathize with roles such as change agents, teachers, and government officials. Frey (1966) found empathy strongly related to geographic cosmopoliteness.

Increased Achievement Motivation and Increased Innovativeness

It can be expected that the cosmopolite orientations of the modern peasant stimulate a desire for higher levels of excellence.

The cosmopolite peasant is likely to be more innovative, both because he is

---

[22] These variables are perceived as interacting, interdependent factors; increments in one are likely to produce increments in others. The word "increase" is used to connote changes in the peasant as he moves from a traditional to a more modern life. In becoming more modern, we are likely to see changes in these aspects of his behavior.

[23] We see initial contact with the external world (or "initial cosmopoliteness") as a possible cause of further cosmopoliteness. The attraction of the urban or larger society is likely to cause the peasant to be more cosmopolite.

[24] Frey's concept of geographical mobility, similar to our cosmopoliteness, summarized the respondent's physical mobility: how often he leaves the village, where he goes, whether he has visited the nearest city of over 50,000 population, and so forth.

aware of more new ideas and because the more innovative peasant is encouraged toward cosmopoliteness in a search for new ideas. It is difficult to see these variables as unrelated,[25] or to decide which precedes the other.

Reduction in Fatalism

Contact with the urban-industrial world shows the peasant that humans can control their environment, which may reduce his fatalistic approach to life. Sen (1962) found "self-reliance," which he views as the opposite of fatalism, to be positively related to cosmopoliteness.

In Summary

Cosmopoliteness is involved in creating initial awareness of the more modern life and in characterizing modern behavior in peasants.

As we turn to the Colombia data, the reader is reminded that the correlational data-analysis does not provide support for the time-order aspects of the model (Figure 7–1). Only the existence of positive or negative relationships can be established between cosmopoliteness and other modernization variables.

MEASURING COSMOPOLITENESS

Most past research on cosmopoliteness has been completed in more developed countries, and as a result the measures of the concept offer little utility for direct application with peasants. Previous inquiries in the United States focused upon cosmopoliteness in communities,[26] and in formal organizations[27] like research bureaucracies, universities, and business and industrial firms.

The measures utilized to operationalize the concept, whatever the exact type of social system involved, were of the following types:

1. *Attitudinal,*[28] in which the respondent is asked to indicate his degree of agreement or disagreement with statements such as: "The most rewarding

---

[25] However, Fliegel (1966) found no significant relationship between innovativeness and trips to urban centers in his study of 142 Brazilian farmers. This is an exception to the results of numerous other investigations.

[26] Community studies usually focus on the orientation of the community's residents to local affairs and organizations, as opposed to national or international affairs. Examples of these studies are Merton (1957), Rogers (1957), Dobriner (1958), MacLean and others (1959), Havens (1960), and Dye (1963).

[27] Organization studies are usually concerned with organizational loyalty versus professional loyalty. Cosmopoliteness is often equated with the professional orientation of the respondent, and is determined by questions such as: "In the long run, would you rather be known and respected (1) throughout the institution where you work, or (2) among specialists in your field in different institutions?" (Davis 1961). Illustrative of these studies are Gouldner (1957), Davis (1961), Glazer (1963), Warden (1964), and Abrahamson (1965).

[28] Investigators of cosmopoliteness who utilized attitudinal indicators are Dobriner (1958), MacLean and others (1959), Havens (1960), Gouldner (1957;1958), Glazer (1963), Abrahamson (1965), Davis (1961), Dye (1963), and Warden (1964).

organizations a person can belong to are local organizations serving local needs" (Dobriner 1958).

2. *Behavioral indicators*, in which the respondent reflects his communication contact with sources external to his social system. Several studies in less developed countries asked peasants how many trips they had taken to urban centers (Goldsen and Ralis 1957; Frey 1966; Sen 1962; and Fliegel 1966). Other behavioral measures used in less developed nations are contact with foreigners (Lerner 1958), and the type of communication source or channel used by peasants[29] (Deutschmann and Fals Borda 1962a).

The main measure of cosmopoliteness in the Colombian study is the number of trips to an urban center by a respondent during the year preceding the interview. Bogotá was the urban center in the case of the three modern villages, whereas a provincial capital served as the parallel referent in the two traditional villages. Number of urban trips is essentially a one-item scale and, as such is subject to relatively low reliability. There is some indication of its reliability over time, since the question was included in both the 1963 and 1965 interviews with the same respondents in Colombia. The correlation between cosmopoliteness in 1963 and 1965 for the three modern villages[30] is .584.[31] Although this correlation is not exceedingly high, it does provide some support for the test-retest reliability of our measure of cosmopoliteness.

In Figure 7–1 it is suggested that factors other than number of trips to urban centers may reflect cosmopoliteness. A factor analysis of four such cosmopoliteness indicators shows that number of urban trips and mass media exposure load consistently (for the modern and traditional villages) on one factor, whereas change agent contact and residence outside the community each loaded heavily on additional factors. This finding may indicate that there are several dimensions to cosmopoliteness. In the analysis of the Colombia data that follows, urban trips will be used as the primary operation of cosmopoliteness.[32]

COSMOPOLITENESS AND MODERNIZATION IN COLOMBIA[33]

Table 7–2 provides an overall impression that cosmopoliteness is quite highly correlated with the other modernization variables chosen for study. In only one village, Nazate, do we notice relatively weaker relationships. Nazate

---

[29] This measure was reviewed in Chapter 6. Other behavioral indicators of cosmopoliteness are the location of formal organizations to which one belongs (Merton 1957; Rogers 1957); news-seeking behavior, such as the type of newspaper or the type of news article read (Merton 1957; Rogers 1957; and MacLean and others 1959).

[30] No reinterviews were conducted in the two traditional communities in 1965.

[31] This correlation is undoubtedly lowered by the fact that the respondents changed their degree of cosmopoliteness during the two year interim between the interviews.

[32] Although all four variables are considered in the factor analysis of modernization variables in Chapter 15. Mass media exposure and change agent contact receive primary attention in Chapters 5 and 8, respectively.

[33] The Colombian data were collected prior to finalization of our cosmopoliteness model, and therefore we do not have adequate measures of all the concepts discussed earlier.

is the most remote and isolated village, and perhaps the lack of variance in the number of trips to cities (the average number for all respondents is only 1.4 per year) acts to depress the correlations of cosmopoliteness with other variables.

Now let us look in detail at the relationships of cosmopoliteness and other variables in Colombia.

SOCIOECONOMIC VARIABLES

A *social status* rating, based on interviewer observation of material possessions and village prestige, is correlated significantly and positively in four of the five Colombian villages (Table 7-2). *Opinion leadership* in one sense, is a measure of esteem from peers, and hence a social status variable. One might expect that a very cosmopolite peasant would be perceived as deviant from village norms, and would not be respected as an opinion leader. On the other hand, because the cosmopolite peasant possesses information that the more localite peasant does not have, his opinion may be sought about such matters as agricultural and health innovations where local sources are not available or less useful. Opinion leadership is positively and significantly correlated with cosmopoliteness in three of the Colombian villages.[34]

Two indicators of economic status are *level of living* and *farm size*. Level of living is correlated positively and significantly with cosmopoliteness in three of the villages (Table 7-1). Farm size is significantly and positively correlated with cosmopoliteness in all the villages, with the exception of La Cañada, where the size of land holdings is extremely small.[35]

In general, we conclude that *socioeconomic variables are positively related to the degree of peasant cosmopoliteness*.[36]

OTHER REFLECTORS OF URBAN CONTACT

One would expect strong, positive correlations between cosmopoliteness (trips to the city) and other variables that indicate peasant contact with the larger society. Cosmopoliteness and *mass media exposure* show high positive correlations in all five villages.

Having *lived outside of the village* is correlated significantly with trips to ctiesi in three of the five villages. *Extension contact* is strongly correlated with cosmopoliteness in the most modern community and in one of the traditional

---

[34] The extremely low correlation in the traditional village of La Cañada, may support the deviancy hypothesis, as the cosmopolite in the more traditional society is likely to be perceived as more deviant than he would be in the more modern communities.

[35] With so little variance in this dimension, it is more difficult to obtain a high correlation.

[36] We have no data for the other antecedents suggested in our hypothetical model. One personality variable, dogmatism, is correlated $-.088$ with trips to the city in the three modern villages. This relationship is in the expected direction, but does not reach significance.

Table 7–2.   Pearsonian Zero-Order Correlations between Cosmopoliteness and Other Variables in Colombia

Variables Correlated with Cosmopoliteness	Zero-Order Correlations with Cosmopoliteness (Trips to Cities)						
	Pueblo Viejo	San Rafael	Cuatro Esquinas	Modern Villages (Pooled)	Nazate	La Cañada	Traditional Villages (Pooled)
I. Socioeconomic antecedents							
1. Social status	.467[b]	.378[a]	.598[b]	.499[b]	[.222]	.403[b]	.331[b]
2. Opinion leadership	.292[a]	.455[b]	[.167]	.288[b]	.496[b]	[.011]	.235[a]
3. Level of living	[.109]	.455[b]	.343[a]	.276[b]	−.366[d]	.291[a]	[.047]
4. Farm size	.466[b]	.382[a]	.530[b]	.456[b]	.364[a]	[.080]	.207[a]
II. Other reflectors of urban contact							
5. Mass media exposure	.427[b]	.657[b]	.664[b]	.574[b]	.324[a]	.617[b]	.504[b]
6. Lived outside of village	.267[a]	.343[a]	[.119]	.233[b]	[−.188]	.657[b]	.350[b]
7. Extension contact	.392[b]	[−.133]	[.041]	.157[a]	—[c]	.734[b]	.734[b,d]
III. Facilitators of modernization							
8. Achievement motivation	[.219]	.348[a]	[.142]	.222[b]	.325[a]	.237[a]	.255[a]
9. Educational aspirations	.256[a]	.689[b]	.579[b]	.490[b]	[.249]	.666[b]	.498[b]
10. Occupational aspirations	[.116]	.510[b]	[.104]	.209[b]	[.089]	.338[a]	.234[a]
11. Education	.415[b]	.564[b]	.507[b]	.483[b]	[.250]	.509[b]	.405[b]
12. Functional literacy	.269[a]	.531[b]	.193	.308[b]	[.123]	[.255]	[.199]
IV. Modernization indicators							
13. Political knowledgeability	.432[b]	.680	.565[b]	.543[b]	[−.049]	.532[b]	.306[b]
14. Empathy	[.159]	.343[a]	.328[a]	.263[b]	[.277]	.372[b]	.333[b]
15. Agricultural innovativeness	.346[b]	[−.003]	.320[a]	.262[b]	.357[a]	.826[b]	.680[b]
16. Home innovativeness	.523[b]	.755[b]	.529[b]	.590[b]	.446[b]	.485[b]	.463[b]
17. Fatalism	—[c]	—[c]	—[c]	−.219[b]	—[c]	—[c]	—[c]

[a] Significantly different from zero at the 5 percent level.
[b] Significantly different from zero at the 1 percent level.
[c] No correlations were computed in these cases.
[d] There is no extension contact in Nazate, so this correlation is for La Cañada only.

villages. The extent of such change agent contact may be a function not only of the peasant, but also of which clients the change agent selects for intensive work, the innovations he promotes, and his ability to relate to the peasants in a given community.

Cosmopoliteness is positively related to the other reflectors of urban contact.

FACILITATORS OF MODERNIZATION[37]

Achievement motivation is related positively and significantly to urban trips in three of the villages (Table 7–1). Positive and significant correlations between cosmopoliteness and *educational aspirations* exist in four of the five villages. Only in Nazate is the relationship too weak to be significant; it is, however, positive and approaches significance. *Occupational aspirations* are significantly linked to cosmopoliteness in only two of the villages, but they are positively related in all five communities.

Two variables that reflect the peasant's acquisition of skills that may serve· as modern life facilitators, *education* and *functional literacy*, correlate strongly and weakly, respectively, with urban trips. Education is correlated significantly in four of the villages, and approaches significance in the other, while functional literacy correlates significantly in only two of the modern villages.

Cosmopoliteness is positively related to the facilitators of modernization.

MODERNIZATION INDICATORS

The modern peasant has been characterized as possessing a relatively higher degree of political knowledgeability, empathy, innovativeness, and less fatalism than his traditional counterpart.

The peasant whose orientation is outside his immediate village is likely to be more knowledgeable about national political affairs, as well as farm and home innovations. *Political knowledgeability* is strongly correlated with cosmopoliteness in four of the five villages (Table 7–2). *Innovativeness*, both home and agricultural, is correlated positively and significantly with cosmopoliteness in four villages.

Increased urban exposure should be reflected in a peasant's capacity to empathize with higher status and more modern roles. *Empathy* is positively correlated with cosmopoliteness in all five villages, and significantly in three. *Fatalism* is correlated negatively and significantly in the three modern villages,[38] suggesting that cosmopoliteness leads to an attitude that the future is controllable.

---

[37] We have no measures from the Colombia data that serve as indicators of the hypothesized *awareness* step (Figure 7–1), but we do have some variables that might be considered as facilitators of modernization, which are considered in this section.

[38] Fatalism was not measured in the traditional villages.

Cosmopoliteness is strongly and positively related to the other indicators of peasant modernization.

In Summary of the Colombian Findings

Although our correlational data do not permit conclusions about the time-order of cosmopoliteness in the modernization process, there is a *possible* time-order relationship among the variables discussed in Figure 7–2. The notion of socioeconomic antecedents to cosmopoliteness was tested with multiple correlation techniques (Table 7–3). About 31 percent of the variance in cosmopoliteness can be explained in the modern villages, and 16 percent in the traditional villages.[39] The inclusion of other variables considered as

Table 7–3. Multiple Correlation of Cosmopoliteness with Selected Antecedent Variables in Modern and Traditional Colombian Villages

| *Antecedent Variables* | *Percentage of Variance in Cosmopoliteness Explained* | |
	Three Modern Villages	Two Traditional Villages
1. Social status	12.86	13.49
2. Farm size (in land units)	14.03	4.86
3. Opinion leadership	2.39	−0.33
4. Level of living	1.84	0.03
Total	31.12	18.05

antecedents to cosmopoliteness in Figure 7–1, but not measured in Colombia, would probably enable a better prediction of cosmopoliteness.

The consistently strong correlations between cosmopoliteness and most other modernization variables emphasizes the importance of the cosmopoliteness concept in the modernization process.

COMPARISON OF COLOMBIA AND INDIA UNESCO FINDINGS

Essentially, the India UNESCO data reflect the same strong correlations as the Colombia data (Table 7–4). Cosmopoliteness (trips to cities) is significantly and positively correlated with all the modernization variables con-

[39] In addition to this attempt to predict cosmopoliteness, we have included cosmopoliteness along with other variables to predict empathy (Chapter 9), achievement motivation (Chapter 11), fatalism (Chapter 12), and agricultural innovativeness (Chapter 13). The greatest contribution to explaining variance in modernization variables is in the case of innovativeness, where cosmopoliteness explained 22 percent of the variance in the traditional villages.

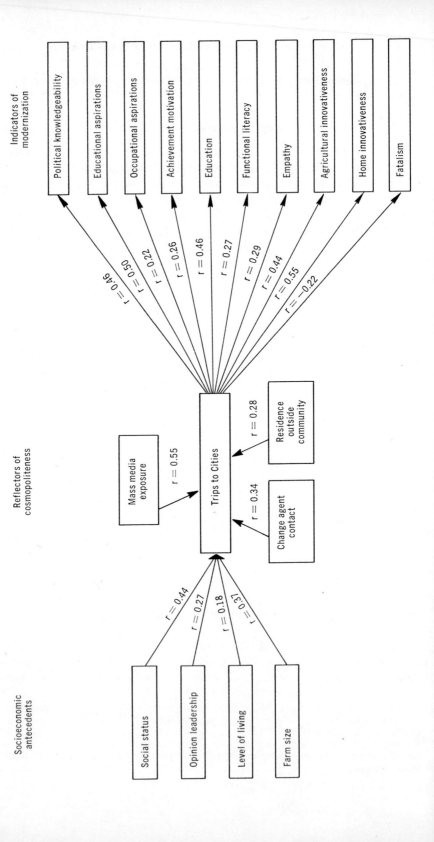

Socioeconomic antecedents

Reflectors of cosmopoliteness

Indicators of modernization

Social status

Opinion leadership

Level of living

Farm size

r = 0.44

r = 0.27

r = 0.18

r = 0.37

Mass media exposure

r = 0.55

Trips to Cities

r = 0.28

Residence outside community

r = 0.34

Change agent contact

r = 0.46

r = 0.50

r = 0.22

r = 0.26

r = 0.46

r = 0.27

r = 0.29

r = 0.44

r = 0.55

r = −0.22

Political knowledgeability

Educational aspirations

Occupational aspirations

Achievement motivation

Education

Functional literacy

Empathy

Agricultural innovativeness

Home innovativeness

Fatalism

Table 7–4   Comparison of Colombian and India UNESCO Zero-Order Correlations of Cosmopoliteness with Other Modernization Variables

Variable Correlated with Cosmopoliteness	Zero-Order Correlations with Cosmopoliteness (Trips to Cities)	
	Five Colombian Villages (Pooled)	India UNESCO
1. Social status	.439[b]	—
2. Sociometric opinion leadership	.269[b]	—
3. Level of living	.178[b]	.60[b]
4. Farm size	.369[b]	.38[b]
5. Mass media exposure	.549[b]	.39[b]
6. Change agent contact	.340[b,c]	.71[b]
7. Political knowledgeability	.462[b]	.72[b]
8. Educational aspirations	.498[b]	.63[b,d]
9. Occupational aspirations	.219[b]	
10. Achievement motivation	.255[b]	.55[b]
11. Education	.456[b]	.32[b]
12. Functional literacy	.268[b]	.28[b]
13. Empathy	.289[b]	.40[b]
14. Agricultural innovativeness	.444[b]	.49[b]
15. Home innovativeness	.546[b]	.47[b]

[a] Significantly different from zero at the 5 percent level.

[b] Significantly different from zero at the 1 percent level.

[c] This pooled correlation includes only four of the Colombian village; there was no change agent contact in Nazate.

[d] This correlation represents a composite of both occupational and educational aspirations.

sidered in the Colombia study; in fact, most of the comparable correlates of cosmopoliteness are even higher in India.

The lure of the city appears to hold across cultures.

Figure 7–2.   Summary Paradigm of Correlates of Cosmopoliteness (Urban Trips) for Five Colombia Villages (Aggregate).

*The reader is cautioned that the time-order indicated in this figure is not supported by the correlations. We have arbitrarily chosen to view the variables as antecedents and consequents.

**All correlations are significantly different from zero at the –1 percent level, with the exception of living level, which is significantly different from zero at the 5 percent level.

FUTURE RESEARCH

Although cosmopoliteness appears to be a crucial factor in peasant modernization, careful studies of the concept are relatively few. Future research should center on the following factors:

1. *Measurement.* Clearly, trips to urban centers measure only one aspect of cosmopoliteness. An individual's orientation to the world outside his immediate social system is indicated in many other ways. We suggest that a composite cosmopolite index should be constructed. Such an index might include, in addition to trips to the city, such variables as number of visitors (from outside the village) received, number of letters received, change agent contact, mass media exposure, previous military service, and residence outside the community.

For the most part, measures of cosmopoliteness reflect the *quantity* of the cosmopolite contacts, rather than the *quality*. We need to content analyze the cosmopolite contact; that is, we need to know the type of article the peasant reads or the type of radio program to which he listens, as well as the type of interaction that occurs on the peasant's urban trips. The reason for the trip and the type of contact the peasant makes must influence the potential impact of cosmopoliteness. For example, different kinds of influence can be expected to occur for (1) the peasant who travels to the city and contacts a transplanted peasant much like himself, and (2) the peasant who goes to the city to buy new farm implements. The general question is how urban and modernizing is the external contact.

2. *Field Experiments.* Field experimentation is a means of collecting evidence to support cause and effect relationships. In order to support our hypothesized model, data are needed from the experimental situation. Many of the "famous" villages that have been investigated by students of modernization, like Saucío in Colombia (Fals Borda 1955), Balgat in Turkey (Lerner 1958) and Tepotzlan in Mexico (Redfield 1941; Lewis 1960b) were subjected to the impact of highway construction that broke their isolation barrier. Unfortunately, careful, controlled inquiry is lacking into the effects of these sudden changes on variables like cosmopoliteness.[40] Using an experimental approach, which involves measuring various modernization variables before and after the impact of sudden changes like highway construction, we would be able to make more definite statements about the development and effects of cosmopoliteness on traditional peasants.

3. *Multivariate Analysis.* The relationships between cosmopoliteness and other modernization variables need to be examined with multivariate statistical techniques. Goldsen and Ralis (1957) found that in Thailand literacy intervenes in the cosmopolite-innovativeness relationship. Among

---

[40] The investigators' observations and inferences seem to indicate that cosmopoliteness was increased by the highway construction, but we lack data from peasant interviews.

illiterate farmers, those who made frequent visits to Bangkok, agricultural fairs, and the nearby city airport were more likely to adopt irrigation pump engines than those who were less cosmopolite. If, however, a farmer could read and write, he was just as likely to adopt the innovation whether or not he had been in contact with urban centers. Perhaps this finding suggests a trade-off in the effects of trips to cities and literacy (and the associated variable of print media exposure). In any event, it illustrates the importance of probing deeper into the complex interrelatedness of cosmopoliteness and other modernization variables.

4. *Personality Variables.* There is little inquiry into the psychological make-up of peasants. Personality configurations must be examined to determine which variables affect the development of cosmopoliteness in peasants. Variables that may enter the picture include self concept and self-awareness, dogmatism, achievement motivation, ability to take risks, interpersonal trust, and intelligence.

5. *Cosmopoliteness across Societal Types.* Cosmopolites have been studied in both more developed and less developed countries. The next step involves comparison. Are cosmopolites in traditional, isolated communities essentially different from cosmopolites in modern systems or can some generalizations be made about cosmopolite behavior that will hold across localite and cosmopolite societies?

6. *Type of Cosmopolite Contact.* What factors affect the type of cosmopolite contact a peasant has? Does the type of cosmopolite contact vary with the peasant's degree of modernization? Perhaps in the early stages of modernization, outsiders entering a village may provide the most frequent type of cosmopolite contact. As the peasant becomes more modern, he may wish to see the larger society for himself, and trips to the city become more frequent. Once literacy skills have been acquired, the peasant may turn to the mass media as his most frequent type of cosmopolite contact.

7. *Relationship of Cosmopoliteness to Other Concepts.* Are cosmopolites also likely to be *opinion leaders* or *gatekeepers?* The fact that the cosmopolite peasant has access to more and varied information may put him in a position of controlling the input of messages to the village, and it may cause other peasants to seek him for opinions.

Does the fact that a peasant maintains cosmopolite interests force him into a position of *marginality* in his local community (or vice versa)?

We know from U.S. studies that migrants to suburban communities often maintain primary interests outside of the residential community. Does the *strangeness* of the peasant in-migrant in a "new" village force him to be cosmopolite?

8. *What is the Cosmopolite?* Is the cosmopolite essentially a localite who also maintains external communication contacts, or is he an entirely different breed? Do external orientations necessarily conflict with internal orientations?

SUMMARY

Cosmopoliteness is the degree to which an individual is oriented outside his immediate social system. We argue that cosmopoliteness plays a central role in the modernization of peasants; the strong empirical relationships found in this chapter support this assertion. Trips to cities were utilized as the primary operation of cosmopoliteness in our Colombian villages. Our paradigm of cosmopoliteness and modernization consists of (1) antecedents to cosmopoliteness, like access to cities, wealth, and so forth; (2) initial cosmopoliteness, which consists of the first contact with the society outside of the village; (3) awareness of modern possibilities; (4) modernization facilitators, such as aroused aspirations, literacy, and active information-seeking; and (5) increased modernization.

Although the time-order aspects of this model could not be tested with a correlational analysis of our Colombia data, socioeconomic variables (like status and level of living) are positively related to cosmopoliteness, which in turn is positively related to such other reflectors of urban contact as mass media exposure and change agent contact. Cosmopoliteness is also related to such modernization variables as achievement motivation, aspirations, education and functional literacy, political knowledgeability, innovativeness, empathy, and (lower) fatalism.

8

Change Agents, Clients, and Change*

I am wont to think that men are not so much the keepers of herds as herds are the keepers of men, the former are so much the freer.   (Henry David Thoreau, in Atkinson 1937:50)

Here is Edward Bear, coming downstairs now, bump, bump, bump, on the back of his head, behind Christopher Robin. It is, as far as he knows, the only way of coming downstairs, but sometimes he feels that there really is another way, if only he could stop bumping for a moment and think of it.   (A.A. Milne, in *Winnie-The-Pooh* 1926:1)

A monkey and a fish were caught in a sudden flood. The monkey scrambled up a tree to safety. Noticing the fish struggling against the current, the monkey was filled with humanitarian desire and rescued the fish from the water. To the monkey's surprise, the fish was ungrateful for this technical aid.

Perhaps this Oriental fable illustrates the relationship of the change agent and his peasant clients (Adams 1960). Motivated by a desire to help, but with a contrasting perspective on change and a different style of life than his clients, the efforts of the change agent are often misunderstood and unappreciated. This chapter discusses the role of the change agent, his relationships with clients, and the various strategies of change he employs to bring about desired effects in his clients' behavior. Perhaps the Thoreau and Milne quotations illustrate the chapter's main themes: (1) the *reciprocity* that characterizes change agent-client relationships, and (2) the greater effectiveness that would be possible if change agents utilized a *strategy* of change.

WHAT IS A CHANGE AGENT?

A *change agent* is a professional who *influences innovation decisions* in a *direction deemed desirable* by a *change agency*.[1] A clearer picture of the role of the change

---

* This chapter was written with the assistance of Robert F. Keith, Assistant Instructor, and Eduardo Ramos, Research Assistant, Department of Communication, Michigan State University.

[1] This definition of change agent is generally consistent with others' conceptions. "Change agent refers to the helper, the person or group who is attempting to effect change (Bennis and others 1962:5). Although these authors do not feel that the change agent must be exogenous to the system, Lippit and others (1958) do. We maintain that he is set off from his clients by the nature of his *professional status* (that is, employment by a change agency), rather than whether he lives in or out (or considers himself a member) of a particular system.

agent can be gained through a detailed consideration of the key terms in this definition.

1. *Influence:* The concept of influence refers to interaction between persons that causes changes in the future behavior or attitudes of the participants (Merton 1957:415). Change agents seek to influence the behavior of their clients. The success of their efforts is measured in terms of (a) client *awareness* of innovations, (b) *persuasion* of the innovation's usefulness, (c) *adoption*, and (d) *reinforcement of continued use*, rather than discontinuance, of the innovations.[2] A change agent must select his strategies of change on the basis of the content of his message, the nature of his audience, the resources at his disposal, and the type of effects he hopes to secure.

2. *Innovation decisions:* Change agents seek to facilitate client decisions to adopt or reject innovations. Individuals adopt new ideas by passing through a cumulative series of stages in the innovation-decision process from (a) awareness (or knowledge) of the innovation, (b) to formation of a favorable attitude toward it, (c) to actual use of the new idea. Efforts in creating awareness and in persuading are aimed at influencing the actual decision. Usually, change agents seek to promote recommended innovations, but they may also oppose new ideas if they feel the innovations would have unfavorable effects on their clients.

3. *Direction deemed desirable:* Change agents operate as tools in the implementation of *planned change* programs. The objectives of these programs presumably represent the change agencies' notion of the directions in which their clients should be changed. Planned change is the alteration of the structure or function of a social system. This results from the efforts by change agents who seek to introduce new ideas in order to reach definite goals. These alterations may occur as the result of mutual undertakings by change agents and their clients, or as the result of coerced change (change without the consent of the client). Most change agents are concerned not only with the promotion of innovations, but also with the development and maintenance of client rapport. However, there are situations when rapport is sometimes ignored in the interest of expediency; for example, in the case of an epidemic, coerced change may become necessary. The change agent's objectives should reflect the clients' needs if the change agent-client relationship is to be kept intact. Planned change programs that take into account the needs of the clientele to determine change objectives stand the greatest chance of success. Thus, clients have at least some effect on the goals of change agencies. This point suggests that there is a good deal of reciprocity in the agent-client interface; each have influence on the behavior of the other in

---

[2] These change agent effects are generally similar to the objective of any purposive communication (Miller 1966:17–18): (1) to increase the acquisition of nonevaluative responses by the receiver (create awareness of new ideas); (2) to affect the acquisition of new evaluative responses by receivers (form attitudes); (3) to alter existing beliefs by affecting the acquisition of different evaluative responses (change attitudes); and (4) to strengthen existing evaluative responses through reinforcement.

reaching mutually satisfying goals through the exchange of knowledge and resources.

4. *Change agency:* Change agents are employees of formal organizations, such as government ministries or commerical companies.

IMPORTANCE OF THE CHANGE AGENT

When it is asked "Why are change agents important?", we are actually posing the question, "Why is planned change important?" In Chapter 1 it was shown that spontaneous change is simply not rapid enough to keep pace with the rapidly rising expectations in less developed countries. It is possible to accelerate the rate of adoption of innovations through the promotional efforts of change agents. Ideally, the change agent also serves as a feedback link from peasants to development planners. He is an organized and routinized communication channel by which plans are put into action, and clients' needs are reflected to the planners. Although a change agent is a potential channel for the upward communication of clients' needs, it seems that he seldom fills this role.

Through the change agent, planned change programs can be modified to suit the particular needs of individuals and villages. Change agents serve to localize innovations and situationally legitimize them. The importance of change agents in less developed nations is emphasized by the huge government expenditures allotted to their training and maintenance. Alternative communication approaches, such as combining mass media and interpersonal channels in media forums, were discussed in Chapter 6. Nonetheless, change agents are still required to organize and to "service" the media forums.[3]

ROLE OF THE CHANGE AGENT

There are seven change agent functions in the process of planned change; each function represents a somewhat different objective in the agent-client relationship (Lippit and others 1958).

1. *Develop a need for change:* The change agent is usually involved in the identification of clients' needs. In some instances, peasants recognize needs and approach the change agent for verification or legitimation of the need. In most cases, however, the change agent is faced with the task of making peasants aware of needs. The short planning horizons, low achievement motivation, high fatalism, and low aspirations characteristic of most peasants, mean that the change agent must serve a catalytic function for client needs. He must point out new alternatives to existing problems, dramatize these solutions, and then convince his clients they can solve the problems that confront them.

[3] Although change agents would be needed in smaller numbers than when they carry the main load in diffusing innovations to villagers.

The needs of the peasant clientele must be recognized if change programs are to be successful. Often we "scratch where they do not itch." As a result, change agents are often faced with a high incidence of the discontinuance of innovations following their initial adoption. In one family planning program in India, 40 percent of those who discontinued cited forced (initial) adoption as their main reason for discontinuing the use of contraceptives (Planning Research and Action Institute 1966:62).

Another example from India illustrates the failure of a planned change program when the clients' needs were overlooked. Government officials provided a village with funds to construct irrigations wells which could approximately double crop yields. But the villagers wanted wells for drinking, as they had to carry their water about 2 miles from a river. So the peasants built the wells in the village center rather than in their fields, and drank the water rather than irrigated their crops. If the change agent had based his program upon the felt needs of the villagers, he would have tried to develop a felt need for irrigation by indicating the financial advantages of this innovation.

2. *Establish a change relationship:* Having created or confirmed a need for change, a change agent must foster a belief among his clients that he is competent, trustworthy, and empathetic with his clients' position. This function of the change agent is not easy. Peasants tend to be distrustful in interpersonal relationships, especially with government officials. Nevertheless, establishing rapport and an acceptable level of interpersonal trust between change agent and client is a prerequisite to successful efforts at change.

3. *Diagnose the problem:* The change agent is responsible for analysis of the clients' problem situation in order to determine why existing behaviors do not meet the clients' needs or objectives. To arrive at his own diagnostic conclusions, the change agent must view the situation from his clients' perspective. He must put himself in his clients' shoes.

4. *Examine goals and alternative courses of action, then create the intent to change in the client:* Peasants are often unable to see alternate courses of action that can be taken to meet goals or solve problems. The change agent must try to explore the various avenues that his clients can take to achieve their goals.

When the first innovations are introduced in a traditional village, whose peasants are characterized by authoritarian-submissive attitudes, a change agent may feel that attempts to explore alternative courses of action with his clients are too time-consuming. The clients may expect the change agent to order them to adopt innovations rather than to explore alternatives with them. Perhaps with subsequent innovations, the change agent can begin to improve the decision-making faculties of his peasant clients.

5. *Translate intent into action so that the client innovates:* The change agent seeks to influence his villagers' behavior in accordance with his recommendations. In essence the agent works to promote compliance with the program he advocates. One way in which the change agent can promote innovation

initiative on the part of peasants is to provide assistance at the trial stage in the innovation-decision process. By helping the client try the innovation, the change agent involves the peasant in actual use of the innovation.[4]

6. *Stabilize change and attempt to prevent discontinuances:* Individuals tend to seek confirming information for decisions they make.[5] Change agents may effectively stabilize new behavior by directing reinforcing messages to those clients who have adopted innovations. By providing support for the new behavior patterns, change agents increase the likelihood that the peasant will continue to use the innovation.

7. *Achieve a terminal relationship:* The goal for any change agent is to develop self-renewing behavior on the part of his clients.[6] The change agent should seek to put himself "out of business" by enabling his clients to be their *own* change agents. The change agent must seek to shift the client from a position of reliance on the change agent to reliance on himself. It is difficult for the change agent to "wean" his clients; often they become more dependent, rather than independent.

ENVIRONMENT OR CLIENT MODIFICATION

The change agent is capable of altering two aspects of any planned change situation: the environment and the client. *Client modification* involves the change agent in a *direct* relationship with the client in which his effect is determined by behavioral changes on the part of the client. When the change agent restructures the physical or sociocultural environment, he is attempting to influence his clients *indirectly*.

Modifying the Environment

1. *Physical environment:* There are numerous instances of change agents seeking to change the clients' physical milieu. Peace Corps volunteers and community development workers often initiate change at the village level by assisting with the construction of schools, roads, wells, and latrines.[7] Client utilization of the new facilities is not automatic, but such physical changes

---

[4] However, Deutschmann and Fals Borda (1962a) found that Colombian peasants rarely tried agricultural innovations on a small-scale basis; instead, they jumped immediately to full-scale adoption.

[5] Evidence for this point is provided by Erlich and others (1957) and Mason (1964).

[6] For a more detailed discussion of self-renewal, see Gardner (1964), who expounds the position that both individuals and institutions must be continually changing if they are to be in adjustment with their environment.

[7] In Chapter 1 it was shown that many innovations fail when introduced to peasants by change agents; however, one of the highest rates of failure must certainly be for latrines. Although latrine construction *can* play an important role in environmental sanitation, most outhouses in peasant villages are idle monuments to change agent ambitiousness. In Colombia, I once observed several thousand newly-built latrines; not one had been used. Villagers were accustomed to defecating in a squatting position, and their culturally-conditioned sphincters were not compatible with the sit-down design of the latrines.

make the clients' modernization more likely; for example, the improvement of roads may increase villagers' cosmopoliteness.

2. *Social environment:* The social environment must be able to support change. In less developed countries, one often finds a complete absence of the social organization necessary for implementation of change programs, or else existing social institutions are unable to cope with the problems of change. In this case the change agent must help provide the needed social structures. For example, a change agent might organize a marketing co-operative in order to introduce greater stability and efficiency into a market system that had previously been erratic and uncoordinated. Village development councils may be formed by change agents to support collective innovations like village wells, roads, schools, and so on.

Modifying the Client

Most commonly, change agents seek to modify their clients' behavior directly. In this case the change agent disseminates information to increase knowledge levels about innovations, and exerts influence to alter or strengthen client attitudes and beliefs to the point where they adopt recommended innovations.

LIAISON ROLE OF THE CHANGE AGENT

Change agents serve as a *linkage* or liaison between two or more social systems:[8] (1) the client social system, and (2) the primary innovation source (Figure 8–1). The client social system may be a single village, a number of villages, or selected individuals (for instance, coffee growers) in several villages. In less developed nations the change agency is usually a government

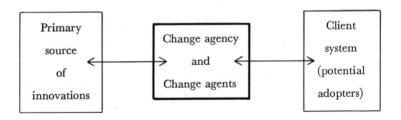

Figure 8–1. Change Agents Are a Communication Linkage between Clients and the Primary Source of Innovations.

[8] Westley and MacLean (1957) posit a general communication model, based upon Newcomb's ABX paradigm, in which C is a role intervening between source and receiver (A and B). C may be a change agent who links B with the source of innovations (the A's). The main function of the C role is the extension of the communication environment of individual B; that is, to link him to more cosmopolite sources of new ideas.

ministry or a company seeking to promote adoption of its products. The primary innovation source is usually an experiment station, university, or some other research organization.

Although it is possible for the primary innovation source to be in direct contact with the client system (Figure 8–1), this is a rather unusual situation in less developed nations. Usually, the change agent must communicate the clients' research needs to the scientists, and in turn disseminate innovations from the research organization to the clients.

Change agents often experience *role conflict* due to their liaison position between social systems with conflicting norms and objectives. Although the change agent is a member of a change agency and with the modernized attitudes and beliefs that accompany development activities, he must also relate to his clientele, who are more traditional. When the norms and objectives of the two systems are more discrepant, the change agent is more likely to experience greater role conflict. Over-identification with either system jeopardizes his relationship with the other group. As a result of his position in cross-pressure, between two reference groups with conflicting norms, the change agent becomes a member of a "third culture."[9]

Priess (1954) found that more successful extension agents in the United States tended to disregard the expectations of the change bureaucracy in favor of those held by their clients.[10] It is doubtful that this finding can be generalized to peasant settings because change agents in less developed nations seem more closely aligned with the change agency than with peasant farmers. The latter often lack the education and sophistication to make them a meaningful reference group for the change agent, and they seldom possess the political power of U.S. farmers over the change agency.

Another source of conflict for change agents is interagency and interagent competition. Change agents promoting similar kinds of programs in the same village are often rivals for clients' attention. Local representatives of ministries of public health, community development, and agriculture all compete for villagers' scarce resources.

[9] Useem and others (1963) use this concept to describe the position of Indian scholars and technicians who have been exposed to Western culture. However, it seems applicable to the role conflict situation faced by most change agents.

[10] An example of similar behavior occurred in Pueblo Viejo at the time of our study. The local school teacher, called "El Professor" by the peasants, had come to Pueblo Viejo a few years before from an urban school. His purpose was to gain an understanding of peasant life through close observation. He was a particularly innovative teacher, introducing such practices as class discussion, localized mimeo books, and coeducational schooling. The latter is forbidden by church and state in Colombia, and El Professor was dismissed from his teaching post in Pueblo Viejo by the Ministry of Education. This is one result of change agent conflict between loyalty to clients and to the change agency. The replacement teacher in Pueblo Viejo immediately reinstated such traditional teaching methods as the lecture method, irrelevant, urban-oriented textbooks, and "segregated" classes. What happened to El Professor? He is now a professor at a teacher training institute in Bogotá, where he influences hundreds of future rural school teachers each year, imbuing them with his desire for educational innovativeness.

CHANGE AGENTS AND CLIENT MODERNIZATION

The previous discussion suggests a complex, multivariate process of modernization at the client level. The *client* and the *change agent* each bring to the situation individual attributes that effect their interaction. Change agent-client interpersonal relationships are expressed in a series of *liaison variables*, which occur in a physical and sociocultural *environment*. The change agent-client relationship is designed to effect changes in the *level of modernization* of the client, which are achieved by utilizing various *change strategies*. These six primary components are diagrammed in Figure 8–2. One can note a basic similarity between this paradigm and the S-M-C-R-E communication model (Chapter 3); the change agent is the source of modernizing messages, which are communicated to his receivers (clients) in order to obtain desired modernization effects.

CHANGE AGENT CONTACT WITH CLIENTS

Although a great many variables undoubtedly determine change agent effectiveness,[11] attention in this section will focus on the degree of *contact* or communication between change agents and their clients. In order for change agents to have new ideas adopted by their clients, they must have contact with them. The change agents' time and energy are scarce resources, so he must concentrate his interpersonal communication on those clients (1) who will be the most responsive, that is, peasants who are already more modernized, of higher social status, and so on, or (2) who need his assistance the most, that is, villagers who are more traditional.[12] *Most change agents have higher contact with clients who are characterized by greater innovativeness, higher social status, and more education, than their counterparts* (Table 8–1). This "eliteness bias," the tendency for change agents to contact their higher status and more modernized clients,[13] is also found in the Colombia villages (Table 8–2), but the correlations are not very strong, and a number are not significant.

When the correlates of change agent contact in Colombia are compared with similar results in India and Kenya (Table 8–2), it can be seen that

[11] A paradigm that includes a number of such variables that might be studied in future inquiries is shown later in this chapter.

[12] This statement implies that the *change agent* determines which clients he will contact. In reality, the clients also determine whether or not they will seek the change agent for information and advice.

[13] Planners of the U.S. War on Poverty programs insisted that the poverty class be represented by its own leaders on citizen committees to guide the programs. However, in practice few of the poor are eager to seek leadership roles, and even if elected, they lack the needed skills of group problem-solving, parlimentary procedure, and regular meeting attendance. As a result, the relatively more elite *among the poor* eventually gravitate into leadersip roles, raising some doubts as to whether the viewpoints of the real poverty class are represented.

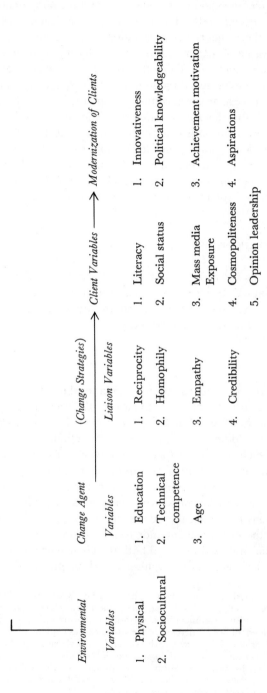

Figure 8–2. Paradigm of Change Agent-Client Communication and Modernization.

formal participation, mass media exposure, social status, and cosmopoliteness are most consistently and strongly related to change agent contact. Tables 8–1 and 8–2 also show that those clients who have more change agent contact are typified by a higher degree of modernization, especially innovativeness. Nevertheless, the relationships shown in Table 8–2 are not very strong, and whereas almost all are in the expected direction, many are not significant.

Relatively little variation in change agent contact is explained in a multiple correlation analysis. In Colombia, 3 variables (formal participation, political knowledgeability, and achievement motivation) account for only 16 percent of the variance; in India, 5 variables (knowledge about change agents, functional literacy, family literacy, indebtedness, and attitude toward change agents) account for only 11 percent of the variance.[14] There is much room for improvement in attempts to explain variance in change agent contact.

CHANGE AGENT-CLIENT RELATIONSHIPS

The nature of relationships between the change agent and his clients involves several variables, that can be viewed as separate concepts, but which must be considered, in reality, as a series of interacting dimensions. They are reciprocity, homophily, empathy, and credibility.

RECIPROCITY

Gans (1962) describes the change agent-client relationship as one of reciprocity; that is, the behaviors of each affect the other. The change agents (social workers) in Gans' study of Boston's urban poor thought that they were helping their clients to learn middle class values such as punctuality, respect for property, and so on, which would aid them in the world of work. The clients, in contrast, felt that they had control by not causing disturbances at settlement house youth parties and by providing the change agents with large (official) work loads, which the social workers needed to justify the donations and appropriations on which they depended for support. In return, the clients expected the change agents not to seek to tamper overly with their lower class values and attitudes. So both the change agents and their clients viewed their relationship as manipulative and reciprocal. Each

---

[14] In the Colombia analysis, empathy, occupational aspirations, family size, farm size, mass media exposure, opinion leadership, level of living, functional literacy, cosmopoliteness, education, and land tenure did not significantly contribute to the multiple correlation. With all the variables included, only 19.5 percent of the variance was explained; thus the deleted variables accounted for only 2.5 percent of the variance. The deleted variables in the India analysis include farm size, level of living, value of agricultural products, mechanization, empathy, mass media exposure, formal participation, knowledgeability, cosmopoliteness, education, and achievement motivation. These variables together account for only 1 percent of the variance in change agent contact.

Table 8–1. Variables Related to Change Agent Contact[a]

Variables Related to Change Agent Contact	Number of Research Studies Reporting			*Number of Countries in Which Studies Were Done*
	Positive Relationship with Change Agent Contact	No Relationship with Change Agent Contact	Negative Relationship with Change Agent Contact	
I. Client attributes				
1. Social status	45	6	5	7
2. Formal participation	24	0	3	4
3. Education	25	3	1	5
4. Opinion leadership	16	1	0	4
II. Modernization variables				
5. Innovativeness	125	8	0	14

[a] The "data" shown in this table come from the Diffusion Documents Center at Michigan State University, where the findings contained in 1290 publications dealing with the diffusion of new ideas have been content-analyzed.   The unit of analysis in this table is a research publication.

Table 8–2. Cross-Cultural Comparison of Correlates of Change Agent Contact

Variables Correlated with Change Agent Contact	Zero-Order Correlation with Change Agent Contact				
	Colombian Modern Villages (N = 160)	A Colombian Traditional Village (N = 54)[c]	India UNESCO (N = 702)	India Punjab (N = 84)	Kenya (N = 624)
I. Client attributes					
1. Social status	.201[a]	[.234]	.177[b]	—[d]	—[d]
2. Functional literacy	[.086]	[.047]	.158[b]	[−.088]	.156[b]
3. Level of living	[.029]	[.083]	.134[b]	[.109]	.250[b]
4. Formal participation	.332[b]	.337[a]	.141[b]	.293[b]	.172[b]
5. Cosmopoliteness	[.146]	.513[b]	[−.007]	.438[b]	[.077]
6. Education	[−.023]	.297[a]	.146[b]	[.111]	.123[b]
7. Mass media exposure	[.078]	.368[b]	.080[a]	.366[b]	.255[b]
8. Opinion leadership	—[d]	—[d]	.082[a]	.320[b]	—[d]
II. Modernization variables					
9. Agricultural innovativeness	.171[a]	.378[b]	.165[b]	.404[b]	.313[b]
10. Home innovativeness	[.140]	[.184]	.167[b]	[.208]	.295[b]
11. Achievement motivation	.235[b]	[.143]	.166[a]	[.196]	[.031]
12. Educational aspirations	[.031]	.585[b]	.126[b,e]	[−.103]	[−.038]
13. Occupational aspirations	[.058]	[.207]		.314[b]	—[d]
14. Empathy	.228[b]	[.069]	.162[b]	[.211]	—[d]

[a] Significant at the 5 percent level.
[b] Significant at the 1 percent level.
[c] There was no change agent contact in Nazate, so only the 54 peasant respondents in La Cañada could be included here.
[d] These variables were not measured, and so no correlation with change agent contact could be computed.
[e] This correlation represents a composite of both occupational and educational aspirations.

party had certain resources and activities that the other needed; each thought they were helping the other.

We maintain that there is a certain degree of reciprocity in most change agent-client relationships, whether the change agent is a VLW in an Indian village, a school teacher in rural Colombia, or an extension worker in the United States. Unfortunately, there is little scientific inquiry to date on the exact nature of the reciprocal give-and-take between clients and change agents in less developed countries. Perhaps one reason why lower class and less innovative clients have less contact with change agents is because they do not perceive such a communication exchange as rewarding. They may, in fact, misperceive the change agent as an authoritarian disciplinarian (as, in fact, some change agents may be[15]). Likewise, there are organizational pressures on the change agent to produce results, usually in the form of client adoption of new ideas that he is promoting. This forces him to interact most frequently with those clients who he feels are most responsive to his persuasive efforts. These are usually clients who are more innovative and of higher status, and who are most like (that is, homophilous with) the change agent in his characteristics and attitudes.

HOMOPHILY

Homophily is the degree to which pairs of individuals who interact are similar in certain attributes. It has already been pointed out that change agents tend to interact most with their more elite clients.[16] *Communication is more effective when a higher degree of homophily is present;* that is, when source and receiver are more similar in certain attributes. An homophilous pair share common meanings and interests; they are better able to empathize with each other because their roles are similar. Further, greater reciprocity is involved when the change agent and client are more similar to each other.

One implication for change agencies of the homophily-effective communication propostion is that they should select change agents who are as alike their clients as possible. If most of the clients in a target system only possess two or three years of formal schooling, a university-trained change agent will face greater communication difficulties than if he had less education.[17] Evidence for this statement comes from a study by the Allahabad

---

[15] There is reason to expect that change agents may be more authoritarian in their dealings with their more laggardly and lower status clients than with their more elite clients.

[16] In Chapter 10 we show the homophilous nature of interpersonal communication between peasants in our Colombian villages. There is a general tendency, albeit a rather weak one, for peasants to interact with those who are similar in innovativeness, mass media exposure, social status, age, literacy, cosmopoliteness, and formal participation. A higher degree of homophily characterizes friendship pairs than information- and opinion-seeking relationships among our Colombian villagers (Chou 1966).

[17] And he will have the most severe problems in communicating effectively with any but the most highly educated of his clients.

Agricultural Institute (1957) in India. Village-level change agents with only an elementary education were more effective in reaching Indian villagers than were change agents with high school or university education.

Unfortunately, most change agents must try to communicate with clients who are much different than themselves in formal education, attitudes toward change, technical competence, and other attributes. In fact, if the clients did not differ from the change agent on these dimensions, the change agent would not have much of a role to play in the modernization process; the clients would already be as modern as the change agent.[18]

The wide subcultural variability within most less developed nations further aggravates the degree of heterophily between change agent and client. For example, because he spoke a different Ibo dialect than his clients, an Ibo extension worker in Eastern Nigeria, employed only about 70 miles from his home village, was forced to communicate with his clients in pidgin English, which only a few of his clients fully understood. Government change agencies in India select village level workers who are usually from a neighboring village,[19] which helps to ensure linguistic and ethnic homophily with peasant clients. In the Colombian villages of study, the extension change agents were university-level graduates in technical agriculture, who had been raised in urban environments.[20] One of the strategies of change they utilized in the modern villages to bridge the "heterophily gap" with their peasant clients was to work through village opinion leaders. Perhaps a reason why most change agents concentrate their efforts on opinion leaders is to halve the social distance[21] between themselves and the majority of their clients, as well as to gain credibility for their innovations through gaining the tacit endorsement of the leaders. But as will be pointed out in Chapter 10, if the opinion leaders are *too* much more innovative than their fellow villagers, the heterophily gap to effective communication that formerly existed between the change agents and their clients, now exists between the opinion leaders and

[18] In fact, a situation approaching this extreme now occurs in some counties in the United States where farmers are becoming almost as well educated and technically competent as county extension agents, at least in certain specialized types of agriculture, such as fruit and vegetable production, poultry-raising, and mink-growing. Once, the county agent was the only college-educated individual in his county. Now the county extension workers are forced to seek graduate-level education in order to "stay ahead" of their clients; nevertheless, increasing numbers of farmers take their problems directly to agricultural scientists at state universities or commercial companies, thus circumventing local extension agents, who the farmers no longer view as credible.

[19] But not from the same village in which the change agent will be assigned to work, as such a high degree of familiarity seems to lead to lower change agent credibility in the clients' eyes.

[20] This is a common background for agricultural extension workers in most Latin American countries.

[21] Ramos (1966) found that the more social distance our Colombian peasants perceived between themselves and the extension workers, the less favorable attitudes they held toward the change agents, the less credibility they placed in them, and the less interpersonal communication they had with the change agents.

their peers. Many change agents make the strategic mistake of selecting opinion leaders who are too much like change agents, and not enough like their average client. Such too-innovative opinion leaders are often eager to demonstrate new ideas that the change agent is promoting. The problem is that these ambitious opinion leaders are *too* elite; they serve as an unrealistic model for the average client, and he knows it.

So the language of the change agent is often different from the language of the client, and a village opinion leader can only help to bridge this heterophily gap if he is enough like the larger village audience that the change agent is attempting to reach.

EMPATHY

Ramos (1966) found that Colombian peasants' ability to empathize with the change agent role was closely related to the amount of interpersonal contact the peasant had with the change agent. This finding may reflect the tendency for change agents to have more contact with those peasants who are more empathic, or, on the other hand, it could indicate that the more contact clients have with change agents, the more familiar they become with the role, and are thus able to empathize more fully with it. Although the empathic ability of the client has been studied in relationship to his innovativeness and change agent contact, no studies have focused on the empathic ability of the change agent.

The change agent's ability to empathize with his clients is undoubtedly an important factor in his success. In fact, a previously-discussed proposition about homophily and effective communication should now be modified to account for the degree of empathy, so as to read: *Communication is less effective when a low degree of homophily is present, unless the source has a high degree of empathy with the receiver.* Even though his clients may be much different from himself, an empathic change agent can communicate effectively with them.

If empathy is so important in change agent effectiveness, how can it be increased? One way is in the selection of change agents; those who have actually been in the clients' role are probably better to empathize with it. Thus, agricultural change agencies often seek to employ change agents who come from farm backgrounds. Sometimes novice change agents are given empathy training by living with a peasant family for some weeks or months, so that they are able to see the world through the eyes of their clients.[22] Likewise role-playing (in which the change agent is asked to act hypotheti-

---

[22] While in Colombia I helped organize such a training experience for a group of Latin American agrarian reform officials. Each such change agent was required to live with a peasant family in an isolated village for about two weeks. During the first days of this empathy training, these urban-oriented officials complained bitterly about the bad food, poor living conditions (such as rats which prevented them from sleeping soundly), "stupidity" of their hosts, etc. By the end of their visit, however, most of the trainees seemed to be able to see government change programs through the villager's eyes.

cally the role of the client) is sometimes utilized as a technique in the training of change agents to teach them to empathize with their clients. This kind of initial empathy with clients must be maintained over time; continuing empathy with clients is most effectively gained by being feedback-minded and receiver-oriented. The change agent's capacity to obtain accurate feedback from his clients depends, in part, upon the closeness of his rapport with them.

Perhaps there is an ideal level of change agent empathy with clients. Most change agents do not have enough empathy, but it is possible that a change agent could become so empathetic with his clients that he would no longer wish to change them. In this extreme case, he would perceive his program only through his clients' eyes, that is, unfavorably. Although such an instance is probably rare, one is reminded of the anthropological observer among the Pueblo Indians who joined the tribe (Katz 1963:25).

The most appropriate degree of change agent empathy with clients may depend, in part, on the clients' level of empathy with the change agent. Gans (1962) found that most of the social workers in a Boston slum had a relatively low degree of empathy with their clients, whereas the slum residents were able to take the role of the change agents with greater ease. The clients therefore had a certain advantage in their manipulative engagements with the social workers; the clients understood the nature of the change agents' objectives and could act accordingly, but the lack of empathy in the reverse direction worked to the disadvantage of the social workers. There is no parallel research of this nature among peasants in less developed nations, and it is needed.[23]

CREDIBILITY

Credibility is the degree to which a communication source or channel is perceived as trustworthy and competent by the receiver. A basic proposition from laboratory-experimental studies in communication is that the degree to which an individual's attitudes change is positively related to the credibility with which he perceives the source (or channel[24]) of persuasive messages. If a client perceives that a change agent possesses relatively higher credibility than various other sources and channels, the client can be expected to be more receptive to messages from that change agent.

Among the Colombian respondents, we sought to determine the relative credibility they placed in extension change agents in comparison with five other sources of information about agricultural innovations. The peasants

[23] Such inquiry might focus on change agent-client dyads as the unit of analysis. Other variables than change agent and client empathy should be included in this type of investigation, such as perceived reciprocity, authoritarianism, homophily, and credibility.

[24] It is very difficult to distinguish between source and channel credibility in most non-laboratory communication situations, although the usual convention is to speak of "source credibility."

were sequentially presented with these six sources in the form of all possible pairs[25] and asked which source in each combination they felt was more credible. Figure 8–3 shows the high relative credibility attributed to the extension worker, followed by the school teacher, radio, neighbors, commercial farm salesman, and newspapers. This ranking on credibility is only on the basis of agricultural innovations, and might be quite different from other types of messages such as political or international news. One should also remember (1) that the extension change agent was undoubtedly highly competent in technical agriculture, since he was a university graduate and had been working intensively for five or six years in the villages of study, and (2) that the village norms were favorable to innovation and change. Where these conditions are not present, extension change agents may be perceived as less credible. Unfortunately, there is no comparable data from the two traditional villages in Colombia to test this suppostion.[26]

Commercial change agents have much lower credibility in the eyes of the Colombian peasants than the extension worker or the school teacher. The sellers of agricultural products like fertilizers, weed sprays, and seeds are not as technically competent (especially in their level of formal education) as the extension worker. Further, they may not be perceived as trustworthy by our peasant respondents who suspect them of a primary interest in profit, rather than in helping the villagers.[27] A similar low credibility for commercial change agents has been found for U.S. farmers (Rogers 1962).

Why do newspapers have such low credibility among the respondents (Figure 8–3)? It may be due to the lack of content devoted to agricultural innovations in Colombia, where none of our interviewees reported this channel in their adoption of a new weed spray (Chapter 6).

Figure 8–3 masks *individual* differences in the perceived credibility of the extension change agent. Obviously, some peasants view this change agent as more credible than do others. Generally, the respondents with highest extension worker credibility are those with whom he works most closely; they have a higher degree of change agent contact, more social status, and larger farms. This finding suggests that when communication with change agents is

[25] This method of determining source credibility is called the paired comparison technique. Its advantage is that it simplifies the stimuli alternatives presented to the respondent in each question; its disadvantage is that it can require considerable interview time if the number of alternatives is large.

[26] However, Herzog (1967b) reports almost identical credibility rankings for 1307 Brazilian peasants in 20 modern and traditional villages; newspapers scored 0.000; radio, 0.250; and extension change agents, 1.240.

[27] The relatively low credibility of commercial change agents is also suggested by the data on communication channels for 2, 4-D weed spray (Table 6–2), where farm store personnel are reported most often in creating awareness of the innovation and in informing peasants about how to use the spray at the trial stage, but not in convincing them to adopt at the persuasion stage (where credibility is probably most important). A somewhat similar, but less marked, tendency can also be noted for extension workers in Table 6–2, which suggests their proportionately greater credibility.

rewarding (as it evidently was in the present case), those clients with greater contact perceive them as more credible. Or perhaps higher credibility leads to greater contact. In any event, future investigation should indicate those

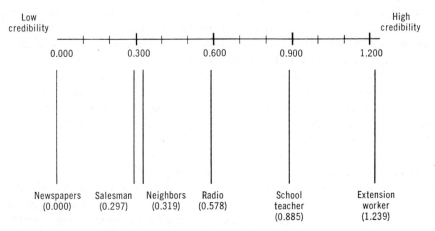

Figure 8-3. Relative Credibility of Six Sources-Channels for Agricultural Innovations in the Three Modern Colombian Villages.

The paired comparison technique was used to obtain these data, which show that the relative credibility of sources (or channels) of agricultural innovations range from extension change agents (highest credibility) to newspapers (lowest credibility). The reader is cautioned that these particular findings may be somewhat idiosyncratic to the three Colombian villages of study, due to their modern norms and the technical competence of the change agent, although they are supported by Herzog's (1967b) data from Brazil.

factors which lead to higher change agent credibility, as well as the modernization consequents of such credibility.[28]

STRATEGIES FOR PLANNED CHANGE

Although the complexity and uniqueness of any specific change situation mitigates against all-inclusive strategies for planned change,[29] some strategy guidelines of a general sort are apparent from past research.

[28] The research of Herzog (1967b) and McLeod and others (1967) suggests there may not be very high relationships between mass media credibility and such modernization variables as political knowledge.

[29] In fact, one of the most unanimous recommendations of 445 technical assistance workers in 13 less developed countries, who were surveyed by Hyman and others (1967: 179), is the importance of utilizing flexibility in selecting strategies of change. Appropriate strategies should be chosen to suit local conditions.

CULTURAL FIT

Programs of change will be more successful if they are relatively compatible with the existing cultural beliefs, attitudes, and values of the clients. Attempts to eradicate the habitat of the tsetse fly in Northern Nigeria, in the hope of reducing the incidence of sleeping sickness disease, were largely unsuccessful because the peasants did not believe there was a relationship between the insect and the illness. Many other change programs fail because they seek to swim against the tide of clients' cultural values. As the discrepancy between existing and advocated positions increases, resistance to change is likely to increase. Change agents must have knowledge of their clients' attitudes and beliefs and their social norms and leadership structure, if their programs of change are to be tailored to fit the clients.

CLIENT PARTICIPATION

Involving the targets (clients) in the planning of change increases the likelihood of success. Such involvement (1) helps insure that the clients' unique *needs* are considered in planning the change program; (2) increases client commitment to decisions which are made, as a result of their participation in the decision-making processes, and (3) helps legitimize collective innovation decisions (such as the construction of a well or road or formation of a cooperative), if the village power-holders participate in the planning process.

CLIENTS' EVALUATIVE ABILITY

The underlying strategy of every change agent should be the improvement of his clients' ability to seek information, to define alternatives, to evaluate these alternatives, and to take action to adopt or reject new ideas. In the process of escalating the rate of innovation adoption, change agents sometimes neglect the development of their clients' evaluative capacities.[30] Self-reliance and self-renewing behaviors should be the goals of any strategy for planned change, leading eventually to termination of the clients' dependence upon the change agents.

OPINION LEADERS

The time and energy of the change agent are scarce resources. By focusing his communication activities upon opinion leaders in a social system, he may increase the rate of diffusion. Economy of effort is achieved because the time

---

[30] When this happens, the change agent has sacrificed long-term progress for the sake of short-run gain. An illustration comes from an agriculural change agent in India, who persuaded his clients to adopt nitrogen fertilizer as the result of an energetic communication campaign, but he did not teach them anything about the principles of how fertilizers stimulate plant growth in the process. The next year, when superphosphate fertilizer became available, the change agent had to repeat his campaign approach, since his clients still had not gained the ability to evaluate innovations by themselves.

and resources involved in contacting opinion leaders is far less than if each member of the client system were to be reached. Essentially, the leader approach magnifies the change agent's efforts. He can communicate the innovation to a few opinion leaders, and then let word-of-mouth communication channels spread the new idea from there. Even such charismatic and dedicated change agents as Christ and Lenin used disciples to increase and rally their followers to new idealogies (Dahl 1961:96).

Furthermore, by enlisting the aid of leaders, the change agent provides the aegis of local sponsorship and sanction for his ideas. Directed change takes on the guise of spontaneous change. Working through leaders improves the credibility of the innovation, thereby increasing its probability of adoption. In fact, after the opinion leaders in a social system have adopted an innovation, it may be impossible to stop its further spread.

Change agents sometimes mistake innovators for opinion leaders. They may be the same individuals, especially in villages with very modern norms, but often are not. The opinion leaders possess a following, whereas the innovators are the first to adopt new ideas and may not have a following. When the change agent concentrates his communication efforts on innovators, rather than opinion leaders, the results may help to increase awareness knowledge of the innovations, but they are unlikely to persuade many clients to adopt because the innovators' behavior is not likely to persuade the average client to follow suit. A related difficulty occurs when a change agent correctly identifies the opinion leaders in a system, but then procedes to concentrate so much of his attention on these few leaders that they may become *too* innovative in the eyes of their followers, or may be perceived as too friendly and overly-identified with the change agent.[31]

NEEDED RESEARCH ON CHANGE AGENTS, CLIENTS, AND CHANGE

Several types of needed research, such as on change agent contact, empathy, and change agent credibility, have already been suggested in this chapter. In this section two further types of future inquiry will be described, one dealing with an explanation of change agent success, and the other with a systems analysis of vertical communication in change agencies.

EXPLAINING SUCCESS AND FAILURE OF VILLAGE PROGRAMS OF PLANNED CHANGE

We already know a good deal, and have ambitious plans to learn more, about the modernization of *individuals* in less developed countries. Unfortunately a parallel type of research on development in which one seeks to

---

[31] Further detail on this point is provided in Chapter 10.

explain the relative success of programs of planned change with the *village* as the unit of analysis has been almost ignored. There are vast numbers of single village studies by anthropologists and sociologists; these community ethnologies serve only in a "for-instance" sense to the administrators of national change agencies in less developed countries. Planners of change need to know "less" about "more"; specifically, they require guidelines concerning the kinds of villages in which new change programs should be first launched in order to achieve a high likelihood of success. Further, administrators and planners need an understanding of why the same program of planned change succeeds in certain villages and fails in others. Is success or failure explained by the nature of the village social structure, by the level of modernization of the village (especially its leaders), by the strategies of change utilized by the local change agent, or by a combination of these factors?

These queries can be answered only with data from a *number* of villages that are representative of a less developed nation, or a region or province within it. Two such inquiries are now underway on a multinational basis. One research project,[32] headquartered at Michigan State University,[33] is investigating the relative success of planned change programs in 69 Brazilian communities, 71 Nigerian villages, and 108 Indian villages. Pairs of villages are contrasted in this approach; in one member of each pair, the change program has been successful in securing the adoption of new ideas (mostly agricultural), whereas the same program has been relatively unsuccessful in the other village.

Among the antecedent variables utilized in this study are the following:

1. *Village social structure* indicators, such as the degree of clique differentiation, opinion leadership concentration, and the concensus of village leaders.

2. *Village modernization levels* as measured by the degree of institutional development,[34] external communication contact, and the modernization of village leaders.

3. *Change agency variables*, such as the degree of feedback to the local change agent about his program's success, rapport with his clients, and how favorably he is perceived by them.

A paradigm of these, and other, antecedent variables conceptualized as important in explaining the relative success of village change programs is

[32] The other investigation has recently been initiated by Professors George Dalton and Erma Edelman at Norhwestern University. The objective is a secondary analysis of existing social science data about villages in Mexico, Nigeria, and India to explain success-failure of village programs of planned change.

[33] Conducted by faculty members in the Department of Communication; see Whiting (1967) and Fliegel and others (1967).

[34] A concept measured by the presence in the village of cooperatives, schools, various types of businesses, and so on. Such an index was constructed for 24 Mexican villages and for 54 peasant communities in the world by Young and Young (1962). It is hypothesized that the adoption of new ideas is facilitated when village institutions are well-developed, as such an institutional base is needed for the adoption of many innovations.

depicted in Figure 8–4. To date, early analysis of the Brazilian data suggests that a rather high percentage of the variance in the dependent variable is explained by the effect of the antecedent variables (Whiting and others,

ANTECEDENT VARIABLES[a]   *CONSEQUENT VARIABLES*

I. VILLAGE SOCIAL STRUCTURE
  1. —Clique differentiation
  2. +Opinion leadership concentration
  3. +Social status concentration
  4. +Consensus on village problems and solutions

II. VILLAGE MODERNIZATION LEVEL   RELATIVE SUCCESS OF
  1. +Institutional development   CHANGE PROGRAM IN
  2. +External contact   THE VILLAGE
  3. +Modernization of village leaders

III. CHANGE AGENCY VARIABLES
  1. +Degree to which needs and motivations of villagers are recognized by change agents
  2. +Adaptation to the social-cultural values and social structure of the village
  3. +Feedback orientation of the change agent
  4. +Rapport with villagers
  5. +Perception of change agent by clients
  6. —Bureaucratic versus client-orientation of the change agent
  7. +Credibility of the clients in the change agent
  8. +Change agents' knowledge of strategies of change.

Figure 8–4. Paradigm of Variables Explaining Success-Failure of Village Programs of Planned Change.

 [a] The positive or negative sign preceding each antecedent variable indicates the expected direction of its relationship with the consequent variable.

1967; Fliegel and others, 1967). Further, the change agency variables in the paradigm seem to be especially important in explaining the success of change programs.

A SYSTEMS ANALYSIS OF VERTICAL COMMUNICATION IN CHANGE AGENCIES

Observers of change agencies in countries like India point out that (1) communication *within* a change agency is often a greater problem than (2) communication *from* local change agents to their clients. In other words, it is more difficult to change the change agents' behavior than the farmers'.

When one looks at the nature of the entire communication system in most less developed countries, he is struck by the many dysfunctions that ultimately act to impede the dissemination of innovations and their adoption by peasants. A considerable time has been spent discussing the communication breakdowns that occur at the level of the peasant village, assuming that adaptable, potentially profitable innovations exist as a result of competent research, that effective change agencies are available to transmit this technology from scientist to client, that the peasant has access to adequate credit and markets, and so on.

The research evidence to date leads us to question seriously such implicit assumptions. For example, in the case of agriculture:

1. Most less developed countries lack a ready stock of culturally and climatically adapted agricultural innovations at the present time.[35] Many nonadapted innovations diffused by agricultural change agencies, like extension services, have failed when adopted by peasants. This leads to further reinforcement of negative attitudes toward new ideas in farming and to lower change agent credibility in the farmers' eyes.

Why do we lack adapted innovations? Most agricultural research is done in temperate climates. The results of such investigation must be subjected to extensive adaptation research in tropical and semitropical settings before useful innovations result.[36] More often than not this latter step is ignored.

The farmers' *needs* for research are seldom communicated "up" to agricultural scientists. This may be due to the fact that change agencies like extension services are largely oriented to "downward" communication. Another aspect of the problem lies in the attitudes and communication styles of the agricultural scientists themselves. For example, a leading fertilizer researcher at an agricultural experiment station in one Latin American country proudly showed me a file case of data accumulated from years of research. He acted surprised when asked why he had not disseminated his findings to extension workers or farmers.

2. There is often a lack of coordination between the organizations responsible for research, extension (diffusion), and change agent training in agriculture. Rather than striving through mutual teamwork to improve farm production, these organizations often compete with one another. Similarly, cooperative relationships are seldom found between agricultural agencies

---

[35] There are few innovations with a potential profitability of 20 to 30 percent (over existing practice), which some observers feel is necessary in order to convince villagers to adopt. Some even estimate minimum profitability at a higher level: "To induce farmers to change, the potential pay-off must be high — not 5 to 10 percent but 50 to 100 percent" (President's Science Advisory Committee 1967:16).

[36] This adaptation type of research is necessary not only in agriculture, but also for every kind of innovation introduced in less developed nations. When new ideas are not properly adapted, development efforts are like an attempt to transplant cut flowers that do not have roots in the indigenous culture (Dart 1963). The flowers wilt and die because of the eager haste. The whole process suggests an attempt to present the Hoover Dam power system to St. Thomas Aquinas.

and their counter parts in community development, health, and public education, even though all of these organizations are trying to assist the same peasant clients to higher levels of living.

3. Most change agencies are characterized by ineffective vertical communication across hierarchical lines. As a result, national policies seldom reach the local change agent, and feedback from the operational level rarely reaches the top administrator.[37] Those at the top are thus forced to make decisions with less than full knowledge of the situation at the operational level.

4. Local change agents are often technically incompetent in agriculture, as well as in their understanding of the strategies of change. This is due in part to a lack of coordination between agricultural research and the training institutions that produce change agents. The result is that many peasants have little faith in agricultural change agents, extension workers reach relatively few farmers, and those contacted are seldom the village opinion leaders who could informally spread the change agents' messages.

5. Lastly, the number of extension workers is far from adequate.

Our view of the problem illustrates the nature of the general inefficiency and ineffectiveness of may institutionalized communication systems in less developed countries. A *systems analysis* of agricultural communication, from the origin of the innovations to their adoption by farmers, is needed. Such a systems approach to investigating a *total system* of innovation diffusion is a natural outgrowth of various research efforts already underway.

A great deal of useful knowledge about within-village (horizontal") diffusion of innovations is being learned. Such data give us understanding of the communication system from the veiwpoint of the peasant and the local change agent. This is a rich data base upon which to build, but it is just a starting point.

Problems of agricultural communication bear a similarity to those in parallel ministry structures like education. Since 1965, a research project has been underway on the diffusion of educational practices in Thailand.[38] Data have been gathered from a national sample of Thai secondary schools through interviews with teachers, principals, and their ministry supervisors about ten educational innovations (examples are objective tests, classroom discussion, school libraries, slide projectors, and so on) recommended and

[37] This ineffective vertical communication traces, at least in part, to the great heterophily between hierarchical levels in these change agencies; the top administrators differ widely from local change agents in amount of education, attitudes, technical knowledge, and so on. Upward negative feedback is particularly rare, as lower-level bureaucrats do not wish their superiors to know about failures.

[38] Sponsored by Michigan State University, the University of Pittsburgh Consortium for Institution-Building, the Ford Foundation, and the United States Agency for International Development, and conducted jointly by the Department of Communication and the Institute for International Studies in Education at Michigan State University.

promoted by top ministry officials. Many of these innovations, which teachers have been persuaded to adopt, have not been correctly utilized.[39]

The essential feature of systems analysis involves gathering data from all levels in a total system; that is, from all the subsystems, as to how they presently function and the interrelationships or interactions among these subsystems.[40] Such a systems approach is expected to yield implications for improvement in the functioning of the entire system.

To date, there has been no such attempt to perform a systems analysis of the entire communication process for a particular type of innovation (like agriculture, family planning, or education) in a less developed country; a great deal could be gained from such inquiry.

SUMMARY

A *change agent* is a professional who influences innovation decisions in a direction deemed desirable by a change agency. The role of the change agent includes the following: developing a need for change among the clients; establishing a change relationship with them; diagnosing the client's problem; examining the clients' goals and alternatives; then creating the intent to change in the client; encouraging the client to innovate; stabilizing the changed behavior so as to prevent discontinuance; and achieving a terminal relationship with the client. Thus the change agent has a role to play at each stage of the clients' innovation-decision process. However in the case of 2, 4-D weed spray in Colombia, change agent contact was most frequently mentioned at the awareness and trial stages, and least at the persuasion stage (Chapter 6).

Essentially, the change agent serves as a communication linkage between his clients and the primary innovation source. As such, the change agent is often subject to role conflict because of his loyalty to two reference groups who have different norms regarding change.

Most change agents have higher contact with clients who are characterized by greater innovativeness, higher social status, and more education. This eliteness bias in change agent contact was found in Colombia and also in the companion investigations in India and Kenya, but the relationships were not very strong.

The change agent-client relationship is characterized by reciprocity in that each expects to exchange with the other. Less elite clients may not

[39] Another finding of the Thailand study is that many new educational ideas flow upward from teachers to principals and supervisors, rather than downward, from ministry officials to teachers, as it had expected would be the case.

[40] The analysis of these "relational data" will certainly call for use of relationships (like dyads) as the units of analysis rather than individuals, as has been the case, often inappropriately, in most past social science inquiry (Coleman 1958).

perceive potential rewards from interaction with change agents, and this perception may explain their lower contact. *Homophily* is the degree to which pairs of individuals who interact are similar in certain attributes. Communication is more effective when a higher degree of homophily is present. This is further reason for the eliteness bias in change agent contact; they interact with those clients who are most like themselves (that is, more educated, innovative, and of higher social status). If the source, like a change agent, has high empathy with his receivers, communication may be effective even when low homophily is present.

Credibility is the degree to which a communication source or channel is perceived as trustworthy and competent by the receiver. Among the peasants in modern Colombian villages, extension change agents were perceived as highly credible sources for agricultural innovations.

Change agents' programs are more likely to be successful if they (1) fit the clients' cultural beliefs and values, (2) involve clients in planning change, (3) increase clients' ability to evaluate innovations, and (4) use opinion leaders to spread the program.

Future research is especially needed on explaining change agent success or failure, and on a systems analysis of vertical communication in change agencies in less developed nations.

A basic assumption that is implied throughout this chapter is that change agents should use strategies of change so that their efforts are maximized. Unfortunately, many change agents simply try to engage in *more* communication activities (such as conducting demonstrations, holding meetings for clients, and so on). They do not follow strategies of change, seemingly being too busy to do so.

9

Empathy: Lubricant of Modernization*

What would you do if you were President of Turkey?
(Research Interviewer)

My God! How can you ask such a thing? How can I . . . I cannot . . . President of Turkey . . . Master of the whole world!!
(Turkish peasant with low empathy, quoted by Lerner 1958:3)

One of the best known noneconomic theories of modernization, proposed by Professor Daniel Lerner (1958) of MIT, is based on the concept of empathy. This "capacity to see oneself in the other fellow's situation" is claimed by Lerner to be the lubricant which facilitates the modernization process in which literacy, mass media exposure, and other variables alter a traditional individual's style of life. Although some social scientists have criticized various aspects of this social-psychological theory of modernization, few adequate replications of Lerner's work have been attempted, and few alternatives to Lerner's paradigm have been suggested. Lerner's model of modernization is particularly appealing because of its communication point of view: he depicts the transformation of traditional lifeways occurring as a result of modernizing messages.

Our intention is to conceptualize further and examine the role of empathy in modernization, to develop an adequate measure of empathy, and to determine the antecedents and consequences of empathy among Colombian villagers. We shall also test the cross-cultural validity of our findings in six Middle East countries and in India.

DEFINING EMPATHY

Ever since Theodore Lipps (1909) coined the German word *einfuhlung* (later translated into English as empathy), the concept has been subject to varied interpretations. Lipps originally intended the term to denote a process in

* This chapter was written with Cesar A. Portocarrero, AID Fellow, Department of Communication, Michigan State University, and is based on his M.A. thesis (1966), *Empathy and Modernization in Colombia*.

195

which an individual observes the gesture of another, imitates it, evokes through the imitation a previously-experienced feeling, and then projects that feeling to the other person. Later usage of the term empathy centered on a narrower meaning than intended by Lipps, but one that still emphasizes feeling into another's emotions.

At present, there are two approaches to the concept of empathy: inference theory and role-taking theory (Berlo 1960).

1. *Inference theory* is psychologically-oriented. It hypothesizes that an individual can directly observe his own behavior and thus relate it symbolically to his internal psychological states. In this way meanings are derived and a self-concept is developed from one's observations and interpretations. On the basis of his first-hand interpretations of himself, an individual makes inferences about the internal states of others.[1] Inference theory assumes that man cannot understand internal states in other people that he has not experienced himself.

2. *The role-taking[2] theory* of empathy is based largely on the sociological writings of George Herbert Mead (1934) dealing with the development of the self. Mead argues that in order to develop the ability to take the role of others meaningfully, a person must be able to adopt an abstract, composite picture of the others. He must mentally build a "generalized other," which provides a set of expectations as to how he should behave and how others will behave. Mead's theory suggests that the concept of self does not precede communication, but is developed through communication with others. As one gains role-taking or emphatic ability, he becomes able to see himself through other's eyes. The development of self-conceptions parallels the development of empathy.

Both sociological and psychological approaches must be taken into account if an acceptable understanding of empathy is to be obtained.[3] An individual probably empathizes by utilizing both inferences and role-taking. Perhaps one gains empathy first through role-taking, thus constructs a conception of self, and based on this conception, begins to make inferences about other people. If our inferences are not correct or rewarding, we go back to role-taking in order to redefine our self so that our inferences will become more accurate. The perpetual cycle of role-taking, inference, role-taking, and

---

[1] An example of inference occurs when you perceive that you often pound the table when you feel angry, then you observe someone else pounding the table; so you infer that he too is angry (Berlo 1960:122–123).

[2] Role-taking is "the symbolic process by which a person momentarily pretends to himself that he is another person, projects himself into the perceptual field of another person, imaginatively 'puts himself in the other's place' in order that he may get an insight into the person's probable behavior in a given situation" (Coutu 1951).

[3] In any event, we cannot empirically test whether the inference theory or the role-taking theory is more correct; they are really better labelled as "assumptions" than as "theories."

inference, facilitates an individual's adjustment to a changing environment.

Empathy is defined as the ability of an individual to project himself into the role of another person.[4] The high-empathic individual will understand the other person's feelings, and take them into account when dealing with him. This definition relies heavily on Lerner's (1958) and Mead's (1934) notions, and on inference theory. Our definition of empathy is essentially similar to the meaning provided by Smith (1966:19): "The core idea of *empathy* is the ability to transpose oneself imaginatively into the feeling, thinking, and acting of another."[5]

From our point of view, empathy usually leads to the utilization of role-taking skills in structuring and interpreting social and interpersonal relationships. To be able to project oneself and understand another person's mind is empathic *ability;* it enables one to *act* in accordance with this understanding.

Empathy defined as the ability to project oneself into another's role, marks empathic ability as somewhat akin to, but distinctive from sympathy, imagination, and identification. Our notion of empathy as a Walter Mitty syndrome is crucial to the effectiveness of any kind of communication, whether in theatrical acting, nursing, counseling, or in mass communication. Willingness to put oneself in another's role is fundamental to communicating effectively with that individual.

Viewing the communication process in terms of empathic elements, two varieties of empathy can be distinguished: (1) *source empathy* with receiver, and (2) *receiver empathy* with source or message. In general, the effectiveness of a communication depends on the ability of the source to feel into the role of

---

[4] This other person may, but need not necessarily, represent a new and unfamiliar role. After reviewing various definitions of empathy, both Allport (1954:3–56) and Strunk (1957) conclude that role-taking or "putting oneself in the other fellow's place" was consistently present in all of the definitions. Gompertz (1960) refuses to offer a definition of empathy, "Perhaps as someone has said, empathy is impossible to understand unless one is able to empathize." Dymond (1949) defined empathy in terms widely accepted by psychologists: "The imaginative transposing of oneself into the thinking, feeling and acting of another and so structuring the world as he does." This definition is essentially similar to ours, although the operations of empathy utilized by psychologists differ a great deal. They often ask a respondent to predict the feelings of another person as indicated by a paper-and-pencil inventory.

[5] This meaning of empathy is a broad one, and is a conceptual brother to what Smith (1966:3) defines as social perceptiveness or *sensitivity*, "The ability to predict what an individual will feel, say, and do about you, himself, and others." In another more limited (but related) sense, Smith (1966:19) regards empathy as one of six determinants of the broader concept of sensitivity; in *this* usage, empathy is "the tendency of a perceiver to assume that another person's feelings, thoughts, and behavior are similar to his own." The use of the term empathy in this book is more analogous to Smith's definition of sensitivity than to his definition of empathy.

the receiver, to "try on the audience's skins."[6] For example, journalists are encouraged to "know" their audience, in order to write more effectively for that audience. Likewise, counselors are urged to empathize with their clients so they are able to offer more appropriate advice. A communication message is also likely to have greater effects when the receiver is able to empathize somewhat with the role of the source or with the persons described in the content of the messages. This latter type of receiver empathy (with the message) is particularly important in peasant modernization.

MEASURING EMPATHY

Lerner's (1958) original empathy scale consisted of nine items. Three of the items asked the individual to describe what he would do if he were the head of a newspaper, a radio station, and the national government. These were the only questions that definitely called for role-taking on the part of the respondent. This type of counterfactual,[7] role-taking item is generally the only type retained in later empathy scales: Eister (1962), Frey (1964), and Rao (1963:299). The other six items in Lerner's scale asked the respondent for *his* opinions, not those of *others*, and are not really measures of role-taking empathy.[8]

[6] Communicants are more likely to have empathy when they are homophilic, or similar in their personal characteristics, value-orientations, and beliefs, than when they are heterophilic. So effective communication depends on empathy, which may often rest on homophily (Katz 1963:6–7). This point is nicely illustrated by the novel *One Hundred Dollar Misunderstanding* (Gover 1961). A college student buys a prostitute for the weekend, but the two soon find that the meanings attached to their words are quite different, and few ideas are accurately transferred. A similar, although less spectacular illustration of this comes from Schatzman and Strauss (1954), who conclude that lower-class hillbilly respondents in Arkansas could not effectively communicate a picture of their experiences in a tornado to research interveiwers, becasue they could not empathize with the investigators.

[7] Perhaps the Lerner-type empathy scale item measures hypothetical counterfactuality as much as it does role-taking ability. Conterfactuality, the capacity to think of oneself other than as he is, to be able mentally to manipulate abstract roles, and to reconstruct them in an unfamiliar and ungiven manner, is certainly central to being modern. But is it properly part of empathy, or only a closely related mental skill (Lane, 1966)? Perhaps a certain degree of the counterfacuality dimension might be removed from the empathy items if they were reworded in a form such as, "What do you think the President of the Village Development Committee should do next year?" rather than being asked as "If you were President of the Village Development Committee, what would you do next year?" The five item empathy scale was asked in both of these two forms in the three Colombian villages of Pueblo Viejo, San Rafael, and Cuatro Esquinas in 1963 and 1965. Correlation between the two types of empathy scores is only .076. This low relationship may be due to a lack of scale reliability over time, as well as to differences in the question wording.

[8] These six nonrole-taking items in Lerner's "empathy" scale asked the respondent (1) what he misses by not getting a newspaper, (2) how people who attend movies differ from those who do not attend, (3) in what other country he would like to live, (4) what he would like to know most about that country, (5) what problems people like himself face in life, and (6) what people like himself can do to solve these problems. In a sense, the last two items measure role-taking ability with roles *like* oneself. Eister (1962) reports some evidence

In order to measure the concept of empathy with others' roles in the Colombian villages, we developed a five-item scale. The scale asked our peasant respondents to take five public roles, which varied from local to national.[9] Except for the empathy scale item dealing with the President of the Village Development Committee, a problem of concern to the role was specified, such as highway improvement, and the respondent was asked to address himself to the stated problem in his answer.

The five empathy questions were:

1. If you were President of the Village Development Committee, what would you do next year?

2. If you were the Extension Service worker, what would you do to improve the price of potatoes in this village?

3. If you were Mayor of the town, what would you do to obtain a better highway for the community?

4. If you were Minister of Education, what would you do for the rural schools in Colombia?

5. If you were President of the Republic, what would you do to suppress the bandit violence?

To what extent were the respondent's empathy scores a function of the interviewer who gathered the data? We categorized the interviewers as more competent and less competent in such interviewing abilities as rapport-building, amount of previous interviewing experience, and productivity (measured as the number of interviews completed per day). We found there was no difference in respondents' mean empathy scores on the basis of the competence of the interviewer.

The responses to the empathy questions were scored by Colombian research investigators (who were trained in the meaning of empathy and in the scoring procedures[10]), on a three point system.

(0)   Low empathy: no answer or a response completely unrelated to the question.

---

from 462 villagers in West Pakistan that the role-taking items in Lerner's scale are positively related to the non role-taking items. A latent-structure analysis of the Lerner empathy items by Marsh (1953) provides somewhat similar evidence. Nevertheless, there is adequate conceptual logic for only including the role-taking type of item in an empathy scale if we define the concept in the terms utilized in the present chapter.

[9] Lerner (1964:7) found that his respondents expressed highest empathy with roles (1) that appeared most frequently in the mass media, and (2) that they had more frequent interaction with. We did not, however, find supportive evidence for this point in Colombia.

[10] We tried to establish scoring procedures that would exclude the dimension of role knowledge from our empathy measure by training our judges not to give points for protocols that indicated higher knowledge of the five roles, as opposed to ability to take these roles. In the 1965 interviews we asked respondents if they knew the kind of work performed by individuals in the roles of extension worker, mayor, and so on. Correlation between the resulting role knowledge scores and the five-item empathy scores is .224, which is significantly different from zero, but does not indicate a very high relationship. So we have some evidence that our empathy dimension is largely independent of role knowledge.

(1) Medium empathy: a general, nonspecific answer, but with some relevance to the question asked.

(2) High empathy: a specific and relevant answer showing ability to take the role indicated.

A criticism of the present measure is that all five questions ask the respondents to take roles that are more modern and of higher social status[11] than themselves. So perhaps scale items such as these measure only what might be called "modern role empathy." However, in the 1965 interviews in Colombia we also determined the respondents' empathy with two lower status and less modern roles. We found that modern role empathy and traditional role empathy are positively related, but the correlation is not very high.[12] Thus, the two varieties of empathy seem to be similar, but not identical. It should be remembered throughout the following sections that we have operationalized *modern* role empathy.

RELIABILITY

A scale is said to be reliable if, when applied to the same sample of respondents, it consistently yields the same results. Using the split-half method of determining scale reliability, the coefficient of reliability of the empathy scale (when corrected by the Spearman-Brown formula) is .75, which is fairly respectable for an instrument composed of only five items.[13]

A high degree of interjudge reliability in scoring the empathy protocols is indicated by correlations of .830, .840, and .860 among the scorings by the three judges. Furthermore, after a lapse of one year, the items were scored again by one of the original judges; his judgments over time were correlated .970.[14]

INTERNAL CONSISTENCY

The degree to which scale items are interrelated is internal consistency, which is usually determined by item-to-total score correlations, and item-to-item correlations:

[11] So perhaps it is no surprise that the present measure of empathy is correlated .595 with social status, a relationship significantly different from zero. However, Whiting (1967b) found a similar measure of empathy was not correlated with social status among Brazilian peasants.

[12] The lower status and less modern roles were those of "oldest man in the village" and "most traditional villager." Empathy with these roles was detemined via interviews with peasants in the three villages of Pueblo Viejo, San Rafael, and Cuatro Esquinas. Correlation with the five-item modern role empathy scores is .190 which is significantly different from zero at the 1 percent level.

[13] The coefficient of reliability is generally higher for scales containing more items.

[14] However, in Brazil Whiting (1967b:141) found a test-retest reliability over a six months period of only .29 for a three-item empathy scale.

1. The five item-to-total score correlations ranged from .668 to .753, with a median correlation of .726;

2. The ten item-to-item correlations ranged from .323 to .480 with a median correlation of .407.

This is rather encouraging evidence of the scale's internal consistency. As further evidence, a McQuitty elementary linkage analysis was performed (McQuitty 1957); it indicated that all the scale items were highly interrelated.

Although there is much need for improvement in empathy operations with peasant respondents,[15] the empathy scale in Colombia exhibited satisfactory levels of reliability and internal consistency.[16]

EMPATHY IN THE PROCESS OF MODERNIZATION

With the publication of Lerner's (1958) book, which featured empathy as central in the process of modernization, the concept came to be regarded by many social scientists[17] as an important variable in modernization. Although, to our knowledge, no explicit replication of Lerner's total modernization model has appeared, his empathy index has been used in several studies in less developed countries.[18]

It is our belief that the ability to envision oneself in someone else's role is an important step to peasant modernity. Every individual must be able to predict the behavior of those with whom he interacts in order to survive. Viewed in this light, even traditional peoples can be said to have a simple type of empathic ability. It might be called minimum or "horizontal" empathy, since they are able to empathize only with individuals whose roles are very similar to theirs. This enables them to function in an environment with an extremely limited range of role-differentiation. It is unlikely that the peasant exposed only to village leader and follower roles will be able to empathize

[15] We tend to agree with Eister (1962), who doubts "whether the factor labeled *empathy* has been defined sharply or clearly enough to be employed and whether the indices so far devised to measure it would stand a thorough test of their validity." Just one of the conceptual-methodological difficulties is the great number of synonyms utilized by various authors for the concept of empathy: "identification facility" (Lerner 1953), "marginal projectivity" (Marsh 1953), "psychic mobility" (Lerner 1958:52), and many others.

[16] Some further evidence of the utility of these role-taking scale items is recently provided by Whiting's (1967b) analysis of four types of empathy indicators among 775 Brazilian village leaders: role-taking, ease and skill in impersonal situations, imaginativeness, and facility with hypotheticals. Results of a factor analysis indicate that the role-taking empathy items "hang together" in one factor, somewhat distinct from operations of the other strains of empathy.

[17] Eister (1962) in West Pakistan, Frey (1964) in Turkey, Rao (1963) in India, and Whiting (1967a) in Brazil.

[18] Modification of the original scale items usually consists of utilizing only the role-taking type of items in Lerner's scale.

with roles other than these.[19] Stewart and Hoult (1959) support this view, arguing that individuals raised in restricted environments, such as isolated peasant villages, will have low empathy because they are not exposed to a wide variety of roles and so never learn how to take the roles of others that are different from themselves.[20] The typical peasant plays one role in life, never learns other roles, and can seldom empathize beyond the usual village roles.

Those individuals living in more modern and complex social environments should be more empathic.[21] Moderns are exposed to many different roles that are constantly changing, and they must learn to empathize with multiple roles in order to survive. They also must empathize with heterophilic individuals, such as those of both higher and lower status.[22] Unfortunately, in many instances, individuals from modern, urban environments learn to empathize in an upward direction, but are *less empathic with roles of much lower status*. For example, North Americans and Europeans who possess a high degree of empathy with the modern-urban roles depicted in the mass media, often are unable to empathize with the lower-status, more traditional role of peasants. This is a special problem when these individuals become change agents in health, agriculture, and education in less developed nations. The Americans and Europeans fail to empathize adequately with their peasant clients, and they often introduce inappropriate innovations, or introduce them in inappropriate ways, and fail.

Although the social environment is an important factor in developing empathic ability, there are also individual differences that make some persons more empathic than others regardless of environment. A concrete style of thinking, "stimulus-bound, unreflective, unanalytic, unsynthetic, and unimaginative" (Lane 1966) seems to characterize the low empathic individual.

---

[19] Mead (1964:54) argues that primitive man is highly imaginative and empathic, but there is little evidence for this point.

[20] Stewart and Hoult propose that this lack of role-taking ability in turn leads to authoritarianism and a lack of tolerance for those different from oneself.

[21] If, indeed, moderns are more empathic than traditionals, the burden of empathizing lies with the more modern individual because the reverse process is unlikely. The interview situation between a (modern) research interviewer and a traditional respondent, brings this point home. It is up to the interviewer to assume the respondents' view of the world. If he expects the peasant respondent to adopt *his* frame of reference in answering the interview questions, little effective communication is likely to occur. Evidence of this point is suggested by Schatzman and Strauss (1955) on the basis of research interviews with Arkansas hillbillies.

[22] Of course a more modern urban environment does not necessarily produce more empathic individuals. Gans (1962:100–101) notes a lack of empathy among his urban slum respondents, stating that his findings bear considerable similarity to the results of Lerner's (1958) Middle Eastern study. West Enders (residents of the west end of Boston) have gone a step further, in that they can place themselves into other roles, but if they have to empathize, they redefine the role so it fits a familiar situation. "Whereas the Middle Eastern peasant would not be able to see himself as mayor of his town, a West Ender can describe what he would do if he were mayor of Boston. He would redefine the job, however, into that of the mayor of the West End."

He is unable to imagine himself in unfamiliar roles, so when he interacts with them, he is unlikely to be an effective *receiver* of new ideas. For instance, the low empathic peasant may be exposed to mass media messages about urban people, but not affected by them because he is unable to project himself into the urban roles. Low empathy mentally insulates many peasants from modern ideas. With empathy comes greater susceptibility to mass media messages.

More empathic individuals are characterized by an open, flexible approach to life. Psychologically more adaptable, such individuals usually interact more effectively with persons in different roles because they can imagine themselves in these other roles and life styles.

Lerner (1965) argues along parallel lines that the empathic person is able to adapt himself to new situations, and thus has capacity for neoteric living. "Rearrangement of the self-system is [empathy's] distinctive role. The mobile person is distinguished by a high capacity for identification with new aspects of his environment; he comes equipped with the mechanisms needed to incorporate new identifications and demands that arise outside of his habitual experience."

The highly empathic peasant is more likely to be affected by mass media exposure, trips to cities, and contact with change agents. Of course, it can also be argued that peasants who have higher mass media exposure, and take more trips to cities, will become more empathic as a result of their exposure to a wider variety of social roles.[23] It is difficult to say which is antecedent and which is consequent — empathy or the other modernization variables. The closest we can come to untangling the chicken-and-egg nature of these concepts is to say that they are related, probably in an interdependent fashion. In other words, more empathy leads to more modernization, which leads to more empathy, and so on. Nevertheless, in the analysis that follows, tentative antecedent and modernization consequences to empathy will be posited.

A PARADIGM OF EMPATHY AND MODERNIZATION

In order to provide a better understanding of the functions of empathy in the process of modernization, empathy will be related to other modernization variables. This analysis will explore the possible conditions (antecedent variables) that enhance or promote empathy, as well as search for consequent variables that are related to empathy. Figure 9–1 is a representation of this approach to analysis. It should be cautioned that the terms "antecedents" and "consequents" are used here to imply a *probable* time-order relationship,

[23] In fact, a proposition might be suggested: the more personal contact one has with a role (for example, with change agents), the higher empathy one will have with that role. In Chapter 8 evidence was reviewed that supported this proposition in the case of our Colombian respondents and their contact with (and empathy with) extension change agents.

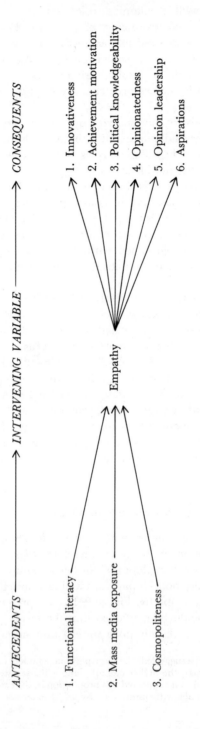

Figure 9–1. Paradigm of the Role of Empathy in the Modernization Process.

and not necessarily a cause-effect relationship. Also, the basis of the antecedent-consequent categorization is rather arbitrary, albeit logical and consistent with the theoretical viewpoint of the modernization process presented throughout this book.

ANTECEDENTS OF EMPATHY

The paradigm in Figure 9–1 indicates the belief that certain variables are especially important in the development of empathic ability: functional literacy, mass media exposure, and cosmopoliteness. All three are means of (or prerequistites to) achieving higher exposure to the more modern world outside of the village.[24]

FUNCTIONAL LITERACY

In an earlier chapter literacy was defined as more than the simple skill of reading and writing. The exact nature of literacy varies with different roles. As the requirements for a given position in society vary, so does the degree of literacy required to adequately cope with the position. For example, the level of literacy required for functioning as a subsistence farmer is very different from that required for a university professor.

Lerner (1958) used literacy as a central concept in his model of modernization, considering it both the index and agent of the second phase of the modernization process. In relating literacy to empathy he contends: "The very act of achieving distance and control over a formal language gives people access to the world of vicarious experience and trains them to use the complicated mechanism of empathy which is needed to cope with this world" (1958:64). He found a strong relationship between literacy and empathy, using data from Syria and Turkey.

The Colombian data (from Pueblo Viejo, San Rafael, and Cuatro Esquinas) substantiates this positive relationship between empathy and literacy. The zero-order correlation between the two variables is .363,[25] which is significantly different from zero. Expressed in another way, literacy accounts for 13.2 percent of the variance in empathy.

[24] One might ask whether more empathy is always desirable for the individual. In very highly media-saturated societies like those in the United States and western Europe, the individual is bombarded with so many messages every minute that it may be dysfunctional for him to empathize with every message.

[25] The correlations between empathy and literacy in the five Colombian villages (of Pueblo Viejo, San Rafael, Cuatro Esquinas, Nazate, and La Cañada) are .437, .568, .143, .420, and .411. All but one are significantly different from zero. Table 9-1 shows a correlation of .363 between empathy and literacy for the three modern villages, which is slightly different than the .371 obtained by pooling .437, .568, and .143. The difference also occurs for all the other correlations in Table 9-1, and is due to a slightly smaller sample size in the table (where only the respondents reinterviewed in 1965 are included).

Suspecting that age and/or social status might intervene[26] in the relationship between empathy and functional literacy, a partial correlation controlling on age and social status was performed.[27] The results (Table 9–1) indicate that neither social status nor age intervene in the empathy-literacy relationship.

The relationship between empathy and literacy thus appears to be positive and independent of factors such as age and social status. *Empathy and literacy are positively related.* With the development of literacy skills, an increase in the individual's ability to empathize with roles outside of his particular environment can be expected. Perhaps literacy facilitates exposure to the larger society, and hence develops empathy.

MASS MEDIA EXPOSURE

Historically, physical mobility was the only means of making contact with the rest of the world, now the mass media provide a route for imaginative access to faraway places. The isolation caused by inadequate roads and means of transportation is easily overcome by radio and to a lesser degree by newpapers, magazines, and books, which put individuals in contact with new places, new situations, and new ways of approaching old problems. Exposure to these media enhances the individual's empathic skill to a point where he can imagine himself as a strange person in a strange situation.

Finding that peasants had higher empathy with the Prime Minister of Turkey than with a minor government official (the county manager), Frey (1964) suggests that the minister's wide public exposure in the mass media better acquainted peasants with his role. More fully aware of the prime minister's responsibilities and actions, they are better able to empathize with him than they are with an official whose function remains relatively unkown. Similarly, it might be easier for most Americans to empathize with the President, than with the role of a cost accountant.

Whereas Lerner perceives the mass media to be a mobility multiplier, Rao (1963) views it as a facilitator of smooth transitions from traditional to modern ways. He argues that when channels of information are few, and they are controlled by power-holders who have almost sole access to them, there is

[26] This expectation was based on the rather high zero-order correlations between empathy scores and both age and social status. These variables were regarded as possible intervening variables, rather than as antecedent or consequent variables, because (1) of their relatively static nature, and (2) of the absence of much theoretical interest in their role in modernization.

[27] A partial correlation analysis is performed in order to eliminate the influence of a third (or fourth) variable on the correlation between two variables. The significance of the partial correlation from zero can be tested by students. The significance of the difference between a zero-order and a partial correlation can be obtained by transforming both correlations into z scores and testing the difference between the two z's. Significant differences between the z scores mean that the two r's are significantly different (McNemar 1962: 165–167).

Table 9–1. Zero-Order Correlations and First-Order Partial Correlations (Controlling on Age and Social Status) of Empathy with Selected Variables in Three Modern Colombian Peasant Villages

Variables Correlated with Empathy Scores	Zero-Order Correlation with Empathy Scores While Not Controlling on Age		Partial Correlations with Empathy Scores While Controlling on Age		z Value for Effect of Controlling on Age	Does Age Intervene?	Partial Correlations with Empathy Scores Controlling on Social Status		z Value for Effect of Controlling on Social Status	Does Social Status Intervene?
	r	r^{2a}	r	r^{2a}			r	r^{2a}		
1. Functional literacy	.363c	13.2	.325c	10.6	[.40]	No	.203c	4.1	[1.54]	No
2. Mass media exposure	.520c	27.0	.500c	25.0	[.25]	No	.290c	8.4	2.46c	Yes
3. Cosmopoliteness	.282c	8.0	.259c	6.7	[.19]	No	[.036]	0.1	2.20c	Yes
4. Agricultural innovativeness	.255c	6.5	.227c	5.2	[.19]	No	[.011]	0.0	2.18c	Yes
5. Achievement motivation	.279c	7.8	.249c	6.2	[.26]	No	[.139]	1.7	[1.20]	No
6. Political knowledgeability	.448c	20.1	.418c	17.5	[.33]	No	.222c	4.9	2.31c	Yes
7. Opinionatedness	.388c	15.1	.367c	13.5	[.19]	No	.396c	15.7	[.10]	No
8. Opinion leadership	.281c	7.9	.258c	6.7	[.18]	No	[.062]	0.4	1.87b	Yes
9. Educational aspirations	.417c	17.4	.398c	15.8	[.21]	No	.249c	6.2	1.70b	Yes

[a] The coefficient of determination or r^2 expresses the percentage of variance shared in common by two variables.

[b] Significant at the 5 per cent level.

[c] Significant at the 1 percent level.

likelihood of resentment and conflict on the part of the nonelites. If, on the other hand, the channels of information are numerous and unrestricted, change can be brought about more smoothly. The economic, social, and political ideas transmitted by the mass media increase the villager's sphere of knowledge, thus promoting the understanding and consensus necessary for a more modern society.

Whether viewed as a transition-smoother or a mobility-multiplier, mass media exposure is directly related to empathy. In fact, the correlation between media exposure and empathy is one of the highest obtained in the Colombian study. The zero-order correlation between these two variables is .520[28] (Table 9–1). Media exposure is more highly related to empathy than is functional literacy, a finding that perhaps suggests that literacy alone may not be "enough." Once reading and writing skills are acquired, they must be used. So exposure to mass media is a better predictor of empathic ability than is literacy.

Partial correlations were computed between media exposure and empathy, while controlling on age and social status. Although age does not affect the mass media-empathy relationship, social status seems to intervene (Table 9–1). The partial correlation of media exposure and empathy, with the effects of social status removed, is still significant at the 1 percent level, however the difference between the zero-order and the partial correlations is also significant. This indicates that *social status has an effect on the media exposure-empathy relationship; however, these two variables are positively related even when the effect of social status is mathematically removed.*

Does social status intervene on the empathy-mass media relationship through its effect on empathy or on media exposure? A part correlation analysis (Figure 9–2) was performed to answer this question. When social status is not controlled, the empathy-media exposure correlation is .520 (Step A in Figure 9–2). When the effect of status is removed, the correlation drops to .290 (Step B). When the effect of the status variable is removed *only* from media exposure (Step C), the empathy-media exposure correlation drops to .228; in Step D, when the effect of status is removed *only* from empathy, the correlation is only .236. Evidently, high empathic ability is particularly characteristic of high status villagers, who also have high mass media exposure. Social status has its effect on the empathy-media exposure relationship both through its covariance with empathy and with mass media exposure.

COSMOPOLITENESS

It seems reasonable to expect that an individual's empathic ability can be enhanced by cosmopoliteness, as Lerner (1958:52) points out, "The historic increase of psychic mobility (empathy) begins with expansion of physical

[28] Correlations between mass media exposure and empathy in the five Colombian villages are: .378, .500, .395, .609, and .376. All are significantly different from zero.

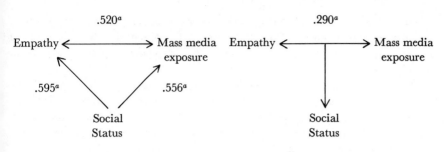

Step A: Zero-order correlations of empathy, media exposure, and social status

Step B: First-order partial correlation of empathy and media exposure, controlling on social status

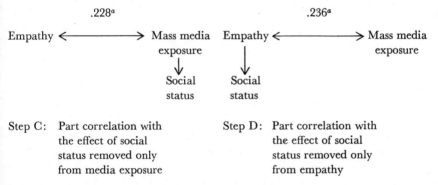

Step C: Part correlation with the effect of social status removed only from media exposure

Step D: Part correlation with the effect of social status removed only from empathy

Figure 9–2. Zero-Order, First-Order and Part Correlations between Empathy, Mass Media Exposure, and Social Status, Which Shows that Social Status Has Its Effect on the Empathy-Media Exposure Relationship through Both the Empathy and the Media Exposure Variables.

[a]Significantly different from zero at the 1 percent level.

travel." If an individual is going to change his mode of life, one source of such inspiration is the world beyond his village. Contact with this outside world is likely to increase his empathic skills as he becomes aware of new roles and situations inherent in a more urban environment. Following the Stewart and Hoult (1959) argument, it can be expected that persons whose social psychological milieu is less restricted and localite will develop greater empathy with roles different than their own.

Rao (1963) found that the key difference between two Indian villages — one of which was very modern and the other very traditional — was the existence of a road that linked the more modern community to a nearby urban center. The villagers were able to travel easily to this small city, where they were exposed to modern technology and urban-industrial roles. When a small industry moved to this village, the people were prepared for it; their receptivity had been modified by their cosmopoliteness. They were better able to take on new industrial roles because of their previous external contact with cities.

The Colombian findings indicate *a positive relationship between empathy and cosmopoliteness.* The zero-order correlation is .282,[29] which is significantly different from zero (Table 9–1). Yet this correlation is considerably lower than that of either of the other two antecedent variables with empathy, and accounts for only 7.9 percent of the variance in empathy scores.

Whereas age does not affect the cosmopoliteness-empathy relationship (Table 9–1), removal of the effects of social status on the empathy-cosmopoliteness correlation results in a partial correlation that is significantly lower. Although the present data do not permit further probing on this point, one might speculate that social status intervenes in this relationship because cosmopolite travel is limited by lack of financial resources, which only villagers with high status possess.

PREDICTING EMPATHY WITH A MULTIPLE CORRELATION APPROACH

At this point, it seems appropriate to discuss the joint relationship of the three antecedents and their ability to predict empathy. It has been previously suggested that the development of literacy skills, exposure to the mass media, and travel to urban centers, is associated with an individual's ability to empathize with others' roles. But how much does each of these three variables contribute to predicting empathic ability independently of the other two antecedents? Analyzed together, the three antecedent variables yields a multiple correlation of .547, which means that they jointly explain 29.9 percent of the variance in empathy scores. The contribution of each antecedent is as follows:

Antecedent Variables	Percentage of Empathy Variance Explained
Mass Media Exposure	23.1
Functional Literacy	6.7
Cosmopoliteness	0.1
Total	29.9

Media exposure explains the greatest percentage of variance in empathy. By such reading and listening, the peasant learns about new roles beyond his immediate environment. Functional literacy accounts for only a small portion of the variance in empathy. Although acquisition of literacy skills opens the

[29] Correlations between empathy and cosmopoliteness in the five Colombian villages are: .159, .343, .328, .277, and .372. Three of the five are significantly different from zero.

way to the more modern world, the individual possessing these skills does not necessarily enter that world. Cosmopoliteness seems to contribute relatively less in explaining empathy, perhaps because trips to cities serve only to awaken interest in the possibilities offered by different ways of life and do not directly teach new roles.[30]

CONSEQUENTS OF EMPATHY

Let us turn our attention to the dimensions that may be effected by the individual's ability to empathize. High empathic and low empathic individuals are likely to differ in their approach to life as well as in specific behaviors; for example, the ability to see beyond one's own role in life is likely to produce a more flexible person capable of seeking new ideas.

INNOVATIVENESS

It is likely that empathy plays a vital role in a person's ability to extend himself beyond the tried and true, the here and now. Empathy is probably a contributing factor to the unique mental abilities of the innovator. Rogers and Beal (1958) found a high relationship between innovativeness and the ability to deal with abstractions. In one sense, empathy is an ability to deal with abstract roles.

Table 9–1 shows *there is a strong positive relationship between empathy and agricultural innovativeness in Colombia*;[31] there is support for the proposition that the ability to empathize contributes to the psychological make-up of the innovative individual. Although age does not intervene in this relationship, social status has a strong effect on the empathy-innovativeness relationship. Past research indicates that innovators are usually of higher social status, since they must possess adequate economic resources to be able to try out new ideas. This might explain, in part, the intervening effect of social status.

ACHIEVEMENT MOTIVATION

Individuals who are able to understand others' roles are often motivated to compare themselves with these new and different roles. When these other roles include a higher level of living and of social prestige, the empathic in-

[30] It is also likely that when peasants travel to cities such as Bogotá, they may interact mostly with other peasants like themselves, who inhabit the same restaurants, taverns, and shops. In fact, I have frequently observed this high degree of homophilic interaction by peasants in cities. Unfortunately, we do not have data on the exact nature of our Colombian respondents' cosmopolite activities.

[31] The correlations between empathy and agricultural innovativeness for each of the five villages are: .267, .291, .185, .550, and .418; three are significant. Empathy is similarly correlated with home innovativeness in the five villages: .188, .528, .255, .415, and .420; three of these correlations are significant.

dividual may be motivated to achieve higher levels of occupational excellence for himself. This expectation is supported by the Colombian data; achievement motivation is correlated .279 with empathy scores, a relationship which is significantly different from zero.[32] Empathy accounts for about 8 percent of the variance in achievement motivation scores.[33] *Achievement motivation is positively related to empathy.*

POLITICAL KNOWLEDGEABILITY

A more empathic individual should possess a higher degree of political knowledgeability. He should be able to put himself in the public roles discussed in the mass media, and thus be more likely to absorb the information than a less empathetic person with the same level of mass media exposure. This expectation is supported by the Colombian data; the correlation between political knowledgeability and empathy is .448, which is significantly different from zero.[34] This relationship is not affected by controlling on age, but is depressed by removing the effect of social status (Table 9–1). But even with status removed, a significant correlation remains between empathy and knowledgeability. *Political knowledgeability is positively related to empathy.*

OPINIONATEDNESS

Opinionatedness is the degree to which an individual has and can express opinions about a variety of issues. Lerner (1958:72) found that the more modern of his Middle East respondents were more likely to have opinions about a number of issues than were his traditionals.[35] The latter adhered more strictly to the beliefs of their ancestors; as such, they did not have opinions about contemporary issues, nor were they accustomed to expressing an attitude about some new idea when it was presented to them. Lerner measured opinionatedness by scoring his respondents on their lack of "don't know," no answer, and other indeterminant responses to a number of attitudinal and opinion questions. A similar type of measure was utilized in the Colombian study.[36]

[32] In fact, achievement motivation is correlated with empathy .259, .491, .331, .482, and .431 in the five Colombia villages. All of these correlations are significantly different from zero.

[33] The effects of age and of social status were not removed from the relationships of achievement motivation and empathy via partial correlation techniques because of the relatively low zero-order correlation.

[34] When computed separately for the five Colombian villages, the correlations between political knowledgeability and empathy scores are .454, .479, .331, .244, and .390; four of the five are significant.

[35] Support for this finding that opinionatedness is positively related to empathy is provided by Eister's (1962) study is West Pakistan.

[36] It must be pointed out that such an operation may include such dimensions as general intelligence, interview rapport, and tolerance for ambiguity, as well as (or as a part of) opinionatedness.

Opinionatedness can be expected to be positively related to empathy. If an individual is able to feel into the role of others, he would be inclined to express his opinion about matters affecting such other persons because, in his own mind, these matters are also his personal concern. It was found that opinionatedness is correlated .388 with empathy in Colombia, which is significantly different from zero, substantiating the conclusion that *opinionatedness is positively related to empathy.*

OPINION LEADERSHIP

Homans (1961:314) states that leaders maintain their positions of influence by rendering valuable and rare services to their group. This requires that the leader be able to put himself in the roles of the group members — that he be highly empathic. Mead (1934) points out that individuals who possess empathic ability are better able to see the needs and goals of their peers, and hence are most likely to become the leaders of a group.[37] This does not mean that the only way to become a leader is through the development of empathy; it does mean, however, that individuals are chosen as opinion leaders by their peers, in part, because they are sufficiently interested in someone else's problems. Therefore, opinion leadership can be expected to be associated with empathy among the Colombian respondents. Such is the case. The correlation is .281 between opinion leadership and empathy, a relationship that is significantly different from zero.[38] *Opinion leadership is positively related to empathy.*

ASPIRATIONS

Role-taking capacity leads to attending to the world outside of the village, and to comparing oneself with others' occupational and educational accomplishments. The Colombian data indicate a correlation of .417 between educational aspirations and empathy, which is supported by the relationship of occupational aspirations and empathy.[39] Controlling on the effect of age does not affect the educational aspirations-empathy relationship. Removing the effect of social status depresses the correlation; however, it remains significantly different from zero (Table 9–1). So *aspirations are positively related to empathy.*

[37] Bell and Hall (1954) provide some tentative experimental evidence for this point.

[38] Some further evidence is supplied by the correlations in the five Colombian villages: .432, .021, .109, .260, and .075. All are in the expected direction, but only one is significantly different from zero.

[39] In the five villages, occupational aspirations and empathy are correlated .369, .218, .036, .318 and .232; all of these are in the expected direction, and two are significantly different from zero. All five correlations between educational aspirations and empathy are significantly different from zero: .381, .345, .375, .415, and .364.

EMPATHY AS AN INTERVENING VARIABLE IN MODERNIZATION

In order to test the assumption that empathy intervenes in the relationship between the antecedents and consequents of modernization, empathy was partialed out of the relationship between the three antecedents and three selected consequents. The comparison between the zero-order correlations and partial correlations shown in Table 9–2 helps clarify the role of empathy in modernization. The results indicate that *empathy does not intervene* significantly in the relationship between (1) the antecedents of literacy, media exposure, and cosmopoliteness, and (2) the consequent variables of innovativeness, political knowledgeability, and educational aspirations, respectively. However, it can be observed in Table 9–2 that all nine zero-order correlations are depressed when the effect of empathy is removed. So the effect of removing empathy from these antecedent-consequent relationships is consistent in all nine cases, and often the reduction in the original covariance is quite large. For instance, when the effect of empathy is removed from the literacy-knowledgeability correlation in Table 9–2, the covariance is reduced from 17.7 percent to 9.6 percent. This result indicates that 8.1 percent (17.7 minus 9.6) of the mutual variance in literacy and political knowledgeability scores is due to their joint covariance with empathy.

Even though removing the effect of empathy from these nine antecedent-consequent relationships did not prove to be significant, the correlations between the antecedent and the consequent variables are consistently lowered. Perhaps if an improved and more sensitive measure of the empathy concept had been utilized, its function in the modernization process could have been more precisely probed.

SUMMARY OF THE COLOMBIAN FINDINGS

1. Significant positive correlations were found between empathy and (a) such antecedents as functional literacy, mass media exposure, and cosmopoliteness; and (b) such consequents as innovativeness, achievement motivation, political knowledgeability, opinionatedness, opinion leadership, and aspirations.

2. Social status strongly intervenes in all the empathy relationships (except those with functional literacy and educational aspirations); therefore it must concluded that *the strength of the relationships between empathy and the other variables is due in part to the social status of the respondent.* Age does not affect any of the relationships of empathy with is antecedents or consequences.

3. Empathy is not an intervening variable in the relationships of modernization antecedents and consequents when (a) functional literacy, mass media exposure, and cosmopoliteness are the selected antecedents, and (b) innova-

Table 9–2. Zero-Order and First-Order Partial Correlations (Controlling on Empathy) of Antecedent and Selected Consequent Variables in Three Modern Colombian Villages

Antecedent Variables	Selected Consequent Variables		
	Agricultural Innovativeness	Political Knowledgeability	Educational Aspirations
I. Functional literacy			
(A) (1) Zero-order correlation (r)	.207[b]	.421[b]	.273[b]
(2) Coefficient of determination (r^2)	4.3	17.7	7.4
(B) (1) Partial correlation controlling on empathy (r)	[.132]	.310[b]	[.140]
(2) Coefficient of determination (r^2)	1.7	9.6	2.0
(C) z value for effect of controlling on empathy	[0.73]	[1.12]	[1.20]
(D) Does empathy intervene?	No	No	No
II. Mass Media Exposure			
(A) (1) Zero-order correlation (r)	.320[b]	.595[b]	.419[b]
(2) Coefficient of determination (r^2)	10.2	35.4	17.6
(B) (1) Partial correlation controlling on empathy (r)	.230[b]	.467[b]	.260[b]
(2) Coefficient of determination (r^2)	5.3	21.8	6.8
(C) z value for effect of controlling on empathy	[0.87]	[1.49]	[1.61]
(D) Does empathy intervene?	No	No	No
III. Cosmopoliteness			
(A) (1) Zero-order correlation (r)	[.135]	.503[b]	.436[b]
(2) Coefficient of determination (r^2)	1.8	25.3	19.0
(B) (1)Partial correlation controlling on empathy (r)	[.064]	.436[b]	.370[b]
(2) Coefficient of determination (r^2)	0.4	19.0	13.7
(C) z values for effect of controlling on empathy	[0.63]	[0.68]	[0.73]
(D) Does empathy intervene?	No	No	No

[a] Significantly different from zero at the 5 percent level.
[b] Significantly different from zero at the 1 percent level.

tiveness, political knowledgeability, and educational aspirations are the selected consequents.

In Lerner's model of modernization, empathy is one of his most central concepts. "For empathy, in the several aspects it exhibits, is the basic communication skill required of modern man" (Lerner 1963 : 342). What general conclusion can be drawn from the Colombian inquiry about the relative importance of empathy in the modernization process? The correlational results that have just been reviewed in this chapter seem to indicate that empathy is hardly *the* most crucial variable in the modernization mix. It is correlated about as expected (in zero-order relationships) with its hypothesized antecedents and consequences, but when partial correlation techniques are utilized, empathy does not significantly intervene in nine selected antecedent-consequent relationships. So empathy appears to be interdependently intertwined with such other modernization concepts as literacy, media exposure, innovativeness. The case is not unlike that disclosed for other concepts in previous chapters of this book. It seems impossible to isolate any single concept from among our ten or twelve leading candidates as *the* central variable in modernization. But the present evidence does show that empathy is *one* important social psychological component of the shift from traditional to neoteric.

4. According to the results of a multiple correlation analysis, the antecedent variable of mass media exposure is the best predictor of empathy. Functional literacy and cosmopoliteness are much less important in predicting empathy. It must be remembered, however, that the predictive power of mass media exposure appears to be, in considerable part, a function of social status; a part-correlation analysis shows that social status has its effect on the empathy-media exposure relationship through both empathy and media exposure. When the effect of social status is removed from media exposure only, and then from empathy only, the empathy-media exposure correlation is lowered.

CROSS-CULTURAL COMPARISONS FROM SIX MIDDLE EAST COUNTRIES AND FROM INDIA

Validity for the findings from the Colombian settings are provided by a cross-cultural comparison which involved reanalyzing data from six Middle East countries and from eight Indian villages. *We generally find support for our findings across these cultures.*[40]

Comparative data were found for four variables in addition to empathy: cosmopoliteness, functional literacy, mass media exposure, and social status. Empathy, of course, is a dependent variable in all three of these studies.

[40] The Middle East data come from Lerner's (1958 : 438–446) sample of 1357 respondents, both rural and urban, in Turkey, Lebanon, Jordan, Egypt, Syria, and Iran.

The data from India are part of the India-UNESCO study of 702 peasants living in eight villages in North-Central India. The data were gathered in 1964 by research interviewers from India's National Institute of Community Development, Hyderabad.

Measurement of all five variables was generally similar to that in our Colombian study.[41]

Table 9-3 presents the zero-order correlations between empathy and the other variables. All of these correlations are significantly different from zero at the one percent level. As in Colombia, social status and mass media ex-

Table 9-3. Cross-Cultural Comparison of Correlates of Empathy in Colombia, Six Middle East Countries and India

	Zero-Order Correlations with Empathy Scores		
Antecedent Variables	Colombia (N = 159)	Six Middle East Countries (N = 1357)	India (N = 702)
1. Social status	.595[b]	.276[b]	.392[b]
2. Mass media exposure	.520[b]	.278[b]	.334[b]
3. Cosmopoliteness	.382[b]	.166[b]	.083[a]
4. Functional literacy	.363[b]	.340[b]	.323[b]

[a] Significantly different from zero at the 5 percent level.
[b] Significantly different from zero at the 1 percent level.

posure are more highly correlated with empathy, and cosmopoliteness and literacy are less highly correlated (except in the Middle East where literacy is most highly related to empathy).

Unfortunately, measures of the consequent variables were not available for analysis from the Middle East study; however, there was general support for the Colombian results with the Indian data.

FUTURE RESEARCH

The present investigation suggests several avenues for future inquiry.

1. With present measures, empathy in traditional cultures appears to be highly related to social status. It is possible that the empathy measures developed to date have been confounded with social status. The empathy scale items, it will be recalled, ask the peasant respondent to empathize with *higher status* roles. Naturally, those villagers who have relatively higher status are less socially distant from such roles as mayor, extension agent, and other government officials, and are more able to empathize with these roles. So it should not be forgotten that a rather specific kind of empathy is being measured — that with higher status (and more modern) roles. Future

---

[41] Although Lerner's measure of empathy in the six Middle Eastern nations included nonrole-taking items, as previously discussed in this chapter.

research might well proceed to improve our empathy operation by including a greater variety of roles, including those of lower status and more tradition than the respondent.[42] Such inquiry could also determine whether role-taking ability is a unidimensional or a multidimensional variable, with the number of dimensions perhaps depending on the types of roles included in the scale.

2. In addition to this attempt to develop improved measures of generalized empathy, there are situations in which a more specific type of empathy could have much research utility. An illustration is the analysis of change agent-client interrelationships. One expects that the effectiveness of communication between change agent and client is positively related to the degree to which change agents are able to take the role of their clients.[43] One might design various field experiments in which the treatments are methods of increasing the degree to which change agents are receiver-oriented (that is, empathic), and the experimental effects are measures of change agent effectiveness in securing altered behavior in their clients.

Not only is empathy (of the variety measured in the present study) likely to be related to peasant innovativeness, as we have just found, but other strains of empathy may be related to special types of innovativeness. For example, Misra (1967:191–199) found that U.S. Negro husbands and wives who had high empathy with each other about family planning matters[44] (that is, they could put themselves into the role of the other regarding number of children desired and attitude toward family planning) were more likely to adopt birth control ideas. High empathy with one's mate was also positively associated with education, income, and being in concurrence with his ideas about family planning.

3. Field experiments might be designed to determine the causal connections between empathy's hypothesized antecedents and consequences. An example of such inquiry is the experiment underway in Brazil (Herzog 1967a) to determine whether the teaching of literacy to adults leads to the expansion of their empathic capacity.

[42] And also by experimenting with different ways of measuring empathy than with the usual Lerner-type empathy items. A promising approach is reported by Wright and others (1967:36). They asked Guatemalan peasants to tell stories about a series of eight projective pictures each of which showed village scenes. The respondents were rated on their degree of empathy, demonstrated by their ability to put themselves into the roles of the pictured characters.

[43] This relationship should hold up to a very high level of empathy, where perhaps the change agent takes the role of his clients so completely that he no longer wishes to change them (Chapter 8). Katz (1963:25) points out a somewhat analogous case of the anthropologist who overidentifies with the natives he studies to the point where he disqualifies himself for dispassionate scientific reporting. An extreme case is that of Frank Cushing, whose empathy with the Pueblo Indians turned out to be permanent. He joined the tribe!

[44] It is important to note that this type of empathy was with a role that is generally equal to one's own in social status and degree of modernization, rather than empathy with a role quite different from one's own.

10

Opinion Leadership and
the Flow of Communication*

Every herd of wild cattle has its leaders, its influential heads.

(Gabriel Tarde 1903:4)

Men nearly always follow the tracks made by others and proceed in their affairs by imitation, even though they cannot entirely keep to the tracks of others or emulate the prowess of their models.

(Niccolo Machiavelli 1961:49)

The Colombian village of Pueblo Viejo, prior to the initiation of intensive change agent activities around 1959, was "ruled" by a small corps of traditional opinion leaders. When extension workers began to spend one day each week in the village, they were opposed by these leaders, and so they concentrated their attention on a new group of younger, emerging leaders like Miguel Gomez. He served as chairman of the village cooperative, which was organized by the extension workers, and as president of the Village Development Committee. Miguel was well-liked by most of his fellow villagers (the data showed that he received a high percentage of the sociometric opinion choices), and he served as an effective liaison between the change agents and his followers. His farm was located at the center of the Y-shaped foot trail over which the peasants of Pueblo Viejo traveled daily, and his social accessibility may have contributed to his influence. Through the efforts of Miguel and the extension workers, a new road was constructed, a piped water system was installed, and the cooperative store flourished. The relative power of the older, traditional leaders gradually shrank in the face of Miguel's development successes until at the time of our data gathering in 1963, the traditional leaders had only a handful of followers.

The rise and decline of these leaders demonstrates an important generalization: opinion leaders conform closely to a system's norms. When the norms

* This chapter was written with the assistance of Teresa Kang Mei Chou Shen, Research Assistant, Department of Communication, Michigan State University. Certain sections in this chapter are adapted from Everett M. Rogers and Johannes C. M. van Es (1964), *Opinion Leadership in Traditional and Modern Colombian Villages*, East Lansing, Michigan State University, Department of Communication, Diffusion of Innovations Research Report 2; and from Teresa Kang Mei Chou (1966), *Homophily in Interaction Patterns in the Diffusion of Innovations in Colombian Villages*, M. A. thesis, East Lansing, Michigan State University.

changed in Pueblo Viejo, so did the leadership.[1] This point will be discussed in more detail after a general consideration of the nature of opinion leadership and the two-step flow of communication. These concepts derive from investigations in Erie County, Ohio, Decatur, Illinois, and similar locales in both the United States and Europe. In this chapter the usefulness of these notions will be shown among the Colombian villagers.

IMPORTANCE OF OPINION LEADERSHIP

The success or failure of programs of planned change depend ultimately upon the ability and cooperation of local leaders at the village level. Change agents are advised to concentrate their efforts in introducing innovations upon village leaders (Chapter 8). Yet little is presently known about the nature of this informal leadership and its role in development and modernization, especially in less developed nations like Colombia.[2] It is strange that such an important topic has gone begging in modernization research. As more is learned abut the nature of village opinion leadership, it will be possible to plan communication strategies more effectively.

As one result of planned change programs, new demands are made on local leadership. At the present time, little is known about the actual impact of change and modernization upon local leadership, and how such leaders meet the demands of modernization. Homans (1961:339) argues that leaders are more conformist to salient group norms than are nonleaders. Therefore, a different type of opinion leader can be expected to emerge as the village becomes more modern. No scientific comparison of leadership in traditional and modern Colombian villages has yet been made. Nor has it been made in any other less developed country.

Our theoretical point of departure is Homans' (1961:314) proposition that leadership is based on the rendering of rare but valuable services to the members of a group. While Homans claims that this proposition will hold true cross-culturally, he admits that not much evidence can be brought to bear from outside the United States. This chapter attempts to determine the applicability of Homan's proposition, with special reference to the way in which the changing demands of the village affect its leadership.

First, however, let us critically review the two-step flow model of communication, a notion that is fundamental to an understanding of opinion leadership.

[1] A somewhat analogous situation was described in the Turkish village of Balgat by Lerner (1958); when the village became linked to Ankara by a highway, the influence of the traditional chief declined (Chapter 7).

[2] Dube (1967:95) points out, "There is very little scientific knowledge regarding the communication situation in the underdeveloped countries . . . Nor is there much scientific information on the opinion leaders who have a seminal role in the dissemination of ideas and adoption of new practices."

THE TWO-STEP FLOW HYPOTHESIS: SHORTCOMINGS AND CONTRIBUTIONS

Early researchers in mass communication thought the mass media were powerful tools in influencing individuals' attitudes and behavior. The "yellow journalism" preceding the Spanish-American War, Goebbel's Nazi propaganda machine, and the power of Madison Avenue advertising led to conceptualization of the so-called "hypodermic needle model."[3] This model assumed that the audience was an atomized mass of disconnected individuals, and that there was a direct and immediate stimulus-response relationship between the sending and receiving of mass media messages (Figure 10–1).

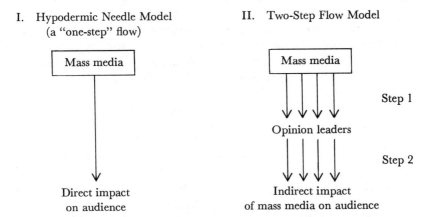

I. Hypodermic Needle Model
(a "one-step" flow)

II. Two-Step Flow Model

Figure 10–1. Diagram of the Hypodermic Needle Model of Communication Effects, and the Two-Step Flow Model that Replaced It.

The hypodermic needle model, with its neglect of the role of opinion leaders, did not mirror reality.

The demise of the hypodermic needle model was brought about by the now-famous Erie County (Ohio) study of the 1950 presidential election by Lazarfeld and others (1944). To the researchers' initial surprise, they found almost *no influence* of the mass media on voting patterns. Instead, interpersonal influence from opinion leaders was recognized as an important intervening mechanism, which operated between the mass media messages and their effects on human behavior. The two-step flow of communication, probably the most exciting idea in the past 25 years of communication research, was postulated: "Ideas often flow from radio and print to opinion leaders and from them to the less active sections of the population" (Lazarsfeld and others 1944:151). Obviously, one of the important implications of the two-step flow

[3] The hypodermic needle model might be termed a *one step flow* model, in that the mass media were perceived to have a direct and uniform effect on the audience.

model was the central place that it awarded to opinion leaders (Figure 10–1) and to their interpersonal communication with followers. It put people back into mass communication. It also implied that the mass media were not as powerful, nor as direct, as once thought.

The major shortcomings of the two-step flow model are the following:

1. It implies that opinion leadership is a dichotomous trait. A given sample of respondents may often be dichotomized into opinion leaders versus followers, but in fact, opinion leadership is a continuous variable, and should certainly be conceptualized (even though not always measured) as such.

2. It implies a competitive rather than a complementary role for mass media and interpersonal communication channels. The two-step flow hypothesis ignores stages in the decision-making process about a new idea. As seen in Chapter 6 mass media channels are most important in creating knowledge or awareness of a new idea, whereas interpersonal communication channels are most important at the persuasion or attitude-change stage.[4] Such channel differences in the knowledge versus persuasion stage exist for *both* opinion leaders and followers; thus it is not only the opinion leaders who use mass media channels.

3. It ignores the so-called time of knowing. Maybe opinion leaders are simply early knowers of a new idea, who pass the innovation along to later knowers.[5]

4. It implies active opinion leaders and a passive audience, while actually many opinions are actively sought by followers from opinion leaders.[6]

The overall criticism of the two-step flow, as originally stated, is that *it does not tell us enough*. The communication process is far more complicated than two steps. Moreover, what is now known about the flow of communication is too detailed to be expressed in one sentence. Nevertheless, several lasting beneficial effects of the two-step flow hypothesis are evident in communication research; one of these is a focus upon opinion leadership.

[4] Put in slightly different words, the two-step flow model did not distinguish between the *knowledge* versus the *persuasion* function in decision-making. Research completed since the early 1940s shows that (1) the mass media probably reach both opinion leaders and followers to create knowledge, but (2) persuasion occurs mainly as a result of interpersonal communication from opinion leaders. Further, studies of the diffusion of news events suggest the generalization that the degree to which mass media communication channels are utilized at the knowledge stage varies directly with the *saliency* of the innovation. When the idea (that is, the news item) has great saliency, mass media channels are less important than when the messages are of medium or low saliency. In the case of a news item such as President Kennedy's assassination, complete strangers often told each other the news.

[5] This supposition is supported by research findings that indicate early knowers make relatively greater use of mass media channels than do late knowers. The two-step flow model states that opinion leaders have higher media usage than do followers.

[6] The original statement of the two-step flow model probably influenced most definitions of opinion leadership to imply an active, opinion-giving role for opinion leaders, or even a passive, "sought" role, but not *both* roles, which in fact is what probably occurs in most communication situations.

OPINION LEADERSHIP

Leadership is commonly defined as the ability to influence other people's behavior in a desired way. Opinion leadership is simply a specific type of leadership, one in which other people's opinions are influenced.[7] *Opinion leadership* is, therefore, the ability to influence others' opinions consistently in a desired way.[8] Theoretical writings about leadership have applicability to the analysis of opinion leadership; likewise, empirical research about the nature of opinion leadership contributes to the verification of hypotheses about general leadership.

Table 10–1. Opinion Giving and Opinion Seeking Roles on the Basis of the Source of Opinion and the Initiation of Communication.[a]

	Source of Opinion or Information	
Initiation of Communication	Opinion Leader (Source)	Follower (Receiver)
Initiator	Opinion leader initiator	Follower initiator
Noninitiator	Opinion leader noninitiator	Follower noninitiator

(The diagram shows diagonal lines labeled *Opinion Seeking*, *Opinion Giving*, and "Opinion Giving" to the left, connecting the four cells.)

[a] This paradigm shows that there are two dimensions to opinion-transmission: the source and the initiator. Opinion leaders are, of course, the source in this situation. Although some opinion leaders initiate the communication flow by seeking receivers for their messages, the most usual occurence is opinion seeking (noted by the solid line above), in which followers initiate the process by seeking the opinion leader.

Table 10–1 indicates two possible dimensions of information and opinion flow. The first dimension is the *source* of ideas; the second is the *initiator* of communication. The opinion leader is always the source of information and

[7] It should also be pointed out that opinion leadership is a type of *informal* leadership, exerted through an individual's ability to influence others' behavior outside of formally-prescribed role relationships. In contrast, formal leadership is exercised by virtue of a titled position that the individual occupies, usually in a formal organization.

[8] We consider this definition an improvement over that of Rogers (1962:251), who defines opinion leaders as those individuals from whom others seek advice and information. The present definition allows for the fact that the receivers may play an *active* or a *passive* role in information and opinion exchange, or both roles.

opinions, but the communication process can be initiated by either the leader or the follower. Basically, there is a distinction between opinion-seeking and opinion-giving in this diagram.

MEASURING OPINION LEADERSHIP IN COLOMBIA

Four different measures of opinion leadership were utilized in Colombia; (1) sociometric; (2) a self-designating opinion leadership scale; (3) a self-anchoring opinion leadership measure; and (4) judges' ratings. The data obtained from the Colombian respondents by the sociometric method serve as the primary measure of opinion leadership in the analysis. The other three measurements are used as validity checks on the sociometric measurement.

Sociometric Measure

All respondents were asked to whom they would go for advice on a number of different topics. The questions covered different aspects of village life: agricultural ideas, the main farm crop, farm credit, health, politics, and marketing products.[9] The following is an example of one of our sociometric questions: "If you needed credit to buy land, which other farmer would you ask about how to obtain it?" Each respondent's score was the number of choices he received from other farmers for each sociometric question. A total sociometric score was computed for each respondent by adding the total number of choices received for all questions. This score appears to be the best single measure of overall opinion leadership in the Colombian villages.

Self-Designating Opinion Leadership

The self-designating opinion leadership scale employed was a shortened version of a scale originally developed for a sample of Ohio farmers (Rogers 1962). The respondents were asked to indicate the tendency for others to seek them for information or advice.[10] Instead of asking respondents "who is your leader?" as in the case of sociometric opinion leadership, they were asked, "Are you a leader?"

[9] In the two traditional villages of Nazate and La Cañada, sociometric questions about marketing and politics were not included.

[10] Some typical items in this scale are as follows (the number in parentheses indicates how each item was scored):
1. Do people come to you for information or advice:
    Yes (2)   No (0)
2. In general, do you think people come to you for information or advice more often than to others:
    Yes (2)   No (0)
3. During the past six months have you talked with your neighbors about new ideas in agriculture:
    Yes (2)   No (0)

Self-Anchoring Ladder Measure

Self-perceived opinion leadership was also measured with a self-anchoring ladder technique.[11] The respondents were given a small card depicting a ten-step ladder during the interviews. The steps were numbered from one to ten, ten being the highest step. The interviewers told each respondent:

> At the highest step of the ladder are the people of this village from whom the other people of the village ask advice, whose opinions are taken into account by the people. At the lowest step of the ladder are the people who are never asked for advice. At which step do you think you are?

Rating by Judges

Judges' ratings of opinion leadership require that each judge be thoroughly familiar with the respondents. Cooperation of adequate judges could only be obtained in the three more modern communities. The local priest, an extension worker, and the school teacher[12] were asked to be judges. They were given cards each containing the name of a head of household in the village, and were asked: (1) to sort out the peasants they did not know, and (2) to place the remaining cards in categories from one to ten according to degree of opinion leadership. Opinion leadership scores were averaged for each respondent across the several judges who rated him.

INTERRELATIONSHIPS AMONG THE OPINION LEADERSHIP MEASURES

Table 10–2 indicates the generally positive interrelationships among the various measures of opinion leadership. This is reassuring in the face of comments by some critical observers that it is difficult or impossible to obtain valid sociometric data from peasant respondents. Where highly trained and qualified interviewers are utilized, and when proper pretesting and development of the sociometric questions is observed, accurate and valid data on sociometric opinion leadership can be gathered.

POLYMORPHIC OPINION LEADERSHIP

A high degree of interrelationship was observed among the responses to the several questions that made up the total sociometric score. Merton (1957: 415) termed this type of opinion leadership as "polymorphic," in that a single

---

[11] Professor Hadley Cantril (1963) of Princeton University developed this self-anchoring ladder technique to measure level of living; it has since been utilized in Asian, African, and Latin American countries. Use of the self-anchoring ladder technique to measure opinion leadership is largely the work of Professor Frederick B. Waisanen of Michigan State University.

[12] The school teacher was used as a judge of opinion leadership in only one village because in the other two villages, the school teachers were on vacation, and could not be contacted at the time of the data gathering.

Table 10–2. Zero-Order Correlations of Sociometric Choices with Other Measures of Opinion Leadership in Five Colombian Villages.

Measures of Opinion Leadership	Correlations with Sociometric Opinion Leadership Choices				
	Pueblo Viejo	San Rafael	Cuatro Esquinas	Nazate	La Cañada
1. Self-designating opinion leadership scale	$.280^a$	[.150]	$.320^a$	$.710^b$	[.010]
2. Self-anchoring ladder measure	$.320^b$	$.350^a$	[.230]	$.380^a$	[.100]
3. Ratings on opinion leadership by judges	$.440^b$	$.450^b$	$.390^b$	—^{c}	—^{c}

^{a} Significantly different from zero at the 5 percent level.
^{b} Significantly different from zero at the 1 percent level.
^{c} No ratings on opinion leadership by judges were available in the two traditional villages of Nazate and La Cañada.

leader is influential about a variety of topics. Opinion leadership in relatively more modern social systems is expected to be more monomorphic; that is, an opinion leader is influential for only one type of information and advice, and other leaders are sought for other topics. Roles are expected to be more specialized and functionally differentiated in modern systems. Different opinion leaders are viewed as credible and competent for different issues.

An example of the high degree of polymorphism of opinion leaders in traditional settings is provided by Lerner (1958:26), who reports the following from an interview with the chief of a Turkish village:

CHIEF: This is my main duty, to give advice.
INTERVIEWER: What about?
CHIEF: About all that you or I could imagine, even about their [the villagers'] wives and how to handle them, and how to cure their sick cow.

In general, a rather high degree of polymorphic opinion leadership was found in the five Colombian villages;[13] that is, a single leader was often influential in providing information and advice on all the topics studied. For instance, in one village, the opinion leader who received the most *total* sociometric choices received the most choices for three of the topics (borrowing capital, politics, and marketing products), was in second place for one topic (agriculture), and tied for second and third place for two topics (main crop grown and health).

Ten percent of the respondents who ranked highest in total sociometric opinion leadership scores in each community, received from 54 to 67 percent of

[13] The polymorphic opinion leadership pattern is further supported by the results of factor analysis in Chapter 14.

all opinion leadership choices on specific topics. This is further evidence of the general polymorphic nature of opinion leadership in the five communities.[14]

The opinion leadership pattern had been expected to be somewhat more monomorphic in the more modern villages. However, *opinion leadership in the three modern villages is no more monomorphic than in the two traditional villages.* Perhaps the range in degree of modernization between the modern and traditional villages is not yet wide enough to affect the degree of polymorphism of opinion leadership.[15]

CHARACTERISTICS OF OPINION LEADERS

In general the Colombian opinion leaders,[16] when compared to their followers[17] (Figure 10–2), in *both* modern and traditional communities, are characterized by: (1) more formal education; (2) higher levels of functional literacy; (3) larger farms (acreage); (4) more farm and home innovativeness; (5) higher social status; (6) lower achievement motivation,[18] (7) more mass media exposure; (8) higher empahy; (9) more political knowledgeability.

In the modern villages, but not in the traditional villages, the opinion leaders are younger in age and more cosmopolite than their followers. How can this finding be explained?

OPINION LEADER-FOLLOWER DIFFERENCES
IN MODERN AND TRADITIONAL VILLAGES

Do village norms help account for opinion leader-follower differences?

Age

Whereas leaders are older than followers in the more traditional villages, they are younger than their followers in the more modern communities (Figure 10–2). Lerner (1958:399) reports a similar relationship between age and opinion leadership in more and in less traditional countries in the Middle East. "The traditional rule that *age brings wisdom* probably worked well in immobile isolated villages, where change was slow and experience was the

---

[14] Although of course the measure of polymorphism is a relative one.

[15] Or perhaps the range of opinion leadership topics (agriculture, health, politics, and so forth) was not very wide in that they were all concerned with village problems.

[16] The opinion leaders are rather arbitrarily considered the 10 percent of the peasants who received the most sociometric choices in each village. In the three modern villages, there were 17 opinion leaders and 143 followers; in the more traditional villages, there were 9 opinion leaders and 86 followers.

[17] For shorthand convenience, the nonleaders are referred to as followers, although in a strict sense they may not all be followers of the opinion leader respondents.

[18] This finding suggests that perhaps the opinion leaders perceive themselves as having "arrived" in terms of occupational excellence.

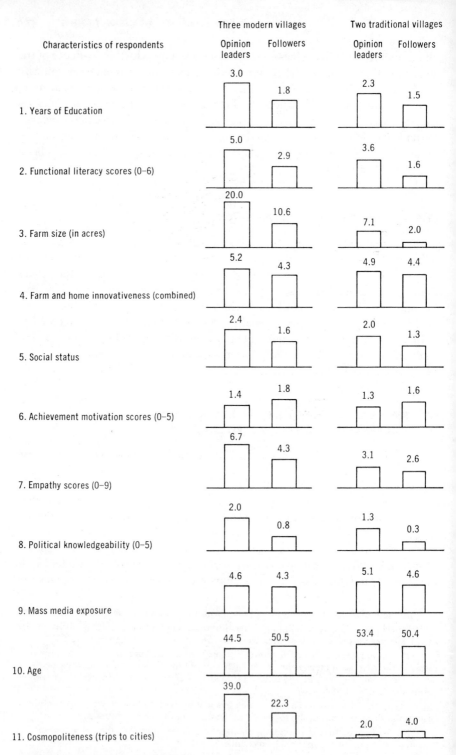

Figure 10-2. Differences between Opinion Leaders and Followers in Modern and Traditional Villages in Colombia.

only teacher. The longer one lived, the more experience he gained and the greater his title to wisdom. Now the young men no longer await their patrimony . . . ." Our village data suggest a similar logic; where change is occuring more rapidly, as in the modern villages, age is no longer a criterion for the selection of opinion leaders. Age is replaced by technical competence, social accessibility, and cosmopolite communication behavior.

Cosmopoliteness

There are extreme differences between the modern and traditional villages in the number of trips to urban centers made by all respondents. The average for all farmers in the modern communities is 24, while the average is 4 in the traditional communities. Followers in the traditional villages average twice as many trips to urban centers per year as do leaders. However, in the modern villages opinion leaders travel to the city much more often than their followers. This finding supports the general notion that leaders are more conformist to social system norms than followers.[19] In the traditional villages, where to be cosmopolite is to be deviant from localistic norms, the opinion leaders are less cosmopolite.[20]

Another somewhat parallel explanation is that the rate of change in the traditional villages was very slow; hence, there was little need for the opinion leaders to be cosmopolite because few ideas were entering these villages from external sources. "It is the opinion leader's function to bring the group into touch with this relevant part of its environment through whatever media are appropriate" (Katz 1957). When external sources are not important as a source of innovations, as in the traditional villages, there is less need for opinion leaders to be cosmopolites.[21]

OPINION LEADERSHIP, INNOVATIVENESS, AND DEVIANCY FROM NORMS

Leaders lead not so much because they possess certain traits or characteristics (in fact, most studies show that leaders are very much like the followers with whom they interact), but rather because they are easily *accessible* to their followers, more *competent* (but not *too* much so) than their followers, and in general *conform* to the norms of the system (Katz 1957). Miguel Gomez is illustrative of these three factors. His home at the fork in the trail made him

[19] It is also a parallel conclusion to that evident in Lerner's (1958) analysis of the localite chief and the cosmopolite grocer in the Turkish village of Balgat (Chapter 7).

[20] Because of the uncertainty of the time-order of these variables, it is also possible that because the leaders in the traditional villages are localistic, the norms are more localistic (at least compared to the modern villages).

[21] Or, in Homans' (1961) words, the importation of innovations from external sources is not a "rare and valuable service" that the opinion leader needs to perform in the traditional village.

accessible. He began learning about new farm ideas from the extension workers and soon became more knowledgeable than the traditional opinion leaders, but not *too* much more knowledgeable and innovative than most of his fellow villagers. And his behavior generally conforms to the relatively modern norms of Pueblo Viejo.

Homans (1961) stated that leaders obtain their position of influence by rendering valuable and rare services to their group. In any system the number of people who produce valuable and rare services is relatively small, and consequently the number of recipients of these services is relatively large. Leader conformity to the group norms is a valuable service to the group, although only a rare one if the conformity is closer than that of other group members. Thus, an important criterion for an opinion leader is to conform closely to the significant norms of the group.[22] "A man of high status will conform to the most valued norms of his groups as the minimum condition of maintaining his status" (Homans 1961:339). Of course, in some cases the high status member of a social system can also violate certain norms with greater impunity.

How can opinion leaders be most conformist to village norms, and also lead in the adoption of new ideas? The answer is, in part, that opinion leaders do not always lead in adopting innovations; in fact, they may influence their followers to reject innovations.[23] Secondly, where village norms favor social change, opinion leaders are more innovative and hence function in close conformity to the system's norms. Where the norms are traditional, opinion leaders again differ very little from their followers; the opinion leaders are not especially innovative. In fact, the innovators in these traditional systems are separate individuals from the opinion leaders; the innovators are viewed with suspicion and often with disrespect by the villagers.

In Colombia, *opinion leaders in the modern villages were more innovative than*

---

[22] A study by Merei (1949) illustrates the importance of leader conformity to group norms. In children's play groups, certain individuals emerged as leaders in initiating new activities. These leaders were removed from their groups while the remaining children continued to play. Shortly, new patterns of play were developed. When the former leaders were reintroduced into the groups they had previously led, they had to adapt to the new patterns. They could again become leaders only if they followed the rest of the group, if they observed the newly-developed norms on play.

[23] Klapper (1960:35) points out that practically no research attention has been paid to the possible influence of opinion leaders in discouraging change. While we did not gather much specific data on the effects of opinion leaders opposing change programs, in Pueblo Viejo, an elderly villager, who had been a village leader prior to the entry of the extension change agents, actively opposed their work. He refused to be interviewed by our interviewers, because he perceived that our investigation was associated with the extension workers. He also encouraged his followers (a small number) to refuse to be interviewed. We have only one other type of data about opinion leaders who oppose change. Each respondent was asked whether anyone had encouraged him *not* to adopt 2, 4-D weed spray. Only a small percent mentioned such negative influence, and the individuals named (those encouraging the rejection of the innovation) were not the same person. Thus we conclude that there was little negative opinion leadership in the case of the weed spray, but this might be due to the fact that it was a very successful innovation that had reached rather widespread adoption at the time of our data gathering.

their followers, but in the traditional villages the opinion leaders were only slightly more innovative than their followers.[24] So our data generally support the notion of opinion leaders as highly conformist to system norms.

The "animation" method of community development in Senegal utilizes an opinion leader approach to change, but care is taken not to alienate the peasants from village norms. Selected leaders are gathered in a two or three week institute or camp, where the discussion method is utilized to fan their motivation for change. Then, the leaders return to their villages to begin community improvement efforts. If the leader were to stay away longer, or be paid by the government, or receive formal schooling, he would be more likely to migrate from the village, or else the villagers would consider him an agent of the government (Hapgood 1965:119).

Another illustration of leader conformity to norms comes from a directed change program in Pakistan. Village leaders are brought to a training center for weekly sessions about agricultural and other innovations. The opinion leaders then return to their villages where they tell their fellows about the new ideas. Ordinarily, the villagers, when working in the muddy rice paddies, wear the bottoms of their *dhotis* (a sort of skirtlike work clothes) high up on their thighs. Nonpeasants, like the change agents at the training center, wear their *dhotis* at ankle length as a sort of status symbol. As time went on, the village leaders in Pakistan began to wear their *dhotis* lower and lower, mimicking the apparel of the change agents, and thus symbolizing their modernization. But when the leaders' *dhotis* crept below their knees, they found that they had lost their followers. The villagers perceived that their former leaders had become too much like the change agents. The moral is that change agents must guard against making village opinion leaders too innovative or too modern, or else they will become ex-leaders, who lost their following by deviating from the village norms.[25]

A MULTIPLE CORRELATION ANALYSIS OF OPINION LEADERSHIP

A review of the research literature discloses only one previous attempt to predict opinion leadership with a multiple correlation approach. Considerable practical benefits for change agents, who are often advised to concentrate their efforts upon opinion leaders, might result if a high degree of variance in opinion leadership could be explained in a multiple correlation analysis. Eight predictor variables were correlated with the dependent variable of

---

[24] Some empirical evidence for this generalization is shown graphically in Figure 10-2; clearer support comes from the results of factor analyses in Chapter 14. However, in a somewhat similar investigation in India, Yadav (1967) did not find entirely supportive evidence. Opinion leadership scores and agricultural innovativeness were more highly related in a modern village than in a traditional village, but the difference between the two correlations was not significant.

[25] A point that suggests that leadership is as much a property of the group as it is a characteristic of the individual.

opinion leadership in Colombia. The eight variables were selected from those utilized in the previous analysis of leader-follower differences, and represented social characteristics, communication exposure and cosmopoliteness, and modernization variables expected to be related to opinion leadership.

Table 10–3 shows the coefficient of multiple determination, R^2, which is the percent of variation in sociometric opinion leadership explained by the eight

Table 10–3. Multiple Correlation Analysis of Opinion Leadership in Five Colombian Villages

Predictor Variables	Percentage of Variation in Opinion Leadership Explained				
	Pueblo Viejo	San Rafael	Cuatro Esquinas	Nazate	La Cañada
1. Functional literacy	−1.96	19.50	4.14	−4.87	4.85
2. Farm size (in acres)	−2.82	−1.49	−2.84	8.91	1.13
3. Agricultural innovativeness	3.96	10.55	27.39	4.66	1.90
4. Social status	7.32	6.49	14.51	10.39	1.02
5. Mass media exposure	6.07	1.69	−4.78	4.80	4.66
6. Cosmopoliteness (number of trips to urban centers)	13.30	.07	−1.36	−.13	−.71
7. Empathy	2.77	14.92	−1.40	−.96	−1.20
8. Political knowledgeability	2.51	1.13	3.95	14.19	29.92
Percentage of variation in opinion leadership explained	33.15	58.86	39.61	36.99	41.57

independent variables for each of the five villages. The highest percentage, 59 percent, is in one of the modern villages, San Rafael. No consistent differences appear to exist between the traditional and the modern villages in the percent of variation explained. In other words, the eight predictor variables (when considered together) explain approximately similar portions of the variance in the dependent variable, opinion leadership, in both the modern and traditional villages.

Three variables, agricultural innovativeness, social status, and political knowledgeability, are consistently effective in explaining opinion leadership. Three other variables, functional literacy, trips to urban centers, and empathy, are each especially important in explaining opinion leadership in one village, but each are relatively less important in the other villages.[26]

[26] It may be worth noting that neither contact with urban centers nor empathy contributed to explaining opinion leadership in the two traditional communities (nor in Cuatro Esquinas, one of the modern villages). In fact, in these locales, they make a negative contribution to the coefficient of multiple determination, which indicates they are more highly related to the other seven predictor variables included in the analysis than they are related to opinion leadership.

Another variable, mass media exposure, explains relatively small amounts of the variation in opinion leadership scores, except in Cuatro Esquinas. The remaining independent variable, farm size, contributes to the prediction of opinion leadership only in the two traditional villages, and especially in Nazate. The present analysis offers little explanation of *why* certain independent variables are important in explaining opinion leadership in some communities and not in others. This explanation must await further research.

COMMUNICATION FLOW IN THREE MODERN COLOMBIAN VILLAGES

HOMOPHILY AND COMMUNICATION FLOW

"Birds of a feather flock together." This old adage reflects the tendency for individuals with similar attributes to interact with each other. A conceptual label — homophily — has only been assigned to this phenomenon in recent years (Lazarsfeld and Merton 1964:23), but the existence of homophilic behavior was noted a half century ago by Tarde (1903:64): "Social relations, I repeat, are much closer between individuals who resemble each other in occupation and education, even if they are competitors, than between those who stand most in need of each other."

Homophily is defined as the degree to which pairs of individuals who interact are similar in certain attributes. In other words, when two interacting peasants are alike in some characteristic, such as social status, they are homophilic. If two villagers are quite different in social status, they are "heterophilic," the opposite of homophily (Lazarsfeld and Merton 1964:23).

How does homophily come about? It may occur (1) due to the basis of *choice* between the interacting individuals, who naturally seem to gravitate toward communicating with others like themselves because they share common meanings and viewpoints, which makes their communication more effective, and hence more rewarding; or (2) as a *result* of previous communication in which messages were exhanged and accepted, bringing about more similar viewpoints.[27] In the first case similarity of attributes precedes communication.[28] The variables are probably in an interdependent relationship: individuals interact with others like themselves; this in turn leads to greater homogeneity in certain attributes, which encourages further interaction between homophilous pairs.

When an individual interacts with someone quite unlike himself, effective

[27] Although of course similarities in age and other demographic characteristics could hardly be explained as a result of previous communication leading to increased homogeneity.

[28] Lazarsfeld and others (1944:139) found in their investigation of the 1940 presidential election that "the changes in vote intention increase group homogeneity," which suggests that previous communication brings about greater homophily, at least in this specific situation.

communication seldom occurs.[29] Heterophily tends to cause cognitive dissonance; that is, exposure to messages inconsistent with one's existing beliefs leads to an uncomfortable psychological state that most individuals

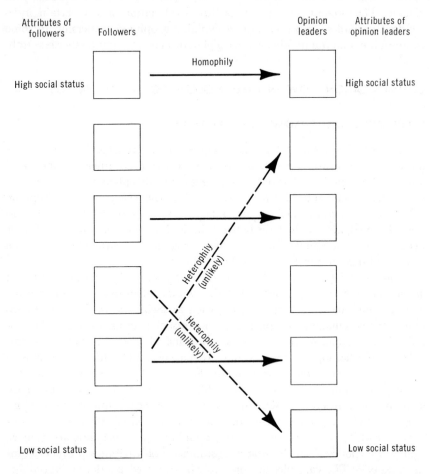

Figure 10–3.   Followers Generally Tend to Seek Ideas from Opinion Leaders Who Are Similar in Social Status (and in Other Attributes); Thus Homophily Is More Likely than Heterophily.

wish to avoid. Communication may occur occasionally between a pair of dissimilar individuals, but probably is not sustained over a considerable period of time. For example, in the Colombian villages there was the tendency

[29] Unless the two individuals have a very high degree of empathy and are thus able to put themselves in each others' roles, even though such roles are quite different from their own.

for informal interaction to occur between farmers of generally similar social status. Seldom did a small farmer initiate a discussion about an innovation with a very large landowner (*hacendado*); perhaps the small farmer thought the *hacendado* would be an inappropriate role model for his adoption behavior or maybe the *hacendado* was socially inaccessible to the small peasant. The lines of communication in a peasant village seem to flow horizontally within social classes, rather than vertically between those of different social classes (Figure 10–3). Opinion leaders probably tend to interact most with others like themselves in social status (and in other attributes).

Numerous research results indicate that homophily generally characterizes most communication patterns, but that the exact attributes on which homophily occurs, may vary.[30] Bose (1967) found a very high degree of homophily among the residents of a village in India on the basis of caste ranking, education, and farm size. In the nearby city of Calcutta, however, income was very important in determining interaction patterns, and caste was unimportant. In a U.S. city, Katz and Lazarsfeld (1955) conclude that most opinion-seeking was "horizontal," that is, from others of similar social status.

Homophily as a Barrier to Communication Flow

In one sense, homophily acts as an invisible barrier to the flow of innovations within a social system. New ideas usually enter a village through higher status peasants, who tend to have more mass media exposure and more cosmopolite relationships. The homophilic interaction patterns of the village cause new ideas to spread horizontally within the village to others of high status, and the innovation trickles down very slowly and indirectly to lower status peasants. Homophily can therefore act to slow down the rate of diffusion of ideas in a system. A Lebanese villager, interviewed by Lerner (1958: 192), reflects the importance of homophily as a barrier to the downward flow of mass media messages, "Townspeople do listen, but I don't know them. Rich people have radios [but] none around me have radios." The attributes on which homophily is based may include not only social status and income, but also mass media exposure, literacy, farm size, and so on.

One implication of the notion of homophily-as-a-barrier-to-idea-flow is that change agents should seek to work with several sets of opinion leaders distributed throughout the social structure. A change agent would only need to concentrate his efforts on one or a few opinion leaders who are near the top in social status or in innovativeness, if the social system were characterized by extreme heterophily. Most peasant villages are, in fact, probably characterized by hompohily. Unfortunately, many change agents continue

---

[30] Yadav (1967) analyzed homophily patterns in interpersonal diffusion in a traditional and a modern Indian village; his results largely support those of our Colombia data-analysis.

to use the heterophilic approach (of concentrating on only a few opinion leaders) in homophilic villages. They would achieve more successful results if they approached opinion leaders at each level in the social structure.

Dyadic Homophily in the Colombian Villages

The degree of homophily can be determined for an individual, a dyadic relationship between two individuals, or for a social system .[31] Almost all survey research utilizes the *individual* as the unit of analysis; he is the unit of response in the sample, and his data are coded and punched on a separate IBM card. Coleman (1958) argues that for many social research purposes, the *dyad*, or pair of individuals, is a more appropriate unit of analysis.[32] The importance of dyadic analysis is apparent for the study of interpersonal communication, such as that between opinion leaders and their followers in a peasant village.

In the three modern Colombian villages, dyadic opinion-seeking relationships were analyzed.[33] Pearsonian zero-order correlation was used as the index of homophily[34]; the higher the correlation coefficient, the greater the degree of homophily present. Table 10–4 presents the degree of dyadic homophily for seven variables; there appears to be a rather low degree of homophily for most of these variables, especially for cosmopoliteness, age, and social status. Even in the case of the highest correlation (for formal participation in San Rafael) in Table 10–4, only about 43 percent of the variance in this variable is explained by homophily in the opinion leader-follower dyad. In addition to formal participation, such variables as functional literacy, agricultural innovativeness, and mass media exposure demonstrate a modest degree of homophily in at least one of the three villages.

We conclude: *the degree of homophily in opinion leader-follower dyads is not a very important barrier to the diffusion of ideas* — at least in the three modern Colombian villages.[35] Evidently, within the Colombian villages most peasants interact freely with each other across status, literacy, and other lines.

[31] A different kind of homophily index, of course, is required for each of these different units of analysis.

[32] The data are usually secured from each member of the dyad, but information about the attributes of both are punched on *one* IBM card to represent the nature of the dyadic relationship.

[33] We obtained data on 68 sociometric dyads in Pueblo Viejo, 27 in San Rafael, and 69 in Cuatro Esquinas. In each case, both members of the dyad were interviewed. The sociometric question was concerned with seeking information and opinions about agricultural innovations.

[34] We feel this is preferable when the variables determining homophily are of an interval and continuous nature; however, when these variables are discrete, Coleman's (1958) homophily index may be more appropriate.

[35] Chou (1966) also reports a generally low degree of homophily for *friendship* dyads in these villages. Yadav (1967) found a rather low degree of homophily in two Indian villages.

Table 10–4. Homophily (Indexed by Pearsonian Zero-Order Correlation) between Leader-Follower Dyads in Three Modern Colombian Villages

	Index of Homophily (*Zero-Order Correlation*)		
Determinants of Homophily	Pueblo Viejo	San Rafael	Cuatro Esquinas
1. Functional literacy	.308[a]	[−.285]	[.103]
2. Agricultural innovativeness	[−.088]	[−.259]	.398[b]
3. Mass media exposure	.263[a]	[.274]	[.233]
4. Cosmopoliteness	[.090]	[.219]	[.136]
5. Formal participation	[.191]	.653[b]	.364[b]
6. Age	[.014]	[.221]	[−.128]
7. Social status	[.132]	[−.160]	[−.080]

[a] Significantly different from zero at the 5 percent level.
[b] Significantly different from zero at the 1 percent level.

Heterophily and Technical Competence

To what extent are the Colombian villagers likely to seek information and advice from opinion leaders more competent than themselves? Let us consider agricultural innovativeness, on which the respondents are classified into adopter categories, as a possible determinant of homophily. There was a tendency for "opinion seekers" to seek information and advice from those in a similar adopter category (that is, for homophily to occur). In fact, 117 of the 177 sociometric dyads (66 percent) are between the same or an adjoining adopter category.[36]

Opinion seekers are more likely to seek information and advice from more innovative individuals than from less innovative individuals. They look to opinion leaders of greater technical competence than themselves. Only 19 percent of the dyadic choices are to a less innovative adopter category, 30 percent are to an equally innovative category, and 51 percent are to a more innovative category. Thus, there is a general tendency for *opinion seekers to obtain information and opinions from opinion leaders who are more competent than themselves in technical knowledge, innovativeness, and so on.* Thus, when heterophily occurs, the opinion-seeker interacts with an opinion leader who is more innovative but not *too* much so.

Homophily in Traditional and Modern Villages

What differences exist between modern and traditional social systems in the degree of homophily across adopter categories? In order to answer this

[36] However, when innovativeness is measured less crudely by an innovativeness score, rather than in terms of adopter categories, as in Table 10-4, the indexes of homophily in the three villages are not very high.

question, an homophily index[37] was computed for the dyadic relationships in the modern and traditional villages. This index is a measure of the degree to which opinion-seekers interact with adopter categories quite different from themselves. The homophily index for adopter categories in the three more modern systems is .80, and for the two traditional villages, .68. Thus, innovativeness acts to impede communication flow to a somewhat greater degree in more traditional communities.[38] In other words, the downward flow of new ideas is more frequently encountered in the more modern villages.

An index was also computed of the degree to which sociometric choices in a social system go to *more* innovative, rather than to *less* innovative individuals, when heterophily does occur. The index for the more modern communities is 0.42 and for the traditional communities, −0.02; this means that in the traditional villages, farmers are slightly more likely to seek opinion leaders who are less innovative than themselves, whereas farmers in modern systems seek more expert opinion leaders.[39] The heterophilous sociometric arrows thus go "downward" to less technically competent peasants in the traditional villages, but go "upward" to more innovative opinion leaders in the modern villages.

Thus, *greater homophily on the basis of innovativeness is found in the traditional villages, where it acts to impede the rate of diffusion of innovations.*[40] Further, *in the traditional villages opinion-seekers tend to interact with opinion leaders less innovative than themselves, whereas in modern villages opinion leaders are sought who are more innovative than the opinion-seekers.*[41]

MASS MEDIA EXPOSURE AND THE MULTISTEP FLOW

One of the assumptions of the two-step flow of communication model, which was discussed earlier in this chapter, is that opinion leaders obtain new ideas from mass media channels and then pass them along to their followers via interpersonal communication channels. Translated into the language of the present investigation, this notion implies that opinion-givers (a term used for the "opinion leader" in the dyadic analysis) have higher mass media exposure than opinion-seekers.

Figure 10–4 shows this tends to be so, at least for the eleven dyadic re-

[37] This homophily index was computed as the average number of adopter categories between opinion seekers and soughts. When the average sociometric choice in a village is across fewer categories, the index is larger.

[38] This may also explain, in part, why these high homophily villages are so traditional.

[39] This again demonstrates the point made earlier in this chapter about opinion leaders' conformity to norms: in the traditional villages the opinion leaders are not innovative, but in the modern villages the opinion leaders are almost the same as the innovators.

[40] Confirmatory evidence is provided by Yadav (1967) from his analysis of data from a traditional and a modern Indian village.

[41] The two generalizations stated here about dyadic homophily on innovativeness were also supported by parallel findings on social status (Rogers and van Es 1964:47).

lationships in one of the three cliques in Pueblo Viejo. *Opinion-seekers have lower mass media exposure than the opinion-givers.* There is a consistent trend in nine of the eleven dyads to seek an opinion-giver with higher mass media

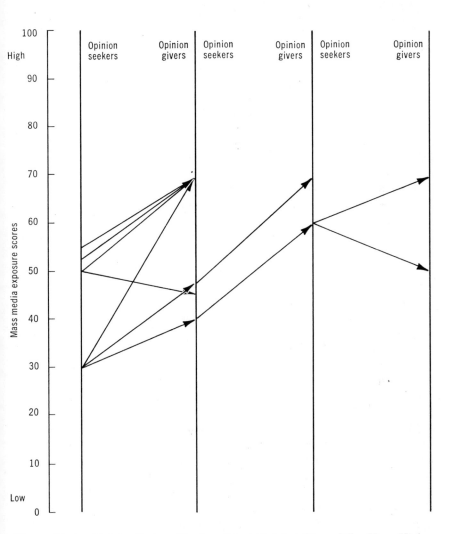

Figure 10–4.   Opinion-Seekers Tend to Select Opinion-Givers Who Have Higher Mass Media Exposure.

This diagram of dyadic opinion seeking about agricultural innovations in one clique in Pueblo Viego shows the tendency for opinion-seekers to select opinion-givers who have higher mass media exposure. Nine of the eleven dyadic relationships shown in this figure are to opinion-givers with higher mass media exposure, and only two sociometric arrows go to peasants with lower media exposure. Generally similar patterns were observed in the other cliques in Pueblo Viego, and in the two other modern villages.

exposure than the opinion-seeker. Further evidence for this generalization comes (1) from the other two cliques in Pueblo Viejo, where tweny-seven of thirty-seven dyadic choices are to opinion-givers with higher mass media exposure, and (2) from the other two modern villages.

The dyadic data in Figure 10–4 suggest further that the *two*-step flow notion is an oversimplification, as suggested earlier. If one looks only at any given dyadic unit in the communication flow, there are indeed two steps involved, but many of these dyads are in turn linked into complex chains of communication flow (Figure 10–4). Thus, on the basis of innovation diffusion patterns in the Colombian villages, it is concluded that the *multistep flow of communication* is a more apt model to describe the reality of idea transmission.[42]

SUMMARY

The present chapter sought (1) to identify the characteristics of opinion leaders and followers in both traditional and modern villages in Colombia, and (2) to analyze the nature of communication flow with dyadic analysis. *Opinion leadership* is defined as the ability to influence others' behavior in a desired way. A sociometric measure of opinion leadership was developed by asking respondents from whom they would seek information and opinions about such aspects of rural Colombian life as agriculture, marketing, credit, health, and politics. Judges' ratings, a self-designating scale, and a self-anchoring ladder measure were also utilized to operationalize opinion leadership. These three measures were correlated with the sociometric measure to provide some evidence of the validity of the latter.

Sociometric opinion leadership was found to be rather polymorphic in both the modern and traditional villages in that generally similar opinion leaders were selected for the different topics studies (such as agriculture, politics, and so on).

In general the opinion leaders, when compared to the followers, in *both* modern and traditional villages were characterized by: (1) more formal education; (2) higher levels of literacy; (3) larger farms; (4) more agricultural and home innovativeness; (5) higher social status; (6) lower achievement motivation; (7) more mass media exposure; (8) higher empathy; (9) more political knowledgeability. Only in the modern villages were the opinion leaders found to have younger age and greater cosmopoliteness than their followers.

Support was provided by the present investigation (in both modern and traditional systems) for a general picture of the opinion leader as one who has more contact with the origins of new ideas than his followers. Most innovations enter Colombian peasant villages from external origins by way of mass

---

[42] Further evidence for this point is presented on the basis of our diffusion simulation approach in Chapter 15.

media channels and interpersonal contact with urban centers. Opinion leaders are characterized by greater mass media exposure and cosmopoliteness (except in the two traditional villages, where levels of cosmopoliteness were very low) than their followers; they display higher social status and more innovativeness. Opinion leaders tend to conform more closely to village norms than do their followers; when the norms favor modernity, the leaders are innovative, but when the norms are traditional, the leaders are only slightly more innovative than their followers.

An attempt was made to explain the variation in opinion leadership scores with eight independent variables, which were combined in a multiple correlation analysis. The amount of variance in opinion leadership explained ranged from about 59 percent in San Rafael to 31 percent in Pueblo Viejo. Three of the independent variables (agricultural innovativeness, social status, and political knowledge) were consistently more important in explaining opinion leadership in the five villages.

Homophily is the degree to which pairs of individuals who interact are similar in certain attributes. When there is a high degree of homophily in a village, the downward flow of new ideas is slowed because innovators interact with other innovators, large farmers with large farmers, and so on. The degree of homophily in opinion leader-follower dyads was not a very important barrier to the diffusion of ideas in the modern Colombian villages. Opinion-seekers tend to obtain information and opinions from opinion leaders who are more competent (but not *too* much so) than themselves in technical knowledge innovativeness, and so forth. There was greater homophily on the basis of innovativeness in the traditional villages, where it acts to impede the rate of diffusion of innovations. When heterophily does occur in traditional villages, opinion-seekers tend to interact with opinion leaders who are more innovative than the opinion-seekers.

It was also found that opinion-seekers have lower mass media exposure than the opinion-givers. This supports an assumption of the two-step flow model — that opinion leaders have higher media exposure than their followers. Further, the sociometric data lend support to the notion of a multistep flow of communication, consisting of complex chains of interpersonal communication relationships.

Homans' (1961) statement that leaders provide rare and valuable services to the group was perhaps supported in the sense that the opinion leaders in villages studied seemed to act as key individuals in the process by which new ideas entered the systems. Thus, in these relatively localite systems, the opinion leaders performed an important group function by linking the village with the outside world.

11

Achievement Motivation*

Question: "*Do you think that a person born in poverty is able to change his economic situation?*"
(Research Interviewer)

Answer: "*Si, señor, for this you need no more than first to think, to have an inspiration to go forward and so thinking, accomplish it.*"
(Colombian peasant with high achievement motivation)

Answer: "*Depending upon God, if He made one poor, he is poor. If He made one rich, he is rich.*"
(Colombian peasant with low achievement motivation)

The citizens of Antioquia, Colombia appear to be quite unlike other Latin Americans in many of the social values and attitudes they hold. The Antioqueños place a high value on hard work, education, and personal advancement. They seem to be natural-born traders, entrepreneurs, and daring businessmen, who are famously "tight" with the peso. They dominate the ranks of captains of industry in Colombia, and are relatively wealthy compared with the average Colombian. In contrast to the aversion for hand-labor found elsewhere in Latin America, Antioqueños work diligently, apparently enjoying manual labor. I remember my surprise, when upon awakening one morning at 4:30 a.m. in an Antiqueño village, I found the darkened streets filled with villagers on their way to work. The rather un-Latinlike values of Antioqueños have prompted their countrymen to term them the "Jews of Colombia," although there is no solid evidence pointing to a Jewish origin (Hagen 1962:371–373).

Why did the Antioqueños, and other entrepreneurially-talented ethnic groups like them (such as the Hindus in Africa, the Chinese in Thailand, the Sikhs in India, the Ibos of Nigeria, the Kikuyus in Kenya, the Hugenots in France, the Jews in the United States, and the Monteros in Mexico), become so success-oriented, so aspiration-centered, and so work-minded? The answer, says one leading social scientist, is achievement motivation.

* This chapter is essentially a distillation of Everett M. Rogers with Ralph E. Neill 1966, *Achievement Motivation Among Colombian Peasants*, East Lansing, Michigan State University, Department of Communication, Diffusion of Innovations Research Report 5.

WHAT IS ACHIEVEMENT MOTIVATION?

Achievement motivation is a social value that emphasizes a desire for excellence in order to attain a sense of personal accomplishment.[1] Achievement motivation has also been referred to as need for achievement, *n* Achievement or *n* Ach. No social motive has been more thoroughly studied than achievement motivation.[2] Most noted for his investigations of achievement motivation is David C. McClelland, a social psychologist at Harvard University. McClelland and his colleagues have primarily utilized college students as respondents; they measure achievement motivation with a modified version of the Thematic Aperception Test (TAT). This type of projective technique[3] may serve as a satisfactory measure under laboratory conditions, but it is not as well suited to field interviewing conditions as another projective measure — a scale composed of sentence-completion items. The advantage of the sentence-completion measure is that it requires much less interview time to administer, is accepted more readily by respondents, and is more easily scored than the TAT measure. Investigations by Morrison (1962) and by Neill and Rogers (1963) demonstrate that measurement of achievement motivation with a sentence-completion scale in field interviews with U.S. farmers is possible. However, the present investigation is the first attempt to measure achievement motivation among peasant villagers in a less developed nation like Colombia. In fact, almost no research has been completed on achievement motivation in developing nations, especially among peasant respondents.

ACHIEVEMENT MOTIVATION AMONG PEASANTS

Why study achievement motivation among peasants? For one reason, most descriptions of peasant life seem to imply that most peasants are characterized by extremely low achievement motivation. The peasant's life-situation includes limited resources, blocked opportunities, authoritarian child-rearing, and exploitation by others. These environmental factors tend to produce individuals with low achievement motivation. The typical Colombian peasant is pictured in anthropological and sociological studies as fatalistic in his out-

---

[1] This definition is based upon McClelland (1961 and 1963b:76). At a later point in the present chapter, it will be argued that achievement motivation should be regarded as a rather special type of social value.

[2] As LeVine (1966:12) points out.

[3] A *projective technique* is "an instrument that is considered especially sensitive to covert or unconscious aspects of behavior, it permits or encourages a wide variety of subject responses, is highly multidimensional, and it evokes unusually rich or profuse response data with a minimum of subject awareness concerning the purpose of the test" (Lindzey 1961:45). Examples of projective techniques are TATs, word association, the Rorschach test, and sentence-completions.

look on life and low in achievement motivation. "Resignation, docility, and fatalism were the natural result of the settled, unbending conditions created during colonial times" says Fals Borda (1955:245), who argues that low levels of aspiration may be functional for peasants whose opportunities have historically been severely limited. Similarly, Rosen (1964), describing one reason for the lower levels of achievement motivation that he found among Brazilian urban boys when compared to their North American counterparts, states: "Where poverty is widespread and opportunity for advancement very limited, where only a few enjoy power and independence while most are powerless and dependent, the belief that the individual has little control over his environment is perhaps inevitable — and probably psychologically functional."

It is a common notion in Colombia that peasant boys who possess higher levels of achievement motivation are likely to migrate to the cities where there may be greater opportunities for fullfilling their achievement values. One result of this selective farm-city migration is to drain off those village youths with higher levels of achievement motivation, thereby perpetuating peasant pools of low achievement motivation.

Nevertheless, one of the assumptions of the present study is that differences in achievement motivation exist among peasants, that peasants are not completely homogeneous in this regard.[4] It is further assumed that these differences in achievement motivation are measurable, and have important consequences for development and modernization.

The analysis of the Colombian data is aimed at probing the relationship of achievement motivation with certain of its antecedents such as childhood personality socialization, communication exposure, and other modernization variables. Further, if significant relationships can be shown between achievement motivation and modernization consequents such as excellence in farming, we shall be one step closer to understanding modernization among peasants. Finally, by comparing the Colombian findings regarding antecedents and consequences of achievement motivation with findings from a different cultural setting such as India, hopefully some cross-cultural consistencies regarding peasant achievement motivation can be established.

THEORIES OF SOCIAL VALUES IN ECONOMIC DEVELOPMENT

WEBER

Weber (1930) postulated that the rise of capitalism in Europe was associated with a basic change in social values that occurred as a result of the Protestant Reformation. He described the essential elements of the Protestant

---

[4] Even though peasants throughout the world are relatively lower in achievement motivation than urbanites, there are still important individual differences in this dimension among villagers.

Ethic as a belief in the value of work, an emphasis upon savings and thrift, and a desire for upward social mobility. In a more general sense, Weber was pointing out the relationship between a change in social values and the resulting increase in economic development.

ROSTOW

Rostow (1961) represents the viewpoint of several social scientists who conceptualize the economic development process as composed of a series of stages: (1) traditional society; (2) preconditions for take-off; (3) take-off; (4) drive to maturity; and (5) age of high mass-consumption. At the take-off stage, in which a widespread desire for economic development is expressed by society, Rostow recognizes that a new type of entrepreneurship must emerge, "It is evident that the take-off requires the existence and the successful activity of some group in the society which is prepared to accept innovations . . . ." Rostow states that a corps of entrepreneurs must arise at the take-off stage in order for economic development to occur, but he does not specify the social values that these new elites must possess.

HAGEN

Hagen (1962:ix) sought to answer the question, "Why have the people of some societes entered upon technological progress sooner or more effectively than others?" The answer, Hagen feels, lies in the social-psychological processes of childhood personality development, where social values are learned. He stresses the role of value changes in causing economic development, and suggests that two social values, achievement and autonomy, are most central to national economic development. These values, Hagen feels, historically arise when some elite group in a traditional society suffers "withdrawal of status respect" by being conquered or losing political power. After a period of retreatism and inferiority, the offspring of these former elites emerge with a high degree of achievement and autonomy as a result of their nonauthoritarian childrearing. These relatively deprived minority groups then demonstrate their entrepreneurial ability in economic growth.

McCLELLAND

McClelland (1961) sought to show that an essential ingredient of entrepreneurship leading to economic development is achievement motivation. In comparison to previous theories, McClelland's has the advantage of a more limited scope, a sounder social-psychological basis, and a greater potential for empirical testing.

The central social value[5] in McClelland's model — achievement motivation — is not specifically defined,[6] but he equates it to an inner concern with achievement, a disposition to engage in activities in which doing well or competing with a standard of excellence are important.[7] He emphasizes that achievement motivation is a desire for excellence, not so much for the sake of social recognition, but rather to attain an inner feeling of personal accomplishment. The similarity between achievement motivation and certain aspects of the Protestant Ethic is noted by McClelland (1961:47), "Certainly, Weber's description of the kind of personality type which the Protestant Reformation produced is startlingly similar to the picture we have drawn of a person with high achievement motivation."

McClelland and his students[8] present a wide range of evidence for his hypothesis that levels of achievement motivation are related to national economic development. The societies investigated are ancient Greece, pre-Inca Peru, Spain in the Middle Ages, England from 1500 to 1850, 22 countries from 1925 to 1950, and 39 countries from 1950 to 1958. Critics of McClelland's work point to (1) the inadequacy of his measures of achievement motivation and economic development in some cases, (2) the implication that a *causal* relationship exists between achievement motivation and economic development, and (3) the usage of nations as the unit of analysis, an aggregation that masks the nature of many relationships. However, certain of McClelland's (and his students') investigations indicate that economic success at the individual level is related to achievement motivation. This relationship has been found for U.S. businessmen (McClelland 1961), Turkish businessmen (Bradburn 1960:103), and artisans in India (Fraser 1961).

Although correlational analysis can tell us much about the *relationships* of achievement motivation to other variables, it cannot prove that achievement motivation *causes* individual economic success and national economic development. The time-order aspect of cause-and-effect relationships[9] can

[5] A question might be raised at this point as to whether achievement motivation is a social value. Certainly, achievement motivation is somewhat different in nature than, for example, the social value on work. Nevertheless, in terms of commonly-accepted definitions of social values, we feel that achievement motivation can be considered as a type of social value. Rosen (1964) prefers to speak of the "achievement syndrome," in which he includes achievement motivation and such "achievement values" as activism, independence, and future orientation. In general, most authors seem to regard achievement motivation as a rather special type of social value.

[6] McClelland's book, *The Achieving Society* (1961), was criticized by Hagen (1961) for its lack of a precise definition of achievement motivation.

[7] McClelland and others (1953:110) state, "Success in competition with some standard of excellence . . . is our generic definition of n Achievement." Further, McClelland (1964a) regards achievement motivation as " . . . a spontaneously expressed desire to do something well for its own sake rather than to gain power or love, recognition or profit."

[8] These studies are summarized in McClelland (1961). Among the works of McClelland's students are Bradburn and Berlew (1961) and Cortes (1961).

[9] But probably not the "forcing quality" of one variable upon another, which is the other basic ingredient of cause-effect relationships.

be better determined by experiments over time; McClelland and his followers have completed several recent analyses of this type which suggest that by raising levels of achievement motivation through counseling or special training, the likelihood of success is increased among college students (Burris 1958), high school underachievers (Kolb 1963), and U.S., Mexican, and Indian businessmen (McClelland 1964a and 1964b).[10]

Thus, considerable evidence exists for McClelland's hypothesized relationships between achievement motivation and (1) individual excellence, and (2) national economic development. No study has yet investigated this hypothesis among peasants in a developing country. The present inquiry was designed to test a part of McClelland's model with data from peasants in Colombia and India.

A MODEL OF ACHIEVEMENT MOTIVATION AND MODERNIZATION

In the present investigation, achievement motivation is defined as a social value that emphasizes a desire for excellence in order to attain a sense of personal accomplishment. It is possible for an individual to display achievement motivation in numerous types of activities, such as in school, sports, sex, or work. In this study, the primary concern is with the *occupational* expression of achievement motivation. Achievement motivation is limited at the operational level to occupational success because of the desire for comparison with the recent research of McClelland (1961), Morrison (1962), and Neill and Rogers (1963), and the conceptual importance of occupational expressions of achievement motivation as a predictor of economic development. The present investigation is therefore operationally limited to the study of the occupational aspects of achievement motivation.

The present study is further limited to expressions of achievement motivation in one occupation, agriculture. Economic growth in a developing nation must usually start in the agricultural sector. Until peasants adopt new farm technology and become more productive, adequate food cannot be provided for an increasing population, and the prospects of rapid and balanced economic growth are hampered.

Figure 11–1 presents the theoretical paradigm, closely based upon that of McClelland's (1961), which is utilized in this study. Two basic hypotheses derive from this model: the first proposition deals with possible consequences, and the other with antecedents of achievement motivation.

1. *Levels of achievement motivation vary directly with the nature of family structure and personality socialization, communication exposure, and modernization variables.*

[10] Perhaps it is significant that these recent field experimental studies by McClelland and his colleagues suggest that achievement motivation can be increased (through intensive training sessions), leading to corresponding increases in occupational performance. Hence both McClelland and Lerner share an assumption with the present authors that *adult* modernization can occur; Weber, Rostow, and Hagen imply that changes in social values occur mainly as part of childhood socialization.

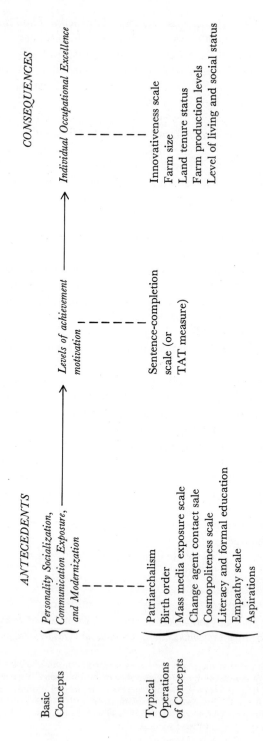

Figure 11–1. Paradigm of Antecedents to Achievement Motivation and Its Consequences.

2. *Individual occupational excellence varies directly with levels of achievement motivation.*

The model depicts achievement motivation as developing from various modernization antecedents, and in turn leading to expressions of occupational excellence.

A SENTENCE-COMPLETION MEASURE OF ACHIEVEMENT MOTIVATION

Past research and theory suggest the difficulty of measuring achievement motivation with direct questions. Individuals often have inaccurate perceptions of their level of achievement motivation. The TAT-type measure of achievement motivation widely used by McClelland and his associates with college student respondents requires considerable time to administer in field interviews (our experience indicates this is somewhat more than 30 minutes in the case of Colombian farmers), and seemed to meet resistance on the part of our respondents when they were asked to tell stories about what was going on in the four TAT pictures.[11] They would answer probe questions about the TAT pictures, but generally they would not volunteer stories or lengthy answers.

The research of Morrison (1962) and Neill (1963) indicates that a sentence-completion measure of achievement motivation was satisfactory for use with U.S. farmers. Such a measure can be administered in a few minutes of interview time, encounters less respondent resistance than the TAT, and adapts more easily to peasant conditions in Colombia.

Only sparse and somewhat contradictory evidence existed in the research literature[12] on the use of sentence-completion items as a measure of achievement motivation until the Morrison (1962) study among Wisconsin farmers. He developed an eight-item, sentence-completion measure of achievement motivation.[13] The items were constructed on the basis of McClelland's scoring

[11] Recently, Wright and others (1967:36) report an evidently successful experience in using a series of eight projective pictures to measure achievement motivation in personal interviews with Guatemalan peasants. The pictures showed village scenes, and perhaps this is one reason for their effectiveness with the respondents. However, the authors reported that many respondents were still unable to provide meaningful data.

[12] Studies which have utilized sentence-completion measures of achievement motivation are Lindzey and Heinemann (1955), McClelland and others (1953:254–257), and Mitchell (1961).

[13] Not only did Morrison (1962) find some evidence for the "construct validity" of his sentence-completion measure (that is, his scale behaved about as expected in its relationship to measures of farm success), but he also administered the McClelland-type TAT measure of achievement motivation to a subsample of 37 of his 335 respondents. He found a significant correlation of +.33 between the TAT and the sentence-completion measure. Both measures tended to operationalize the same concept (although far from identically), and the sentence completions did so in a more appropriate manner in terms of farmer respondents. Furthermore, Morrison reports that his sentence-completion scale correlated at least as consistently (that is, as expected on the basis of theory) with measures of farm success as did the TAT measure of achievement motivation.

rationale for the TAT measure. Typical item stems were "A farmer today should . . .", "A good farmer . . .", and "A 400 acre farm . . . ." The responses were scored using a version of McClelland and others' (1953) scoring guide, originally developed to quantify TAT protocols.

Both the Wisconsin and the Ohio studies (by Neill 1963; and Neill and Rogers 1963) generally indicate the potential for measuring achievement motivation among farmers with sentence-completion items. However, no attempt has been made to measure achievement motivation with sentence completion items in a less developed country like Colombia,[14] where farmers are obviously much different from those in Wisconsin or Ohio.

SCALE ANALYSIS

Validity

A scale is said to be *valid* if it measures the concept that it is designed to measure. Although it is the most critical aspect of scale analysis, validity is the most difficult to determine. In Colombia, McClelland's TAT measure of achievement motivation was administered to a small subsample of our respondents, as well as the sentence-completion scale. The low but positive relationship found between the measures provide some tentative evidence for validity of the sentence-completion scale.[15]

Internal Consistency

Internal consistency is the degree to which items in a scale measure the same dimension. For the present scale items, internal consistency was determined by correlating each scale item with total scores, because the total scores represent the best available measure of the total concept. These item-total score correlations are somewhat spurious because the contribution of each item is also included in the total scores, but this difficulty is less serious with a greater number of scale items.

The final items included in the sentence-completion scale for each Colombian village are shown in Table 11–1, with the internal consistency correlations of each item with the total scores. A rather high degree of internal consistency can be noted. A somewhat different set of scale items was utilized to measure achievement motivation in each community. This is due in part to

[14] Phillips (1965) reports utilizing sentence completions with Thai peasants, although not to measure achievement motivation.

[15] After the present scale analysis was largely completed, the conclusions of Morrison (1964), were encountered: "While these data hardly provide a firm basis for concluding that the TATs and sentence-completions are tapping the same dimension, they seem to give some support to this notion. They most certainly do not give a basis for regarding TATs as an unequivocally 'known' measure of *n* Achievement for a sample of this sort". We agree on the basis of the present results.

Table 11–1. Item-to-Total Score Correlations for the Sentence-Completion AchievementMotivation Scale for Six Colombian Communities.

| Scale Item Stems | Item-to-Total Score Correlations for the Six Communities[a] | | | | | |
	Támesis	Pueblo Viejo	San Rafael	Cuatro Esquinas	Nazate	La Cañada
1. "If I lost an arm in an accident at work (or on my farm), I would . . ."	.260	—	—	—	.460	.540
2. "For a better life on my farm, I need . . ."	—	—	—	—	.670	.260
3. "I wish that my eldest son . . ."	.270	—	—	—	.500	.390
4. "In the next 10 years, I'm going to . . ."	.700	.380	.500	.550	.600	.560
5. "My greatest aspiration in life is . . ."	.280	—	—	—	.730	.560
6. "The thing most necessary for my farm is . . ."	—	.450	.440	.210	.460	.330
7. "Today, to have success in farming one . . ."	.460	—	—	—	.520	.420
8. "Farmers in this country need . . ."	—	.430	.330	.390	.430	.280
9. "A good farmer must have . . ."	.390	.490	.280	.460	.420	.350
10. "That which I wish to do on my farm in the future is . . ."	.600	—	—	—	.660	.610
11. "A good man is one that . . ."	.410	.460	.360	.130	.220	.230
12. "If my work did not progress, I . . ."	.360	.570	.410	.500	.620	.240
13. "To have 15 head of cattle is . . ."	—	.520	.460	.480	—	—
14. "To earn a good return from farming, a farmer must have . . ."	—	.460	.430	.250	—	—

[a] The dashes indicate that this particular scale item was not used in that community.

the subcultural differences among the three main study areas.[16] In any event, these differences in scale items suggest that the items used in the present investigation should be subjected to scale analysis again before they are utilized in future research to measure achievement motivation in Colombia or in other countries.

Reliability

Reliability is the degree to which a scale consistently produces similar results when administered to the same individuals at different times. In the split-half method of determining scale reliability, the items in a scale are divided into two subscales, and the correlation between these two subscores is computed. It is argued that administering two forms of the same scale at one point in time is approximately equivalent to administering the scale to the same individuals at two different times. The split-half coefficients of reliability for the six villages ranged from .20 to .75, which indicates a modest degree of scale reliablity.[17]

A second method of determining scale reliability, the test-retest technique, consists of administering the same scale items to the same respondents at two different times. Time and travel costs prevented the determination of test-retest reliabilities in each of the six villages, but retest data were gathered from sixteen respondents living in one of the six communities about ten weeks after the original interviews. The sentence completion scale was administered in its original form to the sixteen respondents, and the protocols were scored for level of achievement motivation by the same scorer. The coefficient of correlation between the test and retest scores is $+.24$, which offers very limited evidence of the reliability of the present instrument.[18]

Scoring Agreement

Scoring agreement is the similarity of one researcher's reading of an instrument with the readings made by other researchers. In the present investigation, the judges scoring the protocols were investigators from the National

[16] Where these regional differences were not encountered, among the three geographically-clustered Facatativa villages (Pueblo Viejo, San Rafael, and Cuatro Esquinas), it was possible to select eight items that functioned adequately in all three villages. Likewise, in Nazate and La Cañada (both located in the same region of Colombia), twelve common scale items were selected after analysis. This is one indication of the importance of subcultural differences in the development and selection of achievement motivation scale items in a culturally heterogeneous nation like Colombia.

[17] In fact, the coefficients of reliability in five of the six communities are over .44.

[18] This test-retest reliability coefficient obviously leaves much to be desired. Andrews (1963) reports test-retest reliability correlations ranging from $-.02$ to $+.57$ for the TAT measure of achievement motivation among Harvard University freshmen, Mexican businessmen, and children. He summarizes his findings by stating that " . . . It seems fairly clear that when n Ach is measured for stability over fairly long time-periods, the results are orderly and meaningful, not pure error variance." Andrews contends "That the TAT n Ach score is measuring 'something', in a consistent way, even when that score changes rather markedly over time." Kagan (1959) reports similarly low test-retest reliabilities for a TAT measure of achievement motivation, which was administered to eighty-six children at three-year intervals.

University of Colombia, who were thoroughly trained in the nature of achievement motivation and its measurement, who had served as field interviewers in the present investigation, and who were instructed in the use of a standard scoring guide. This protocol scoring system awarded zero points for an answer (to each scale item) indicating variables other than achievement motivation (such as patriotism, familism, or honesty); one point for a partial indicator of occupational achievement motivation (such as material concerns with property, work, or prosperity), and so forth, up to five points for definite indications of achievement motivation (such as responses dealing with need, attempt, and intention). As illustrations of use of this scoring guide, the reader's attention is again called to the responses from two farmers presented at the beginning of this chapter. The first peasant's answer ("To have an inspiration . . .") is scored "5," whereas the second peasant ("Depending upon God. . . .") is scored "0."

In order to determine interjudge scoring agreement, each of the protocols for the achievement motivation scale from one village were scored by three judges. Intercorrelations computed among the total scores assigned by each judge were .78, .62, and .75. In general, this reflects a rather high level of interjudge agreement, which is similar to the experience reported by Morrison (1962) and by Neill (1963).

Another method of determining judge agreement is for the same judge to score the same protocols at two different points in time; this is essentially one type of scoring reliability. One judge rescored the sentence-completion achievement motivation protocols for four of the six villages after a two month period. The coefficients of correlation ranged (by village) from .96 to .99. A very high judge reliablity over time is evident.

It has been shown that the sentence-completion measure of achievement motivation possesses a certain degree of validity, internal consistency, reliability, and scoring agreement.

ANTECEDENTS OF ACHIEVEMENT MOTIVATION

Does peasant achievement motivation vary directly with the nature of personality socialization, communication exposure, and modernization variables?

PERSONALITY SOCIALIZATION

Past writings generally indicate that an individual's level of achievement motivation is, at least in part, a function of certain family structural variables. For example, McClelland (1964c:185) stated " . . . There is substantiating evidence that n Achievement is a motive which a child can acquire quite early in life, say, by the age of eight or ten, as a result of the way his parents have brought him up."

Patriarchialism is defined as the degree to which family power is concentrated in the hands of the father. It is argued that authoritarian fathers usually produce sons with low achievement motivation because " . . . the son does not learn to set his own achievement goals and to learn to find his own ways of achieving them" (McClelland 1963a:173). One indicator of patriarchialism is whether the father is absent or present in the home during the years of childhood personality socialization — Colombian peasant fathers (when present) are generally quite patriarchal. Thus, if the father is absent from the home, there is greater likelihood that the son will develop higher achievement motivation. McClelland (1964c:186) states, "The extent to which the authoritarian father is away from the home while the boy is growing up may prove to be another crucial variable in higher achievement motivation." Bradburn (1960:133–135) found that Turkish college students who had lived in village institutes since age 14 had higher achievement scores than similar students who had lived with their parents. Furthermore, three samples of university education students, business students, and senior business executives whose fathers had died or lived apart from them had higher achievement motivation scores than comparable samples who had lived with both of their parents.

Data were available in the present investigation from only a subsample of the respondents with whom tape-recorded interviews were conducted. These data show a slight tendency for higher achievement motivation scores to be associated with father absence from the home before age 12 (due to such causes as death, separation, chronic illness, and so on) giving some rather tentative support for our hypothesis that *achievement motivation is negatively related to patriarchialism*.[19]

Rosen (1961) found that U.S. boys who were first born had higher achievement motivation than those later in birth order. The argument is that first born individuals are usually trained for higher achievement standards during childhood in order to assume greater responsibility for younger brothers and sisters. Findings from a sample of students in India (McClelland 1961:374) and of businessmen in Japan (Abegglen 1958), however, indicate that younger sons may have higher achievement motivation.[20] The findings in Table 11–2 provide *no evidence of a relationship between achievement motivation and birth order among Colombian peasants*.

---

[19] Investigation of the relationship of authoritarianism to achievement motivation, and to other modernization variables, is needed in future studies. Elder (1965) found that individuals possessing an autocratic family ideology (probably one indicator of generally authoritarian attitudes) were fatalistic, low in formal education, lacking in interpersonal trust, and low in political knowledge. Elder's respondents were urbanites in the United States, Great Britain, Germany, Italy, and Mexico.

[20] These findings support the argument that in cultures where the oldest son is the prime inheritor, and younger sons must "find for themselves," the younger sons are more apt to be highly motivated entrepreneurs, and generally more achievement-oriented.

Table 11–2. Zero-Order Correlations between Achievement Motivation Scores and Personality Socialization, Communication Exposure, and Modernization Variables for Six Colombian Villages

Personality Socialization, Communication Exposure, and Modernization Variables	Zero-Order Correlations with Achievement Motivation Scores by Village						
	Támesis	Pueblo Viejo	San Rafael	Cuatro Esquinas	Nazate	La Cañada	All Villages Combined
1. Respondent's birth order	—	—	—	—	[.130]	[−.038]	[.079]
2. Mass media exposure	[−.032]	[.169]	.373[a]	[.181]	.511[b]	.457[b]	.336[b]
3. Political knowledgeability	[.146]	[.176]	.411[a]	[.244]	.503[b]	.354[a]	.331[b]
4. Cosmopoliteness	[.084]	[.219]	.348[a]	[.142]	.325[a]	.297[a]	.236[b]
5. Extension change agent contact	[−.074]	[.236]	[−.019]	.375[b]	—	[.219]	.245[b]
6. Literacy	.332[a]	[.219]	[.285]	.294[a]	.436[b]	.353[a]	.301[b]
7. Years of formal education	.355[a]	[.048]	[.244]	[.083]	.462[b]	.349[a]	.254[b]
8. Empathy	—	.259[a]	.491[b]	.331[a]	.482[b]	.431[b]	.397[b]
9. Educational aspirations	—	[.020]	[.293]	.332[a]	.470[b]	.312[a]	.264[b]
10. Occupational aspirations	—	[.008]	[.101]	[.088]	.395[a]	[.120]	.129[a]

[a] Significantly different from zero at the 5 percent level.
[b] Significantly different from zero at the 1 percent level.

COMMUNICATION EXPOSURE

It is our belief that exposure to communication sources and channels (such as the city, mass media, or change agents) that reflect a more modern way of life will prompt peasants to achieve a higher level of living. The contents of the mass media in Colombia are highly urban-oriented and development-minded. Exposure[21] to such media content should help instill higher levels of achievement motivation. Table 11–2 shows one negative and five positive correlations (of which three are significant), indicating a generally *positive relationship between mass media exposure and achievement motivation.*

An indirect indicator of communication linkage with sources external to the village is the political knowledgeability scale, which represents knowledge of political events and leaders outside the village. Table 11–2 shows all six correlations are positive, and three are significant. *Achievement motivation is positively related to political knowledgeability.*

Cosmopolite villagers are oriented to a social system external to their own. This out-system orientation was measured with the number of trips to urban centers. The cosmopolite villager is more apt to strive toward the higher levels of living reflected in urban centers than is the village localite. The six positive correlations (three of which are significant) offer support for the *positive cosmopoliteness-achievement motivation relationship.*

Farmers who have a greater degree of contact with extension service change agents are expected to have higher achievement motivation. Table 11–2 shows three positive correlations (one of which is significant) and two negative correlations between achievement motivation scores and extension contact.[22] Our data, therefore, supply *little evidence that achievement motivation is positively related to extension contact.*

MODERNIZATION VARIABLES

Although modernization variables are arbitrarily shown as antecedents to achievement motivation in Figure 11–1, it is difficult to establish the time-order relationships between achievement motivation and variables such as literacy, formal education, empathy, fatalism, and aspirations. For example, one could argue that literacy and formal education increase the need to achieve, or on the other hand, that achievement motivation impels the peasant to attend school or adult literacy classes in order to learn to read. Rather than argue the case for a particular set of time-order relationships, let us merely point out that high achievement motivation characterizes a more

[21] Mass media exposure was measured by the frequency of reading, listening, and watching the five mass media available in Colombian villages: newspapers, magazines, radio, TV, and films (see Chapters 3 and 5 for details about the mass media exposure scale.)

[22] No correlation could be computed in Nazate because none of the respondents indicated any extension service contact.

modern peasant,[23] as do the other modernization variables. So perhaps these modernization indicators accompany achievement motivation, rather than precede it.

Among the Colombian respondents there was evidence to support the conclusion that *achievement motivation is positively related to literacy and to formal education.* Table 11–2 show that all twelve correlations are positive, and seven reach significance.

It is interesting to note that of all the "antecedent" variables correlated with achievement motivation, *empathy is most consistently and significantly related to achievement motivation.* Empathy evidently contributes to the individual's ability to internalize mass media messages and cosmopolite experiences. Empathic respondents should be able to imagine themselves psychologically in the roles of urban people, and therefore, perhaps be motivated to achieve a comparable level of living.

Achievement motivation seems to be in direct opposition to a fatalistic outlook on life. One could hardly be motivated to achieve, if he feels the determinants of his fortune lie in supernatural causes. A content analysis of tape-recorded answers to queries dealing with what the respondent felt to be the cause of crop failure, good luck, and so forth, revealed that Colombian peasants high in achievement motivation have a mean fatalism score of 31.3, and those low in achievement motivation average 46.1, a significant difference. Fatalism scores on an eight-item scale (see Chapter 12) administered in the three modern villages, correlate −.191 with achievement motivation, which is significantly different from zero. Our conclusion is that *achievement motivation and fatalism are negatively related.*

The positive correlations (Table 11–2) between aspirations (both educational and occupational) that our respondents held for their sons, and achievement motivation, support the conclusion that *achievement motivation is positively related to both educational and occupational aspirations.*

In general then, the modern peasant is more likely to be high in achievement motivation, and in a way that was expected.

CONSEQUENCES OF ACHIEVEMENT MOTIVATION

Does achievement motivation produce results? Does it predispose an individual to be innovative, and to advance economically in terms of greater production and relatively higher levels of living? One of the objectives of this chapter is to determine whether such individual excellence in farming varies

[23] Research leads us to believe that more modern peasants are also likely to be younger, therefore we would expect achievement motivation to be negatively related to age. Such is the case in Colombia, as reflected by the negative correlations in all six communities, two of which are significant: −.169, −.197, −.056, −.313, −.387, and −.030.

directly with levels of achievement motivation. Past research results[24] among U.S. farmers indicate that the correlations between measures of farming excellence and achievement motivation are generally low, but in the expected direction.

INNOVATIVENESS

Individuals with high achievement motivation are expected to engage in innovating and risk-taking activities (McClelland 1964c:182–183). Low, positive relationships between achievement motivation and the adoption of innovations were found in four studies of U.S. farmers.[25] Innovativeness is one indicator of farming excellence. The adoption of technological innovations indicates one way in which a peasant can improve his farming performance and gain higher levels of farm production and greater profit.

The correlations (Table 11–3) between agricultural innovativeness scores and achievement motivation scores are significant in Nazate and La Cañada, positive but not significant in three other communities, and negative in one. Although the evidence is not compelling, agricultural innovativeness seems to be positively related to achievement motivation. The strongest relationships are in the two most traditional villages — settings where the author feels the respondents are relatively more heterogenous in both agricultural innovativeness and achievement motivation. The greater variability may be one reason for the higher correlations.

Among subsistence peasants, the distinction between farm production and household consumption activities is not very clear-cut. Thus, adoption of home innovations is also considered one indicator of farming excellence, partly because farming financial success often provides the resources with which to purchase home innovations. Table 11–3 shows that correlations between home innovativeness scores and achievement motivation scores are positive in all six communities and significant in San Rafael and Nazate, providing more evidence to support the conclusion that *innovativeness and achievement motivation are positively related.*

FARM SIZE

One partial indicator of excellence in farming is farm size, whether measured in land units or in labor inputs. A farmer with a larger-sized operation is generally considered by his peers to be more successful, although of course there are many possible reasons for a large operation other than farming ability, such as inheritance or off-farm employment. Nevertheless, it

---

[24] Examples are the studies of Morrison (1964) in Wisconsin, Neill (1963) and Neill and Rogers (1963) in Ohio, and Ramsey and others (1959) in New York.

[25] These researchers are Morrison (1964), Neill (1963), Neill and Rogers (1963), and Ramsey and others (1959).

Table 11–3. Zero-Order Correlations between Achievement Motivation Scores and Indicators of Individual Excellence in Farming for Six Colombian Villages

Indicators of Individual Excellence in Farming	Zero-Order Correlations with Achievement Motivation Scores by Village						
	Támesis	Pueblo Viejo	San Rafael	Cuatro Esquinas	Nazate	La Cañada	All Villages Combined
1. Agricultural innovativeness	[.039]	[.149]	[−.186]	[.231]	.479^b	.324^a	.226^b
2. Home innovativeness	[.078]	[.079]	.373^a	[.246]	.352^a	[.254]	.226^b
3. Farm size (in land)	[−.069]	[.023]	[.029]	[−.020]	[.193]	[.192]	[.080]
4. Farm size (in labor)	[.103]	[−.101]	[.122]	[.135]	−[.167]	[.030]	[.109]
5. Desire to increase farm size	—	—	—	—	[.205]	.541^b	.414^b
6. Land tenure status	[.061]	[−.160]	[.159]	[.061]	[.298]	[.184]	.158^b
7. Farm production per hectare	—	—	—	—	.381^a	[.141]	[.168]
8. Social status	—	[.181]	.357^a	.339^a	.442^b	[.265]	.300^b
9. Level of living	—	[.062]	.507^b	[.201]	[.302]	[.130]	.245^b

[a] Significantly different from zero at the 5 percent level.
[b] Significantly different from zero at the 1 percent level.

might be argued that a farmer with low ability would not be able to operate a large unit successfully for long, even if he inherited it. There are low but positive correlations between farm size in land units and achievement motivation in four of the communities, and very low negative correlations in two (Table 11–3).

Because some of the farm land in the Colombian villages was almost impossible to cultivate, whereas other farms could be operated intensively, the measure of farm size in labor inputs (number of days of family or hired labor utilized on the respondent's farm in the past year) may be more accurate than the measure of farm size in terms of land units. There are low but positive correlations for four of the communities, and negative correlations in Pueblo Viejo and Nazate (Table 11–3).

In two of the communities an attitudinal-aspirational aspect of farm size was also measured — the *desire* to increase farm size. This was felt to be a particularly important variable in Nazate and La Cañada, where there was great pressure on land resources, and where desires for larger operations were often blocked by the unavailability of farm land. Table 11–3 shows that desire to increase farm size varies directly with achievement motivation scores. There are positive correlations in both communities and a significant correlation in La Cañada.

Another aspect of the farm size variable (as an indicator of farming excellence) is land tenure. It was measured as the percentage of the respondent's farm that he owned. Thus, the land tenure measure is independent of farm size in land units. Table 11–3 shows positive (although not significant) correlations in all of the six communities except Pueblo Viejo, where the correlation is negative.

The rather inconsistent evidence allows the *tentative conclusion that a positive relationship exists between farm size and achievement motivation.*

FARM PRODUCTION

Another indicator of farming excellence is the level of farm production. In fact, from the viewpoint of agricultural development, farm production is one of the most important expressions of farming excellence.[26] In the present study,

---

[26] It is rather curious that few investigations of the adoption of agricultural innovations have considered farm production, rather than agricultural innovativeness, as the main dependent variable to be explained. These studies halted with the task of explaining the variance in innovativeness (with such independent variables as literacy, mass media exposure, change agent contact, and so forth), rather than continuing the analysis one step further to analyze the relationship of these independent variables (and innovativeness) upon levels of farm production. One likely reason for this omission is the difficulty in accurately measuring levels of farm production in personal interviews with peasant farmers.

farm production was measured as the respondent's yield per hectare of his major crop, which was potatoes in Nazate and coffee in La Cañada, the only two villages for which satisfactory measures of farm production could be developed.[27] Correlations in both communities are in the expected direction, and one is significant (Table 11–3), suggesting that *farm production is positively related to achievement motivation.*

SOCIAL STATUS AND LEVEL OF LIVING

It might be argued that social status[28] is a partial indicator of farming excellence. All of the present respondents are occupied in a common occupation. Efficient farming is probably one of their primary means of earning higher social status. Table 11–3 shows positive correlations in all five of the six communities where a status measure was available; three of the five are significant.

Level of living is indicated by the possession of status-conferring material objects. The present level of living scale[29] included items like brick house walls, glass windows, and certain items of household equipment. Possession of adequate resources to purchase these level of living items is one indicator of excellence in farming. Table 11–3 shows positive correlations (in all five of the communities where the hypothesis is tested), one of which is significant. *Achievement motivation appears to be positively related to social status and to level of living.*

CROSS-COMMUNITY CONSISTENCY OF RESULTS

What can be concluded about the consistency across the six communities of the empirical relationships between achievement motivation and other variables? This is an important question because the villages studied represent a range in modern-traditional norms on social change.

[27] This measure could not be utilized in the other communities where the nature of farm production proved to be less specialized; the farmers grew small amounts of numerous crops, thereby prohibiting an accurate, standardized estimate of production.

[28] The interviewers categorized the respondents' social status in five categories on the basis of such indicators as ownership of material possessions, prestige, education, and community leadership. As such, the ratings represent a subjective composite of the various social status indicators. The interviewers were well-acquainted with the nature of the concept of social status, and they were trained in standardized procedures for making the ratings.

[29] In the communities of Pueblo Viejo, San Rafael, and Cuatro Esquinas, a self-perceived measure of relative level of living was utilized, rather than the measure based upon possession of material objects.

An index was constructed of cross-village correlations in consistency.[30] It can be seen (Table 11–4) that there is generally less consistency for the correlations across villages in the case of the antecedent variables, than for the consequent variables. So although there are higher correlations (that is *stronger relationships*) for the antecedents of achievement motivation, these variables are *less consistently* related across the six villages than are the consequent variables. Among the antecedents, birth order and literacy are the most consistent correlates of achievement motivation; social status and farm size (in land) are most consistent among the indicators of occupational excellence.

MULTIPLE CORRELATION ANALYSIS OF ACHIEVEMENT MOTIVATION SCORES

Multiple correlation is a method of explaining the variance in a dependent variable, achievement motivation in the present case, through its relationships with a series of independent variables. The advantage of the multiple correlation approach is that instead of determining only the zero-order relationships between each independent variable and achievement motivation scores (as in Tables 11–2 and 11–3), the joint effects (interaction effects or overlaps) can be determined of all of these independent variables *together* upon achievement motivation scores. For example, Table 11–2 showed that in Pueblo Viejo, achievement motivation scores are correlated .259 with empathy scores and .219 with functional literacy. Yet, empathy and literacy are known to be positively related; perhaps the zero-order correlation of achievement motivation with literacy is due, in part, to the mutual covariance of both variables with empathy. Thus, multiple correlation analysis can tell us

[30] The following procedures were followed in constructing this index:

1. Each of the zero-order Pearsonian coefficients of correlation between achievement motivation scores and an indicator of farming excellence, such as agricultural innovativeness in Table 11-3, were converted to z scores. The z transformation is linear in function (that is, a z score of .40 indicates twice as high a degree of relationship as a z score of .20), while the coefficient of correlation is not linear.

2. The z scores for an indicator of farming excellence were averaged across the six communities (when available in all six communities), keeping the sign (positive or negative) of the original correlation.

3. The standard deviation of these z scores is the index of cross-village inconsistency; that is, the higher the degree of consistency of these correlations, the smaller the size of the inconsistency index.

In order to illustrate the use of this index of inconsistency, consider two extreme cases:

1. In one case, there are two correlations, between achievement motivation scores and an indicator of farming excellence, that are identical; for example, both r's are .50. The z scores are .549 and .549; their standard deviation or inconsistency index is 0.

2. Assume there are two maximally different correlations; one is +.99 and the other is −.99. Both z scores are 2.647 (one is positive and the other is negative). Their standard deviation, the index of inconsistency, is 2.647.

Thus, the inconsistency index can range from 0 to 2.647. One advantage of this index is that it is largely independent of the number of villages for which correlations are available between a particular indicator of farming excellence and achievement motivation scores.

Table 11–4. Inconsistency Indexes for Antecedent and Consequent Correlates of Achievement Motivation in the Colombian Villages.

Correlates of Achievement Motivation	Number of Communities for Which Correlations with Achievement Motivation Were Computed	Cross-Community Inconsistency Index
I. Personality socialization, communication exposure, and modernization variables		
1. Respondent's birth order	2	.119
2. Mass media exposure	6	.507
3. Political knowledgeability	6	.354
4. Cosmopoliteness	6	.251
5. Extension change agent contact	5	.390
6. Literacy	6	.144
7. Years of formal education	6	.396
8. Empathy	5	.234
9. Educational aspirations	5	.353
10. Occupational aspirations	5	.319
II. Indicators of individual excellence in farming		
1. Agricultural innovativeness	6	.223
2. Home innovativeness	6	.124
3. Farm size (in land)	6	.099
4. Farm size (in labor)	6	.116
5. Desire to increase farm size	2	.198
6. Land tenure status	6	.145
7. Farm production per hectare	2	.129
8. Social status	5	.098
9. Level of living	5	.173

the multiple-order relationships of achievement motivation with the independent variables; it controls or removes the effects of the interrelationships among the independent variables in explaining the variance in achievement motivation.

Six independent variables were selected for the multiple correlation analysis on the basis of (1) their zero-order correlations with achievement motivation scores, (2) their theoretical importance, (3) their measurement in all six of the communities,[31] and (4) their representation of the general dimensions of farming excellence, communication exposure, and modernization variables.

[31] However, social status and empathy were not measured in Támesis.

Table 11–5 Multiple Correlation Analysis of Achievement Motivation Scores in Six Colombian Villages

Independent Variables	Támesis	Pueblo Viejo	San Rafael	Cuatro Esquinas	Nazate	La Cañada
			Approximate Percentage of the Variance in Achievement Motivation Scores Explained in the Six Villages			
1. Years of formal education	8.32	−0.98	−0.50	−1.29	1.34	8.78
2. Literacy	7.68	3.80	−3.27	9.52	2.87	1.23
3. Social status	—[a]	0.24	−2.27	9.03	−3.11	10.16
4. Mass media exposure	0.67	0.93	4.23	−1.94	16.97	16.51
5. Cosmopoliteness	0.37	4.40	7.15	0.09	−1.28	3.13
6. Empathy	—[a]	4.52	23.61	6.41	13.77	3.85
Total variance explained ($R^2_{y.123456}$) in Achievement Motivation	17.04	12.91	28.95	21.82	30.56	43.66

[a] Social status and empathy were not measured in Támesis.

Table 11–5 shows that . . .

1. The highest percentage of the variance in achievement motivation scores $(R^2_{Y.123456})$ is explained in the most traditional villages, Nazate and La Cañada, where 31 percent and 44 percent, respectively, of the variance, is explained.

2. Empathy is consistently one of the most effective independent variables in explaining variance in achievement motivation scores; however, there is no one best predictor of achievement motivation scores across all the villages.

3. Mass media exposure and cosmopoliteness (trips to urban centers) seem to play a complementary role in explaining variance in achievement motivation scores, especially in the two most traditional villages where mass media exposure is of greater importance than cosmopoliteness. This might be due to the relative isolation of Nazate and La Cañada; the mass media seem to be a more important link to the urban world than trips to cities, which are much less frequent than in the other four villages.

4. Social status is most important as a predictor of achievement motivation scores in Cuatro Esquinas and La Cañada; elsewhere it was of almost no importance, and was negative in two communities.[32]

5. Literacy and formal education seem to play a complementary role in predicting achievement motivation scores; perhaps this is due to the high correlation between literacy and formal education. These two variables are relatively better predictors of achievement motivation scores in Támesis and La Cañada, the least and the most traditional villages.

SUMMARY OF THE COLOMBIAN FINDINGS

Achievement motivation is a social value that emphasizes a desire for excellence in order to attain a sense of personal accomplishment. The present investigation sought to study the antecedents and consequences of occupational achievement motivation among Colombian peasants in six communities. A measure of achievement motivation was developed that could be utilized in personal interviews with Colombian peasants. No previous research of this nature had been completed among peasants in a less developed country. A measurement technique consisting of sentence-completion scale items which had been utilized in three studies of U.S. farmers was adapted for use in the present investigation. After various types of scale-analysis, the sentence-completion measure of achievement motivation was found to possess modest levels of validity, internal consistency, reliability, and scoring agreement.

[32] An independent variable will explain a negative portion of the variance in the dependent variable when it is more highly related to the other independent variables than it is to the dependent variable; it thus makes a negative contribution as one of the predictors of the dependent variable. In San Rafael, for example, social status is evidently more highly related to formal education, literacy, mass media exposure, cosmopoliteness, and empathy than it is to achievement motivation scores.

The number of items in the achievement motivation scale ranged from 8 to 12 in the different communities; this suggests the importance of repeating the scale analysis procedures in future investigations before a final set of scale items can be developed, which possess general applicability throughout Colombia or other nations.

Levels of achievement motivation were found to vary directly with the nature of personality socialization, communication exposure, and modernization variables. It was found that achievement motivation scores were related to the following: (1) father absence from home during childhood socialization; (2) greater mass media exposure; (3) political knowledgeability; (4) cosmopoliteness (trips to urban centers); (5) literacy; (6) more years of formal education; (7) greater empathy; (8) fatalism (negatively); (9) higher educational aspirations; and (10) higher occupational aspirations.

Expected relationships were not found between achievement motivation scores and birth order, and extension change agent contact. A multiple correlation analysis indicated that empathy was generally one of the best predictors of achievement motivation, when the effects of other variables are also considered.

It can be concluded, we feel, that individual occupational excellence varies with levels of achievement motivation. Achievement motivation scores were related to such indicators of farming excellence such as: (1) agricultural innovativeness; (2) home innovativeness; (3) farm size in land units; (4) farm size in labor units; (5) desire to increase farm size; (6) land ownership; (7) farm production per hectare; (8) higher social status; and (9) higher levels of living.

In general, stronger evidence for most of the hypotheses was found in the more traditional villages. What might explain this tendency? It seems that Nazate and La Cañada, the two most traditional villages, are relatively retarded in the process of social change; although they contain some modern individuals who are literate, empathic, cosmopolite, and who have high mass media exposure, *most* residents of these two villages are still quite traditional. There is a greater range of variability in the variables studied among the respondents in Nazate and La Cañada than in the other four villages, where the process of modernization has proceeded more completely and where urban influences are more pervasive. With more heterogeneous respondents in the two more traditional villages, higher correlations can be expected.

One gains the impression from inspecting Tables 11–2 and 11–3 that most of the correlations with achievement motivation scores are in the expected direction, but none are very high. The highest correlation in either of the tables is .541. Perhaps these generally low correlations suggest the need for further research on achievement motivation. In explaining the generally low relationships found in their study, Ramsey and others (1959) point out that "There has been much fundamental thinking about values, their nature, and their relationship to social change. However, little has been done to advance the correspondence between measurement and concept." A priority step for future research should be to refine further the existing measures of achievement motivation, and to develop adequate operations for other social values.

RESEARCH ON ACHIEVEMENT MOTIVATION IN OTHER CULTURES

Since the present data-gathering was conducted in 1963–1964, several investigations have been designed in other cultures, which utilize an essentially similar approach to the study of achievement motivation. Among these samples are 50 farmers in 4 Malaysian villages; 27 small-scale industrialists in Delhi, India; 92 small industrial entrepreneurs in Punjab state; 84 farmers in 2 Punjabi villages served by the Intensive Agriculture District Programme, Ludhiana, India; and 702 farmers in 8 villages in Uttar Pradesh, India. All of these researches utilized a version of the sentence-completion achievement motivation scale developed in the Colombian study. Hence, as the results of these varied investigations become available in the near future, further evidence will be accumulated about certain of the hypotheses tested in the present investigation as well as the measurement techniques that were used.

CROSS-CULTURAL CONSISTENCY OF RESULTS BETWEEN INDIA AND COLOMBIA

The last investigation mentioned (of 702 farmers in 8 Indian villages) bears close similarity to the design of the Colombia study; hence a cross-cultural comparison of results can be made. The India data were obtained through personal interviews with all heads of farm households by trained interviewers from the National Institute of Community Development, Hyderabad, India. After pretesting a more lengthy instrument, the sentence-completion achievement motivateion scale was reduced to six items,[33] which were similar to the items included in the final versions of the Colombia scale. The scoring procedure for the interview protocols was also comparable to that utilized in Colombia.

Nine antecedent variables are correlated with achievement motivation scores in the eight Indian villages (Table 11–6). All of these variables are measured in a similar way in India as in Colombia, except the following: (1) change agent exposure in India is a composite of contact with various types of government change agents, while in Colombia it is only with extension workers; (2) educational and occupational aspirations are combined into

---

[33] The six items are: (1) "For a better life on my farm, I need . . . ," (2) "My greatest aspiration in life is . . . ," (3) "Farmers in our country are . . . ," (4) "A good farmer must have . . . ," (5) "A true man is one who . . . ," and (6) "What are your plans for the next five years?" The latter item was not asked in sentence-completion style. The items are correlated .49, .49, .42, .51, .40, and .56 with total achievement motivation scores. These correlations are for the total sample of 702 respondents; the item-total score correlations are generally similar in magnitude and all are positive, when computed separately for each of the eight villages.

a single score in India because of their high interrelationship, while they are treated separately in Colombia.

Table 11–6 shows that levels of achievement motivation vary directly with communication exposure and modernization variables in India.[34] Of the 72 correlations with achievement motivation scores by village in Table 11–6, 11 are not in the expected direction, 28 are in the expected direction but not significant, and 33 are in the expected direction and significant. There are generally lower levels of consistency for the antecedent variables in India (Table 11–6) than in Colombia (Table 11–4).

Seven consequent variables are correlated with achievement motivation scores in India; these seven variables are measured in as similar a way to Colombia as possible. However, there are some minor differences; for example, farm production per land unit was computed for the three major crops grown in the Indian villages and only for one major crop in Colombia.

Table 11–7 shows evidence from India that individual excellence in farming varies directly with levels of achievement motivation. One exception occurs in the case of farm production per land unit that is not significantly, nor very consistently, correlated with achievement motivation scores in the eight villages. Of the 48 correlations by villages (Table 11–7), 4 are not in the expected direction, 25 are in the expected direction but not significant, and 19 are in the expected direction and significant. These results are approximately similar to those presented earlier for the six Colombian villages. Also, the lowest level of cross-community consistency in India is for agricultural innovativeness, as was the case in Colombia, and the highest consistency is for farm size in land units.

Not only can the consistency of these findings be compared across communities, but also across the two countries. Although social scientists give widespread support to the notion that propositions should hold true cross-culturally, there are relatively few investigations designed to provide cross-cultural tests of hypotheses.[35] Tables 11–6 and 11–7 include an index of cross-cultural inconsistency between India and Colombia for four of the six consequent variables and for each of the nine antecedent variables. The index is computed by essentially the same formula as the index of cross-community inconsistency. The comparisons in Tables 11–6 and 11–7 are for (1) the eight Indian villages pooled, with (2) the three modern Colombian villages pooled. There is very high consistency for the correlates of achievement motivation across the two cultures. In fact, there is much higher consistency *across* the two cultures than among the villages *within* each country.[36]

[34] Measures of personality socialization are unfortunately not available in the India study.

[35] Although ours undoubtedly leaves much to be desired, there are even fewer that seek to develop a quantitative measure of cross-cultural consistency.

[36] This suggests that pooling correlations across villages within the same country loses one type of variability, much as might be expected. A somewhat parallel example is provided in Chapter 14, when aggregate and individual units of analysis are compared.

Table 11-6. Zero-Order Correlations between Achievement Motivation Scores and Antecedent Variables in Eight Indian Villages

Antecedent Variables	Zero-Order Correlations with Achievement Motivation Scores by Village Studied								All Eight Communities Combined (N = 702)	Cross-Community Inconsistency Index	Cross-Cultural Inconsistency Index (India and Three Colombian Villages)
	Karimabad (N = 80)	Bhuhar (N = 61)	Barawan Khurd (N = 139)	Dasdoi (N = 82)	Sikanderpur Kurd (N = 39)	Uttardhavna (N = 141)	Atrivli (N = 60)	Bahadurpur (N = 100)			
1. Mass media exposure	[.07]	[-.05]	.30[b]	[-.12]	.39[a]	.33[b]	[.07]	[.10]	.17[b]	.523	.080
2. Political knowledgeability	.27[a]	.32[a]	.30[b]	[.10]	.46[b]	.36[b]	.32[a]	[-.02]	.23[b]	.428	.024
3. Cosmopoliteness	.22[a]	[.11]	[.13]	[.04]	[.02]	.16[a]	[.07]	[-.07]	.09[a]	.491	.050
4. Change agent exposure	.27[a]	[.10]	[.08]	.25[a]	[.28]	.20[a]	[.20]	[-.14]	.17[b]	.379	.094
5. Literacy	[.11]	[.10]	.23[b]	[.00]	[.24]	.20[a]	[.20]	.27[b]	.21[b]	.245	.034
6. Years of formal education	[.19]	[-.12]	.26[b]	[.01]	.33[a]	.18[a]	.38[b]	.37[b]	.24[b]	.488	.060
7. Age	[.04]	[-.12]	[.03]	[-.10]	[.00]	[.04]	[.01]	[.02]	[-.03]	.169	.090
8. Empathy	.24[a]	.52[b]	.45[b]	.22[a]	.45[b]	.41[b]	.32[a]	[.00]	.38[b]	.494	.054
9. Educational and occupational aspirations[c]	[-.08]	.39[b]	[.15]	[.05]	.34[a]	.24[b]	.28[b]	[.12]	.24[b]	.432	{ .054 / .100

[a] Significantly different from zero at the 5 percent level.
[b] Significantly different from zero at the 1 percent level.
[c] Educational and occupational aspirations were pooled in India, but not in Colombia.

Table 11-7. Zero-Order Correlations between Consequent Variables and Acheivement Motivation Scores in Eight Indian Villages

Consequent Variables	Zero-Order Correlations with Achievement Motivation Scores by Village Studied								All Eight Communities Combined (N = 702)	Cross-Community Inconsistency Index	Cross-Cultural Inconsistency Index (India and Three Colombian Villages)
	Karimabad (N = 80)	Bhuhar (N = 61)	Barawan Khurd (N = 139)	Dasdoi (N = 82)	Sikanderpur Kurd (N = 39)	Uttardhauna (N = 141)	Atravii (N = 60)	Bahadurpur (N = 100)			
1. Agricultural innovativeness	.37[b]	.30[a]	.34[b]	[−.02]	[.10]	.28[b]	.33[b]	.26[b]	.32[b]	.440	.140
2. Home innovativeness	.32[b]	[.10]	.31[b]	[−.06]	[.19]	[.14]	[.17]	[.05]	.18[b]	.347	.045
3. Farm size in land units	[.14]	[.16]	.23[b]	[.06]	[.20]	[.08]	[.24]	.24[a]	.22[b]	.194	.070
4. Farm size in labor units	[.15]	.90[b]	.27[b]	[.01]	[.06]	[.10]	.31[a]	.24[a]	.19[b]	.295	—[c]
5. Farm production per land unit	[−.06]	[.17]	.18[a]	[−.04]	[.02]	[.01]	[.06]	[.16]	[.04]	.256	—[c]
6. Level of living	[.21]	.40[b]	.29[b]	[.04]	.48[b]	.26[b]	.36[b]	[.18]	.31[b]	.399	.050

[a] Significantly different from zero at the 5 percent level.
[b] Significantly different from zero at the 1 percent level.
[c] Comparable measures were not available from the three Colombian villages.

NEEDED RESEARCH

In addition to the basic methodological need for improved measurement of achievement motivation, several substantive suggestions for future investigation may be offered. In Table 11–5 the highest amount of variance explained in achievement motivation scores was 44 percent in one of the six villages. This suggests that much variance in achievement motivation remains to be explained by future research.

Undoubtedly, it is an oversimplification to conclude that achievement motivation is related to such behavioral consequences as occupational excellence in *zero-order* relationships; often its effects occur through, and in relationship to, other value-orientations. Attention needs to be devoted to conceptualization and measurement of these other value-orientations. For a start, the following deserve priority attention:

1. *Familism*   The subordination of individual goals to those of the family, is a variable that merits future investigation. Until an individual's level of familism decreases to a certain minimum, his achievement motivation may have little relationship to his occupational excellence. This is to say that until an individual has majority control of his own business decisions, his values will not bear much relationship to his business performance because it is not his, but rather his family's business.

2. *Machismo*   The Latin American masculinity complex is believed by some observers to explain such varied behaviors as reckless automobile driving, high rates of prostitution, the frequency of beauty queen contests, and large family size. Many of the responses to the sentence-completion scale items in the Colombia investigation were clearly indications of *machismo*, even though the items were not designed to measure this concept. An adequate sentence-completion measure of *machismo* could be developed, and perhaps it would be related with achievement motivation, at least in some of its occupational expressions in Latin cultures.

3. *Need for affiliation*   McClelland (1961:160) defines this concept as a concern . . ."over establishing, maintaining, or restoring a positive affective relationship with another person." Need for affiliation may act as a deterrent to innovativeness; a potential innovator with high need for affiliation may hesitate to adopt a new idea that will mark him as a deviant to his peers in a social system. It would be interesting to determine the joint relationships of need for affiliation and achievement motivation upon innovativeness among peasants.

4. *Need for power*   McClelland (1961:167) defines this as a concern . . . "with the control of the means of influencing a person." Perhaps opinion leadership in a peasant community is particularly characteristic of individuals who are high both in need for power[37] and in need for affiliation.

---

[37] Or in *need for influence*, which Uleman (1966) differentiates from need for power as an altruistic motive to help the other person, rather than to help or gratify oneself.

Not only do these and other value-orientations need to be investigated in connection with achievement motivation, but additional measures of consequences of achievement motivation also need to be examined. For example, Neill (1963) found that the variable most highly related to achievement motivation among Ohio farmers was a measure of farm labor efficiency. In the present investigation we were unable to develop adequate measures of agricultural production efficiency (such as labor efficiency, capital return, cost per pound of gain in livestock, and so on) due to difficulties in securing this data from peasant farmers. Future researchers should study the relationship of farm efficiency to achievement motivation.

The consequences of achievement motivation on migration out of agriculture also need to be investigated. It is commonly observed in Colombia that to become rich, one must leave agriculture because of its limited opportunities. The design for this type of investigation would involve measuring the achievement motivation of early teenagers in a peasant village, and then following up the respondents about a decade later to determine the levels of achievement motivation among those who did and did not migrate to urban centers.

Lastly, inquiry is needed on the role of achievement motivation in leading to entrepreneurial success on the part of the Antioqueños in Colombia, and similar ethnic groups in other less developed countries. It is not fully understood how and why the Antioqueños gained their entrepreneurial and innovative attitudes, but an analysis of their achievement motivation may provide an important key to such insight.

12

Fatalism*

Fatalism is our religion; the church just supplies the pageantry of life.
(Southern Italian peasant quoted by Sangree 1952:87)

The anthropologist Malinowski (1948:14) describes the role of magic in the lives of the Trobriand Islanders in the South Pacific: On the inner lagoon of their coral atoll, where a living was easily forged by poisoning fish, the food supply was stable and secure. Here magic was generally unknown; but on the outer reef of the island, the Trobrianders fished in the open sea from rafts. The fishermen might sail for days without sighting food, and then in a few hours they would haul in a week's catch. Storms would occasionally destroy their rafts at sea. Under these hazardous and risky conditions, the Trobrianders observed complicated magical rituals, and fatalistic explanations for fishing success were widely believed.

Now suppose that your task as a change agent among these Trobrianders is to introduce an improved, safer type of fishing boat. Would the fatalistic beliefs of the outer Islanders cause resistance to the adoption of your innovation? Once you were able to secure the widespread adoption of the safer craft, would the need for fatalistic explanations of fishing success decrease?

THE CONCEPT OF FATALISM

Fatalism is the degree to which an individual perceives a lack of ability to contol his future.[1] Fatalistic individuals believe that the events of their lives are preordained and determined by fate or supernatural forces. Their attitudes toward self-control of future events involve passivity, pessimism, acceptance, endurance, pliancy, and evasion.

* This chapter was written with assistance from Elssy Bonilla de Ramos, formerly Research Assistant in Communication at Michigan State University, and is based, in part, on her M.A. thesis (1966), *Fatalism and Modernization in Colombia*, East Lansing, Michigan State University.
    [1] Hence fatalism is a sort of generalized sense of powerlessness, one of the five dimensions of alienation postulated by Seeman (1959), which he defines as "the expectancy or probability held by the individual that his own behavior cannot determine the occurrence of the outcome, or reinforcements, he seeks." The other four dimensions of alienation are isolation, self-estrangement, meaninglessness, and normlessness.

273

Such fatalistic beliefs are pervasive among most peasants;[2] for instance, in rural Colombia when an infant dies, the parents are likely to say, "It was his destiny not to grow up." Whenever a Colombian announces his intention to undertake some future activity, the counter remark is often an automatic, "*Ojalla*," which is a linguistic bastardization of the Arabic expression, "If Allah wills;" similar epitaphs may be encountered throughout Latin America, the Middle East, and India and Pakistan. Erasmus (1961:52) describes Latin American attitudes toward death: "Much of the peasant's seeming apathy and unconcern results from the prevalent attitude that it does not really matter what is done to help a person, if his time has come to die . . . ." One can imagine the difficulties the change agent encounters with such clients if he is bent on introducing vaccination or improved sanitation measures to decrease the death rate. Likewise, efforts to promote adoption of chemical fertilizers and other crop innovations are unlikely to be fruitful if villagers believe that only supernatural forces control their crop production.[3]

Why are peasants fatalistic? One reason is that they have a relatively low degree of mastery over their natural and social environments (Foster 1962: 52–59). Peasants lack the knowledge, skills, and resources necessary to cope with phenomena such as drought, floods, and famine. The causes of these conditions are looked upon as a visitation from gods or evil spirits, whom man can propitiate but not control. Under circumstances that condemn a farmer to subsistence living and a comparatively short life span, it is not surprising that villagers have few illusions about the possibility of improving their lot. A fatalistic outlook, the assumption that whatever happens is the will of God or Allah, is perhaps the best adjustment the individual can make to an apparently hopeless situation. Indeed, fatalistic attitudes may have been highly efficient and functional in the past as means of psychological adaptation to a harsh environment.[4] But in today's era of planned change, these historically efficacious attitudes toward fate probably act as impediments to the adoption of innovations. Change agents generally wish that peasants' traditional despair was replaced by a "Rotarian bounce" (Lerner and Riesman 1955).

This leads to the central theme of this chapter: How does fatalism affect an individuals' propensity to change, to become more modern? Two views of the role of fatalism in modernization will be presented and the Colombia data will then be brought to bear on these two approaches.

[2] Perhaps it is significant that the major religious belief systems in Latin America, Africa, and Asia often have fatalism as a central tenet. Examples are the concept of *karma* (or predestination) in Buddhism and Hinduism, and the similar notion of *kismet* in Islam.

[3] In terms of Kluckhohn and Strodtbeck's (1961) major value orientations, fatalism is closely synonymous with subjugation to nature and with a lack of future orientation.

[4] Gans (1962:248–249) suggests that this is true not only among peasants, but also among the urban poor. "It is this belief in fate that allows the West Ender [an Italian slum dweller in Boston] to face illness and even death with resignation when there is little chance of recovery, and that softens the blow for his survivors, allowing them to continue to function."

FATALISM AND MODERNIZATION: TWO VIEWS

FATALISM AS A BARRIER TO CHANGE

It has been asserted that fatalism stands as a barrier to modernization. This line of argument goes as follows: Peasants believe in the inevitability of happenings. They perceive they have little or no control over the events of their own lives. Believing they are powerless to control their future, they prefer to accept their lot rather than engage in behaviors to improve their level of living. The use of supernatural factors to explain frustrations and failures eventually leads to the establishment of extremely limited expectations, which in turn promotes a generally pessimistic mental stance toward new ideas. Proponents of the "fatalism as a barrier" school of thought go on to argue that the process of modernization itself can promote fatalism. Encouraged to want more than they can have or possibly get, peasants are frustrated by the difference between aspirations and actualities, and they are likely to develop a retreatist and fatalistic disposition toward change. In Chapter 1 it was mentioned that the "revolution of rising expectations" of the 1950s has given way to a "revolution of rising frustrations" in the 1960s as peasants' expectations soared higher than their actual levels of living (Lerner 1963:349).

Hunt (1957:318) views the religious beliefs prominently held throughout the less developed world as essentially fatalistic, and characterizes them as blocks to economic development.

The tradition-bound rigidity of Islam, the other-wordly emphasis of Buddhism, the asceticism of Hinduism and the fiesta-laden Catholicism of countries with Spanish tradition, may embody important teachings, but their emphasis is not calculated to provide industrious workers, thrifty capitalists or daring promoters.

Change agents who believe that fatalism is an intervening variable in the change process, are likely to ask: What factors are likely to reduce fatalism, thereby increasing the probability of innovation adoption? Following Lerner's (1958) suggestion concerning antecedents of modernization, it could be argued that literacy, empathy, cosmopoliteness, and mass media exposure are likely to increase an individual's self-perceived control of his life, thereby decreasing his fatalism, and promoting such modernization consequents as higher innovativeness, aspirations, achievement motivation, and so forth. A paradigm of such a model is presented in Figure 12–1. Here fatalism is viewed as an intervening variable in the process of modernization.

FATALISM AS A POST HOC RATIONALIZATION

Before turning to an examination of the Colombian data, it is useful to look at fatalism from another point of view, which in the end may also provide

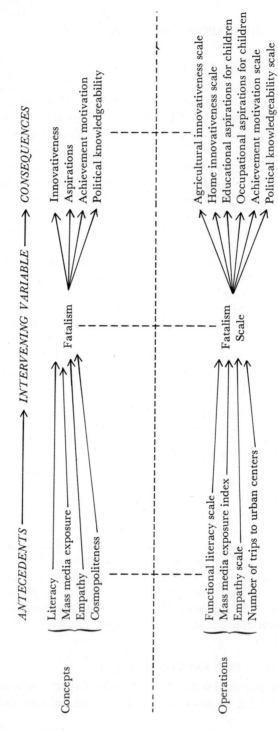

Figure 12–1.   Paradigm of the Role of Fatalism as Intervening in the Modernization Process.

a meaningful insight into the role of fatalism in modernization. This approach holds that fatalism is not an impediment to modernization, but merely is a *post hoc* rationale by peasants to account for perceived and real limitations imposed by their daily existence. Fatalism in this instance is a matter of personality adjustment, which allows individuals on the traditional rungs of the modernization ladder to cope with their daily tensions and frustrations. Therefore, fatalistic attitudes serve as a marvelous mental mechanism for reduction of cognitive dissonance. As such, fatalism need not directly impede progress. It is simply used as an explanation and excuse for the lack of modernization.

This view of fatalism as a rationalization for failure is supported by Niehoff and Anderson (1966) who conclude, after a review of numerous case studies dealing with planned change in less developed countries, that fatalism is not an important variable in explaining the adoption or rejection of innovations. Niehoff (1966b) further surmises from his review of research on fatalism in Asia that there is little evidence that fatalistic attitudes actually affect behavior. "Fate or destiny is normally blamed for unfortunate events only after they have occurred. Thus [fatalism] serves principally as an explanatory device rather than a determinant of action."

Seen as a rationalization device, the fatalism of peasants might even be used to advantage by change agents. For instance, a Peace Corps volunteer in a Bolivian village attributed part of his success to the peasants' fatalistic acceptance of failure. Fatalism served to protect his credibility as a communication source of new ideas after the first innovation that he attempted, the artificial insemination of sheep, failed completely. His clients blamed the failure on fate, not on him. And so he was able to proceed with the introduction of other new ideas, some of which were successful.

Although fatalism may prevent an active search for new ideas from the outside world and discourage an active attempt to change one's life situation, it does not necessarily cause avoidance of innovations injected to the villager from external sources. The fatalistic peasant is likely to endure the introduction of new ideas by change agents with apathetic passivity.

Often, and mistakenly, fatalism is equated with essential pessimism. But this is not so, because the peasant may attribute both good and bad to fate.[5] So while fatalism may lead to resignation and acceptance of one's lot because it is perceived to be in the control of some outside force, fatalism does not necessarily lead to pessimism concerning the outcome of all future events.

Fatalistic attitudes permit the possibility of innovation successess as well as failures, and may allow for the acceptance and accommodation of change agents and their activities. A peasant under pressures to modernize will

---

[5] Although, as Arensberg and Niehoff (1964:114) point out, "Fatalism is usually a negative attitude; that is, it more often explains why unpleasant things happened than the reverse. It explains why someone died or why the crop failed, rather than why some person remained healthy or why there was a good crop."

likely accept the influence of outside change agents with a fatalistic attitude.

Knowing that fatalism is common among peasants, and assuming that it does not necessarily intervene in the modernization process, a reduction in fatalism as a consequence of modernization might be expected. The paradigm for such a model is: modernization antecedents → reduction in fatalism (and other consequences). The modernization antecedets include: literacy, mass media exposure, cosmopoliteness, and so on.

This view of reduction-in-fatalism as a consequence of modernization has not received as much attention by social science researchers as has the other approach to fatalism, that is, as a block to modernization. In designing the Colombian investigation the latter approach was followed originally; fatalistic attitudes were conceived as an intervening variable in the modernization process. The data do not provide a clear-cut test of the two approaches to fatalism, but they do shed some light on the matter. For this reason both approaches to the role of fatalism in modernization will be discussed toward the end of this chapter.

MEASURING FATALISM

PREVIOUS APPROACHES

Before turning to the empirical results of the study of fatalism in Colombia, we must first discuss our measurement of the concept. Although much has been written in the past about fatalism,[6] most attempts to measure the variable have been rather impressionistic, intuitive, and imprecise. One exception is Sariola's (1965) development of a crude attitude scale to measure fatalism among Colombian peasants. His four-scale items asked respondents for fatalistic versus nonfatalistic reasons for farming success, crop failures, and so on.[7] Sariola's work demonstrates that fatalism can be measured with an attitude-type scale among peasants, but no evidence was provided as to the scale's validity or reliability.

A more useful guide for construction of the fatalism scale is the conceptualization by Niehoff and Anderson (1966), who see the concept as composed of three subdimensions: (1) supernaturalism, (2) situational fatalism, and (3) project negativism.

Supernaturalism consists of traditional theological beliefs and magical notions which, by their manipulation, provide the individual with a fatalistic

---

[6] Much past research and writing about fatalism has been done by anthropologists such as Laura Thompson and Louise and George Spindler, who have focused on the role of fatalism in acculturation.

[7] Incidentally, the majority of his respondents gave fatalistic responses like "luck" or the "will of God" to this type of query.

escape from daily insecurities. For example, rather than apply chemical fertilizer to his potatoes in order to obtain higher yields on his eroding soil, a fatalistic Colombian peasant will burn an extra candle at Sunday mass. The Trobrianders' ritualistic magic in connection with fishing on the open sea is another illustration of supernaturalistic fatalism.

Situational fatalism is an attitude of apathetic passiveness that stems from an accurate understanding of limited possibilities for improving life conditions.[8] The individual comprehends the precariousness of his life situation and feels a need for improvement, but perceives the unavailability of means to reach these desired ends. So his relatively hopeless situation creates a feeling of fatalism, one that is more-or-less based on a realistic appraisal of his limited resources.

Project negativism is a type of fatalistic apathy toward innovations that is founded on their previous failures. This brand of fatalism is a product of the current age of development rather than stemming from a traditional culture or difficult conditions. "Some people are so poor, have so little land and resources, and have previously failed to better their own conditions so often that they simply do not believe they can improve their own circumstances" (Niehoff 1966a:38). As many externally induced innovations fail among villagers, a higher degree of project negativism is created, which makes it even more likely that the next innovation will fail. "Project positivism" may, of course, result from the successful introduction of an innovation, but project negativism is often a more common occurrence in less developed countries.

Although the theoretical division of fatalism into three subtypes on the basis of the *origin* of fatalistic attitudes has much to commend it, Niehoff and Anderson (1966) did not proceed to construct a fatalism scale to measure each of these three dimensions.[9] We sought to do so.

MEASURING FATALISM IN COLOMBIA

Fatalism is the degree to which an individual perceives a lack of ability to control his future.[10] We will now describe the steps we followed in measuring this concept. After pretesting a much greater number of possible scale items in Colombia, ten items were selected, which include each of the three differ-

---

[8]Niehoff (1966b) also refers to the situational variety of fatalism as "realistic fatalism" in the sense that it is based on real, limited possibilities in this world.

[9] They were analyzing case studies of the success-failure of innovations, and so their data would not allow them to develop a fatalism scale, even if they had wished to do so.

[10] This definition implies that fatalism is a type of *attitude* or opinion, a view of the world and man's role in it. Our fatalism scale, to be described shortly, includes only attitudinal items. However, it may be possible to measure fatalistic *behavior* as well as attitudes. Respondents would be asked, for example, the fatalistic activities in which they engaged, such as buying a rabbit's foot, making libations to their ancestors, and so forth.

ent dimensions of fatalism just discussed: supernatural, situational, and project negativism.[11] The items[12] are the following:

1. "The success in business of a person depends on his luck and not on his intelligence." (situational fatalism)
2. "When an epidemic or bad luck arrives, man has to endure it." (supernatural fatalism)
3. "When man is born, his life is determined and he cannot modify it." (supernatural fatalism)
4. "New techniques and machines work better than good weather in assuring good crops." (situational fatalism)
5. "Only if I win a lottery can I better my conditions." (supernatural fatalism)
6. "Man can plan the future because the future depends on man." (project negativism)
7. "It is better to accept things as they come and not to plan for the future." (supernatural fatalism)
8. "To make plans for the future will cause unhappiness." (supernatural fatalism)
9. "During his life, it is better for a man to work than to have good luck." (supernatural fatalism)
10. "When a man behaves badly, illness will punish him." (situational fatalism)

The ten scale items were administered to all 135 heads of farm households in the 1965 reinterviews in Pueblo Viejo, San Rafael, and Cuatro Esquinas. During the personal interviews, the respondents seemed able to comprehend the nature of the statements fairly easily, and generally responded readily in terms of whether they agreed or disagreed, and to what extent.

The scale was analyzed in terms of its reliability and its unidimensionality. The split-half coefficient of reliability is .516, which seems fairly adequate for a ten-item scale. In order to determine whether the scale items measured three subdimensions of fatalism, or one general fatalism dimension, the scale response data were subjected to three types of factor analysis[13] in order to determine the main dimensions or factors that are involved. Essentially,

[11] Selection of items to measure project negativism was particularly difficult because of village-to-village differences in the exact nature of innovations and change projects which had failed. As a result, almost all of the tentative scale items developed to tap project negativism "washed out" in the pretesting, and the one item (6) that was retained in the final ten-item scale leaves much to be desired as a measure of project negativism.

[12] Agreement with items 1, 2, 3, 5, 7, 8, and 10 indicates a fatalistic attitude, as does disagreement with items 4, 6, and 9; the fatalism score for each respondent was computed to reflect this positive or negative direction of the ten items.

[13] The three types of factor analysis are principal axis solution, varimax rotation, and quartimax rotation. We will only present the results of the principal axis solution (in Table 12-1), as the varimax rotation and quartimax rotation results are very similar (Bonilla 1966).

factor analysis is a method of obtaining abstract dimensions that run through a set of scale items by analyzing the intercorrelations among each of the scale items with every other scale item.

The evidence clearly suggests the existence of three dimensions of fatalism (Table 12–1). All items measuring supernatural fatalism (2, 3, 5, 7, 8 and 9)

Table 12–1.   Factor Analysis of the Fatalism Scale Items Using the Principal Axis Solution

Fatalism Scale Item Number	Scale Item (Abbreviated)	Item Correlations with Factors		
		I "Supernatural Fatalism"	II "Situational Fatalism"	III "Project Negativism"
1. Business success depends on luck.		.5571[a]	.4054[b]	−.2603
2. Must endure epidemic or bad luck.		.6335	.2080	.0587
3. Man's life is predetermined.		.6549	−.0525	.2757
4. New techniques explain good crops.		−.0848	.7409	.2702
5. Winning a lottery betters my condition		.6172	.0949	−.5030
6. Man can plan his future		−.1395	.1957	.7927
7. Do not plan for the future		.7324	−.1763	.2189
8. Future planning causes unhappiness		.7161	−.2527	.1975
9. Work is better than good luck		.4400	.2387	.0854
10. Illness punishes bad behavior		−.1447	.5981	−.2202
Proportion of the total variance explained by each factor		28.12	13.16	12.44

[a] Dashed underlining indicates that item 1 was expected to load most highly with factor II, but it actually loaded somewhat more highly with factor I.

[b] Solid underlining indicates the factor on which each item was expected to load most highly, and with which it actually loaded most highly.

loaded very highly on factor I. Items 4 and 10 were designed to measure situational fatalism, and loaded very highly on factor II. Item 1 was also intended to measure the situational dimension, but showed no dominant loading on any of the three factors. Item 6, designed to measure project negativism, loaded highly on factor III, which might be labelled a project negativism factor.[14] Item 5, designed to measure supernatural fatalism, also loaded fairly heavily on factor III, which means that it measures project negativism as well as supernatural fatalism.

The results of the factor analysis in Table 12–1 show that construction of

[14] But this may also include some other residual dimensions of fatalism. The evidence is less clear-cut here than in the case of factors I and II, which rather definitely seem to measure supernatural fatalism and situational fatalism, respectively.

separate scales to measure each of the three dimensions of fatalism would probably be a difficult, and perhaps fruitless task. Even items with very high loadings on one factor, for example scale item 2, often have small, positive loadings on the other two factors. Also the percentage of the total variance in all of the scale items that is explained by each of the three factors is far from overwhelming; it is 25 percent for factor I, and only about 44 percent for the three factors combined. Therefore the ten-item scale will be utilized as a measure of the entire fatalism concept, remembering that it represents each of the three hypothesized subdimensions of fatalism.[15]

CORRELATES OF FATALISM

To permit an interpretation of our findings from both viewpoints (fatalism as a barrier to modernization versus a reduction in fatalism as a consequence of modernization) suggested earlier in this chapter, the correlates of fatalism are not categorized as antecedents or consequences. The zero-order relationship of fatalism to each of the following variables — literacy, mass media exposure, empathy, cosmopoliteness, innovativeness, aspirations, achievement motivation, and political knowledgeability — will be discussed.

LITERACY

Literacy is one of the variables that unlocks the peasant's mind for exposure to modern ideas beyond his village. Among these external ideas are rational, scientific explanations of the occurence of daily phenomena. This knowledge can give the villager greater control over future events that affect his style of life. So functional literacy should be negatively related to fatalism; that is, literates should have less fatalistic attitudes than illiterates. Table 12–2 indicates that the correlation between literacy[16] and fatalism is −.330, which is significantly different from zero. While the expected negative relationship between fatalism and functional literacy was found, only 11 percent of the variance in fatalism and literacy occurs in common. This indicates that one must look to other variables to explain further the variance in fatalism. Although the amount of covariance is relatively modest, we conclude that *fatalism is negatively related to literacy.*[17]

[15] And that the ten-item scale represents the supernatural fatalism variable more strongly, with the situational fatalism and project negativism subdimensions represented somewhat less thoroughly.

[16] Years of formal education, a variable that we know from previous analysis highly overlaps with functional literacy, is correlated −.398 with fatalism, which is significantly different from zero.

[17] This relationship holds even when the effect of age (but not when the effect of social status) is removed by partial correlation techniques.

Table 12–2.   Zero-Order Correlates of Fatalism in Three Colombian Villages

Variables Correlated with Fatalism	Zero-Order Correlation(r) with Fatalism	Percentage of Variance in Fatalism Explained(r^2)
1. Functional literacy	$-.330^b$	10.9
2. Mass media exposure	$-.306^b$	9.4
3. Empathy	$-.214^b$	4.6
4. Cosmopoliteness	$-.323^b$	10.4
5. Agricultural innovativeness	$[-.027]$	0.1
6. Home innovativeness	$-.396^b$	15.1
7. Educational aspirations	$-.179^a$	3.2
8. Occupational aspirations	$[-.122]$	1.5
9. Achievement motivation	$-.191^a$	3.6
10. Political knowledgeability	$-.342^b$	11.7

^{a} Significantly different from zero at the 5 percent level.

^{b} Significantly different from zero at the 1 percent level.

MASS MEDIA EXPOSURE

The mass media can be a liberating force that break the bounds of distance and isolation, and transport the villager into a more modern milieu (Schramm 1964:24). Exposure to such mass media should be associated with a lower degree of fatalism. Our data indicate a significant negative correlation, $-.306$, between media exposure and fatalism, supporting the conclusion that *fatalism is negatively related to mass media exposure.*[18]

EMPATHY

If a peasant is able to put himself in the role of more modern others, such as an extension change agent, one expects that he would also assume a more modern explanation rather than fate as a determinant of successes and failures in his daily living. *There is a negative relationship between empathy and fatalism* indicated by a correlation of $-.214$, which is significantly different from zero.[19]

COSMOPOLITENESS

Exposure to urban ways of life should lead the individual to perceive of man as in control of his environment. Almost inherent in the development of a city is man's ability to manipulate nature and the environment. Urban life

[18] This relationship is not lowered significantly when the effect of age is removed, although it is lowered when social status is partialled out.

[19] This relationship is not affected by controlling on the effects of age, although it is lowered significantly when the effect of social status is removed via partial correlation.

presents the subsistence farmer with a different explanation of happenings. As the peasant comes in closer contact with city ways, there should be a reduction in his fatalism. This line of reasoning is supported by Sariola's (1965) results regarding fatalism in two Colombian villages: one village was quite isolated, whereas the other was located on a main highway outside the industrial city of Medellin. Sariola found a much lower level of fatalism in the more cosmopolite village.

The Colombian findings show that *fatalism is negatively related to cosmopoliteness*, measured as the number of trips in the past year to a major city; the correlation is −.323, which is significantly different from zero.[20]

INNOVATIVENESS

The adoption of new ideas — fertilizers and crop varieties, vaccinations and latrines — is in direct opposition to being fatalistic. All such innovations represent attempts by an individual to control his future agricultural production, his personal and his family's health. In Colombia, home innovativeness and fatalism are correlated −.396, which is significantly different from zero. In fact, as Table 12–2 indicates, this correlation is the highest of any of the variables related to fatalism. However, agricultural innovativeness is only correlated −.027 with fatalism, which is not significantly different from zero, even though it is in the expected direction. We can offer no adequate explanation as to why agricultural innovativeness is not more highly (negatively) related to fatalism. Although the evidence is less adequate than we would like to have, it can be tentatively concluded that *innovativeness is negatively related to fatalism.*[21]

ASPIRATIONS

Only when peasants have contact with the outside world of opportunities can they become aware of the status levels that their children may achieve through higher levels of education. Exposure to the modern world often brings about the understanding that education is needed to compete with others in reaching desired goals. The hypothesis of an *inverse relationship between fatalism and educational and occupational aspirations* is somewhat sustained by our data. The correlation (−.179) between educational aspirations and fatalism (Table 12–2) is negative and significantly different from zero.[22] The correlation between occupational aspirations and fatalism (Table 12–2) is negative, but not significantly different from zero.

[20] This correlation is not changed significantly by controlling on the effects of either age or social status.

[21] This relationship is not affected by removing the effect of age, but it is significantly different when the effect of social status is controlled.

[22] The relationship of educational aspirations to fatalism is lowered significantly when the effects of age and of social status are removed.

ACHIEVEMENT MOTIVATION

It has been suggested that low levels of aspirations, a lack of achievement motivation, and a sense of fatalism may be highly functional for peasants whose opportunities have been severely limited. Achievement motivation, the desire for occupational excellence, is expected to be negatively related to fatalism. A fatalistic individual would not recognize the concept of personal accomplishment, since he does not perceive that man has control over his destiny. A significant negative correlation, −.191, was found; *achievement motivation and fatalism are negatively related in Colombia.*[23]

POLITICAL KNOWLEDGEABILITY

If one has a grasp of political events, he probably is interested in how the governmental institution is controlled. The pure fatalist would not perceive any utility in understanding political matters, since he feels powerless to affect political decisions. A correlation of −.342 was found between political knowledgeability and fatalism in Colombia, which is significantly different from zero.[24] This supports the assertion that *political knowledgeability is negatively related to fatalism.*

FATALISM AS AN INTERVENING VARIABLE

It has been seen that all of the selected correlates of fatalism are in the expected direction, and eight of the ten are significantly different from zero. Yet none of these zero-order correlations explains a very large part of the variance in fatalism. The largest covariance shown in Table 12–2 is 15.1 percent in the case of home innovativeness.[25]

PARTIAL CORRELATION ANALYSIS

The evidence (in Table 12–2), considered in general, leads to the conclusion that fatalism is of *some importance* in the modernization process. In this section it will be statistically determined whether fatalism intervenes between

[23] This relationship is not significantly lowered when the effect of age is partialled out, but such is the case when social status is controlled.

[24] This zero-order correlation between political knowledgeability and fatalism is not significantly changed when the effects of age and social status are removed.

[25] Actually, one other variable not included in the present discussion — dogmatism — correlated even more highly, +.422, with fatalism. Dogmatism refers to the strength with which beliefs are held, and was measured with the Troldahl and Powell (1965) short form of Rokeach's (1960) dogmatism scale. The positive empirical relationship between dogmatism and fatalism is not unexpected on logical grounds, and is not very important to the main conceptual thrust of this chapter.

selected "antecedents" and "consequences" in this process.[26] The method of probing, partial correlation, is familiar from its use in previous chapters. The first-order partial correlation between a selected pair of antecedent and consequent variables (with fatalism partialled out) is compared with the zero-order correlation between the same two variables. To the extent that fatalism intervenes, the first-order partial correlation should be reduced, and be significantly different from the zero-order correlation.

Table 12–3 shows 20 empirical tests of whether fatalism intervenes between selected pairs of antecedent-consequent variables.[27] In *none* of the 20 cases did controlling on fatalism significantly affect the relationships between the five antecedents and the four consequents. We conclude that *fatalism is not an important intervening variable between the antecedents and consequences of modernization.*

MULTIPLE CORRELATION OF FATALISM

A multiple correlation analysis was utilized to determine the relative importance of selected predictors of fatalism.[28] Of the eight antecedent variables included in the analysis, the most effective predictors of fatalism are education, literacy, and cosmopoliteness. A total of about 19 percent of the variance in fatalism is explained by the eight antecedents; their relative share of the variance explained is as follows:

Antecedent Variables	Percentage of Variance in Fatalism Explained
1. Education	8.55
2. Literacy	3.69
3. Cosmopoliteness	3.45
4. Level of living	2.66
5. Social status	1.72
6. Farm size (in acres)	0.27
7. Empathy	−0.15
8. Mass media exposure	−1.11
Total	19.08

[26] For simplicity of nomenclature in this section, literacy, mass media exposure, empathy, and cosmopoliteness are termed as antecedents, and agricultural innovativeness, home innovativeness, educational aspirations, achievement motivation, and political knowledgeability as consequences of fatalism, even though it has not yet been definitely established that these are indeed antecedents and consequences of fatalism.

[27] The four antecedent and five consequent variables included in Table 12–3 are nine of the ten main variables correlated previously in this chapter with fatalism (Table 12–2). The exception is occupational aspirations, which we found was correlated only −.191 with fatalism in the three Colombian villages. In view of this low relationship, it is unlikely that fatalism could significantly intervene in the relationships of various antecedent variables with occupational aspirations, so it was not incorporated in the analysis summarized in Table 12–3.

[28] The eight predictors included the four antecedent variables postulated in Figure 12–1 (literacy, cosmopoliteness, empathy, and mass media exposure), plus formal education and three status indicators level of living, social status ratings, and farm size).

Table 12–3. Zero-Order Correlations and First-Order Partial Correlations (Controlling on Fatalism) of Selected Modernization Antecedent and Consequent Variables

Selected Consequent Variables	Literacy				Mass Media Exposure			
	Zero-Order Correlation	Partial Correlation (Controlling on Fatalism)	z Test for Difference of Correlations	Does Fatalism Intervene?	Zero-Order Correlation	Partial Correlation (Controlling on Fatalism)	z Test for Difference of Correlations	Does Fatalism Intervene?
1. Agricultural innovativeness	.207	.208	0	No	.320	.331	.090	No
2. Home innovativeness	.426	.418	.098	No	.563	.574	.123	No
3. Educational aspirations	.273	.234	.352	No	.419	.391	.295	No
4. Achievement motivation	.272	.230	.352	No	.316	.277	.451	No
5. Political knowledgeability	.421	.457	.402	No	.595	.580	.262	No

(Continued).

Table 12–3. (Continued).

Selected Consequent Variables	Empathy				Cosmopoliteness			
	Zero-Order Correlation	Partial Correlation (Controlling on Fatalism)	z Test for Difference of Correlations	Does Fatalism Intervene?	Zero-Order Correlation	Partial Correlation (Controlling on Fatalism)	z Test for Difference of Correlations	Does Fatalism Intervene?
1. Agricultural innovativeness	.268	.303	.189	No	.135	.135	0	No
2. Home innovativeness	.366	.353	.295	No	.603	.597	0	No
3. Educational aspirations	.417	.394	.180	No	.436	.426	.098	No
4. Achievement motivation	.279	.259	.205	No	.282	.279	0	No
5. Political knowledgeability	.448	.433	0	No	.503	.495	0	No

By no means do these possible antecedents provide a very complete explanation of fatalism scores among the Colombian peasants. In fact, such usual antecedents of modernization as mass media exposure and empathy do not explain any of the variance in fatalism that is not also explained by other predictor variables.[29]

Thus two different types of empirical evidence have been obtained for the conclusion that fatalism does not seem to play a very central role in the modernization process. First, fatalism did not intervene between 20 pairs of antecedent-consequents of modernization. Further, 8 possible predictors of fatalism, when combined in a multiple correlation approach, explain only about 19 percent of the variance in fatalism.

CAN FATALISM PREDICT MODERNIZATION CONSEQUENTS?

The question remains: will knowledge of a peasant's fatalism, plus certain other predictor variables, permit us to predict (with multiple correlation techniques) such consequents as agricultural innovativeness, educational aspirations, and achievement motivation? We sought to determine whether fatalism could predict a unique portion of the variance in the dependent variable not explained by the other eight predictor variables. The results show that *fatalism did not contribute significantly to the prediction of agricultural innovativeness, aspirations, or achievement motivation* (Bonilla 1966).

So again there is evidence that fatalism does not seem to play a very central role in explaining modernization consequences.[30] Although the time-order of fatalism in this process cannot be determined, the research results suggest *the possibly greater utility of viewing a reduction in fatalism as a result of previous modernizing activities, rather than as a barrier to modernization.*

SUMMARY AND CONCLUSIONS

Fatalism is the degree to which an individual perceives a lack of ability to control his future. Three varieties of fatalism, conceptualized by Niehoff and Anderson (1966), were represented in the ten-item fatalism scale. Supernaturalism consists of traditional theological beliefs and magical notions which, by their manipulation, provide the individual with a fatalistic escape from daily insecurities. Situational fatalism is an attitude of apathetic passiveness that stems from an accurate understanding of limited possibilities for

[29] Both empathy and mass media exposure actually make very small *negative* contributions to explaining the variance in fatalism scores. This suggests, for instance, that empathy is more highly related to the other seven predictor variables than it is to fatalism.

[30] This conclusion about the relative unimportance of fatalism in explaining modernization is supported by the analysis of case studies of directed change in less developed countries by Niehoff and Anderson (1966).

improvement of life conditions. Project negativism is a type of fatalistic apathy toward innovations, founded on their previous failures. Factor analysis of the intercorrelations among the ten scale items indicated a basic underlying dimension of fatalism, but with the subdimensions of supernaturalism, situational fatalism, and project negativism each seeming to constitute a factor.

In the three Colombian villages of Pueblo Viejo, San Rafael, and Cuatro Esquinas, fatalism was negatively related to literacy, mass media exposure, empathy, cosmopoliteness, innovativeness, aspirations, achievement motivation, and political knowledgeability. However, the correlates of fatalism were generally low (the highest covariance with fatalism was 15 percent in the case of home innovativeness), but in the expected direction.

Fatalism did not significantly intervene in the relationship between 20 pairs of selected antecedent-consequent relationships. The conclusion, therefore, is that fatalism is not a very important intervening variable in the modernization process, a point further supported by multiple correlation attempts (1) to predict fatalism with eight antecedent predictors, and (2) to predict such modernization consequents as agricultural innovativeness, educational aspirations, and achievement motivation, respectively, with fatalism and eight other independent variables. The results show that fatalistic attitudes do not occupy a very central position in explaining modernization. At best, fatalism is one of the less important of the 10 to 12 variables that were expected to be involved, theoretically and empirically, in modernizing peasants.

These results also suggest that fatalism may be less a barrier to modernization than a post hoc rationalization for modernizing activities already completed. Evidence on this point is far from definitive. More research is needed before a decision can be made as to which of the two viewpoints of fatalism is more correct.

The present measure of fatalism was entirely attitudinal in nature, and one of the steps for future scholars of fatalism is to construct a scale that measures fatalistic *behavior*, rather than just fatalistic attitudes.

13

Innovativeness as an Indicator of Modernization*

In this country we have a genius of not putting to use our existing knowledge.
(P.C. Mahalanobis, India Planning Commission, as quoted by Guka-Thakurta, 1966)

Whoever could make two blades of grass to grow upon a spot of ground where only one grew before, would deserve better of mankind, and do more essential service to his country, than the whole race of politicians put together.

(Jonathan Swift in *Gulliver's Travels*)

Even in very traditional villages one is apt to find a handful of peasants who take the lead in adopting new ideas. These innovators, as they are called, dare to be venturesome in their struggle against the prevailing current of traditional village norms. They play a key role in the drama of development and change in less developed countries. How are such individuals, seemingly without group support, motivated to adopt new ideas? What characteristics set the innovators off from their fellow villagers?

Answers are provided by considerable research literature on the diffusion of innovations, which began in the United States and then spread to less developed nations like Colombia, where generally similar conclusions have been reported. This chapter primarily reports results of our investigation of variables correlated with innovativeness[1] — the concept most central to all diffusion researches.[2]

INNOVATIVENESS AND MODERNIZATION

There are several possible reasons why innovativeness is a key variable in the modernization process. First, it offers a kind of "hard data" about the extent to which modernization has occurred; ultimately, the degree to which

---

* This chapter was prepared with the assistance of Lytton Guimaraẽs, Diffusion Research Fellow, Department of Communication, Michigan State University.

[1] *Innovativeness* is defined as the degree to which an individual adopts new ideas relatively earlier than others in his social system.

[2] A content analysis of over 900 diffusion publications in the Michigan State University Diffusion Documents Center, containing some 7000 coded two-variable generalizations about diffusion, shows that innovativeness is the dependent variable in about 60 percent of the generalizations.

an individual has accepted "a more complex, technologically-advanced, and rapidly changing style of life" is best indicated by his actual use of new ideas in agriculture, health, and family living. Increasing his literacy, cosmopoliteness, and mass media exposure are all designed, in the end, to encourage him to adopt new ways of life. *The best single indicator of his degree of modernization is innovativeness*, indicating a behavioral rather than a cognitive or attitudinal change.

There is also much practical usefulness for change agents if they can identify the potential innovators (and laggards) in their audience, and then utilize different strategies of change with each of these subaudiences. If change agents and development planners can understand the antecedent variables that may lead to innovativeness among peasants, they can use this knowledge as a useful "handle" to prime the pump of planned change.

Figure 13–1 shows our conception of the role of innovativeness in the modernization process. Innovativeness is seen as consequent of such ante-

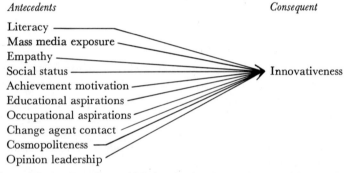

Figure 13–1.   Paradigm of Modernization Antecedents and Innovativeness.

cedents as literacy, mass media exposure, change agent contact, and cosmopoliteness, all of which indicate a peasant's relationship to the modern, urban society. Empathy allows the individual to benefit from a given quantity of such communication contact. A number of attitudinal and motivational variables, such as achievement motivation, educational and occupational aspirations, are also shown as antecedents to innovativeness. If these attitudes lead to overt behavioral change, one would expect it to be expressed as innovativeness. Although age and social status could also be depicted as antecedents to innovativeness, we have somewhat less theoretical interest in them than the other variables shown. Older peasants are expected to be less innovative, as are those of lower status, who likely have less wherewithal to afford new ideas.

S-SHAPED ADOPTER DISTRIBUTIONS FOR INNOVATIONS IN COLOMBIA

Fundamental to our measurement of innovativeness and adopter categories is the notion of an S-shaped curve when the rate of adoption of an innovation is plotted over time (Rogers 1962:152–158). Figure 13–2 shows the S-shaped adopter distributions for three innovations in both the modern and traditional Colombian villages. Such an S-shaped curve is a *normal* cumulative frequency, a fact that is important for adopter categorization. None of the innovations demonstrate a complete S curve, however, since none reach 100 percent adoption. In the more modern villages, a higher level of adoption for each of the three innovations was reached than in the traditional villages. In one sense, the striking differences between these two types of villages in level of innova-

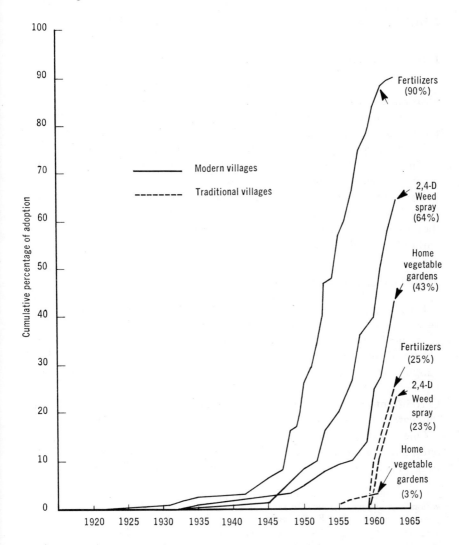

Figure 13–2. Adopter Distributions in Both Modern and Traditional Villages Are S-Shaped, but the Rate of Adoption in Traditional Villages Is Much Slower.

tion adoption is strong empirical evidence that our classification of the village norms as traditional and modern is appropriate. When viewed in a slightly different way, the different levels of adoption in the villages (at least since the initiation of change agent activities in the modern villages in the late 1950s) show the contrast between the effects of planned change and of selective change.[3]

MEASURING INNOVATIVENESS AND ADOPTER CATEGORIZATION

INNOVATIVENESS

Innovativeness is defined as the degree to which an individual adopts new ideas relatively earlier than others in his social system. Innovativeness scales were computed for all household heads in the 5 Colombian villages, based on their reported time of adoption of each of 12 to 15 new agricultural ideas, such as weed sprays, fertilizers, new crop varieties, farm machinery, and animal vaccination. A similar procedure was followed in the construction of a home innovativeness scale composed of 10 to 12 health, nutrition, sanitation, and home equipment innovations. The exact number of both agricultural and home innovations varied somewhat from village to village, but in general they were all important new ideas that had been introduced in the village within the last decade.

ADOPTER CATEGORIZATION

For many purposes, a continuous measure of innovativeness, such as the agricultural and home innovativeness scales just discussed, is satisfactory. A continuous variable is most appropriate when correlating antecedent variables with innovativeness. Occasionally respondents must be classified into adopter categories[4] in order to look at differences between the earlier and later adopters of new ideas, or between the innovators and noninnovators. Certain antecedent differences may be significant in determining who will innovate and who will not.

One procedure is to classify adopters into categories on the basis of the two parameters of the normal curve, which are the mean and the standard deviation.[5] These parameters are used to divide the adopter distribution into five

---

[3] A similar point was made in Chapter 1 to explain the different rates of change for innovations introduced in Saucío before and after a change agent began work in the village (Deutschmann and Fals Borda 1962a).

[4] *Adopter categories* are classifications of individuals within a social system on the basis of innovativeness (Rogers 1962:148).

[5] The mean is the average for all the individuals in the social system; in the present case it is the average year of adoption of an innovation (or the average innovativeness score). The standard deviation is a measure of the range or "spread" of the distribution.

categories, labeled as innovators, early adopters, early majority, late majority, and laggards. The percentage of individuals included in each of these five adopter categories is shown on a normal frequency distribution in Figure 13–3.

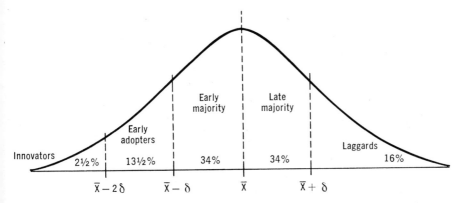

Figure 13–3.   Adopter Categorization on the Basis of Innovativeness.

The area lying to the left of the mean time of adoption minus two standard deviations includes the first 2.5 percent of the individuals to adopt an innovation — the *innovators*. The next 13.5 percent to adopt the new idea are included in the area between the mean minus one standard deviation and the mean minus two standard deviations; they are labeled *early adopters*. The next 34 percent of the adopters, called *early majority*, are included in the area between the mean date of adoption and minus one standard deviation. Between the mean and one standard deviation to the right of the mean are located the next 34 percent to adopt the new idea, the *late majority*. The last 16 percent are called *laggards*.

This method of adopter classification is probably the most widely used in current diffusion studies. However, as can be observed, it is not a symmetrical classification in that there are three adopter categories to the left of the mean, and only two to the right. One solution would be to break laggards into two categories, such as early and late laggards, but laggards seem to be a fairly homogeneous category. Similarly, innovators and early adopters could be combined into a single class to achieve symmetry, but their quite different characteristics mark them as two distinct categories.

Another difficulty in our method of adopter classification is incomplete adoption, which occurs for innovations that have not reached 100 percent use at the time of their study. This means that our fivefold classification scheme is not completely exhaustive. But the problem of incomplete adoption or nonadoption is eliminated when a series of innovations is combined into a composite innovativeness scale.

Respondents in the five Colombian villages were categorized into the fivefold classification system for both agricultural and home innovations (Table 13–1). In general, the categories approach the expected percentages

Table 13–1. Adopter Categories on the Basis of Agricultural and Home Innovativeness in Five Colombian Villages.

Adopter Categories	Percentage Distribution in Each Adopter Category		
	Theoretical for Perfect Normal Adopter Distribution	Actual for Agricultural Innovativeness in Colombia	Actual for Home Innovativeness in Colombia
1. Innovators	2.5	3.1	3.1
2. Early adopters	13.5	13.3	13.0
3. Early majority	34.0	30.6	34.1
4. Late majority	34.0	26.7	29.4
5. Laggards	16.0	26.3	20.4
Totals	100.0	100.0	100.0

in each category with the exception of the last two categories, late adopters and laggards. One reason for this is that in the two traditional villages (especially La Cañada), there are too many peasants who have not adopted any (or almost any) of the innovations.[6]

CHARACTERISTICS OF ADOPTER CATEGORIES

Generalizations about (1) the personal characteristics, (2) communication behavior, and (3) social relationships of adopter categories, are available from past studies, largely completed in the United States (Rogers 1962:172–192). Earlier adopters are usually: younger in age; higher in social status; in a more favorable financial position, involved in more specialized operations; and better able to deal with abstractions than later adopters.[7] The communication behavior of earlier adopters also distinguishes them from later adopters. Generally, earlier adopters utilize communication channels that are less interpersonal (more mass media) and more cosmopolite in nature than

[6] Both innovativeness scales in Colombia have one serious shortcoming in that they depend upon *recall* data. Obviously, recall of adoption dates may be inaccurate for some individuals and for certain types of innovations. For example, Menzel (1957) found that the time of adoption of a new medical drug as reported by physicians in personal interviews did not exactly jibe with druggists' prescription records. The precision with which adoption dates are recalled by peasants is certainly less than desired.

[7] There is a tendency for the characteristics discussed to increase or decrease consistently from earlier to later adopters.

Table 13-2. Characteristics of Adopter Categories for Three Modern Colombian Villages.

Characteristics of Adopter Categories	Adopter Categories[a]				
	Innovators	Early Adopters	Early Majority	Late Majority	Laggards
1. Percentage literate	80	43	41	31	25
2. Number of times per day the respondent listens to radio	6.4	3.3	3.4	1.3	2.2
3. Number of newspapers read (or read to) per week	5.6	3.5	2.7	1.0	1.6
4. Number of magazines read (or read to) per month	3.4	1.3	0.5	0.4	0.4
5. Number of movies seen in the past year	5.4	3.4	3.7	2.3	2.2
6. Number of TV shows seen in the past year	3.6	1.0	0.9	0.3	0.7
7. Empathy score	6.2	5.7	4.9	4.0	3.6
8. Social status score (ratings by interviewers)	2.8	2.3	1.9	1.4	1.2
9. Farm size (in acres)	22.8	22.4	15.6	4.1	4.4
10. Achievement motivation score	12.6	12.0	11.4	11.7	11.2
11. Educational aspiration for oldest male child (in years)	7.0	4.5	3.9	2.7	2.9
12. Occupational aspiration for oldest male child	3.4	2.2	2.5	2.0	1.9
13. Number of extension worker contacts in the past year	1.8	0.9	1.3	0.7	0.2
14. Number of trips to cities in past year	41.0	20.0	19.3	7.3	12.1
15. Sociometric opinion leadership score	27.6	9.9	5.6	1.9	1.2

[a] On the basis of agricultural innovativeness scores.

Table 13–3. Characteristics of Adopter Categories for Two Traditional Colombian Villages

Characteristics of Adopter Categories	Adopter Categories[a]				
	Innovators	Early Adopters	Early Majority	Late Majority	Laggards
1. Percentage literate	67	18	20	23	14
2. Number of times per day the respondent listens to radio	3.3	2.4	1.3	1.1	0.9
3. Number of newspapers read (or read to) per month	5.0	0.4	0.8	0.2	0.2
4. Number of magazines read (or read to) per month	1.3	0.5	0	0	0
5. Number of movies seen in the past year	2.0	0.5	0	0	0.3
6. Number of TV shows seen in the past year	0	0	0	0	0
7. Empathy scores	7.0	3.5	3.6	2.5	1.6
8. Social status score (ratings by interviewers)	2.7	1.9	1.7	1.5	0.9
9. Farm size (in acres)	1.8	1.3	1.2	1.0	0.3
10. Achievement motivation score	33.0	18.7	19.0	15.4	14.7
11. Educational aspirations for oldest male child (in years)	9.7	5.7	4.5	4.1	4.0
12. Occupationl aspirations for oldest male child	2.3	2.3	1.8	1.8	1.5
13. Number of extension worker contacts in the past year[b]	3.0	0.8	0.1	0	0.3
14. Number of trips to cities	30.0	2.5	2.8	3.8	0.3
15. Sociometric opinion leadership score	2.3	2.8	2.3	0.8	0.6

[a] On the basis of agricultural innovativeness scores.
[b] There is no contact with extension service change agents in Nazate.

later adopters. They also utilize a greater number of different channels than do later adopters. With respect to social relationships, innovators and early adopters are more cosmopolite and generally have higher opinion leadership than later adopters.

The Colombia findings (summarized for the three modern villages in Table 13–2, and for the two traditional villages in Table 13–3) show that the characteristics of adopter categories in the Colombia villages are substantially similar to the characteristics derived largely from studies of U.S. farmers.[8] The Colombian innovators score consistently higher on most of the modernization variables (literacy, aspirations, cosmopoliteness, mass media exposure, and so forth) than respondents in the other adopter categories in both the modern and traditional villages.

The one exception to a general pattern of similarity between the modern and traditional communities is the amount of opinion leadership accorded to innovators. In the three more modern communities, innovators are opinion leaders, whereas in the more traditional communities (where the innovators are very much more modern than the other members of their social system) they are accorded relatively little opinion leadership.[9] *The innovators in the traditional villages seem to be perceived as deviants by their peers* (Figure 13–4). Although they are not influential in persuading their peers to follow suit, the small handful of peasant innovators in the traditional communities at least create an *awareness* of modern possibilities.

The Colombia data show that innovativeness[10] in both modern and traditional villages is positively related to the following variables; (1) literacy; (2) mass media exposure; (3) empathy; (4) social status; (5) farm size; (6) achievement motivation; (7) educational aspirations; (8) occupational aspirations; (9) extension change agent contact; (10) cosmopoliteness.

PREDICTING INNOVATIVENESS

METHODS OF PREDICTION

One purpose of the social sciences is to develop a rationale to serve as a basis for reliable, empirical prediction of human behavior. Although such

[8] The two tables show that, except for anticipated differences in the *level* of modernization variables, adopter categories in the three modern and the two traditional villages exhibit similar characteristics. In other words, there are parallel relationships between innovativeness and the various antecedent variables in both the modern and traditional settings.

[9] We believe that one reason these innovators are not perceived as opinion leaders is because they are so much more modern than their followers. In fact, the innovators in the traditional villages even outscore the innovators in the modern villages on such modernization variables as empathy, achievement motivation, and aspirations.

[10] General supportive evidence for these correlates of peasant innovativeness is provided by a great number of investigations; the most comprehensive is Loomis (1967) who reported data from a national sample of about 7200 Indian villagers.

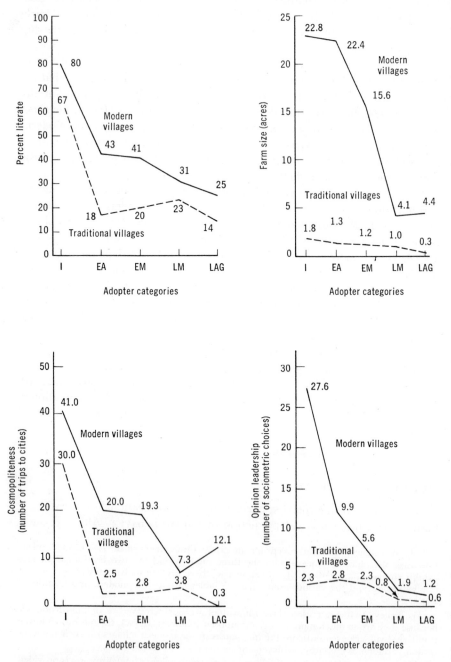

Figure 13–4. Characteristics of Adopter Categories in Modern and Traditional Villages in Colombia.

prediction is obviously important to the scientist pursuing scientific knowledge, it is perhaps even more useful and relevant for those whose immediate concern is action (such as development planners, administrators, change agents, and so on).

The two general approaches to predicting human behavior are *clinical* and *statistical*. The clinical method of prediction is used primarily in medicine, psychiatry, and clinical psychology where each case is viewed as somewhat unique, requiring an assessment of the total complexity of antecedent symptoms before a prediction can be intuitively offered. Niehoff and Anderson (1965) and Niehoff (1966a), in their attempt to predict the success or failure of change agents in introducing innovations in less developed countries,[11] represent one of the few uses of clinical prediction methods in the social sciences.

Statistical methods of prediction are more commonly used to predict innovativeness. Probability (or stochastic) models are used to forecast the likelihood of individuals behaving in a particular manner. *Multiple correlation* techniques and the *configurational* method are perhaps most useful for predicting innovative behavior.

MULTIPLE CORRELATION APPROACH

Multiple correlation is a statistical procedure designed to analyze and explain the variance in a dependent variable into components attributable to the joint effect of independent variables. Rogers (1962:287–289) summarizes eleven U.S. studies that used multiple correlation to examine the relationships of innovativeness with other variables. These independent variables explained from 17 to 64 percent of the variance in innovativeness scores.

Since 1962, several additional investigations have been completed, seven in more developed nations and nine in less developed countries. A summary of these nine studies is provided in Table 13–4. While all of these studies used the same basic approach to prediction, differences in conceptualization and measurement of the independent variables make comparisons somewhat difficult. The most common independent variables included in these investigations are economic, attitudinal, communication, and group relationship variables. The explained variance in innovativeness in these analyses ranges from a low of 17 percent, to a high of about 88 percent, which was obtained by Wish (1967) in his study of retail food establishments in Puerto Rico.

The independent variables for inclusion in our multiple correlation analyses were selected in accordance with the following criteria:

[11] Professor Niehoff developed a set of antecedent variables, which he uses to predict whether or not the change attempt was successful.

Table 13–4. Comparison of Multiple Correlation Attempts to Explain Innovativeness in Less Developed Countries

Investigator	Respondents	Some of the Main Independent Variables Utilized	Percent of Variance in Innovativeness Explained (r^2)
Deutschmann and Fals Borda (1962a)	Colombian peasants	Mass media exposure Farm size Education Cosmopoliteness Awareness of innovations Use of written farm accounts	56.3 (68.9 when using 21 more independent variables)
Junghare (1962)	Indian peasants	Extension worker contact Formal participation Socioeconomic status Education Economic status Age	23.8
Madigan (1962)	Household heads in the Philippines	Education Preference for democratic leadership Level of living	17.1
Havens (1963)	Colombian peasants	Mass media exposure Level of living Age	47.5

Beal and Sibley (1966)	Guatemalan Indian farmers	Scientific attitudes Fatalism Achievement motivation Knowledgeability Age Education Literacy Cosmopoliteness Source credibility Farm size	78 when using 51 variables, and 42 when using 6 variables
Moulik and others (1966)	Indian peasants	Attitude toward an innovation Knowledge about an innovation Economic motivation Opinion leadership Extension worker contact	81
Whittenbarger and Maffei (1966)	Colombian peasants	Information-seeking activity Knowledgeability Farm size Attitude toward credit	44.4
Wish (1967)	Retail food stores in Puerto Rico	Sales Store size Education of owner Interpersonal trust Hoarding propensity (plus 30 other variables)	87.5
Chattopadhyay and Pareek (1967)	Indian peasants	Fatalism Authoritarianism Liberalism	59

1. Each independent variable should be highly related to the dependent variable in a zero-order relationship.

2. Each independent variable should have low interrelationships with all other independent variables.

3. The total number of variables should be minimized to increase practical use of the results.[12]

4. There should be theoretical and practical relevance for the relationship of each independent variable with the dependent variable.

Agricultural Innovativeness in the Modern and Traditional Villages in Colombia

A total of 35 independent variables were initially included in the multiple correlation analysis of agricultural innovativeness for the three modern Colombian villages. The amount of variance explained in agricultural innovativeness (r^2) with 35 variables is 45.3 percent. The final multiple correlation analysis includes only five independent variables, since the relatively less effective predictor variables were successively eliminated.[13] Empathy, opinion leadership (about a marketing problem), size of farm (in labor units), size of farm (in land units), and school teacher contact explain 34.9 percent of the variance in agricultural innovativeness in the three modern villages (Table 13–5). The best predictors of agricultural innovativeness appear to be empathy and opinion leadership.

Table 13–5. Percentage of Variance Explained in Agricultural Innovativeness by Five Independent Variables in Three Modern Villiages in Colombia.

Independent Variables	Percentage of Variation Explained(r^2)	Percentage of Contribution to Total Variance Explained
1. Empathy	9.6	27.6
2. Opinion leadership (about a marketing problem)	8.2	23.4
3. Farm size (in labor units)	4.3	12.4
4. Farm size (in land units)	6.5	18.6
5. School teacher contact	6.3	18.0
Total	34.9	100.0

[12] Up until about 1960, the number of independent variables was usually limited to five or six by computational time requirements. With the advent of computer use, the number of independent variables rose dramatically, and now we often find studies employing 50 to 60 independent variables for prediction purposes.

[13] This is done by a computer program called "least squares delete" because it successively drops independent variables from the multiple correlation analysis in reverse order of their contribution to explaining the dependent variable.

In the two traditional villages, 76.5 percent of the variance in agricultural innovativeness was explained with 37 independent variables.[14] Reducing the number of independent variables to eleven — magazine exposure, sociometric opinion leadership for farm innovations, farm size in land units, empathy, farm land cultivated, farm production, home innovativeness, desire to increase farm size, farm intensification, self-perceived innovativeness and sociometric reputation as a good farmer — we were still able to explain 66.4 percent of the variance in agricultural innovativeness in the two traditional villages (Table 13–6). Magazine exposure is the best single predictor of agricultural innovativeness in the traditional villages.

Table 13–6. Percentage of Variance Explained in Agricultural Innovativeness by Eleven Independent Variables in Two Traditional Villages in Colombia

Independent Variables	Percentage of Variance Explained (^2r)	Percentage of Contribution to Total Variance Explained
1. Magazine exposure	20.3	30.5
2. Home innovativeness scores	13.5	20.3
3. Empathy scores	11.4	17.1
4. Farm size (in land units)	11.0	16.9
5. Sociometric opinion leadership (for farm innovations)	7.2	10.8
6. Farm intensification scores	4.5	6.7
7. Farm production	3.9	5.9
8. Desire to increase size of farm	1.5	2.2
9. Self-perceived innovativeness	−0.8	−1.2
10. Farm land cultivated	−1.6	−2.4
11. Sociometric reputation as a good farmer	−4.5	−6.8
Total	66.4	100.0

When the five best predictors of agricultural innovativeness in the modern villages are compared (Table 13–5) with their eleven counterparts in the traditional villages (Table 13–6), there are only three variables in common: opinion leadership, empathy, and farm size (in land units). Evidently the best determinants of agricultural innovativeness in modern and traditional systems are rather different. Few of the attitudinal-motivational variables indicating social psychological modernization (like educational aspirations, achievement motivation, and so on) explain significant amounts of variance in farm innovativeness, when the effects of all other variables are removed.

[14] The amount of variance explained in the traditional villages is much higher than the 34.9 percent explained in the modern villages.

Home Innovativeness in Modern and Traditional Villages

The initial correlation analysis to predict home innovativeness for the three modern villages includes 35 independent variables. They explain 58.7 percent of the variance in home innovativeness in the three modern villages. Using only seven variables: cosmopoliteness (number of trips to cities per year), political knowledgeability, social status, self-perceived opinion leadership, lack of farm fragmentation, farm size (in land units), and functional literacy, 53.0 percent of variance can still be explained (Table 13–7).

Table 13–7. Percentage of Variance Explained in Home Innovativeness by Seven Independent Variables in Three Modern Villages in Colombia.

Independent Variables	Percentage of Variation Explained (r^2)	Percentage of Contribution to Total Variance Explained
1. Cosmopoliteness (number of trips to cities per year)	21.9	41.3
2. Political knowledgeability	12.3	23.2
3. Lack of farm fragmentation	7.9	14.9
4. Social status	7.3	13.8
5. Self-perceived opinion leadership	6.6	12.5
6. Functional literacy	5.2	9.8
7. Farm size (in land units)	−8.2	−15.5
Total	53.0	100.0

Cosmopoliteness is the best single predictor. Farm size (in land units) is the only independent variable that is a significant predictor of both agricultural and home innovativeness in the modern villages.[15]

In the traditional villages 69.1 percent of the variance was accounted for by using 37 independent variables in the initial multiple correlation analysis. With seven variables: contact with the federal agricultural bank; present debt; cosmopoliteness (trips to cities); empathy; farm size (in labor units); farm intensification; and formal education, 52.9 percent of the variance in home innovativeness in the traditional villages (Table 13–8) was explained.

Differences in Predicting Agricultural and Home Innovativeness

The two best predictors of agricultural innovativeness for the two traditional villages are magazine exposure and home innovativeness scores,

---

[15] This variable actually makes a negative contribution in explaining the variance in home innovativeness scores.

whereas the two best predictors of home innovativeness are amount of debt and cosmopoliteness. The latter variable is one of the best predictors of home innovativeness in both the traditional and the modern villages, whereas it is

Table 13–8. Percentage of Variance Explained in Home Innovativeness by Seven Independent Variables in Two Traditional Villages in Colombia

Independent Variables	Percentage of Variance Explained (r^2)	Percentage of Contribution to Total Variance Explained
1. Present debt	14.1	26.7
2. Cosmopoliteness (trips to cities)	14.1	26.7
3. Empathy scores	13.5	25.6
4. Formal education	9.3	17.5
5. Farm intensification scores	5.1	9.6
6. Farm size (in labor units)	4.9	9.3
7. Contact with federal agricultural bank	−8.1	−15.4
Total	52.9	100.0

relatively unimportant in explaining agricultural innovativeness. This seems reasonable; when peasants travel to cities, they largely see home innovations rather than agricultural ideas.

Conclusions

What can generally be concluded about the attempts to predict innovativeness in the Colombian villages?

1. The amount of variance in innovativeness explained in the Colombian villages is about the same as in parallel studies in more developed countries, and somewhat less than in some of the studies recently completed in less developed countries (Table 13–4), where up to 87 percent of the variance in innovativeness has been explained.

2. The amount of variance explained in agricultural innovativeness in the traditional villages (66.4 percent) exceeded that predicted in the modern villages (34.9 percent), but this was not true in the case of home innovativeness. About 53 percent of the variance in home innovativeness was explained in both modern and traditional villages, although by somewhat different variables.

3. In fact, *there are few common independent variables retained in the final multiple correlation analyses for the two types of innovativeness, and for the two kinds of villages.* This is a discouraging conclusion for change agents who seek a succinct number of universal variables by which they can identify innovators and other adopter categories among their peasant clientele. This fact emphasizes

the need for further research on multiple correlation prediction of innovativeness among different villages in the same country, and cross-culturally.[16]

4. *In none of the multiple correlation analyses do attitudinal variables (like aspirations) appear to be as important as predictors of innovativeness as are economic, external communication, and social relationship variables.*

One shortcoming of the multiple correlation method is that it does not tell us about possible "interaction effects" among the independent variables in predicting innovativeness. One must assume that the independent variables act separately in association with the dependent variable. It is likely that the relationship of certain independent variables with innovativeness is affected by the presence of other independent variables. Mass media exposure, for example, may have a greater effect on innovativeness in the presence of empathy. These interaction effects can better be determined by configurational analysis.

CONFIGURATIONAL ANALYSIS

The configurational approach to prediction consists of dividing a sample of respondents into relatively homogeneous categories on the basis of several independent variables. Each category or configuration is maximally homogeneous in regard to the independent variables. This isolation of the variance serves to help predict the dependent variable. There are two versions of the configurational method: the symmetrical version of Stuckert (1958), and the nonsymmetrical Sonquist-Morgan approach (1964).

Stuckert Symmetrical Approach

In this approach, each homogeneous subsample, resulting from successive breakdowns on the basis of the independent variables, is regarded as a separate unit of analysis. This approach was utilized with data from the modern villages in Colombia (Rogers and Bonilla 1965). Five independent variables, empathy, cosmopoliteness, village norms, mass media exposure, and literacy, are related to the dependent variable — adoption of home vegetable gardens. The innovation is an important nutritional idea among the respondents, whose diets are otherwise generally lacking in vitamins and protein. Home gardens were promoted in the three modern villages for about five years before the data gathering by extension change agents. The independent variables were dichotomized, and arrayed in a configurational tree, so as to predict adoption or nonadoption of the innovation. A number of deviant cases

---

[16] We replicated the present attempt to predict agricultural innovativeness with the same statistical technique and with approximately similar variables with 702 India peasants, who were interrogated as part of the UNESCO study (described in Chapter 3). We were able to explain 39.5 percent of the variance; the best predictor variables are value of farm production, level of living, and sociometric reputation as a good farmer. So we see little similarity in the best predictors with our Colombia villagers.

were observed in this configuration. For example, there was a peasant who did not adopt, but was high in empathy and media exposure; usually those peasants who were highly empathic and who had high media exposure were adopters. Kendall and Wolf (1949:152–179) call attention to the importance of analyzing deviant cases[17] such as these. Such analysis may reveal additional independent variables not previously considered, as well as lead to refinement in the measurement of variables used to identify the deviant cases.

Ten of the twenty-four most deviant individuals shown by the Stuckert configurational approach were reinterviewed in a follow-up attempt to examine in more detail the reasons for such deviancy from the predicted outcomes. The following reasons (Rogers and Ramos 1965) were found:

1. *Perception* of the innovation. Respondents who perceived the innovation as contributing to improved health and nutrition, were likely to adopt even though they were unlikely to do so on the basis of the five predictor variables (empathy, literacy, and so forth)

2. Adequacy or lack of *knowledge* about the innovation.

3. Possession of a *plot* that could be utilized for a vegetable garden.

A second Stuckert configurational tree that included these variables, as well as the five original independent variables, showed a considerable increase in the success of prediction.

Sonquist-Morgan Approach

The Stuckert method of prediction successively breaks down each subsample through each independent variable, whereas the Sonquist-Morgan approach interrupts this breakdown whenever the variance in the dependent variable is maximally separated by any combination of the independent variables. This approach also allows an independent variable to be utilized more than once in the prediction process, as long as the variable is divided at a different point each time it is used. The mutually exclusive series of subcategories are chosen (by a computer program) in such a way that at each step in the procedure, the subcategory means account for the greatest possible variance in the dependent variable; that is, they reduce the predictive error more than the means of any other equal number of subcategories (Sonquist and Morgan 1964:4).

It was indicated previously that one limitation of the multiple correlation method is that it does not provide for possible interactions between variables. The Sonquist-Morgan approach allows this type of analysis. The neccessity of a large sample of respondents precluded the use of this method with the Colombia nrespondents, so data obtained in the India-UNESCO study were subjected to the Sonquist-Morgan analysis. The criterion for splitting into configurations was the minimization of the variance in the dependent variable

---

[17] These individuals are deviants from the prediction in a statistical sense, rather than in being nonconformists to system norms.

within each configuration; twenty-five was the minimum number of respondents allowable in any configuration. The outcome of the India analysis is shown in Figure 13–5.

The same predictor variables as were included in a multiple correlation analysis were utilized to gain additional information with the Sonquist-Morgan analysis. Opinion leadership, for example, is found to be an important predictor only for respondents with a high value of farm products sold and a high level of living. Similarly, farm size is important only for those individuals with a low value of farm products sold and a high level of living. This is evidence of interacton effects among the independent variables in predicting innovativeness. The Sonquist-Morgan configurational method also arrays the results of prediction in a format that is easily visualized, and hence more easily communicated to change agents.

CONCLUSIONS ABOUT PREDICTION APPROACHES

Briefly, the major advantages and disadvantages of each of the three prediction methods are the following:

1. Multiple correlation is the most common method utilized in past research on predicting innovativeness. With the present state of computer technology, it is possible to include up to 50 or 60 independent variables in such an analysis.[18] The coefficient of multiple determination, r^2, is an easily comparable index of relative prediction success. On the other hand, the multiple correlation method necessitates the assumption of linearity in relationships and can be utilized only with continuous independent variables. The lack of "visibility" to the researcher, or practitioner, of the complex relationships among his variables (including greater problems in spotting deviant cases than with the configurational approaches), may obscure important interaction effects leading to "inaccurate" conclusions.

2. Both configurational approaches — Stuckert and Sonquist-Morgan — offer the researcher an opportunity to become intimately acquainted with the interaction effects among his data. Configurational analyses result in a picture of relationships, and therefore, might be more easily understood by field practitioners, such as change agents. Although configurational methods do not offer a standard index of relative prediction success, as does multiple correlation, perhaps one could be developed.

   a. The Stuckert approach requires no more complex equipment than an IBM card counter-sorter. The arbitrary decisions, regarding the order in which independent variables are utilized in the configuration tree, may hamper the success of the prediction.

   b. The Sonquist-Morgan version of the configurational approach

---

[18] This is a major increase over the practical limitation of five or six variables in the desk calculator era of multiple correlation analysis, which existed up to about 1960.

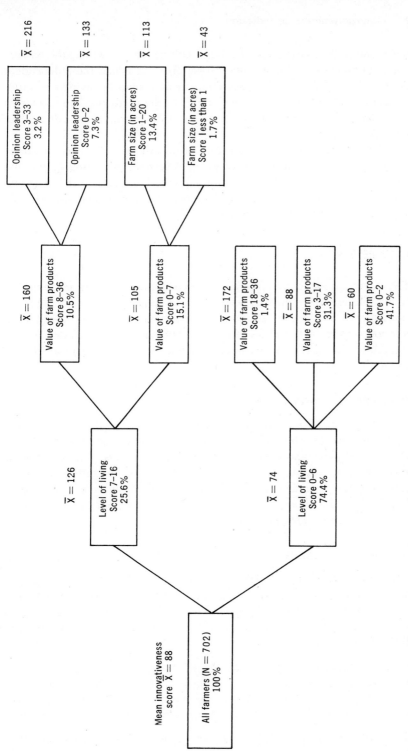

Figure 13–5. Sonquist-Morgan Configurational Prediction of Agricultural Innovativeness Scores.

requires computer assistance and a large sample size. However, the basis of major data-analysis decisions (such as the order in which the independent variables will be utilized in the prediction, at what point to divide a continuous variable, which variables to exclude from the prediction, and so forth) are soundly based on maximum partitioning of the variance in the dependent variable.

3. All methods of prediction, as utilized in past research, are essentially "postdiction" rather than true prediction. A second, validating sample has not been utilized to test the success of a prediction equation derived from multiple correlation or configuration methods. The use of validating samples is an important step in future research.

NEEDED RESEARCH

The directions for future research on peasant innovativeness are indicated by the limitations of completed research. Especially important are (1) study of nonmaterial innovation diffusion; (2) inclusion of economic variables in prediction studies; (3) analysis of attitude behavioral discrepancy; and (4) inquiry into the direct and indirect consequences of technological innovations.

NONMATERIAL INNOVATIONS

To date, most diffusion research has concentrated on the study of technological innovations that have a *material referent*. Studies are needed of nonmaterial ideas like communism, the Alliance for Progress, and news events. On the first page of this book it was pointed out that the diffusion of news events has rarely been analyzed outside of the United States. To what extent will generalizations about technological innovations hold for nonmaterial innovations? We do not yet know.

ECONOMIC VARIABLES

The economist Schultz (1964) recently argued against the prevailing view that sociocultural variables are important determinants of behavioral change among peasants in less developed countries. He said that economic stimuli greatly affect peasants — to the extent that we do not need to attend to cultural factors.

Studies of the observed lags in the acceptance of particular new agricultural factors show that these lags are explained satisfactorily by profitability . . . . Since differences in profitability are a strong explanatory variable, it is not necessary to appeal to differences in personality, education, and social environment (Schultz 1964:164).

This rather extreme statement has been welcomed by many social scientists, especially economists, in spite of the scanty evidence cited by Schultz.

He ignores a myriad of research studies[19] showing cultural factors to be of great importance in explaining peasant behavior, and rests his case primarily on the findings of one of his Ph.D. students (Hopper 1957) in India and an anthropological colleague, Tax (1963), who studied a Guatemala town. Schultz uses the findings from aggregate analyses of price sensitivity among India cotton farmers to support the assertion that peasants are motivated to adopt innovations solely by economic incentives. Unfortunately, reactions to price changes in established crop enterprises tell us little about how peasants adopt *new* ideas.

Schultz *does* have a point, even if it is overstated. Economic considerations *are* one predictor of innovative behavior by peasants, but they certainly do not outweigh sociocultural variables in all instances. For example, the Igbo of Nigeria could realize great savings were they to eat the fish from nearby rivers, rather than importing salt water fish from the North Sea. However, some Nigerians believe that the souls of their ancestors reside in their river fish, so they engage in the highly uneconomic practice of importing ocean fish. Likewise, even were the price of beef to be halved in India, Hindus would not eat cows.

The rate of adoption by peasants is likely to be more rapid if the innovation is more profitable, although the increase in profitability must be rather spectacular to affect the rate of adoption significantly. It has been estimated that the relative economic advantage of a new idea must be as least 25 to 30 percent higher than existing practice for economic factors to affect peasants' rate of adoption. When an innovation promises only a 5 to 10 percent advantage, the peasant farmer may have difficulty distinguishing its economic advantage. His limited skill with numbers, his crude accounting scheme, and his lack of finesse with the scientific method of reaching conclusions, all act to limit his ability to make economic comparisons.

In any event, economic variables need to be incorporated more thoroughly into future attempts to explain peasant innovativeness. A perusal of the independent variables utilized in past research to predict peasant innovativeness (Table 13–4) suggests that when economic variables have been included in these analyses, the amount of variance explained in innovativeness is usually higher. When there are predictions of innovativeness using *both* economic and noneconomic variables, there will be an empirical basis for evaluating the relative importance of each in explaining peasant adoption of new ideas.

ATTITUDE-BEHAVIORAL DISCREPANCY

The consonance of attitudes toward an innovation, with behavior — adoption or rejection of the innovation — is certainly an important variable in its own right. Attitude-behavior consonance is probably a general trait,

[19] Many of which are summarized in books by Foster (1962), Barnett (1953), Paul (1955), Erasmus (1961), and Arensberg and Niehoff (1964).

which is evident in many aspects of a given individual's activities. The notion that there is often dissonance between attitudes and action is illustrated by the popular Latin American saying, "Del dicho al hecho hay muy trecho," or "There is a long distance between what I say and what I do." This dimension, which might be called tolerance of attitude-behavioral dissonance, may be important in explaining the variance between a positive attitude toward an innovation and the actual adoption of that innovation.

CONSEQUENCES

Lastly, investigations are needed of the social results or consequences of technological innovations. To date, social anthropologists seem to be among the few who have avoided the common assumption that the consequences of innovation adoption are universally desirable. Their research attention has often been concentrated on the unanticipated (by change agents) and often negative consequences of innovation adoption in less developed countries.[20] The current emphasis on planned social change demands that more research efforts be placed on the effects of innovativeness.

Several authors have suggested that the consequences of innovativeness may be of two types: direct or manifest, and indirect or latent. The direct consequences are adjustments in the social system that are intended and recognized by the members, whereas the indirect consequences are neither planned nor recognized by the participants of the social system. Adoption of fertilizers by the Colombian respondents led directly to higher crop yields. In the longer run, however, such technological change may reduce the need for a large farm work force, resulting in migration of peasant families to urban slums.

Inquiry must be turned toward the direct and the indirect consequences of technological innovations among peasants.

SUMMARY

Innovativeness is the degree to which an individual adopts new ideas relatively earlier than others in his social system. Because the adopter distributions for most innovations (over time) are S-shaped and approach a normal ogive curve, the mean and standard deviation may be used to classify the members of any social system into five adopter categories: *innovators*, the first 2.5 percent to adopt; *early adopters*, the next 12.5 percent; *early majority*, the next 34 percent; *late majority*, the next 34 percent; and *laggards*, the last 16 percent to adopt new ideas. The basis of classification into adopter

[20] Illustrative of such work are Spicer (1952), Paul (1955), and Arensberg and Niehoff (1964).

categories is innovativeness. The five categories provide a shorthand notion for describing an individual's relative innovativeness.

Innovators, when compared to laggards, are characterized in both the modern and traditional Colombian villages by higher literacy, more mass media exposure, greater empathy, higher social status, larger-sized farms, greater achievement motivation, higher educational and occupational aspirations, more extension change agent contact, and greater cosmopoliteness. In the modern villages, the innovators were also opinion leaders, but in the traditional systems, the innovators were evidently too modernized to command the respect of their fellow villagers. The opinion leaders in Nazate and La Cañada were not innovators.

Two main methods were utilized to predict innovativeness: multiple correlation and the configurational approach. About 35 percent of the variance in agricultural innovativeness was explained in the modern villages, and 66 percent in the traditional communites, using a multiple correlation approach. About 53 percent of the variance in home innovativeness was explained in both modern and traditional villages. This prediction success is comparable with that found in recent studies in the United States, but somewhat less than contemporary inquiries in less developed countries. Few common independent variables were found across the four different multiple correlation analyses that were performed. Economic, communication, and social relationships variables seemed to be relatively more effective in predicting innovativeness than attitudinal-aspirational variables in Colombia.

Two types of configurational prediction methods were also utilized in this chapter: the Stuckert symmetrical method was used to predict the adoption versus nonadoption of home vegetable gardens in our Colombian villages; and the Sonquist-Morgan approach was utilized to predict innovativeness among Indian peasants. The major advantage of the later approach is that it allows one to visualize the interaction effects among one's independent and dependent variables.

Future research is needed on the diffusion of nonmaterial ideas, the relative importance of economic variables in explaining innovativeness, the discrepancy between attitudes toward innovations and their adoption, and the direct and indirect consequences of innovations.

14

The Web of Modernization: Interrelationships among Conceptual Variables*

One of the problems of a multi-variable phenomenon such as diffusion is that we are faced with many individual findings, some consistent and obviously related, others seemingly irrelevant and contradictory. Further, we face many doubts because of the frequent lack of clear-cut results when we examine a single variable.

(Deutschmann and Fals Borda 1962:84)

The preceding chapters focused on some of the major components of the process of modernization: literacy, mass media exposure, communication channels, cosmopoliteness, change agent contact, empathy, opinion leadership, achievement motivation, fatalism, and innovativeness. The statistical methods used to determine the interrelationships among these and other variables were *correlational*. The findings yield sufficient evidence to strongly indicate that *modernization is a multivariate phenomenon*. Indeed, so many variables appear to be important parts of the modernization process that it is a formidable task to put them in some kind of order. In the process of probing the nature of modernization, we now find ourselves unable to see the forest for the trees.

We have tried, in various ways, to impose order among the many modernization variables. For example, in most chapters somewhat arbitrary antecedent-consequent paradigms were proposed. These paradigms likely indicate logical, rather than necessarily valid, representations of reality.

This chapter utilizes a different analytical tool to gain new perspectives on the modernization process; it begins with the conviction that the modernization domain may not be as conceptually confusing as it first appears. The basic tenet is that the multitude of possible modernization concepts are connected in a cobweb of interdependent relationships, such that they function in a state of dynamic equilibrium. Variations in any one variable, therefore, trigger corresponding changes in numerous other concepts.

---

*This chapter was written by Joseph R. Ascroft, Research Assistant, Department of Communication, Michigan State University, and is based in part upon his M.A. thesis (1966), *A Factor Analytic Investigation of Modernization among Kenya Villagers*.

The intention is to search for underlying streams of structural order within the potentially bewildering mass of interlinked variables. Statistical tools such as factor analysis, utilized with computer assistance, now offer a tremendous potential for manipulating data in quantities and combinations previously impossible. By reducing masses of complexly interrelated variables into a few intellectually manageable units of understanding, a top-of-the-hill *Gestaltic* view of the current modernization variables will hopefully emerge.

We are wary, however, of allowing ourselves to fall victim too readily to the simple notion of single-factor determinism. All of the variables in the modernization domain may indeed be interlinked in a single web, suggesting a unidimensional concept of modernization; they also could be clustered into several distinct webs. Determination of the nature and number of underlying structural orders among the modernization variables is the topic for empirical investigation in this chapter.

THE STATISTICAL TECHNIQUE OF FACTOR ANALYSIS

Factor analysis will be used as the principal method of attacking this multivariate problem. "Factor analysis is useful, especially in those domains where basic and fruitful concepts are essentially lacking and where crucial experiments have been difficult to conceive" (Thurstone 1947:56). The essential purpose of factor analysis is data reduction. It enables us to look at a large number of variables, all at once, to determine whether or not their collective variations can be explained by some smaller set of underlying processes called "factors." A *factor* may be regarded as a gathering, under one banner, of all those variables that share common variance and which, therefore, reflect a single dimension that is "causing" the set of variables to associate with each other. Factor analysis may therefore be regarded as an empirical way to search for basic dimensions.

When factor analysis is used in the context of data reduction, it serves a discovery or exploratory purpose, inasmuch as it is usually performed without specific hypotheses as to the number and nature of factors that will be extracted. It is also possible to use factor analysis as a direct means of testing or confirming specific hypotheses or speculations about which variables "hang" together. Indeed, every exploratory factor analysis should be viewed as a prelude to a confirmatory analysis in which the number and nature of factors to be extracted are explicitly hypothesized. The use of factor analysis in this chapter is essentially exploratory, since at this time there are no clearcut hypotheses about the number and nature of factors in the totality of the modernization domain.

Factor analysis yields only succinct numerical statements about a set of data. It tells us in a fairly unambiguous manner that a set of variables form a cluster. It cannot tell us *why* they do so. There may be more, or there may be less to a cluster of variables than meets the eye. So the interpretation of factor analyses are still subject to the vagaries of the investigator.

COMPARABILITY ACROSS FACTOR ANALYTIC STUDIES

Prior to discussing available factor analytic research findings on modernization, it should be noted that comparisons across factor analytic studies are hazardous because of the following limitations:

1. Researchers differ in their *statistical approaches* to factor analyses. Some use oblique, whereas others utilize orthogonal rotations[1] to achieve simple, stable structures among variables. Still other researchers use handy approximations[2] to factor analysis. Comparison of results is made more difficult by the different methods used.

2. Researchers use different *units* in their analysis. Some concern themselves with nations, whereas others are interested in individuals.

3. The *phenomena* that researchers seek to explain are different. Some explicitly specify their main area of concern as modernization, whereas others are more narrowly concerned with explaining such facets of modernization as political development, innovativeness, mass media development, or urbanization, each of which may be conceptually regarded as a subset of modernization.

4. The number and nature of *variables* submitted to factor analysis varies. Deutschmann and Fals Borda (1962a) conclude that "any *particular* factor analysis, of course, is a product of the particular variables chosen for a particular study." To the extent that empirical representatives of some powerful underlying dimension are not included in our factor analysis, that characteristic must fail to emerge.

5. Some studies are *exploratory* in nature, searching for dimensions underlying a particular phenomenon.[3] Others are *confirmatory* in that they specifically hypothesize the number and nature of dimensions which underlie modernization.

Bearing these differences in mind, examinations and comparisons of the cross-national findings of several factor analytic investigations will be essayed;

---

[1] Rotation is essentially a mathematical means of looking at the data from different angles with a view to simplify factor structures and also to identify the most invariant factor structures. Orthogonal rotation maintains independence between any two factors so that their correlation is always zero. Oblique rotations do not place this constraint upon factors. Because of this freedom, oblique rotations may yield a more realistic view of the configuration of variables in factor space, whereas the constraints of orthogonality may produce an artifical view. However, oblique factor solutions are characteristically more difficult to interpret than orthogonal solutions.

[2] For example, McQuitty's (1957) elementary linkage analysis.

[3] Almost all of the studies reviewed in this chapter are exploratory, which is itself a commentary on the degree to which modernization research is still in its infancy.

some of these investigations used nations, and others individual peasants, as their units of analysis. The overall intention is to determine the manner in which the web, or webs, of modernization is structured.

AGGREGATE RESEARCH ON DEVELOPMENT

Some factor analyses of modernization are based upon secondary data. Such sources are termed "secondary" because their data were originally obtained by someone else for uses other than those of subsequent analysis. Frequently used sources include national censuses, registration materials, and change agency records, all of which can provide estimates of a country's characteristics. These kinds of data usually reflect modal characteristics of large sociogeographical entities, rather than of individuals within such entities; thus, studies based on such data are called "aggregate" or macro-level studies. National development, which is a parallel process to individual modernization, is the main concern of aggregate studies (Table 14-1). Generally, there appear to be many common findings across the aggregate studies.

Deutschmann and McNelly (1964), Schnore (1961), and Farace (1961) each observed at least one factor composed of variables that are remarkably similar. Each inquiry yielded a factor on which the economic indices (such as per capita income) and the communication indices (such as mass media development and education) are loaded[4] most highly. This result suggests that at the macro level of analysis, where the unit of analysis is a nation, *the dominant determinants of a nation's degree of development are economic level and ability to communicate with its people.* In general, the economic indices have their highest loadings on the national development[5] factor, and seem to reflect its core. The mass media indices are nearly as highly loaded on this factor, suggesting that economic development is generally accompanied by the widespread availability of mass media.[6]

Both Schnore (1961) and Farace (1965) extracted a single factor in their aggregate analyses (Table 14-1). Schnore regards the single factor solution as evidence of "an approximation of unidimensionality" in national development inasmuch as "the same fundamental variable would appear to be involved in the ostensibly different indices." The single factor result is in con-

---

[4] *Loadings* express the correlations between variables and factors; all factors, like variables, are bipolar.

[5] Once a factor has been extracted, it is a common practice to name that factor in terms of the main variables that make it up. Naming a factor is a highly subjective operation, and it is quite likely that independent researchers evaluating the same factor structure might attach different labels to that factor. The appropriateness of the inferential interpretation depends upon the percent of total variance which the factor explains; the smaller the proportion of total variance explained, the weaker is the inference implied by the label.

[6] Or else that mass media development is often accompanied by higher economic levels.

Table 14–1. Exploratory Factor Analysis of Aggregate Data on Development.

Author	Factor Analytic Approach	Number and Nature of Variables	Main Variables of Interest; Findings	Nature of Factors Extracted
Deutschmann and McNally (1963)	McQuitty's linkage analysis; and *R* analysis of 20 Latin American nations	Sixteen indexes of national development including population size, land area, newspaper circulation, exports to United States, and press freedom.	National development; three factors extracted	1. Developmental (urbanization, education, mass communication indexes 2. Size (population size, land area, size of capital city) 3. Export (export of goods to United States)
Schnore (1958)	Complete centroid method; *R* analysis of nations	Eleven indexes of development including energy consumption, newspaper circulation, per capita income, literacy, and urbanization.	Development; one factor extracted	Development (economic and mass communication)
Farace (1965)	Centroid method with oblique rotations; *R* analysis of 109 nations	Fifty-four indexes of national development including political activity, health and nutrition, climate, agriculture productivity, economic, cultural and population characteristics, and mass media development.	Mass communication and national development; one factor extracted	National development (economic and mass media)

Farace (1966)	Centroid method with oblique rotations; P analysis of 54 indexes of national development	One hundred and nine nations including the most, and the least modern, countries.	Typologies of national development; six factors extracted
			1. Latin America (party/press restraints, Catholic, low literacy)
			2. North America/Western Europe (less press restraint, high life expectancy, dense population, industrialization, high media use)
			3. Asia (low mass media, one party, press restraint, dense population)
			4. Central/South Africa (low literacy, one party, anemist, press restraints)
			5. North Africa/Middle East (low development, one party, low literacy, Muslim, considerable waste-land)
			6. Communist East Europe (high mass media, industrialization, one party, press restraints)

trast with the Deutschmann and McNelly (1964) study in which three factors were extracted; this difference, however, appears to be partly a function of differences in method of analysis.

So far as can be ascertained, Farace (1966) is the only researcher to submit aggregate units to a *P* analysis.[7] His findings suggest that nations can be categorized into six types; the countries within each typology show a common syndrome or pattern of development characteristics (Table 14–1). Gregg and Banks (1965) submitted 68 political variable to *R* factor analysis.[8] Included among these variables were six variables that represent the same six regional typologies of nations found by Farace (1966). An examination of the way in which each of the six regional groupings of nations loaded on each of the seven factors extracted by Gregg and Banks indicates that no two categories of nations loaded both highly and positively on the same factor. This finding suggests that the six regional typologies are relatively independent of each other, which provides some indication of the validity of the national typologies extracted in the Farace factor analysis.

Aggregate studies are frequently criticized on two counts: (1) they do not include sociopsychological measures of attitudes, beliefs, motivations, and aspirations; and (2) they preclude generalization of results to smaller units. The aggregate approach thus loses the "within country" variance in the modernization variables. These criticisms notwithstanding, aggregate studies have utility in yielding useful exploratory estimates of relationships that can then be studied systematically, using more elemental units of analysis such as individuals.[9]

A less defensible criticism of aggregate studies stems mainly from the manner in which the secondary data are obtained. All too frequently, the aggregate data are in the form of crude estimates bordering upon conjecture. Some national governments may falsify certain data in order to bias opinion in a desired direction. For example, a government may under-report its total population or over-report its gross national product, so that per capita incomes appear to have risen. Other sources seek to impart an aura of credibility to data of suspicious authenticity. Although it is not suggested that data from primary sources are entirely devoid of parallel shortcomings, aggregate

[7] *P* analysis is one of two broad approaches to factor analysis. It focuses upon resolving a large number of *persons* (or nations) to underlying typologies. The *P* approach seeks to cluster units that tend to "go together" in the sense of displaying similar characteristics. *Q* analysis differs from P analysis only in the nature, not in the essence, of data-collection.

[8] *R* analysis is the other fundamental approach in factor analysis. It focuses on resolving a large number of *variables* (or responses by individuals) to their underlying dimensions. *R* analysis seeks to cluster variables that tend to "go together."

[9] The generalization of aggregate results to the individual level must be done carefully so so as to avoid the danger of the "ecological fallacy," which is the false assumption that aggregate correlations apply directly to the individual level, where much more between-individual variance is involved, and where parallel correlations are generally lower.

studies nevertheless exhibit relatively greater weaknesses. And with secondary data, analysts lack control over the manner in which the data were initially compiled.[10]

FACTOR ANALYSES OF INDIVIDUAL MODERNIZATION

In contrast to students interested in explaining national development, some researchers are concerned with determining the factors underlying *individual* modernization. They typically restrict their investigations to less developed countries, where the transition from traditional to modern ways of life is currently underway. When communities in more developed countries are examined, the researchers tend, nevertheless, to isolate very traditional communities.[11]

The preoccupation with data from less developed countries in the investigation of modernization is understandable.[12] A microcosmic array of persons at all stages of modernization, from traditional to modern attitudes, beliefs, and behaviors, is thus provided. Not all of the studies summarized in Table 14–2 were specifically designed to probe the modernization process. However, the variables submitted to factor analysis in each of the studies certainly fall within the domain of modernization. Many variables such as age, education, literacy, and mass media exposure are common to all of the studies, thus facilitating comparison of the results.

Each of the studies yield multiple factors. This finding contrasts sharply with the macro-level aggregate factor analyses, which generally yield just one general development factor. Since each factor is mathematically independent of all other factors within each factor analysis, it would seem that *modernization is multidimensional at the individual level, but unidimensional at the aggregate level of analysis.*

The divergent findings in terms of numbers of factors extracted between micro- and macro-level analyses may be purely a function of different methodological approaches. The aggregate researches of Farace (1965) and Schnore (1958) use the centroid method of factor analysis with oblique rotations, whereas the micro-level investigations tend to use principle axis factor

[10] Most aggregate researchers attempt to warn their readers about the doubtful quality of their indices.

[11] Donohew (1967) focused his attention upon two Appalalachian poverty communities in the United States, which in many ways resemble the Colombian and other villages that are described in this book. Similarly, Jain (1965) investigated Mennonites in Waterloo County, Ontario, a very conservative religious group, who have low education and income, and a traditional way of life.

[12] It is, however, unfortunate that companion studies are not conducted in more modern settings for comparative purposes.

Table 14–2. Exploratory Factor Analyses on Individual Modernization

Author and Country	Factor Analytic Approach	Number and Nature of Variables	Main Variable of Interest; Findings	Nature of Factors Extracted
Deutschmann and Fals Borda (1962a) in Colombia	Principal axis verimax rotations; R analysis of 71 Andean villagers in Saucío, Colombia	Twenty-three variables including sex, age, farm size, communication channels, education, literacy, and innovativeness	Innovativeness; nine factors extracted	1. Economic ability to innovate (farm size) 2. Awareness of innovations (knowledge index) 3. Ability to understand communication (education and literacy)
Jain (1965) in Canada	Centroid method verimax rotations; R analysis of 275 Mennonite farmers in Waterloo County, Ontario	Eighteen variables including mass media exposure, age, education, income, traditionalism, family size, and farm size.	Communication channels in diffusions; three factors extracted	1. Socioeconomic status (media exposure, social status, formal participation, income, level of living, and farm size) 2. Family structure (age and family size)
Rahim (1966) in Pakistan	Principle axis varimax rotations; R analysis of 66 peasants in Comilla, East Pakistan	Twenty variables including mass media exposure, formal leadership, sociometric opinion leadership, age, social status, literacy, and land ownership.	Opinion leadership; three factors extracted	1. Ability to understand communication (literacy, education, and print media exposure) 2. Opinion leadership (popularity and formal participation) 3. Cosmopoliteness (electronic media exposure and visits to cities)

Donchew (1967) in the United States	Principle axis verimax rotation; R analysis of 238 Knox County, Kentucky household heads	Twenty-seven variables including mass media exposure, receptiveness to change, social participation, physical mobility, age, education, sex, and income.	Modernization; four factors extracted	1. Projectiveness (print media exposure, communication index, age, and education) 2. Social participation (cosmopoliteness, interpersonal contacts, and formal participation) 3. Housewife (sex and electronic media) 4. Isolation (age, education, income, and cosmopoliteness)
Ascroft (1966b) in Kenya	Principal axis varimax rotations; R analysis of 624 peasants in three Kenya villages	Forty-three variables including communication behavior, family structure, agricultural productivity, health activity, economic activity, educational capability, and demographic characteristics.	Modernization; five factors extracted	1. Ability to understand communication (literacy, education, and print media) 2. Family structure (age, sex, and family complexity) 3. Receptiveness to change (change agent contact and innovativeness) 4. Aspirations (education, aspirations for children, achievement motivation, and opinionatedness) 5. Agricultural productivity (crop indexes, commercialization, and intensification of farming)
Whiting and others (1967) in Brazil	Principle axis varimax rotations; R analysis of 71 Brazilian villages[a]	Forty-two variables including mass media exposure, education, age, empathy, and attitude toward change.	Modernization; four factors extracted	1. Modernization skills (education and most mass media exposure) 2. Interpersonal skills (trust, empathy, and radio exposure) 3. Scale of operations (farm size)

(continued)

Table 14-2 (continued).

Author and Country	Factor Analytic Approach	Number and Nature of Variables	Main Variable of Interest; Findings	Nature of Factors Extracted
Farace and others (1967) in Puerto Rico	Principle axis varimax rotations; R analysis of 172 Puerto Rican peasants	Ninety variables including economic behavior, modernization characteristics, and communication behavior.	Modernization; seven factors extracted	1. General development (education and mass media exposure) 2. Marginal noninnovativeness 3. Interpersonal traditionalism 4. General innovativeness 5. Progressive marketing orientation 6. Traditional negativism 7. Mixed traditionalism
The present study in Colombian modern and traditional villages	Principle axis varimax rotations; R analysis of 160 (modern) and 95 (traditional) peasants	Seventy-two variables (in modern villages) and sixty variables (in traditional villages) including the same variables as in the Kenya study (#5) above.	Modernization; three factors extracted	1. External communication (mass media exposure and education) 2. Orientation to change (empathy and age) 3. Innovative leadership orientation (opinion leadership)

^a The units of *response* in this investigation are Brazilian village leaders and change agents, but the units of *analysis* are villages. Nevertheless, we include the study in this table, rather than in Table 14-1 with the aggregate factor analyses, because the approach used and the results obtained are more closely comparable with the factor analysis of individual modernization.

analysis with orthogonal rotations.[13] On the other hand, the different results may be due to the fact that "within country" variability in modernization variables is lost in aggregate data. Furthermore, no social-psychological measures are included in the macro-level research, thereby precluding the emergence of additional factors on which such variables might have loaded.

Whatever the reasons for the differences in the number of factors extracted, there is nevertheless much similarity in at least one major aspect of modernization. *In each of the studies reviewed, both macro and micro, at least one factor emerges in which mass media indexes are featured prominently.* At the micro-level, the mass media indices are in each case strongly associated with education and literacy. The implication is that a country's capacity to communicate with its people through the mass media is not (in itself) enough: the people must also possess the necessary skills to absorb the mass media messages directed at them.

Apart from this communication factor, however, other factors that emerge from individual level studies do not appear very consistently across the several studies. A major problem in comparing factor structures across studies arises: (1) as a function of the number and nature of imput variables; and (2) due to individual researchers' subjective decisions in terminating rotations at certain points.[14] As a result, different factor analyses yield different numbers of factors. We are thus unable to proceed beyond identifying the mass media/education factor on the basis of the summaries presented in Table 14–2, unless we can control for the number of factors extracted.

In an attempt to achieve this kind of control, a restriction, which allows us to look at those rotations that yielded a three or four factor view, has been arbitrarily imposed. In the case of the data analyzed from Colombia, Kenya, Pakistan, Brazil, and Puerto Rico, access to the original computer output from the factor analyses enabled us to achieve adequate comparison. In the case of the Kentucky and Canada data, three or four factor solutions were reported by the authors. The Deutschmann and Fals Borda (1962a) study is the only analysis for which the objective of comparison could not be achieved.

The rational for fixing an arbitrary restriction upon the number of factors is based largely on the fact that all the studies are exploratory rather than confirmatory. Thus, the justification for limiting the view to an initial search for very basic, rather gross dimensions that essentially serve to sensitize us to the probable way in which modernization variables cluster. This enables

---

[13] Oblique rotations tend to minimize the number of factors extracted, since obliqueness (factor axes are allowed to form acute or obtuse angles) means that factors are correlated. Orthogonal rotations (the angles between factors are kept at 90 degrees) maintain independence among factors and tend to increase the number of factors extracted.

[14] It is possible for the researcher to continue rotating factors orthogonally until as many factors emerge as there are variables included in the factor analyses. In practice, however, researchers place some arbitrary limit upon the number of factors extracted. Very frequently they cease rotation when any one factor has fewer than say, three variables with their highest loadings on that factor.

rough heuristic boundaries to be placed around each constellation of inter-related variables. Consideration of whether or not each cluster should be further divided into separate dimensions is the concern of subsequent analysis.

MAIN DIMENSIONS OF MODERNIZATION

The arbitrary restriction to a three factor view of modernization variables enables us to relate factor structures across studies more meaningfully. Following close scrutiny of the nature of the variables loading on each of the three factors, meanings are inferred for each dimension and each dimension is labeled accordingly. The three dimensions are *external communication ability*, *orientation to change*, and *innovative leadership orientation*.

EXTERNAL COMMUNICATION

The external communication dimension is so named because the indices that load on this factor reflect communication with the world outside the immediate village environment. An examination of the factor structures across the nine studies reported in Table 14–3 reveals a remarkable cross-cultural consistency of results. To interpret the factors, a descriptive approach is adopted in which the make-up of the factor is assumed to convey insight about the way in which variables cluster on that factor.

Generally, *education* and *literacy* seem to facilitate mass media exposure and cosmopoliteness, which in turn lead to greater political knowledgeability and home innovativeness.[15] Higher literacy provides opportunity for greater exposure to the mass media. The mass media, particularly the *print media*, are instruments for increasing empathy. When a peasant reads a newspaper or a magazine or watches a movie or television, he is living vicariously in another world. Literacy, as observed in Chapter 4, becomes a catalyst of modernization, opening the mass media communication channels to the individual.

The external communication orientation of the individual is also reflected in his geographic mobility. *Cosmopoliteness* is closely associated with mass media exposure and other modernization variables, which indicates that the orientation of the individual to the environment beyond his immediate social system is an important concomitant of modernity.

The external communication behavior of the individual is likely to lead to a higher deree of *political knowledgeability* becasue he has access to more, and varied information. The pro-change nature of the majority of messages

[15] In this statement, and in the following discussion, we do not intend to imply time-order relationships, since the results of a factor analysis are correlational in nature.

Table 14–3. The External Communication Factor[a]

Factor Loadings with Factor I, External Communication

Variables	Colombia Modern Villages	Colombia Traditional Villages	Ascroft (1966b) in Kenya	Whiting and others (1967) in Brazil	Rahim (1966) in Pakistan	Donohew (1967) in Kentucky	Farace and others (1967) in Puerto Rico	Jain (1965) in Canada
1. Education	.67	.67	.69	.76	.84	.40	.77	.20
2. Literacy	*	.50	.75	.80	.83	—	—	—
3. Educational aspirations for children	.60	.73	.33	.55	—	.38	—	—
4. Newspaper exposure	.79	.81	.63	.67	.75	.74	.71	.61
5. Radio exposure	*	.48	.50	*	*	*	*	
6. Magazine exposure	.59	.74	.65	—	—	.64	.44	
7. Movie exposure	.41	.66	.39	.38	*	*	—	
8. Television exposure	.63	—	—	.74	—	*	.40	
9. Political knowledgeability	.64	.46	—	.52	—	.57	.67	
10. Home innovativeness	.63	.56	.51	—	—	—	—	
11. Level of living	.52	*	.58	—	—	—	—	.40
12. Social status and/or income	.56	.60	—	—	.87	—	.48	.89
13. Cosmopoliteness (trips to cities)	.69	.70	*	.60	*	*	.56	—

[a] The variables selected for presentation in this table are chiefly those which tended to remain within the same factor through several rotations, and which are all relatively highly loaded on the same factor. Asterisks indicate variables with primary loadings on a dimension other than the external communication dimension, whereas dashes indicate there are no data available regarding that variable for a particular study.

processed by the peasant encourages favorable attitudes towards new ideas, thereby promoting *home innovativeness* and a proclivity to acquire the artifacts of higher *levels of living*.

The fact that *social status* loads on factor I reflects the tendency for individuals who have external communication to enjoy a higher social status than locally oriented peasants. Social status is an integral factor in the external communication of the peasant.

There are, as expected, individual differences within countries; for example, the electronic media, especially radio, are not always associated with the external communication dimension in all studies (Table 14–3). There will be more to say about this observation when the dimension of orientation to change is discussed.

ORIENTATION TO CHANGE

The orientation to change dimension is not as clear-cut in the studies (Table 14–4) as factor I, the external communication dimension. Directly comparable measures across the various studies are not as easy to identify, but the central flavor of the orientation to change factor is apparent. *Age* appears to be a central variable. Younger peasants tend to have a more nuclear, smaller family size. This may be a function of their modernity as well as their fewer years of married life.

In the United States, *radio* is a youth medium; the same phenomenon appears across nations. Age is associated (negatively) with more frequent radio listening, a variable that does not fit with other types of mass media exposure.

More youthful peasants appear to exhibit dissatisfaction with their village. This disenchantment manifests itself in *negative cohesion* with their community (that is, a desire to leave), and in *favorable attitudes towards innovations*. Alternatives to resolve this dissatisfaction include the possibility of out-migration or attempting to change the village in a desired way. Clearly, if the latter alternative gains the upper hand, modernization begins to take place.

Additional variables associated with factor II, especially in the three modern Colombia villages, are self-perceived change-proneness (.46), achievement motivation (.53), attitude toward change (.46), and optimism regarding future levels of living (.55). In contrast, factor I (external communication) mostly includes variables expressing *present* states of being,[16] whereas factor II variables generally indicate *future state of being*. Despite the overtones of change-proneness in factor II, agricultural and home innovativeness are not primarily associated with this factor. Perhaps the youthful peasant must await his opportunity to fully excercise his innovativeness, even

---

[16] One exception is educational aspirations for children. Even in this case, however, a vicarious desire for one's *children*, rather than a *self*-aspiration is involved.

Table 14–4. Orientation to Change Factor.[a]

		Factor Loadings with Factor II, Orientation to Change						
Variables	Colombia Modern Villages	Colombia Traditional Villages	Ascroft (1966) in Kenya	Whiting and others (1967) in Brazil	Rahim (1966) in Pakistan	Donohew (1967) in Kentucky	Farace and others (1967) in Puerto Rico	Jain (1965) in Canada
1. Age	−.46	*	−.55	−.52	−.77	−.68	*	−.72
2. Family size	*	−.42	−.73	—	—	—	*	−.36
3. Radio exposure	.35	*	*	.62	.78	.22	.49	—
4. Attitude to innovations	.47	.50	—	—	—	—	.36	.37
5. Negative cohesion with the village	.32	.49	—	—	—	.34	—	—

[a] The variables selected for presentation in this table are chiefly those that tended to remain within the same factor through several rotations, and which are all relatively highly loaded on the same factor. Asterisks indicate variables with primary loadings on a dimension other than change orientation, whereas dashes indicate there are no data available regarding that variable for a particular study.

when he has a strong desire for change. In fact, in the Colombian villages, several progressive young farmers had to defer to their more traditional fathers in regard to farm decisions.

INNOVATIVE LEADERSHIP ORIENTATION

As in the case of the change orientation factor, the essence of the innovative leadership orientation dimension is not easily demonstrated cross-nationally in Table 14-5. The variability in measures designed to tap essentially the same kind of dimensions are greater for this factor than for the external communication dimension. The variables selected for presentation in Table 14–5 serve, however, to summarize the main notions underlying the leadership orientation factor.

Opinion leadership sets the general tone for this factor. This variable is distinguished as the only concept in the various studies that was not directly elicited from the respondent. Each individual's opinion leadership is identified by independent sociometric assessment from his peers.[17]

In Pakistan and Colombia, opinion leadership appears to be basically polymorphic in the sense that all the measures designed to determine leadership in different roles (agriculture, health, marketing, politics, and so on) load highly and consistently on the same factor, thereby enabling us to sum across the roles to arrive at a general opinion leadership index.

Opinion leaders are known to conform more closely to social system norms than the average individual (Chapter 10). If the village norms are modern, leaders tend to exhibit *agricultural innovativeness*. If the community norms favor tradition, opinion leaders tend not to be especially innovative. One evidence of this point can be observed in the strikingly different factor structures for the Colombia modern versus traditional villages in Table 14–5.[18] Since opinion leaders conform closely to system norms, it is reasonable that they also have high *formal participation* in village organizations.

Opinion leaders are not really technical experts, but they are responsible for passing along messages gained from relevant expert sources. Thus, *change agent contact* appears bound in the same package with opinion leadership and agricultural innovativeness.

THREE COMPONENTS OF MODERNIZATION

Factor analytic investigations of modernization variables across several different cultures and nations yield a genetic, sensitizing view of how these variables act in concert at the micro-level of analysis. Three general constella-

[17] Indeed, self-designated opinion leadership, which usually loads on a different factor, is not necessarily associated with sociometric opinion leadership.

[18] Agricultural innovativeness (and change agent contact) load on factor III in the modern villages, but not in the traditional villages.

Table 14-5. Innovative Leadership Orientation[a]

Variables	Factor Loadings with Factor III, Innovative Leadership Orientation							
	Colombia Modern Villages	Colombia Traditional Villages	Ascroft (1966) in Kenya	Whiting and others (1967) in Brazil	Rahim (1966) in Pakistan	Donohew (1967) in Kentucky	Farace and others (1967) in Puerto Rico	Jain (1966) in Canada
1. Agricultural innovativeness	.45	*	.71	—	—	—	.40	—
2. Change agent contact	.46	*	.66	—	—	.20	—	—
3. Opinion leadership	.76	.86	—	.45	.94	—	—	—
4. Formal participation	.39	*	.62	.47	—	—	.33	—

[a] The variables selected for presentation in this table are chiefly those that tended to remain within the same factor through several rotations, and which are all relatively highly loaded on the same factor. Asterisks indicate variables with primary loadings on a dimension other than innovative leadership orientation, whereas dashes indicate there are no data available regarding that variable for a particular study.

tions of variables are distilled from among a large number of variables initially thought to be within the modernization domain:

1. The capacity for external communication via trips to cities and mass media exposure, combined with the associated ability of individuals to absorb mass communication messages, as indicated by literacy and education.

2. A change-prone generation of young adults who are disenchanted with their life environment, and are pressuring for the acquisition of new styles of life.

3. A cadre of innovative opinion leaders linked with change agents.

These are the major dimensions of modernization that emerge from our analysis, given the nature of the variables on which data were gathered. There may be other factors, which did not emerge because adequate measures to tap them were not included in our survey instruments. Further, the three dimensions extracted are still subject to further subdivision in future investigations. The present concern, however, is to allow the new understandings gained about modernization to crystalize into some kind of conceptual order. How useful are the three modernization factors in explaining differences between the modern and the traditional Colombian villages?

THE WEBS OF MODERNIZATION IN COLOMBIA

Figure 14–1 organizes those variables, which by virtue of their high factor loadings, reflect the core of the three dimensions in the modern and traditional villages, respectively. The variables are diagrammed in weblike fashion with the highest-loading variables placed (generally) in the center, and the remaining variables arranged around them in order of diminishing correlations with the factor. The loading of each variable with the factor is shown in parentheses near each variable.[19] Zero-order correlation coefficients between many of the variables are also provided in Figure 14–1.

The aim in so diagramming the variables is to demonstrate the interdependent relatedness of the variables within each factor. A change in any variable would likely be reflected in a chain-reaction process through which variables in the system would shift until equilibrium is again established. Each system of variables within a factor is diagrammatically analogous to a spider web with the zero-order correlations representing juncture points in the web, and the factor loadings representing the distance of any juncture point from the center of the web. One can envisage changes in the stresses on all other strands that would be caused by altering the stress on any one strand. The greater the pressure one applies to a single strand, the greater the changes in all the other strands forming the web of modernization.

---

[19] With regard to mass media exposure, individual mass media exposure items rather than a composite mass media exposure index were submitted to factor analysis. Thus, we have no factor loading for mass media exposure per se. The zero-order correlations, however, *are* between total mass media exposure and other variables.

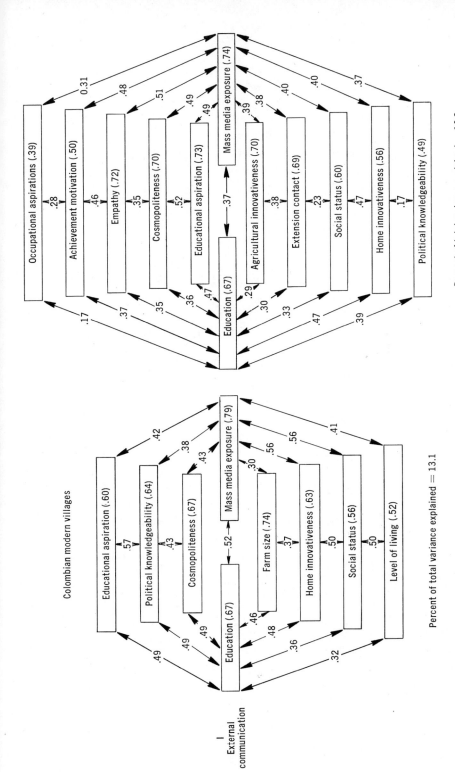

Colombian modern villages

Percent of total variance explained = 13.1

Percent of total variance explained = 16.2

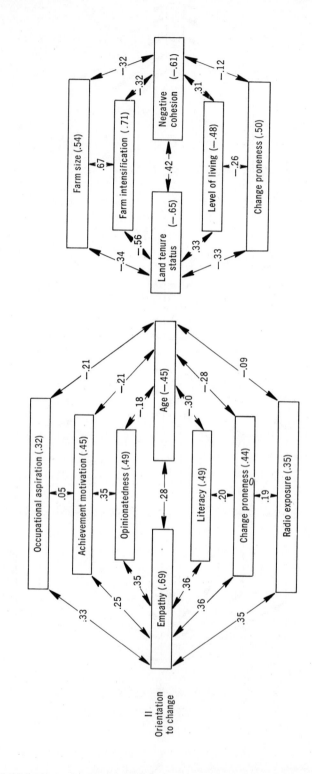

Percent of total variance explained = 9.0

Percent of total variance explained = 9.7

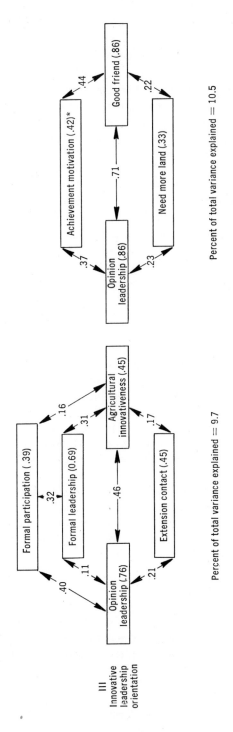

Percent of total variance explained = 10.5

Percent of total variance explained = 9.7

Figure 14–1. Comparison of Modern versus Traditional Colombian Villages Across Three Webs of Modernization.

[a]This is a secondary loading; the primary loading is on the external communication dimension.

It is evident from Figure 14–1 that there are striking differences in the factor structures between the Colombian modern and traditional villages. Factor I, the external communication dimension, contains more variables for the traditional villages than for the modern villages. However, in the case of factors II and III, the reverse occurs. There is a remarkable degree of correspondence between the two types of villages in regard to the variables making up factor I, but there is a striking dissimilarity on the change orientation and the innovative leadership factors. Finally, for the external communication dimension, the degree of association (1) between each variable and the factor (that is, the factor loading), and (2) the zero-order correlations, are consistently higher than for the other two factors.[20] How can these differences across factors, and across types of villages, be explained?

MODERN VILLAGES

In the modern villages, the external communication dimension is characterized chiefly by education, mass media exposure, and cosmopoliteness; the concomitants of which are socioeconomic status, psychic mobility, higher aspirations, the acquisition of political knowledge, and various behavioral aspects of modernizing life styles.

The change orientation factor appears to organize the thrust toward modernization. Lerner's (1958) modern respondents had opinions about issues and could empathize with others. In the orientation to change dimension, empathy is indeed associated with opinionatedness. Age is negatively related, although not very strongly, with this factor, suggesting that village modernity emerges with maturation of a younger generation of peasants. Along with the development of empathic ability is the rise of achievement motivation, occupational aspirations, and change proneness, all of which suggest a general dissatisfaction with current ways of life.

The innovative leadership dimension appears to be a legitimizing facilitator of the thrust to modernization in the modern villages. If opinion leaders and formal organization leaders, along with change agents, place their seal of approval upon a new idea, it is likely to be adopted, and the trend to modernization is expedited.

TRADITIONAL VILLAGES

In the traditional village settings, the external communication web is composed of a larger number of variables than in the more modern settings. It iontains almost all the variables found in the modern web, and several other variables, such as empathy, agricultural innovativeness, and occupational rspirations, which are not included in the external communication web in

---

[20] This is true in both modern and traditional villages.

the modern villages. Why? The orientation to change factor in the traditional villages is remarkable for the absence of a significant loading on age. Factor II expresses a general aura of change-proneness, as in the modern context, but with a difference: the kind of person in the traditional setting that the factor would describe appears to be a small farmer who owns all his land.[21] He apparently does not have the economic ability to augment his small farm by renting additional land. Consequently, he is disenchanted with the village because of his blocked ambitions, and wishes to migrate elsewhere. His dissatisfaction is not tempered by youthful optimism; he would rather migrate than change his environment in a desired way. Age, in fact, is not correlated very highly with any of the three factors in the traditional settings, suggesting there is little difference in life outlook between various age groups. In the modern villages, however, age does make a difference — so much difference that enough strain is brought to bear upon the external communication dimension to pull such variables as empathy, achievement motivation, and occupational aspirations out of factor I to form another age-and-change dimension (factor II). *Age seems to lead to a very striking difference in life outlook between generations in the modern villages, but not in the traditional communities.* Polarization of viewpoints within villages along age lines does not seem to occur until the transformation of traditional lifeways is well underway.[22] Until then, as in the traditional villages, there is only an ancestral homogeniety of thought. As modernization influences begin to creep into the traditional village, a division occurs between the mentality of the youthful, who welcome the ethic of modernity, and the older generation, who resist it.

In the traditional villages, factor III, the innovative leadership dimension, does not include agricultural innovativeness. The opinion leaders in Nazate and La Cañada are "good friends," noted for their sociability and accessibility rather than for their innovativeness. This fact is perhaps one reason why agricultural innovations have not saturated the traditional villages, and why the systems' norms have not shifted from traditional to modern. The leaders seem to safeguard the old norms; this means that social approval is not forthcoming from the leadership structure for the occasional peasant who dares to change. A fascinating subject for future inquiry, perhaps necessitating observational rather than survey research methods, would be to study the process by which village norms and the leaders' degree of innovativeness

[21] Land tenure status was operationalized by a ratio of total land owned by the respondent, to total land owned and operated. Thus, the variable ranged from all land rented (negative pole of the continuum) to all land owned (positive pole).

[22] Our personal impression is that this social splitting of the modern villages along the lines of age (and modern attitudes), as implied by our factor analysis, is quite valid. For instance, in Pueblo Viejo the progressive leaders of change were almost all in their 30s or early 40s, whereas the peasant respondents over 45 generally viewed the developments underway in their village with some alarm. However, in Nazate and La Cañada, our impression is that while intra-village cliques flourished, they were along ethnic-racial and kinship lines, rather than on the basis of age and modernity (Chapter 10).

shift from traditional to modern.[23] Such system metamorphosis is fundamental to the modernization of individual peasants.

In the modern villages the leaders are innovative, but in the traditional villages the leaders are not. The criteria for the selection of leaders in the traditional villages are their sociability and embodiment of the traditional norms.

SUMMARY

This chapter sought to synthesize the results of factor analytic studies (1) of development, where the nation is the unit of analysis, and (2) of modernization, where individuals are the units of analysis. The macro-level investigations show that the most important development factor includes a nation's economic level, as indexed by per capita income, for example, and its ability to communicate with its people, as expressed in mass media communication development. Micro-level factor analyses of individual modernization, in contrast, show that modernization is multidimensional, composed of at least three distinct dimensions: external communication; orientation to change; and innovative leadership orientation.

The first factor is essentially a capacity to communicate by way of urban contact and the mass media, combined with the associated ability of individuals to absorb mass communication messages. Factor II characterizes a change-prone generation of young adults who are disenchanted with their life environment in the village, and are pressuring for the acquistion of new styles of life. The third factor typifies a cadre of innovative opinion leaders linked with change agents. This latter dimension appears to be a facilitator of the thrust to modernization in the modern villages, but it is not yet present in the traditional villages where the leaders are respected for their social accessibility and not for their technical expertise. Age seems to indicate a very striking difference in life outlook (that is, its modernization) between the younger and older generations in the modern villages, but not in the traditional communities, where the effects of modernization are much less pervasive.

Cast in the framework of dissonance theory, in both modern and traditional villages, there are individuals in a state of dissonance aroused by generalized disenchantment with their current ways of life. An essential difference between the two systems rests in the mode of dissonance-reduction utilized by

---

[23] In Pueblo Viejo there was a 60-year-old peasant who had been an important village leader in its former, more traditional era (before the late 1950s). He actively opposed the extension change agents, the school teacher's progressive ideas, and formation of a village development council and a cooperative store. His stubbornness in the face of these advantageous ideas gradually lead to a loss of his followers, until they only numbered a few old cronies. Unfortunately, we lack much further insight into this case study of loss of leadership in the face of changing village norms because the peasant in question refused to be interviewed in our survey, and encouraged his peers to do likewise (Chapter 10).

these disenchanted individuals. In the modern villages, where opinion leaders are active facilitators of change, reduction of dissonance can be accomplished by altering modal patterns of existing styles of life. In the traditional settings, where opinion leaders are opposed to change, reduction of dissonance may occur through psychological or physical departure from the environment.

NEEDED RESEARCH

The main objective in this chapter was to examine available results of factor analyses of modernization variables with a view to distilling a few succinct dimensions with which to represent the modernization domain. This is, however, only a beginning step, subsequent work is needed along the following lines.

1. Additional variables calculated to tap new dimensions of modernization should be included in factor analyses of modernization. In particular, marketing and other *economic* measures are needed. To date, these dimensions have been slighted because economists have not yet engaged in the factor analytic approach represented in this chapter. There is also need to investigate further dimensions of modernization such as deferred gratification, nationalism, and so on (see Chapter 16). The three dimensions extracted in the present factor analyses should be closely scrutinized to determine whether they require further subdivision.

2. Thus far, factor anlytic investigations, with the exception of the Farace (1966) P-analysis, have been concerned with *R* analysis of modernization *variables*, rather than with P-analysis of *people* types.[24] One next step is the isolation of clusters of individuals who are similar across a number of modernization variables. Can peasants within a social system be categorized as to "moderns" and "traditionals" via factor analytic techniques?

3. Inferences need to be drawn about the relative time-order of variables in the process of becoming modern. For example, which comes first, an orientation to change or an innovative leadership orientation? McCrone and Cnudde (1967) demonstrate the usefulness of "path analysis," a casual inference technique using aggregate correlational data, to support Lerner's (1958) contention that urbanization of a nation leads to literacy, which precedes mass media development, which leads to political participation. The way is now clear to utilize path analysis to determine parallel *inferences*[25] about the

[24] In a recent study, Donohew and Singh (1967) utilize Q factor analysis. Their results reveal three fairly clear-cut *types* of individuals in two traditional Appalachian communities. The types are identified as (1) *outgoing*, characterized by high cosmopoliteness, education, and empathic ability, (2) *isolated*, characterized by low dogmatism, low mass media exposure, low educational aspirations, and low income, and (3) *mass media*, considered to be the most modern type.

[25] The reader is cautioned that only highly tentative inferences about time-order of variables can be drawn from path analysis; definitive statements about time-order depend upon the conduct of field experiments (see Chapter 16).

time-order of the central variables in our model of individual modernization: literacy, mass media exposure, empathy, innovativeness, and so forth.

A more useful, though generally more expensive approach to establishing time-order involves the use of field experiments. Thus far, all the studies utilizing factor analysis have been surveys conducted at a single point in time. Repeated studies carried out within the same village setting over a protracted period of time may allow us to demonstrate more clearly how the factor structures alter as a village progresses from traditional to modern lifeways.

4. A final research step suggested is to combine the results of R and P factor analyses. Once the underlying dimensions have been determined among modernization *variables*, and the basic *typologies of people* who are similar to each other on modernization variables, we should attempt to relate the separate findings in a combined analysis. The usefulness of this approach, however, may ultimately be limited by the kind and quality of the modernization variables that are measured, a central topic of Chapter 17.

15

Computer Simulation of Innovation Diffusion in a Peasant Village*

In my experience, the computer is a hard master since it forces one to be specific about the variables in interpersonal behavior and the exact relations between them.

(Paul Hare 1961)

Some refer to computer simulation as a sandbox for scholars.

(Forrest R. Pitts 1964)

Hamlet's "play within a play" attempted to recreate the murder of his father in order to cause the suspected murderer, the King, to admit the crime. "If he but blench, I know my course" (Act II, Scene III). The contrived reality of Hamlet's play so closely approached the actual event, that the King not only "blenched," but rushed from the room, thereby displaying his guilt.

Simulation is a type of social science "play." Like Hamlet's approach, it is an attempt to capture the essential elements of a complex process and reproduce them in coherent form, with a view to gaining insight from the process of reproduction.

IMPORTANCE OF SIMULATION IN THE SOCIAL SCIENCES[1]

Any social process, such as the diffusion of innovations, must be viewed as an intricate complex of interacting variables. Modeling[2] is an attempt to describe succinctly the structure and dynamics of a system or process found in

---

* This chapter is a revised version of J. David Stanfield and others (1965), "Computer Simulation of Innovation Diffusion: An Illustration from a Latin American Village," Paper presented at the American Sociological Association and the Rural Sociological Society, Chicago.

[1] Certain ideas in this section are adopted from Clark and Lin (1965).

[2] A *model* of a social process is a formalization of components and rules that specify the relationships and conditions for change among the components. A model indicates the relevant components in the system or process under study. Empirical evidence and theoreti-

reality. *Simulation* is a technical attempt to imitate a system or process in reality through operationalization of a model. It attempts to mirror the behavioral process in a dynamic manner over time. Simulation has several advantages for the social scientist.

1. It gives *life* to a model. Most models are static descriptions of components and their relationships. Simulation techniques set the model in process, and allow one to view the components as they function. Simulation carries the social scientist one step beyond the usual results of hypothesis testing.

2. Simulation techniques provide the social scientist with a method of testing the *reliability and validity* of a model. This may be done by simulating the model repeatedly, and thus estimating the outcome with a cerain measure of confidence. The simulation outcome is then used to evaluate the validity of the model by comparing the simulation with reality data.

3. Simulation techniques realistically handle *increasing complexity*, as a model incorporates more and more components and conditions. Laboratory experiments and analytic methods must "hold constant" all but a few variables and their relationships. This necessary, but highly unreal, representation of a system's operation requires the scientist to predict accurately from a relatively static system to one in which almost nothing is constant. Simulation presents an opportunity to help close the gap between conventional experiments and the prediction of reality.

The complex nature of social phenomena can be abstracted into formal aspects only by models that are themselves exceedingly complex. Social scientists have found computers to be particularly useful when they are trying to manipulate systems with a large number of variables, poorly defined processes, and either too many or too few observations. Most human behavior change processes are of this type.

Simulation is an attempt to include several variables in a process that mirrors a complex reality. The computer allows the scientist to incorporate more variables and rules in his attempt to approximate reality. The high speed and large storage capacity of computers make them useful tools for simulation researchers.

THE RESEARCH STRATEGY OF DIFFUSION SIMULATION

The result of simulation is an heuristic reproduction of a social process. The process that we are interested in reproducing in this chapter is *diffusion:*

---

cal significance may help to determine which components should be used in the model. The model should also provide rules under which the components operate individually and upon each other. These rules may be derived from theories and from empirical evidence. They guide the transformation of a static listing of components and relationships into an operating system, with whose help the scientist can develop theories, test hypotheses, discover significant components, and negate previously held theories. Model-building usually begins with a minimum number of components and rules, and proceeds toward greater complexity.

the spread over time of a new idea through a social system by way of communication channels (Rogers with Shoemaker 1968). The diffusion process has been studied traditionally by examining slices or cross sections of the process at one point in time. The slice is held stationary artificially, while the researcher performs his analysis. Simulation techniques allow us to capture more accurately the important variables in motion, fusing stationary analysis with over-time considerations. Ability to incorporate the time dimension in a model of the diffusion process gives a much more accurate picture of the real process.

A summary of the usual steps in simulating innovation diffusion is provided in Figure 15–1. The diffusion model is constructed by drawing on the evidence from studies of the diffusion processes under many circumstances; the model is composed of a set of rules which succinctly summarize how diffusion occurs. By comparing this simulated reproduction of the diffusion process with reality data, it can be determined whether our theories, analysis, and model correctly reconstruct the original reality. Should there be a lack of close correspondence between simulation and reality, the model can be changed until its rules yield results that more closely approach reality.[3] For example, if the simulated diffusion process runs too rapidly in comparison to reality in a peasant village, certain constraints can be introduced in the model to slow down the process until it more closely approximates reality.

A model that yields an adequate reproduction of reality can then be tested in similar but different social systems, in order to see if the model will *generally* hold true. For instance, if a model of innovation diffusion that functions properly in a Colombian village, it may then be tested in Indian villages to see if the model accurately reproduces idea flow there. An accurate diffusion model, which reproduces a process in a particular system for a specific innovation, can further be applied to similar social systems where reality data are not available, so as to *predict* communication and change in these systems.

In sum, a simulated model of diffusion for a peasant village could be used: (1) to predict the adoption of innovations at future times in this village, since time can be compressed or expanded in simulation; (2) to predict adoption patterns in similar villages; or (3) to find and test optimum strategies for change agencies that will maximize the rate of change and/or minimize the cost and effort of achieving this change. Simulation techniques could help determine the following: how many change agents are needed to optimize effects; how many and which opinion leaders will best facilitate innovation adoption; how many innovators must adopt an innovation before further promotional efforts are unneeded; what economic or communication incentives are most efficient in causing adoption; and the desirable and undesirable social consequences of the program of directed change.

---

[3] Thus, in one sense the simulation approach to research tests a whole bundle of hypotheses at once, when one determines the fit between simulation and reality.

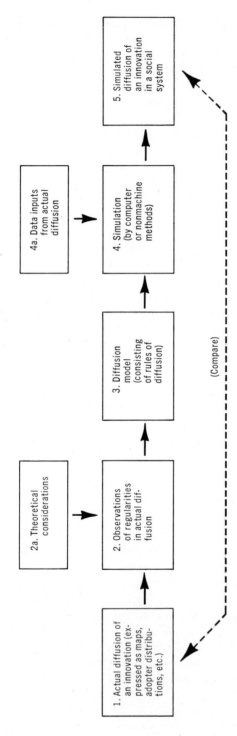

Figure 15-1. Paradigm of the Usual Steps in Innovation Diffusion Simulation.

After proceding from steps 1 through 5 in the above diagram, the simulation researcher may do the following.

1. He may compare 5 with 1 to determine the relative success of the diffusion simulation in approaching reality. The tests of equivalence (of 5 with 1) include the goodness-of-fit of the shape of the adopter distributions, of the geographical or social coverage of those who have adopted, or of the relative time-order in which individuals adopt an innovation.

2. If the comparison of 5 with 1 is unsatisfactory, he may alter 3 in accordance with knowledge of 2 and 2a to improve the simulation, and thus add to theoretical understanding of the diffusion process.

3. Once a satisfactory simulation model has been developed, it may be used to perform 4 with data imputs (4a) different than 1 to test the predictive power of the diffusion model (3) in other social systems; to predict the point of origin of the innovation in the social system by running 4 in reverse direction over time; or, by altering the diffusion model (3), test the effect of various alternative strategies of planned diffusion that might be used by agencies of change, so as to determine optimizing policies for change agencies, or for the training of change agents.

Following a brief review of past research on the simulation of innovation diffusion, the results of SINDI, a computer simulation attempt to capture the reality of diffusion in the Colombian village of Pueblo Viejo, will be presented.

ORIGINS IN SPATIAL DIFFUSION SIMULATION

Professor Torsten Hägerstrand, a quantitative geographer at the Royal University of Lund, Sweden, is the father of diffusion simulation research. His work on computer simulation began in the early 1950s and predates efforts in the United States to simulate political behavior (Pool and Abelson 1961; Pool and others 1964), small group interaction (Coleman 1962), and role conflict (Gullahorn and Gullahorn 1965). Only recently has Hägerstrand's work come to the attention of North American researchers. Language, spatial, and disciplinary barriers hindered the diffusion of the Hägerstrand approach to diffusion simulation.[4]

Spatial factors in the diffusion process provide the central focus for Hägerstrand and his followers. Spatial simulation models endeavor to predict the geographical distribution of an innovation as it diffuses. A principle of diffusion utilized in most spatial simulation models is called the "neighborhood effect." This principle argues that as spatial distance between a previous adopter and another individual increases, the likelihood of that individual adopting the innovation decreases. This inverse relationship between distance and probability of adoption is based on the fact that communication between two individuals is less likely as the distance between them becomes greater.

Another of Hägerstrand's contributions was the Monte Carlo technique, which gives lifelike qualities to the simulated diffusion process through random sampling.[5] The exact path that an innovation takes in spreading from individual to individual at each time period or "generation" is determined through assigned probabilities and random procedures.

Presently, an enthusiastic coterie of quantitative geographers are carrying forward Hägerstrand's approach. Examples of spatial diffusion simulations are summarized in Table 15–1 in terms of the innovation studied, the locale, and the primary research objective. The Tiedemann and Van Doren (1964) simulation of the diffusion of hybrid seed corn in Iowa is a good example of a spatial diffusion model based on research findings of earlier, nonsimulation

[4] For many years an adequate English description of Hägerstrand's work could only be found in three published works (Hägerstrand 1952; Karlsson 1958; Bunge 1962), all of which originally appeared in Sweden. However, this "paper curtain" was cleared away by Hägerstrand (1965a and 1965b).

[5] Monte Carlo procedures are especially valuable in simulating diffusion because there *is* a certain amount of randomness involved in the process by which innovations spread. For example, two peasants happen to meet on a village path and discuss a new agricultural idea. We do not yet know enough about the determinants of interpersonal communication within a village to predict exactly who will interact with whom.

Table 15–1. A Summary of Diffusion Simulation Studies

Researcher	Innovation Studied	Locale of the Study	Objective of the Research
Hägerstrand (1952)	Subsidized pasture improvement	Sweden	Trace spatial diffusion and social diffusion with computer simulation
Karlsson (1958)	A hypothetical new idea	None	Develop a nonmachine simulation of the diffusion of new ideas with synthetic data
Deutschmann (1962)	A hypothetical farm innovation	Latin American village	Construct a preliminary model of diffusion illustrated with synthetic data
Pitts (1964)	Hand tractors	Japan	Geographical diffusion within a nation
Tiedemann and Van Doren (1964)	Hybrid seed corn	Story County, Iowa	Geographical diffusion of hybrid corn from seed dealers to farmers
Yuill (1964)	Hypothetical innovations	None	Effects of barriers on spatial diffusion of ideas utilizing synthetic data
Gould (1964)	Cooperatives	East Africa	Social and geographical diffusion leading to modernization
Bowden (1965)	Irrigation wells	Colorado	Geographical diffusion to predict future use of water resources
Hägerstrand (1965a)	Such innovations as a church movement, public bath houses, and dairy cattle vaccination	Sweden	Spatial spread of innovations
Brown (1966)	Artificial dairy cattle insemination and television sets	Sweden	Spatial spread of innovations
Wolpert (1967)	Tractors and automatic self-binders	Sweden	Regional simulation incorporating a two-step flow of communication

diffusion research.[6] Using the Ryan and Gross (1943) finding that Iowa farmers usually heard of hybrid corn from commercial seed-sellers, but they were persuaded to adopt by their neighbors, Tiedemann and Van Doren mimicked a sort of two-step flow of communication with the simulation model.

THE SOCIAL STRUCTURE APPROACH TO DIFFUSION SIMULATION

Most of the diffusion simulation studies suffer from a heavy emphasis upon spatial variables to the partial exclusion of other social structural and social psychological variables, which past research indicates are of great importance in affecting the diffusion of innovations. Karlsson (1958), a Swedish sociologist, proposed a number of simulation models that center on nonspatial variables and processes, but unfortunately he did not provide data illustrating the use of these models. Karlsson expanded Hägerstrand's spatial principle of the neighborhood effect to include the notion of social distance. Karlsson argues that the probability of effective communication of a new idea between two individuals increases with greater source-receiver homophily (similarity) in such characteristics as social status, resistance to the innovation, and source credibility.

Some of the simulation procedures developed by Karlsson were modified by Deutschmann to approximate the communication environment of a Latin American peasant community. Unfortunately, his model was not tested with empirical data. We developed a computer program incorporating some of Deutschmann's and Karlsson's ideas to *S*imulate *IN*novation *DI*ffusion (SINDI).

THE SINDI MODEL

SINDI models the diffusion of awareness about an innovation in a small, relatively isolated peasant community in Latin America. The focus on diffusion simulation in a peasant village setting was chosen because: (1) it is a relatively small social system; (2) it has relatively closed boundaries; (3) we had personal knowledge of the diffusion process within a village; and (4) reality data from a Colombian village, Pueblo Viejo, were available against which to test our simulation.[7]

---

[6] Simulation research, by its nature, is most appropriate when it can incorporate in the model the results of previous investigations. Unfortunately, the original work of Hagerstrand (1952) and that of many of his followers was influenced slightly by the results of the some 1290 diffusion publications of a nonsimulation nature.

[7] The village setting is viewed as a starting point for our simulation research, which later may be applied to other more complex types of systems, such as a formal organization or perhaps an entire communication system, from scientists through change agents to clients.

Research findings that are incorporated in SINDI specify that innovations are transmitted to a Latin American village through external channels; further spread of the new idea then occurs through interpersonal channels within the village. The model also includes the notion that the majority of the peasant members of the village are divided into cliques, which is often the case in small Latin American communities. These notions were incorporated into SINDI through the calculation of the following parameters:[8]

1. The number and composition of cliques within the village.

2. The number of messages about the innovation introduced per time period from external channels.

3. The number of villagers exposed to each message.

4. The probablity of any nonknower (about the innovation) becoming a knower as a result of contact with messages from each external channel.

5. The probability of a nonknower becoming a knower through contact with a teller of his own clique.

6. The probability of a nonknower becoming a knower through contact with a teller of another clique.

The following discussion describes how each of these six parameters were computed.

CLIQUES

The villagers were divided into four cliques and a fifth group of isolates on the basis of sociometric data obtained in response to an interview question about whom the villager sought for agricultural information. The sociometric question[9] on general agricultural information was utilized (rather than other sociometric questions) because we were concerned with diffusion simulation of *agricultural* innovations. Cliques were delineated by plotting a sociogram on a map of the village. The peasants were then categorized into cliques so that most of the sociometric choices of a set of individuals were within (rather than outside) the clique[10] (Table 15–2). Most of the within-clique choices were to geographically-near individuals.[11]

---

[8] Data gathered by personal interviews with the 67 farm household heads in Pueblo Viejo were used to arrive at numerical values for these parameters in most cases; others were estimated.

[9] Each respondent was allowed to name four other villagers whom he sought for agricultural information.

[10] In order to check whether any of the apparent isolates should have been placed in a clique, we examined how often each isolate was chosen on five other information-seeking sociometric questions. If a villager received more than two such choices, he was placed in the clique of the peasants who made the choices. Two such "isolates" were placed in an appropriate clique.

[11] This suggests that the spatial focus of the quantitative geographers in their diffusion simulation research is not entirely inappropriate when the social system is a Colombian village. Here, the ecological pattern is for peasant homes to be located on their farms, rather than in a clustered center.

Table 15–2.   SINDI Parameters for the Colombian Village of Pueblo Viejo.

Identification of Clique	Number of Members in the Clique	Number of Opinion Leaders in the Clique	Number of Villagers with Each Type of External Channel Contact			
			Extension Agent		School Teacher	
			Opinion Leaders	Non-leaders	Opinion Leaders	Non-leaders
Clique 1	7	2	0	1	1	1
Clique 2	17	4	1	4	2	3
Clique 3	17	3	1	4	1	6
Clique 4	4	0	0	0	0	1
Isolates	22	0	0	7	0	4
Totals	67	9	2	16	4	15

EXTERNAL CHANNELS

Two types of external message channels were chosen: extension service agents and school teachers. In Colombia, the extension change agent usually lives and has his office outside the village. He visits the village regularly with the intent of communicating new agriculture information. The teacher usually lives in the village and has closer rapport with the villagers. He generally has greater allegiance and contact with the outside world than the average villager, and is likely to bring new ideas to the villagers from these contacts. The extension agent often works through the teacher in introducing new ideas to the community. It therefore seemed appropriate to utilize the extension change agent and school teacher as the chief channels of external innovation messages.[12] The degree to which each opinion leader[13] and non-leader was oriented to one or both of the two change agents was determined from the relative frequency with which he reported having personally communicated with them in the past year (Table 15–2).

The number of external messages introduced in the simulation model per time period may be varied.[14] One innovation message was chosen per time period, which would symbolize one trip to the village per month by the extension worker during which he mentions the innovation, or the similar introduction of such a message by the teacher.

[12] Other possible channels for external communication messages concerning an innovation are the mass media, commercial farm suppliers, or cosmopolite trips by villagers. We know that the mass media are unimportant in diffusing innovations in Pueblo Viejo (Chapter 6), but they may be, nontheless, important in other village settings.

[13] Opinion leaders were arbitrarily considered to be those villagers who received three or more sociometric choices from their peers as sources of agricultural information.

[14] This enables experimentation with the model to yield the optimum level of effort that change agents need to expend in order to diffuse knowledge of innovations.

EXTERNAL MESSAGE CONTACT

Each message introduced in a time period reaches a certain number of peasants. The number of villager contacts made by the extension change agent (referred to as "channel 1" from now on) was estimated at 12 per time period, that is, per year, and the number of contacts by the school teacher ("channel 2") at 24 per time period. Although the extension worker makes relatively few trips to the village per year, the school teacher resides there and should, therefore, make more interpersonal contacts about the innovation.

BECOMING A KNOWER FROM AN EXTERNAL CHANNEL

The probability that villagers oriented to the two channels would become aware of the innovation was calculated. Eighteen villagers (Table 15–2) were primarily oriented to channel 1, the extension change agent; that is, they each had more interpersonal communication with the extension worker than with the school teacher. These 18 peasants had a total of 34 contacts with channel 1, and 17 contacts with channel 2. The probability of learning from channel 1, given primarily a channel 1 orientation, was rather arbitrarily established at .50.[15] The probability of learning about an innovation from channel 2, given a channel 1 orientation, is 17/34 x .50 or .25. The 19 villagers oriented primarily to channel 2, the teacher, had 55 contacts with channel 2 and only 10 contacts with channel 1. Thus, for those oriented primarily to channel 2, the probability of becoming a knower about the innovation from channel 2 is (arbitrarily) .50, and the probablility of awareness from channel 1 is .10. The remaining 32 peasants in the village had no contact with either the extension agent or the teacher.

BECOMING A KNOWER FROM A FELLOW-CLIQUE MEMBER

In each clique, the probability of a nonknower becoming aware of the new idea upon contact with a knower-teller (or opinion leader) of his own clique had to be determined. This probability in clique 1 is .58.

In a similar fashion, the probability for a nonknower learning from a knower-teller in clique 2 is 13/64 or .20, and for clique 3 the probability is 11/48 or .23. There are no opinion leaders in clique 4 or for the isolates (Table 15–2), so there is a zero probability of learning of the innovation in such a manner.

---

[15] This level of probability was chosen on the basis of rather intuitive observation that in about half of the extension change agent's interpersonal contacts with villagers, he created awareness of a new farm idea. Similar reasoning applies to the case of the teacher.

BECOMING A KNOWER FROM A NONCLIQUE PEASANT

The final parameter in SINDI is the probability that a person in one clique will become a knower upon contact with a knower-teller in another clique; that is, the probability of interclique diffusion of the innovation. In the villages of study, there are only two cliques, 2 and 3, with mutual contacts. The probability of interclique contact was calculated in an analogous fashion to the calculation of the within-clique probability. The total number of peasants in clique 2 contacted by knower-tellers in clique 3 is 5, while the total number of possible contacts is 51.[16] Therefore, the probability of clique 2 members being contacted by clique knower-tellers in clique 3 is .10. Similarly, the probability of contact of clique 3 members by clique 2 knower-tellers is 6/68 or .09.

NEEDED IMPROVEMENTS IN PARAMETER ESTIMATES

It seems appropriate to note where these parameter estimates are particularly weak, and where more specific data are needed.

1. The method for dividing the villagers into cliques could be made more precise with matrix multiplication procedures, such as that described by Hubbell (1965).

2. Limitation of external channels to the extension worker and to the school teacher is arbitrary. A third channel by which new ideas enter a village are the trips made by villagers to towns and cities. Not only should the number of such cosmopolite trips be considered in the SINDI model, but also the nature of such contact; for example, whether interaction is with urbanities, store personnel, or other villagers in the city. Mass media channels should also be included in models that attempt to simulate diffusion in villages where mass media are available and are known to be important diffusion channels.

3. Finally, the isolates in the SINDI model are really "too isolated." These villagers have no opinion leaders (knower-tellers) from whom agricultural innovations may flow from external sources, nor do they have any contact with opinion leaders in other cliques. Therefore, it is impossible (in terms of the parameters of the model) for them to become aware of the innovation. Perhaps part of the problem is that the dichotomization of villagers as opinion leaders and nonleaders implies a two-step flow of communication, whereas in fact ideas diffuse in a multistep manner. On the other hand, a peasant village often *does* contain some isolates who never are reached by new ideas. The impression remains, however, that our parameter estimates are too extreme in cutting the isolates completely off from new ideas.

---

[16] The total number of possible contacts is estimated as the total number (3) of knower-tellers in clique 3, times the total number (17) of members in clique 2, which is 51.

OPERATION OF SINDI

The SINDI program[17] starts by randomly selecting members of the village, and matching each peasant so chosen against both of the external communication channels. The probability of a villager becoming aware of the innovation as a result of an external channel contact is determined by matching his probability for such occurence, whose calculation was discussed previously, with a random number drawn by the computer. If the random number (in percentage form) is equal to or less than the specified probability, the individual is designated as a new knower; otherwise, he remains a nonknower. The SINDI computer program then checks all the knowers and matches them against randomly selected villagers who are nonknowers. Whether the nonknower becomes a knower depends on: (1) the knower being a teller (or opinion leader); (2) the random number drawn; and (3) the matching of this random number against the probability of the nonknower being told.[18] In each time period, individuals become knowers either through external message contact, or by interpersonal communication within the village. A time period (or generation) ends when all possible communication matchings have been tried by the computer.

The same procedure is followed in the next generation with another quota of external message channels and personal contacts (from knowers of the previous generation). Further generations are halted at a specified time period or when a certain number of the villagers become knowers, such as 100 percent.

An important feature of the SINDI model is that multiple iterations or "runs" of the simulation are facilitated. If a complete run of SINDI from the first to last generation is regarded as a random[19] sampling of one diffusion process from the many possible patterns of diffusion in the village, a number of such elements are certainly needed in the total sample to be able to estimate sampling error and the true parameters. SINDI can easily iterate or repeat the complete simulation run as many times as specified, so that a sampling distribution of diffusion patterns is obtained, and estimates about the true

[17] SINDI is written in FORTRAN language and was run on the Control Data Corporation 3600 computer at Michigan State University. A copy of the SINDI program may be obtained from the authors for the cost of card reproduction.

[18] This depends, as explained previously in the discussion of the model's parameters, on (1) whether the teller and potential knower are members of the same clique or not, and (2) whether the teller is an opinion leader or not.

[19] It is random in the sense that SINDI is Monte Carlo simulation in which each run will be somewhat different from every other one, due to the numerous decisions in the simulation procedures which the computer makes randomly. To a certain extent, each actual simulation output represents one of a population of possible simulation outputs, each of whom have an equal chance of occurring.

parameters can be made. Such iteration has been absent in previous diffusion simulation research, where only a single run has been made, and this in itself is a strong argument for *computer* simulation, which is much speedier than nonmachine methods. Some idea of the ease of iteration is provided by the fact that only about three minutes of computer time are required for fifty runs of the SINDI model. Of course, another reason for using a computer is that more complex processes can be simulated than by nonmachine methods. As Hare (1961) points out in the case of computer simulation of small group interaction, "Its special value lies in its ability to make predictions by considering in a systematic way far more variables and relationships than an individual could hope to handle in the short run."

COMPARISON OF THE SIMULATION WITH REALITY DATA

In order to evaluate the simulation model, its results are compared with the actual diffusion of awareness of 2, 4-D weed spray in the Colombian village of Pueblo Viejo. These "reality" data were obtained through recall by the 67 peasants as to when they first heard of the innovation, so that reliability of the survey data is probably low.[20] Nonetheless, the data are probably fairly accurate in the aggregate, in indicating the distribution of new knowers per year over a period of 16 years. By aggregating to the rate of awareness for the *village*, much of the unreliability of *individual* awareness dates has been cancelled.

How close do the simulation results copy or reproduce the diffusion pattern that actually occurred in the Colombian village? SINDI was run 50 times to obtain an average number of new knowers for each consecutive time period. Thus, the estimate of the rate of new knowers is a summary, or the mean, of 50 different simulated diffusion patterns. Figure 15–2 shows the cumulative percentage of new knowers for both the simulation[21] (averaged over the 50 runs) and for the survey data. *The distribution for simulation and reality appear to be quite different,* an impression confirmed by: (1) the Kolmogorov-Smirnov goodness-of-fit test;[22] (2) a chi square test for a 2 x 2

[20] Menzel (1957) presents data on time of adoption of a new medical drug obtained from druggists' prescription records and from physicians' recall, to show that the latter are not completely accurate. The precision with which innovation awareness dates are reported by peasants over a much longer time period is probably even lower. Nevertheless, the reality data (as can be observed in Figure 15–2) generally approach an S-shaped distribution, which is what we would expect on the basis of theoretical reasoning and other empirical data.

[21] Since per year data provided the basis for calculation of the simulation's parameters, the simulation results are a rough approximation of the annual diffusion of awareness.

[22] The Kolmogorov-Smirnov analysis indicates that the two distributions differ more than could be due to chance in 1958, 1959, 1960, 1961, and 1962.

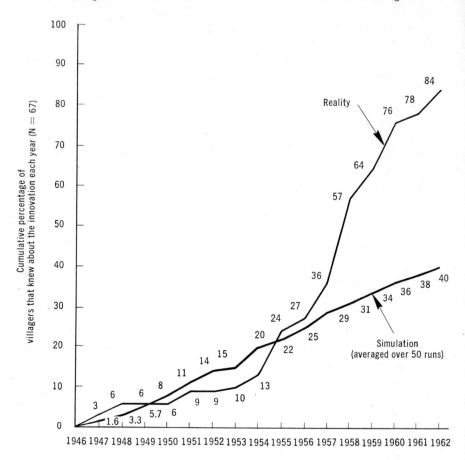

Figure 15–2. Cumulative Percentage of Knowers about an Innovation for Each Time Period in a Colombian Village for Similation and for Reality Data.

breakdown of those aware versus those not aware of the innovation for simulation and reality;[23] and (3) a rank ordering of the rate of awareness for 16 time periods for the simulation and reality.[24]

[23] Twenty-seven of the villagers became aware of the innovation in the simulation runs, whereas the reality data indicated 56 were aware by the end of the sixteenth generation ($X^2 = 26.6$, which is significant at the 5 percent level).

[24] Spearman rank-order correlation between the two rankings (for simulation and reality) on rate of awareness is .251, which is not significantly different from zero. Thus, the two distributions are not significantly related.

DISCUSSION AND FUTURE RESEARCH

The two distributions of knowers about the innovation are different; the simulation output is not similar to the actual diffusion pattern in this Colombian village. What went wrong with the diffusion model?[25]

1. SINDI's results show that about 27 people (40 percent) became aware after 16 time periods, whereas the reality data from Colombia indicate that 56 of the 67 peasants (84 percent) became aware in the 16 years between 1947 and 1962. SINDI underestimates the number of knowers at the end of 16 generations.

2. Figure 15–2 shows that reality and simulation were rather similar for the first ten generations, but then the reality diffusion process picked up speed much more rapidly than did SINDI in the last six generations. The simulated rate of awareness approximates a straight line.

Deutschmann (1962) and Hägerstrand (1965a) suggest that a psychological resistance (to the innovation) factor be introduced in simulation models. Repeated contacts with knowers would then be necessary to break through the screens of selective exposure and perception in order to create awareness, and that the number of these required contacts might vary for different individuals. Thus, introduction of an individual resistance factor in the simulation model might provide the spurt in rate of awareness in the last six generations to the point where simulation would approach reality in this last stage of the diffusion process. Rather, incorporation of the individual resistance factor in the model would primarily help attain closer simulation-reality correspondence in the first ten generations.

Another alteration in SINDI's rules of diffusion, and one that is expected to yield greater improvement in the goodness-of-fit of simulation to reality in the later generations, *is changing the model from a two-step to a multistep flow of communication.*[26] In the present model, the rate of awareness through inner-village diffusion from opinion leaders to nonleaders is hindered by a too-strict modeling of the two-step flow hypothesis. Once the simulated opinion leaders learn about the innovation and they tell an immediate corps of followers, these followers are heuristically prevented from acting as "secondhand" opinion leaders in distributing the new idea to later potential knowers; that is, those who should have become aware of the innovation after about

---

[25] As already pointed out, the unreliability of our reality data may also cause part of the simulation-reality difference. Perhaps in future research an attempt might be made (1) to obtain reality data about the rate of awareness of a battery of several innovations, or (2) to secure data on rate of adoption from records of the sellers of the new product, so as to overcome in part the unreliability of recall data.

[26] Logistical and cost considerations unfortunately precluded making this substantial structural change in the present SINDI model, but in future diffusion modeling we hope to include this and other refinements.

1956. The model's "false dichotomization" of opinion leadership, which in reality is a continuous variable, leaves a large number of sociometric isolates unreached by the innovation at the conclusion of the 16 stimulated generations.[27]

Perhaps this shortcoming of the 50 simulated diffusion patterns illustrates one of the important contributions of the simulation approach to research. Through simulation some of the theoretically interesting properties of the process can be isolated, and this can lead to improved understanding of the empirical data we seek to explain.

In fact, the present explanation of the model's inappropriate basis in the two-step rather than the multistep flow of communication has a close parallel in the interpretation by Coleman and others (1957) of the distribution of adopters (of a new medical drug) over time for their "integrated physicians" (that is, those linked by social relationships). This curve was of a chain-reaction or snowball nature, similar to the S-shape of our reality data in Figure 15–2. The adopter distribution for the relatively isolated medical doctors demonstrates a more constant rate of increase that is approximately a straight line, similar to our simulation data in Figure 15–2.

In future work with the present simulation model, the simulation's diffusion rules will be altered to allow for multistep diffusion. This should achieve a closer fit between simulation and reality.[28] Other steps in diffusion simulation are:

1. To simulate *adoption* decisions, as well as the awareness of an innovation.

2. To simulate not only aggregate (that is, social system) rates of diffusion and adoption, but also *individual* awareness and adoption of innovations. For example, we might seek to predict the relative time-order by which individuals in a village adopt a new idea, or the level of adoption of innovations that a change agent is able to secure among his clients by use of various diffusion strategies.[29]

SUMMARY AND CONCLUSIONS

This chapter described the development of research on the simulation of innovation diffusion, and presented results of one computer diffusion simulation, SINDI, which was developed to mimic the diffusion of a new agricul-

[27] In retrospect, we feel that we were led, at least in part, to this dichotomization of opinion leadership by the rather simple nature of the data on opinion leadership in the Colombian village. Thus, the nature of the input data led to distortion of a theoretical relationship when expressed as a simulation parameter.

[28] This strategy perhaps illustrates one of the possible pitfalls of the simulation research approach in which one rule in the model is altered in order to obtain an improved fit with reality, and as a consequence a poorer fit occurs elsewhere in the process. This danger is more likely to be avoided if changes in the model's rules are based on conceptual reasoning as well as goodness-of-fit considerations. In any event, simulation-reality fit should not be overemphasized as the sole goal of simulation research.

[29] Efforts to develop a computer-based diffusion game for the training of change agents is currently underway at Michigan State University.

tural idea in a peasant village with a Monte Carlo, computer program. SINDI's parameters include such variables as: external communication channels by means of which innovations enter the village; opinion leaders; and within-village cliques that affect the probability of interpersonal diffusion from leaders to nonleaders. Reality data on the diffusion of a new weed spray were gathered from the 67 farm household decision-makers in Pueblo Viejo, so as to provide parameter estimates for SINDI and so that the diffusion simulation results could be compared with reality. The comparison between (1) 50 runs of the SINDI model across 16 generations, and (2) the reality data on the diffusion of awareness about the weed spray from 1946 to 1962, indicate that the two distributions are generally similar in the first 11 generations, but they differ significantly in the last five generations. In addition to the possible unreliability of the reality data, reasons for this lack of simulation-reality fit suggest the need for (1) the addition of an individual variable indicating the degree of psychological resistance to an innovation; and (2) the alteration of the diffusion model rules so as to simulate a multistep, rather than a two-step, flow of communication. The latter procedure is likely to have the greatest payoff in improving the SINDI model of diffusion. It implies consideration of opinion leadership as a continuous variable, rather than as a false dichotomy of leaders and followers, and stresses the sequential diffusion of a new idea from opinion leaders with external channel contact, to their immediate followers in the village via interpersonal communication channels, and from them to still other villagers.[30]

Karlsson (1958:29) predicted the widespread use of simulation in the social sciences, especially Hägerstrand's method of Monte Carlo diffusion simulation. "This . . . is a situation that will probably become more and more common in the social sciences . . . . The normal course of action will be to do as Hägerstrand did . . . . In principle his solution of the problem is correct and feasible and will be accepted by more and more social scientists."

Perhaps it is surprising that in some 15 years since Hägerstrand's first English publication on Monte Carlo methods, or in the 10 years since Karlsson's prediction of widespread use of this simulation approach by social scientists, only a handful of quantitative geographers (and almost no other social scientists) have utilized Monte Carlo simulation. Consideration of improved methods of diffusion simulation is a priority investment for those engaged in scientific investigation of communication and modernization processes.[31]

---

[30] These considerations were held to be important in the previous discussion of the two-step flow of communication (Chapter 10).

[31] Subsequent research with the SINDI model, completed after the present chapter was written, revealed a programming error that when corrected, yielded a cumulative curve of knowers that very closely approximated the reality data shown in Figure 15–2.

16

Next Steps in
Modernization Research

And no man putteth new wine into old bottles; else the new wine doth burst the bottles, and the wine is spilled, and the bottles will be marred: but new wine must be put into new bottles.

(Mark II:22)

The modernization process is under study by researchers from a number of different social science disciplines. Despite the differences in gardening tools, all are toiling in the same vineyard. One might ask what has been achieved to date through the efforts of social scientists, and further, what more can social scientists contribute to the solution of development and modernization problems?

SOCIAL SCIENCES AND THE CHALLENGE OF LESS DEVELOPED NATIONS

There can be little doubt that social scientists recognize the challenge offered by less devloped nations.[1] For evidence, one has only to look at the increasing number of social science studies being conducted in countries like Colombia, Kenya, and India. Throughout this book the results of hundreds of such studies conducted by anthropologists, economists, psychologists, sociologists, political scientists, communication analysts, and so on have been referred to, citing the contributions that have been made to theory, measurement, and practical solutions to modernization problems. In spite of these numerous completed studies, we maintain that the social sciences have not yet reached their full potential in solving development problems.

Some of the major reasons why the social sciences have not yet made their full contribution to the identification and solution of development problems are listed below.

1. To date, there has been inadequate focus on the *social aspects* of development. Much of the research in less developed nations has been strictly

---

[1] In fact, Inkeles (1967a:v) comments that if the rate of economic growth and change in less developed countries were directly proportional to the increase in research on them, the problem of underdevelopment would be solved.

360

economic in nature, ignoring social-psychological variables and cultural aspects of the development problem (Inkeles 1967a:v) as a result, much more is known about gross national products and per capita income in less developed countries than about perceptions, attitudes, and beliefs of peasants. It is increasingly apparent that these sociocultural dimensions are often instrumental in the success or failure of development programs.

2. The social sciences cover a wide range of disciplines. Unfortunately, there has been *little cooperation among the disciplines* in studies of modernization and development. Much could be gained if research teams included members of several different research orientations. Each social science may be able to explain a portion of human behavior; no one discipline can offer a complete explanation. An interdisciplinary attack on modernization problems is needed.

3. There are *inadequate resources* for behavioral research in less developed countries. First of all, government leaders in less developed nations have been slow to realize the role that social scientists can perform in moving their countries closer to their development goals. To a certain extent the failure to recognize the potential of the social sciences is reflected in the lack of well-trained social scientists in less developed countries.[2] Social science research in less developed countries is itself not yet very well developed.

4. There has been a tendency on the part of researchers from more developed countries to engage in *data mining*, rather than *institution building*. In the past, sojourning scientists engaging in "safari research" traveled to the host country, gathered data, and departed for their home countries to analyze the data and publish the results. Their impact has been about as permanent as that of a finger removed from a glass of water. Little effort has been made to improve the research capability of the host country institutions, so that social science research would be conducted competently after the sojourner leaves. One of the most efficient ways of accelerating the emergence of a group of trained social scientists is to have "budding" scientists from less developed countries "engage in joint research activities employing similar methods, theories, and research designs" (Jacobson 1966). Although such a procedure is neither simple nor easy, it is one direct means of meeting the challenge to the social sciences in less developed nations.

5. The *culture-bound research methodology* of social scientists from more developed countries hinders social research in less developed nations.[3] There are important sociocultural differences between more and less developed countries, many of which have not been incorporated in sampling procedures, data gathering techniques, measurement, or analysis. Often researchers have settled for squeezing less developed countries into methodological molds devised for more developed countries, rather than making new molds to fit

[2] "Most social scientists live in the United States" (Tenune 1966).

[3] We shall return to a more specific discussion of this problem later in the present chapter.

the specifications of the new research situation. An *international social science* must emerge from research in the less developed countries, a science predicated upon indigenous adaption and application. The result will be a social science with cross-culturally valid generalizations and principles, as well as a more rapid rate of development and modernization.

A FOCUS: THE GAP BETWEEN ELITES AND PEASANTS

The potential contribution of the social sciences can best be realized if future efforts have a coordinated focus. A key problem in all less developed countries is the lack of adequate communication between "power-elites" and the majority of the population — the peasants.

The Problem

Most less developed countries are controlled by a small group of elites who were educated abroad and who share little but a national identity and (perhaps) a common language with the peasant masses. Little effective upward or downward communication occurs between these two groups.

Too often the needs, the aspirations, and the capabilities of the peasants who comprise nearly three-fourths of the populations of the developing countries, and who produce one-half of their income, are not adequatley communicated to their governments and thus are not reflected in the centrally designed development formulas.[4]

Those who manage the development programs have little regard or understanding of the realities of peasant living. The elites discuss and plan, but the peasants rarely listen or participate in carrying out the development designs.

Presocial Science Attempts

This is not a new problem, nor is it only recently recognized. In the presocial science era, the intelligentsia realized the necessity for bridging the gap to the masses, but they utilized generally ineffective means to achieve this goal. For instance, in nineteenth centruy Russia, many intellectuals returned to peasant villages as part of the Norodniki movement (Pool 1966). This early version of the Peace Corps was motivated by a desire to understand the masses. Unfortunately Norodnism and similar movements in other countries[5] provided only partial and impressionistic mental pcitures of the peasants. In the contemporary milieu of rapid change and massive development programs, attempts to reach and understand the peasants have proven equally unsatisfactory.

[4] Quoted from a U.S. government report by the Subcommittee on International Organizations and Movements of the U.S. House of Representatives (1967:9).

[5] The "people's houses" in Turkish villages, for example, were part of Kemal Ataturk's modernization program in the 1920's and 1930's. These village centers featured adult literacy classes and libraries, and were expected to act as a cultural bridge between the local villagers and the volunteer teachers who came from towns and cities.

Potential of the Social Sciences in Bridging the Gap

Of the hundreds of development projects launched by local and national governments and by international agencies since the end of World War II, "relatively few have been analyzed by techniques adequate for measuring their actual effectiveness or for guiding them towards increased effectiveness" (Hayes 1966:5).

In order for develpment programs to be effective, there must be *reliable data about the masses*. Therefore, the collection of reliable social science data might be considered as one way in which the gap can be bridged.

1. All too often the data on which planners have to depend are incorrect, unreliable, and insufficient.[6] An illustration is the number of infant deaths in five Egyptian villages reported by a health center contrasted with the number of such deaths disclosed by a survey of the villages. The survey of households indicated that 238 infant deaths had occurred in a one year period, whereas the administrative records of the health center showed only 84 deaths, an under-reporting of 65 percent (Moss 1965). Social research techniques can therefore help provide more reliable data as a basis for development planning. It is indeed difficult to plan without facts.

2. Reliable data are needed on the perceived needs of the potential clients of change agencies. Too often, we have "scratched where the masses did not itch." Data that reflect the attitudes, desires, and needs of peasants aid developers in planning change programs that will be more readily accepted by the intended audience.

3. Feedback data are also needed. Change agency officials must know how their programs are functioning at the operational level in order for these leaders to manage the programs efficiently.[7]

Social science research methods can offer the ruling elites a more effective avenue to the peasant mind. Without the contribution of the social sciences, "the process of development, if it ever occurs, will be very much slower, more painful, more violent, more cruel, more arbitrary, and more unequal" (Pool 1966).

The role of the social sciences should be increased in both development planning and evaluation. Before this role can be trenchantly fulfilled, social scientists must take heed of the methodological problems in current modernization research.

---

[6] Planning is often based on national censuses or administrative records of change agencies.

[7] A humorous illustration of this point was related to me by an anthropologist in an African nation. The U.S. Agency for International Development symbol, which appears on all its vehicles, equipment, and publications, is a handshake. This symbol is viewed with bemused surprise by a major tribe in the African country who believe that the handshake signifies agreement to engage in sexual intercourse.

NEED FOR A CULTURALLY APPROPRIATE METHODOLOGY[8]

The social sciences were founded in Europe, grew to methodological sophistication in North America, and were then transplanted to less developed countries. Concepts, theories, and methods have been taken from Western-industrial nations, and utilized elsewhere. Severe problems of cultural limitation have been encountered that prohibit attainment of the same level of precision achieved in more developed countries. One must wonder how different the social sciences would be if they had been founded by Kenyans, Japanese, or Bolivians.

What are the main characterisics of less developed nations that act to limit the transfer of Western social science research methods? These countries are typified by much greater *variability* in most sociocultural dimensions: their vast range of languages, life styles, levels of living, attitudes, ethnic backgrounds, religions, and other human characteristics, is almost impossible to imagine. None of the less developed nations, even the smallest, approach the "mass culture" of the United States and western Europe, where the mass media reach a mass audience in a way that tends to produce common values, standardized speech and dress, and similar viewpoints.[9] Safe generalization of research findings to broad populations in less developed nations becomes much more difficult due to the varied conditions in these systems.

Another restrictive aspect of research in less developed countries is *unfamiliarity* of the research setting. The social researcher often begins an investigation without the helpful legacy of an accumulated body of past research. Further, the investigator is likely to be markedly different from his respondents, which makes it difficult for him to become familiar with them in a relatively short period of time. Such dissimilarities make effective communication between the two very difficult. Researcher and respondent simply do not share the same frames of reference, meanings, and often language. Data gathering is essentially a communication process, and in less developed nations source-receiver heterophily poses grave problems between the researcher and the researched: the former are often urban and middle class or uppermiddle class, the latter are usually peasants or urban poor. The social chasm between the two is widened much further when the researcher is a sojourning scientist from another country.

How is the hiatus of unfamiliarity and dissimilarity to be bridged? The researcher must be able to take the role of the respondent, as the opposite is unlikely to occur. The traditional target of study is almost always less able to be empathic than the more modern researcher. One way for the investigator

---

[8] Certain ideas in this section are adopted from Rogers (1966a). Further detail may be found in Hursh (in process).

[9] As Crutchfield (1963:208) points out, "The vast growth of mass communication makes ever easier the mass homogenization of thought."

to gain empathy is to learn as much as possible about his respondents through reading, discussion, and exploratory data-gathering. In short, the scientist should seek to make the unfamiliar sociocultural system more familiar. Beginning with less structured data-gathering methods (like case studies, observation, focused interviews, and so forth) before moving to more highly-structured techniques like personal interviews is an in-process method for gaining familiarity with the setting and the respondents. The research strategy, then, is to *progress from less to more highly structured research methods, in order to gain familiarity with and understanding of one's respondents.*

Whether one is in Katmandu, Dar-es-Salaam, or Des Moines and whether the research study lasts a few months or several years, the basic steps in the research process are about the same. The actual procedures involved at each step, of course, must vary. The stages in the research process form a natural, chronological organization for the discussion that follows. Since *survey research*[10] is the most commonly used approach in modernization investigations, our comments shall be concentrated accordingly, but not entirely to the exclusion of other social science approaches.

FORMULATION OF THE RESEARCH PROBLEM

The body of concepts, hypotheses, and findings from social science research in more developed countries too often form the model for similar investigation in less developed countries. Major differences in the sociocultural environment make it imperative for the social scientist to look beyond the research completed in more developed countries. Otherwise, he is likely to select the "wrong" variables as explanations of human behavior in the peasant world.[11]

Concepts that have little relevance in a modern country may prove to be the most important in a more traditional environment, and vice-versa. In a mass society like the United States, for example, where almost everyone is

[10] *Survey research methods* are all those techniques of scientific investigation utilized to gather data from the field in order to generalize from a sample to a larger population. Our central concern in surveys is with the ability to *generalize*. This implies that the number of respondents who are interrogated is generally adequate to allow generalization to a specified population. Seldom does a survey sample consist of only one or a few individuals. Our desire for generalizing also necessitates a relatively structured data-gathering instrument so as to facilitate quantification of the responses into categories and numbers. A comparison of the survey with the laboratory and field experiment is provided later in this chapter.

[11] Naturally a social scientist's perception of the situation that he is researching is structured by the concepts and theories he has been taught. He "sees" cosmopoliteness, empathy, and fatalism because he has internalized these ideas. They limit his perception of the world; they affect his choice of concepts and research methods. The scientist's problem is an example of the Sapir-Whorf viewpoint that man's environment affects his language, which in turn structures his perceptions. A certain Eskimo language contains twelve words for different kinds of snow, whereas English only has one word. The Eskimo is thus able to perceive 12 kinds of snow, while English speakers can only distinguish one kind. Likewise, the social scientist perceives fatalism among peasants because he has a concept for it.

literate and has easy access to public transportation and all forms of mass media — literacy, cosmopoliteness, and empathy are likely to account for much less variance in innovativeness, than among peasants in Colombia.

Personal health is another variable that probably holds little significance in more developed countries, but does in less developed nations, as a factor explaining the adoption of innovations. A peasant farmer whose digestive system is infected with parasites, who has a low level of nutrition, and who has little opportunity or desire to take advantage of modern medicine, is seldom motivated to adopt improved farming methods. The gravity of the health factor is illustrated by data from one Colombian village in which the average farmer reported he was physically unable to work for about 40 days per year due to illness. The "belly theory" of innovativeness could be substantiated by assessing the rate of adoption of agricultural ideas in a community both before and after a successful public health campaign to eliminate internal parasites.

On the other hand there are variables that have proven important in more developed countries, but that seem to have little relevance in less developed countries. The United States has an extremely well-developed agricultural extension service, and contact with extension personnel is a significant factor in explaining variance in innovation-adoption patterns of individuals. In our most traditional village in Colombia, none of the farmers had *any* contact with extension workers. The complete absence of such cosmopolite communication contact meant that this variable was completely useless in explaining individual differences in innovativeness. One might even find extremely traditional and isolated villages where no one has adopted *any* innovations, and hence, there would be no range in innovativeness.[12]

When the formulator of modernization research studies in less developed societies is from a more developed country, he must be careful not to transplant concepts and hypotheses about human behavior without proper regard for the different conditions.[13] Certainly the foreign researcher will benefit from host country participation in the definition of culturally-relevant variables. In turn, he should consider it an obligation to train host country investigators,[14] who will then have the advantage of a culturally relevant framework within which they can apply the newly acquired social science research techniques.

[12] Although the complete lack of mass media exposure, extension contact, or the adoption of innovations in an extremely traditional community may prevent measuring *individual* differences in these variables, these communities could prove useful in comparisons, and in definition of the traditional-modern continuum.

[13] This is easier said than done. Too often the assumptions we make about human behavior are so implicit that it is difficult to bring them to the surface when faced with a culture where human behavior changes may result from vastly different stimuli.

[14] Care must be taken, however, not to superimpose culturally-bound assumptions during the training of indigenous social scientists.

DATA-GATHERING METHODS

Speaking from personally experienced frustrations, it is folly to consider studying a similar problem (such as the diffusion of ideas) in a less developed nation with the same research methods used in a more developed country. One cannot assume, as is often done in the United States, that a random sample of respondents will willingly provide accurate responses to structured questions in field interviews.[15]

In general, it is difficult to gain the cooperation of peasant respondents in interviews. Suspicious attitudes toward strangers, a misperception that research interviewers are government employees (such as tax collectors), greater physical and social isolation in terms of communication and transportation, and a lack of prior experience with scientific surveys all serve as blocks to interview rapport.

Field interviewing is susceptible to many and varied problems. In one Latin American community local rumors were spread that the researchers conducting the field interviews were really looking for farm children to send to a sausage factory. In the case of the Colombian study, an increase in local property taxes was announced by the government during the data collection. The farmers were asked as part of our interviews, how many animals they owned and how many acres they operated. Naturally, they assumed a direct causal link between the information they were giving and the tax increase. Interviewing was brought to a halt by noncooperation until the community leaders, who fortunately understood the nature of the investigation, had an opportunity to explain the situation to their neighbors.

These examples point up the necessity of clarifying the field interviewer's role with village respondents. Personal interviewing should be initiated only after explanations have been made to the community leaders, and their sanction has been obtained. A particularly useful field interviewing technique[16] requires that data-gatherers live in a community for a period of time before they begin asking questions from an interview schedule. Observation and unstructured interviewing techniques can be combined with use of an interview schedule to obtain a more accurate picture of modernization variables. Further, the get-acquainted period permits the interviewer more opportunity to gain the respondent's frame of reference.

A totally different problem that the researcher must face when he uses personal interviewing as his major data-gathering device, is the "Si, Señor" complex — better known as *courtesy bias*.[17] Some peasant respondents simply

[15] Field interviews are probably the most standard digging tools of researchers studying peasant modernization. While we do not suggest that this favorite intellectual spade be abandoned, we recommend that personal interviewing be supplemented with other measurement methods, usually of a less structured nature.

[16] Anthropologists are probably the most successful at using this technique.

[17] Since the wording of questions also effects the tendency to offer falsely positive responses, we shall return to a discussion of courtesy bias in regard to measurement.

agree with all questions they are asked, including attitude scale items. This overwhelming positiveness is commonly encountered in Latin American and Southeast Asian nations, where farmers think it extremely impolite to disagree with a guest (as they perceive the interviewer to be). The traditional farmer who, when asked whether his parents were alive, responded, "Yes . . . but they are both dead," provides an illustration. When the peasant interviewer does not offer an explanation of his "yes" response, as this respondent did, it may not be obvious to the interviewer that the information he is gathering is totally inaccurate.

Such problems lead us to advocate strongly that *field interviews be supplemented with other data-gathering methods to provide external validity checks on the survey data.* To be most useful, these techniques should be unobstrusive and disguised in nature, so that the respondents are not fully aware of the variables being assessed. An excellent catalogue of unobstrusive measuring devices is provided by Webb and others (1966); examples are (1) calibrating the selective erosion of floor tiles around a chick-hatching exhibit in a museum to index the popularity of the display; (2) counting empty bottles in ash cans to estimate whiskey consumption in a "dry" town where store sales records were not available; and (3) measuring the degree of fear induced in a ghost story-telling session by noting the shrinking diameter of a circle of seated children. Although these illustrations come from U.S. research, parallels might easily be thought of for peasant settings.[18]

Modernization researchers must stretch the boundaries of their methodological thinking. Creativity should characterize the development and use of new research methods as well as the adaption and combination of existing techniques.

SAMPLING

Sampling is a complex task in less developed nations, where experience with national samples is virtually unknown. Maps and adequate census-type information are often unobtainable. The lack of a sampling frame, such as a list of names or an adequate area map, often means that a complete census must be taken of every household in an area before a sample can be drawn. These difficulties frequently preclude the use of probability samp-

---

[18] For example, a technique used by zoologists to trace deer migration patterns could be easily adapted for the study of interpersonal communication patterns in a peasant village. Miniature electronic devices could be planted on each peasant in a given village for a sample of time periods. These devices are activated by close proximity to another sensing device (as when two peasants are within speaking distance). The activation of the devices is electronically recorded, so that the researcher can later compute a "whom-to-whom" matrix of interpersonal communication that would serve as an external validity check on sociometric data gathered with an interview schedule. Accurate data on interpersonal communication patterns is a priority need in the types of analyses described in Chapters 10 and 14.

ling.[19] The great advantage of probability samples over judgement or other types of nonprobability samples is that they allow one to *generalize* from his respondents to the larger population.

A problem related to sampling is the selection of the respondent. Who should he be? One cannot assume that each unit in a social system has the ability or power to make his own decisions. For example, the extended family, the clan, the plantation, or other such groupings may in fact be the decision units regarding farm and health innovations. In mainland China, for instance, most agricultural decisions are made by directors of communal farms; the workers are then ordered to carry them out. In one rural Colombian community about 95 percent of all the land was held by five large farmers who made the farm decisions, and then hired farm workers to carry out these decisions. If the farm workers were interviewed in either of the aforementioned cases, the innovation-decision process could not be reconstructed with any degree of accuracy.

MEASUREMENT

Measurement techniques are apt to be one of the most culture-bound aspects of the entire research process, and as such are likely to cause the international social science researcher the biggest headache. The problems inherent in measurement are especially difficult when the researcher is working in an unfamiliar environment.

Take the simple problem of wording an interview question. Within developing countries there are usually many regional differences in language, and frequent subcultural differences in meanings. A researcher cannot be sure that a question will mean the same thing in one village that it does in another, even if the basic language is the same. One can imagine the problems of conducting a national sample in a country like Nigeria, where over 200 different language groups have been identified.[20]

An illustration may serve to bring out another problem related to question wording. A field interviewer, who was driving along a main road in search of a particular village, inquired of numerous villagers en route, "I'm going in the correct direction for Village A, aren't I?" "Si, señor," was invariably the reply. Not until he had overshot his destination point by 50 miles did he realize that he had fallen victim to the courtesy bias. Perhaps if he had inquired, "Where is village A?" he would have been told that he was headed in the wrong direction.

A similar instance of the courtesy bias occurs when farmers are asked, "How many cattle do you have?" Some will respond with a number, even though

---

[19] A *probability sample* is one in which each unit in the population has a known probability of being selected in the sample.

[20] This is probably one reason why a national sample has not yet been undertaken.

they have no cattle. The question implies that the farmer has some cattle, and he affirms the implication with a number response, so as not to seem impolite.[21]

Peasant respondents often take other than the truth into account when responding to questions. Foster (1967:109) concludes that his Mexican peasant respondents obscured "the line between truth and fasehood to the point where most people do not think in this way at all. Will an answer work? Will it please? Will it be the simplest solution?" How does one obtain valid data from village respondents when their replies to research questions are framed by such criteria as these?

When a survey researcher attempts to use an attitude scale, further problems become apparent. Although most attitude scales imply a continuum of attitude belief, many peasant respondents seem to think in dichotomous terms. Various mechanical or visual methods have been used to aid respondents in reacting to attitude scales, but they sometimes lead to further problems. For example, one ingenious researcher in Brazil used a 10-stepped ladder on a small wooden paddle. The peasants were asked to indicate their attitudes toward a number of issues by inserting a peg in one of the 10 holes, corressponding to steps on the ladder. Unfortunately, some respondents perceived this instrument as being connected with black magic, and therefore refused to respond.

Perhaps the most effective way of meeting some of the measurement problems in less developed countries is through careful and extensive pretesting of the instruments. The survey researcher should be prepared to spend proportionately more of his time and resources in pretesting the instruments than he would in more familiar sociocultural situations. Improved operaationalization of modernization concepts will inevitably lead to a higher quality of survey research in less developed nations.

DATA ANALYSIS AND INTERPRETATION

An interesting data analysis problem was encountered in one of the Indian villages discussed in this book. Sociometric opinion leadership data were collected by asking respondents to name peers who they sought for agricultural information. Fifteen of the approximately 100 household heads in the village had identical names, were of the same caste, and in some cases had the same father. The problem of analyzing the sociometric data was resolved only when it was determined that the villagers had bestowed different nicknames on the 15 men.

In addition to such problems as these, all the difficulties described under formulation of the research problem are relevant at this final stage of the

---

[21] One solution to this problem, as illustrated by this example, is to precede the question about the number of cows with a "filter" question: "Do you have any cows?" Only if the respondent answers the filter question positively is he then asked how many cows he has.

research process.[22] The general problem is the culture-bound nature of the concepts and models on which the data analysis and interpretation are based.

Only some of the problems facing survey researcher in less developed countries have been highlighted. Even fewer specific solutions have been suggested, as their exact amelioration depends on the particular nature of the sociocultural conditions, the research objectives, and the researcher's skills in combining research methodologies into hybrid forms.

Creativity and a search for culturally-appropriate methods are urged for those undertaking survey research in less developed countries. The eventual, though presently far-off, goal of such activity is a culture-free research methodology that will facilitate the construction of an international social science, consisting of cross-culturally valid understandings of human behavior.

FIELD EXPERIMENTS ON MODERNIZATION

As noted earlier, survey research tends to be the most popular approach among social scientists investigating modernization problems in less developed nations. In survey research, the obtained consequent measures of respondents' knowledge, attitudes, and behavior are typically correlated with selected antecedent variables. The *survey* allows the researcher to generalize these results from the sample to a larger population. Although this is an important advantage, the difficulty in controlling the effect of unwanted variables makes the survey a less-than-perfect research approach for many social science problems.

The *experimental* approach to social science research in less developed countries may involve exposure to a communication message, whose effects are evaluated in terms of the amount of change in knowledge, attitudes, or behavior of individuals studied before and after the message exposure. These effects are often compared to those of similar individuals (in a control group) who have not been exposed to the treatment message.[23] The differ-

---

[22] Plus at least one other — the occasional danger of suppression of research publications by government or other authorities in less developed countries. This appears to be a more serious problem in these settings than in more developed nations. Research topics of great potential value are also often highly sensitive, and there are many examples of government attempts at the censorship or suppression of research reports. One instance recently occurred in an African nation when a ministry of agriculture official refused to allow the distribution of a survey report, which described the nation's peasants as illiterate, poor, and so forth. The government leaders felt the publication was correct, but that it reflected a negative image of their countrymen.

[23] Respondents should be assigned to the treatment and the control group on a random basis, so as to remove the effects of all possible antecedent variables other than the treatment variable.

ence between the treatment effects among the experimental and the control groups indicates the effect of the treatment independent of all other variables.

The *field experiment* allows the researcher to combine some of the advantages of both the survey (such as the ability to generalize to a larger population), and the experiment (like control). The "before" and "after" measurements are taken by surveys, and the experiment is conducted in the field, rather than the laboratory, permitting a test under more realistic conditions.[24] A comparison of laboratory, survey, and field experimental approaches is featured in Table 16–1.

Communication research on modernization[25] began largely with correlational analyses of survey data. The information derived from these correlational studies aids in probing the nature of the modernization process, in sensitizing us to the elements of the subculture of peasantry, and in establishing *relationships* or associations among variables. Field surveys do not permit a very high level of control over possibly intervening variables.[26] Further, they cannot establish a clear *time-order relationship* between the variables investigated.

The present research generation of survey results provides a solid basis for the design of future field experiments on communication and modernization; for experiments, like simulations, are most efficient when they are based on a considerable body of previous findings. Survey results help narrow the multitude of possible antecedent variables associated with a particular consequent; they provide a basis for selecting the concepts that should be incorporated in an experiment, and those that should be excluded with control procedures.

Dodd's (1934) study of the effects of health campaigns in Syria was probably one of the first field experiments on modernization. Although his design and methods are considered crude by today's standards, he recognized the importance of the peasant village setting for field experimentation. The vil-

---

[24] Field experiments can also provide insights into the approximate cost of a communication treatment in order to obtain a unit of change in human behavior. The obvious usefulness of such information to development planners emphasizes the importance of the field experiment approach. An illustration of input-output estimates of the economics of change secured in radio forums in India is provided by Schramm and others (1967a and 1967b).

[25] Communication research conducted in the United States often reflects a sequential combination of the laboratory-field approach; that is, research topics are often explored under laboratory conditions from which a series of generalizations are then tested in a field situation to determine their validity. The persuasion research initiated by Carl Hovland provides an example of the laboratory-field approach. His early laboratory studies on attitude change were followed with field experiments and surveys, which are reviewed by Festinger (1964). Of course, the usual sequence is occasionally reversed; that is, field surveys lead to laboratory experiments.

[26] The main type of control possible with correlational analysis of survey data is *statistical*, such as with partial correlation. Statistical methods of control can only be utilized with variables that have been adequately measured, whereas experiments enable control over *all variables* through randomization procedures.

Table 16-1. Comparison of Three Research Approaches: The Laboratory Experiment, the Survey, and the Field Experiment

Characteristics of the Research Approach	Research Approaches		
	Laboratory Experiment	Survey	Field Experiment
1. Main advantage of the research approach	Control over possibly interviewing variables	Ability to generalize results from a sample to a larger population	Ability to generalize and to control
2. Main disadvantage of the research approach	Artificiality of the results because respondents are seldom typical of a population of interest	Difficulty in controlling on possible interviewing variables	Depends on much prior research to isolate the crucial variables for inclusion in a field experiment
3. Method of control over possibly intervening variables	Randomization in the assignment of respondents to treatment(s) and control groups	Statistical (like partial correlation)	Randomization (when possible) in the assignment of respondents to treatment(s) and control groups
4. Can time-order of variables be determined?	Yes	No	Yes
5. Can forcing quality of the variables be determined?	No[a]	No	No[a]
6. Main purpose	To determine the time-order of relationships with other variables controlled	(1) to describe a population, or (2) to determine the covariance or relationships among two or more variables	To determine the time-order of relationships with other variables controlled
7. Usual sequence in the chronological development of a research tradition	First	Later	Latest

[a] The experimental methods do allow the researcher to rule out certain antecedent variables as possibly forcing a consequent variable, but they cannot tell him which variable(s) definitely has a forcing quality on the dependent or consequent variable. Inferences about the forcing quality of variables can only be gained from theoretical insight, and not from a strictly empirical basis.

lage makes a meaningful unit for treatment application because it is relatively isolated, and thus generally less susceptible to contamination by naturally occurring processes, which may be uncontrollable by the researcher.

In previous chapters findings were reviewed from the India radio forum experiment by Neurath (1960 and 1962), the analysis of media effects in Ecuador (Spector and others 1963), and the Menefee and Menefee (1965 and (1967) experiment on community newspapers in India. These studies might be considered representative of the small handful of field experiments conducted in villages of less developed countries.[27] They represent both impressive potential on one hand, and the discouraging methodological weaknesses inherent in a new avenue of investigation on the other.

The time is now ripe. We must capitalize on what has been learned in correlational studies and early field experiments, and move forward in a series of carefully designed and conducted field experiments on communication and modernization. An important reward can be knowledge of the direction in which the arrows in our modernization paradigms should point; we can more adequately determine the time-order relationships among the variables involved in the modernization process.

CONCEPTS FOR INVESTIGATION

The Colombian investigation (and its counterparts in other nations that were drawn upon in this book) serve not only to establish empirical relationships among our main variables, but also to point to other concepts that might be fruitfully studied in future investigations. The directions that this future modernization research might take are the subject of the following discussion.

INTERPERSONAL TRUST AND VILLAGE CONSENSUS

Interpersonal trust is the predisposition of an individual to enter an ambiguous situation where the outcome depends on another person. Development, modernization, and acceptance of such collective innovations as village irrigation schemes and cooperatives, depend on mutual interpersonal cooperation, which in turn is a function of the degree of trust among members of a social system.

As was indicated in Chapter 2, there is a tendency for peasants to be distrustful in interpersonal relations. Take the Nigerian farmer, who when asked in a research interview whether he thought he should let his relatives know everything about his life, responded "No, even my wife does not know or she will take advantage of me." Although most peasants tend to be distrustful,

---

[27] Another important investigation in this tradition is the Berelson and Freedman (1964) field experiment on the role of mass media and change agent contact in diffusing family planning innovations in Taiwan.

some are more trusting than others. In other words, there is variance in this variable among villagers.

Is there greater institutional development and success in collective decision making in villages where the residents are characterized by higher levels of interpersonal trust? Stanfield (1968) is attempting to answer this and other questions dealing with modernization consequences of interpersonal trust in his study of Brazilian peasants.

Interpersonal trust may be an important antecedent to *village consensus* which is defined as the degree to which members of a social system are in agreement. Collective innovation decision making about innovations that require "group adoption" (for example, the building of a village road or the joint purchase of a tractor or irrigation pump) is facilitated by consensus, which in turn may be determined by such variables as effective communication, absence of within-village cliques, strong leadership,[28] and interpersonal trust. Future research should provide more insight into the social-psychological conditions that give rise to consensus in a village setting, and to the consequences of trust for cooperative village efforts at development.

STATUS INCONSISTENCY AND SOCIAL MARGINALITY

Status inconsistency[29] is the relative lack of similarity in an individual's ranking on various indicators of social status.[30] School teachers in the United States are generally characterized by status inconsistency; that is, they have a relatively high educational level and occupational prestige, but a relatively low income.

Past research on status inconsistency indicates that it is positively associated with a desire for social change, with modern rather than traditional attitudes and liberal political attitudes. Such research provides support for the theory that status inconsistency leads to a feeling of *social marginality*, an ambiguous position in a social system. This ambiguous status is uncomfortable to the individual. A change in the extant social situation favors those in positions of status inconsistency, so they innovate in the hope of changing existing conditions. Peasants characterized by status inconsistency are likely to be the innovators in modernization.

Sen's (1962) research with Indian villagers shows generally positive rela-

[28] This is perhaps measured as the degree of concentration of opinion leadership in the village. *Concentration* is the degree to which one or more units in a social system possess a given attribute in greater strength than other units in the social system. The Gini index is often used to operationalize the degree of concentration or inequality.

[29] Inconsistency refers not to the *degree* of social status (high or low), but to how *discrepant* or unlike the various measures of social status are for a given individual.

[30] The concept, originally referred to as "status crystallization," was called to scientific attention by Lenski (1954). Recent methodological advances in measuring status inconsistency have been reported by Mitchell (1964) and Hyman (1966).

tionships between status inconsistency (measured as the discrepancy between such status indicators as caste, occupational prestige, income, and education) and modern attitudes. Although no research study has explored the relationship between status inconsistency and innovativeness, one would expect it to be positive. Likewise, status inconsistency ought to be related to other modernization indicators like achievement motivation, aspirations, and cosmopoliteness.

It is relatively easy to incorporate a status inconsistency index in a study, since the measurement of status inconsistency does not necessarily require the addition of questions to the interview schedule. Usually the respondent is asked about such factors as income, education, occupation anyway, and so it is only necessary to compute a status inconsistency index from these data. In addition to a general measure of status inconsistency, specific measures of inconsistency can also be computed for pairs of social status indicators, such as occupation-income, income-education, and so forth.

To date there have been exciting research leads to follow on the role of status inconsistency in modernization, but there has been little evidence.

INDUSTRIALIZATION AND URBANIZATION

The effects of urbanization and/or industrialization on the modernization of traditional people is clearly of import, but it has not yet been studied adequately. One of the relatively few inquires into industrialization effects is a multination investigation conducted by Professor Alex Inkeles of Harvard University. This study concentrates on the effects of factory experience in Argentina, Chile, India, Israel, Nigeria, and Pakistan.[31] The preliminary findings indicate that "Each year in the factory contributes to significant change, and the process is continuous, so that after ten years in a factory the typical worker will, on our measures of individual 'modernity,' far outscore his compatriot who continued in his native village" (Inkeles 1967a:vi).

The task before researchers is not an easy one, for it will be difficult to separate the effects due to industrialization and those due to urbanization, both are intricately entangled. Most factories are located in cities and towns. Is it the effect of the occupation, or of residence in the city, which produces changes in the traditional individual? Can we determine that industrialization is responsible for cerain kinds of changes, whereas urbanization is responsible for others? Kahl (1962) attempted to determine the consequences of both urbanization and industrialization on individual modernization in Brazil. His correlational analysis of survey data indicates that both variables strongly effect modernization.

The procedural and methodological problems involved in studying the

---

[31] The study is entitled the Harvard Project on Social and Cultural Aspects; its results are to be summarized in a forthcoming book, *Becoming Modern*, by Inkeles and others.

effects of industrialization and urbanization[32] do not diminish the need for their investigation. Less developed countries have relatively little industry now,[33] but it is certain to increase. It is important to understand how the trends to industrialization and to city living will affect the peasant population.

Perhaps the knowledge gained from such stabilization effects studied could also be used to prevent certain social problems from occurring, such as the streaming of peasants to urban unemployment, the growth of urban slums, and so forth.

DEFERRED GRATIFICATION

The postponement of immediate satisfaction in anticipation of future rewards is called *deferred gratification*. Anticipated gratifications are perceived by an individual to be of greater value than immediate rewards. Deferred gratification implies a choice point; immediate or short-term goals constitute one set of alternatives, while long-term objectives and their associated rewards constitute the other.

It was pointed out in Chapter 2 that peasant farmers are typified by immediate or impulse gratification, rather than deferred gratification.[34] This tendency affects the adoption behavior of peasants in that the rewards from most innovations are not very immediate. If a peasant has a certain amount of money to spend, he is more likely to buy objects that will give immediate pleasure, than to invest in a tractor or in fertilizer that will improve his crops next year. The inability of the villager to postpone rewards thereby retards adoption of agricultural innovations.

Perhaps it is strange that there are no research studies which explore the relationship of deferred gratification to modernization consequents, but as yet we even lack a fully adequate measure of the concept.[35]

NATIONALISM

Many peasants living in isolated villages do not even realize that they are members of a nation-state. If the process of national development requires an increasing commitment of citizens to their country and a willingness to make

[32] One might wish for a panel survey study over a period of years in which the same sample of individuals are interviewed before and after urban migration and industrial work experience.

[33] Inkeles (1967a:vii) points out that "If they [less developed countries] must wait for industrialization to bring about the psychological modernization of their people, they must wait a long time indeed."

[34] Chu (1967) found that levels of deferred gratification were very low among Taiwanese banana-growers until at least a minimum level of living was reached. This suggests that perhaps deferred gratification is a luxury that one must be able to afford.

[35] Several attitudinal-type items suggested by Doob (1965b) seem to tap the deferred gratification dimension. Examples are: "It is better to live pretty much for today and let tomorrow take care of itself," and "If I had a choice, I would rather be promised a large sum of money one year from now than to be given a smaller sum to be spent immediately."

individual sacrifices for the good of the nation, *nationalism*, or the degree to which an individual places his nation's interests above those of any other collectivity, becomes an important variable for study.

Although considerable discussion has been devoted to the concept of nationalism, national images, national character, and so forth, there is need for a "genuine cross-cultural study, such as one relating some measure of nationalism[36] to other social or psychological factors" (Doob 1964). There is almost no research on variables correlated with nationalism, and therefore, there is little evidence to support propositions like the following: cosmopoliteness and attention to the mass media are accompanied by heightened nationalism. We assert that feelings of nationalism are an important modernization indicator, and should be subjected to investigation.[37] It is possible that nationalism may motivate certain expressions of neo-traditionalization, the process by which individuals change from a modern way of life to a more traditional style of life.

POLITICAL POWERLESSNESS

Peasants in less developed countries have generally been found to possess low levels of political efficacy, to distrust their government (at least the levels of government other than the local village chief), and to feel helpless in influencing the nature of public political decisions (Chapter 2). Political *powerlessness* is the degree to which an individual perceives his efforts are inadequate to influence public political decisions. One can see conceptual parallels between powerlessness, political apathy, and peasant fatalism.[38]

Widespread feelings of powerlessness may be one reason for the failure of self-help community development programs in peasant villages. If powerlessness is prevalent, then change agent strategies must accomodate this feeling and perhaps even use it to advantage. Research can determine the extent to which political powerlessness influences peasant behavior, and point to ways in which powerlessness can be overcome or utilized. Despite a number of investigations dealing with this concept in the United States,[39] there is a vacuum of research on this dimension in less developed countries.

[36] We lack an adequate measure of the concept of nationalism. Doob (1965b) suggests items such as "What is good for my country is not always good for all of us citizens," and "In general, my country has become much more important to me than my tribe."

[37] Almond and Verba (1963) studied a closely-related concept, "pride in country," in five nations, but only one — Mexico — is less developed.

[38] Powerlessness is conceptualized by Seeman (1959) as one of five dimensions of alienation. The others are (1) meaninglessness, where the individual is unclear as to what he ought to believe; (2) normlessness, the breakdown of social norms regulating behavior; (3) isolation, in which the individual assigns low value to goals or beliefs accorded high value in a given social system; and (4) self-estrangement, or dependence of a given behavior on anticipated rewards which lie outside the behavior itself.

[39] Powerlessness and other alienation variables are explored in Dean (1969), Neal and Rettig (1963), Neal and Seeman (1964), and Thompson and Horton (1960).

SATISFACTION WITH LEVEL OF LIVING

All programs of planned change in less developed nations aim to raise clients' levels of living. The *level of living* of an individual or family is the degree to which the basic needs of nutrition, clothing, housing, and health are met. The concept is usually measured by the possession of such material objects as a brick house, tin roof, household equipment, and so forth.

The people of most nations have standards of living that are higher than their levels of living. A *standard of living* is the desired degree to which a person's basic needs are met, whereas the level of living represents the actualities that exist.

Satisfaction with level of living is the degree to which an individual's expectations (or standard of living) are fulfilled by his actualities (or level of living). The state of disequilibrium that exists when an individual has a higher standard of living than his level of living, results in dissatisfaction and a desire to improve his level of living. Dissatisfaction with one's level of living may be caused by mass media exposure, which provides individuals with comparative information about others' levels of living. Change agents may seek to increase dissatisfaction with present levels of living as a means to motivate their clients to adopt new technological ideas which should eventually result in higher levels of living. Of course, it is important that increasing dissatisfaction with existing levels of living be accompanied by means which higher levels of living may actually be attained.[40]

Research is needed on the relationship of variables such as cosmopoliteness, media exposure, and change agent contact, to dissatisfaction with level of living. Further, the assumption that levels of frustration are rising in less developed nations must be tested empirically. We must also ascertain the point at which dissatisfaction no longer serves as a motivating force, but rather leads to revolution and social disorganization. Of course, such research presumes an accurate measure of satisfaction with level of living, whose construction is a scientific task still to be met.[41]

[40] In chapter 1, the present development era was characterized as one of rising frustrations because villagers are encouraged to want more than they can get.

[41] We used a very tentative operation of satisfaction with level of living, by asking our Colombian respondents how satisfied they were (on a one-to-ten step ladder rating of the type developed by Professor Hadley Cantril at Princeton University) with their level of living. In the three modern villages, this crude measure correlates positively (.325) with farm size in land units, .495 with level of living scores, and .479 with social status ratings (Stickley and others 1967). The relationships are all in the expected direction. The magnitude of the correlations between satisfaction and indicators of level of living, indicates they are empirically, as well as conceptually, distinct. Surprisingly, satisfaction is *positively* related to media exposure (.398) and to cosmopoliteness (.338) This may only reflect the fact that those individuals who can "afford" media exposure and trips to the city are relatively well-off, and perceive themselves as such.

SUMMARY AND CONCLUSIONS

Social science research in less developed countries can contribute to more effective communication between top government officials and the people. Development planners need reliable data about the masses, especially concerning their needs for change and their reactions to the functioning of change agencies at the operational level. Past social research has not given enough focus to social-psychological or to cultural aspects of development, there has been little interdisciplinary cooperation, and adequate resources for behavioral research have been lacking in less developed nations. Further, a data-mining rather than an institution-building approach has often been evidenced in past social science research by sojourning scholars. Most serious, however, has been the inappropriate use of culture-bound research methods (largely developed in the United States) in survey studies in less developed countries.

At least two characteristics of these new research settings necessitate major overhaul of survey methods: their much greater variability in most sociocultural dimensions, and their relative unfamiliarity to most social scientists. The appropriate research strategy under these conditions is to progress from less to more highly structured research methods, so as to gain familiarity and understanding of one's respondents. Inappropriate cultural biases are apt to affect the survey research process at each of its major steps: (1) formulation of the problem; (2) choice of data-gathering methods; (3) sampling; (4) measurement; and (5) data-analysis and interpretation. Needed in future studies of modernization are field experiments, which can provide evidence of the time-order nature of modernization variables.

Future inquiries on modernization should consider giving more attention to the following concepts: (1) *interpersonal trust*, defined as the predisposition of an individual to enter an ambiguous situation where the outcome depends on another person, and village *concensus*, the degree to which members of a social system are in agreement, (2) *status inconsistency*, the relative lack of similarity in an individual's ranking on various indicators of social status; (3) industrialization and urbanization; (4) deferred gratification; (5) *nationalism*, the degree to which an individual places his nation's interests above those of any other collectivity; (6) political *powerlessness*, the degree to which an individual perceives his efforts are inadequate to influence public political decisions; and (7) satisfaction with level of living.

We have seen in this chapter (and throughout this book) that social science research methods face special problems and require particular adaptation when used in the unfamiliar sociocultural systems frequently found in less developed countries. New concepts and new methodological approaches must be utilized in future modernization research, as we strive toward an international social science.

Then indeed we shall have new wine in new bottles.

APPENDIX

The Colombian Villages
and Villagers

The purpose of this appendix is to present a succinct word picture of the Colombian villages and villagers that provided the main empirical basis of this book.

Table 17–1 describes the peasants in the six Colombian villages in terms of their education and literacy, mass media exposure, and adoption of agricultural and home innovations. The peasants in the relatively modern villages generally have more formal education, more media exposure, and higher levels of adoption than their counterparts in the two more traditional villages.[1]

Although a complete ethnological account of each of the six Colombian villages is beyond the scope of the present appendix, certain selected aspects of village life in these settings can be summarized as follows: the respondents reflect many elements of the Latin American style of life. Their language is almost entirely Spanish; few Indian words remain in their dialect. While the majority of their blood is Indian, the centuries of Spanish influence have left a firm mark on their attitudes and institutions. The Roman Catholic Church is an important presence in their lives; all are officially members, and most are active participants in religious services and holiday activities. The *municipio* (county) is the significant and local level of government, although three of the villages have recently founded village development committees, which engage in certain self-help community activities. Each of the six villages has a local elementary school that offers the first few years of schooling. The teacher is an employee of the national Ministry of Education, but the school building was built, and is maintained, by the local villagers.

Subsistence agricultural production is the predominant pattern. Farms are small in size and the farmers are poor, in relation to commerical farmers or urbanites in Colombia. Some food, drink, and farm supplies are available from cooperatives or private stores in the villages, but most other economic services come from stores in towns or cities. The peasants live on their farm lands in a "scattered farmstead" fashion; the village center consists only of a couple of homes near a school or a store. Nevertheless, the village is a viable social system and represents a meaningful and powerful reference group to

[1] This was also pointed out in Chapter 3, where full detail on the basic classification of the villages on the modern traditional continuum is provided, as well as on the methods of data gathering that were utilized.

Table 17-1. Characteristics of the Villagers in Six Colombian Communities.

Characteristics of the Villagers	More Modern Communities				More Traditional Communities	
	Támesis	Pueblo Viejo	San Rafael	Cuatro Esquinas	Nazate	La Cañada
1. Mean years of education	3.2	1.6	2.1	2.2	1.2	1.8
2. Percentage of respondents with formal education	—	70	50	68	39	63
3. Percentage of respondents who are functionally literate	—	27	39	49	24	15
4. Percentage of respondents reading[a] a newspaper at least once a week	—	54	61	67	22	18
5. Percentage of respondents reading[a] a magazine at least once a month	—	18	17	19	0	11
6. Percentage of respondents having seen a film in the past year	—	69	72	63	0	20
7. Percentage of respondents listening to radio at least once a week	—	55	56	68	56	35
8. Percentage of respondents having watched TV in the past year	—	10	17	14	0[b]	0[b]
9. Percentage of respondents using chemical fertilizer	—	90	94	95	72	8
10. Percentage of respondents using a weed sprayer	—	79	89	82	53	0
11. Percentage of respondents possessing a latrine	—	8	78	60	0	43

[a] In the case of both newspaper and magazine exposure, these percentages also include someone else reading to the respondent.
[b] No television programs could be received in Nazate or La Cañada because of their distance from transmitting stations.

most of its members. Interaction patterns are highly concentrated within the village, with the exception of some cosmopolite peasants who travel frequently to towns and cities.

The family is also an important reference group to the typical individual. Most families are nuclear in the sense that the adult farmer, his wife, and children constitute most households, although some homes also contain another relative or two (such as a grandparent or uncle or aunt). The pattern of child-rearing is highly authoritarian and patriarchial. Attitudes of distrust and suspicion of nonfamily villagers are common, and in fact, it is our intuitive impression that most of the Colombian respondents are typified by the ten elements of the subculture of peasantry (described in Chapter 2). They are fatalistic, limited in time and distance perspectives, lack deferred gratification, and so forth.

Now let us turn to a brief description of each of the six communities.

TÁMESIS

Támesis is characterized by a large number of small-sized farms located on steep mountain slopes in the Andes. In fact, the *municipio* takes up the largest part of one mountainside.

The major crops of Támesis are coffee, which is grown at medium altitude in a band across the width of the *municipio*, and bananas. Támesis probably represents a higher degree of farm commericialization than the other five villages (largely due to coffee-growing), but its farmers are, nevertheless, oriented mainly to subsistence food production. Cultivated crops are corn, sugar cane, beans, and potatoes. The diversity of crops is largely due to the range in altitude. The farms are generally small; more than one-third are less than 5 acres in size. Ninety percent of the farmers of Támesis own the land they cultivate.

The level of living in Támesis is higher than in the other Colombian communities studied. Eighty percent of the homes have electricity. The Federation of Coffee Growers, the National Institute of Food (INA), and Acción Comunal (a Colombian community development program) have change agents working in the *municipio* to improve agricultural production and family living conditions.

PUEBLO VIEJO, SAN RAFAEL, AND CUATRO ESQUINAS

The three *veredas*[2] of Pueblo Viejo, San Rafael, and Cuatro Esquinas are located in the western edge of the plateau of Bogotá near the town of Facatativa, which is the marketing center for the farmers in the area. Although these

---

[2] A *vereda* in Colombia is a locality group providing certain institutional services, usually a school and a general store-tavern, and containing between 25 and 150 rural families. The *vereda* is probably similar to a rural township in the Midwestern United States in the 1930s. Throughout this book we generally refer to these *veredas* as "villages" or "communities," which they are in a sociological sense, although they provide their residents with a minimum of institutional services.

villages border the plateau, most of the farmland is located in the foothills of the Andes Mountains. The town of Facatativa provides most of the institutional services for the three villages, but elementary education and such economic services as food and farm supplies are located in each of the villages.

Pueblo Viejo

Pueblo Viejo, one of the relatively more progressive villages near Facatativa, contains 93 households. Most landowners have very small plots of land, characteristic of the *minifundia* (small land holding) pattern of Colombia. However, there are also a few *haciendas* (large farms) in the community.[3] Homes are located in a scattered fashion on the farms.

Agricultural extension service personnel from Facatativa spend one day each week in the village conducting programs of planned change. They cooperate closely with the local school teacher, who plays a very prominent role in introducing change in the community. The extension program includes a village development committee, a home economics club, a 4-S (similar to 4-H) club, and a marketing and supply cooperative.

The social center of the village is the school and the cooperative store. Both are located on the main road and near the center of the village (there are also four or five small taverns in the village). The main road passing through the village is of great importance in explaining external communication patterns. A bus service operates three times daily along the main road to Facatativa, where a bus leaves each hour for Bogotá. There are frequent contacts with Bogotá, and many of the youth migrate there to work in factories or in households as maids.

The major crops are potatoes, wheat, barley, and corn. Almost every farm has a few chickens, rabbits, hogs, or sheep.

San Rafael

San Rafael, which contains 61 households, is located northwest of Facatativa. The homes are scattered along both sides of a 2-mile long, dead-end road that begins on the plateau of Bogotá, crosses several ridges, and ends in a valley. The boundaries of the village are quite clear-cut, and consist of mountain ridges on three sides and the plateau of Bogotá on the fourth. The main crop grown by the small farmers is potatoes, whereas the large farmers are mainly cattle breeders.

The extension service has had an active program in the *vereda* since about 1959. Their organizations include a village development committee, a home economics club, a 4-S club, and a cooperative store. The co-op was reor-

---

[3] Characteristic of most of Colombia (and other Latin American nations), is their pattern of "upside-down" farming in Pueblo Viejo; the more level and fertile land is owned by the large farmers and is used mostly as cattle pasture. The steep, less fertile soil is operated intensively by small farmers. This strange farming pattern arose historically when the Spanish conquerors took over the best land, and forced the Indians up into the mountain slopes.

ganized in 1962 after its near-failure the previous year. It now functions with moderate success, and recently moved into a new building. A piped water system has recently been completed to supply water to several homes near the co-op. Both projects were started by extension service personnel, who also have a home rebuilding program underway.

There is no bus service in the village, and only a jeep or truck is able to traverse the entire distance of the dead-end road, and then not in rainy weather. Compared to Pueblo Viejo, San Rafael is somewhat more isolated. The level of living, however, does not appear to be lower; in fact, more than two-thirds of the farm households have latrines.

Cuatro Esquinas

Cuatro Esquinas, a village consisting of 73 households, is located about 6 miles northeast of Facatativa. The village stretches for about 5 miles along a passable road in the foothills just off the plateau of Bogotá. The village center consists of the school and a tavern.

The extension service has been active in the village since 1961. Their program is generally similar to those in the other two villages near Facatativa, but generally has been less successful.

Bus service operates only twice weekly, and residents of the village have relatively few contacts outside of the community. Villagers travel to church services and to the market day in Facatativa by foot or by animal.

NAZATE AND LA CAÑADA

Nazate and La Cañada are located in the state of Nariño in the southwestern part of Colombia bordering Ecuador (Figure 1–3). This is a very mountainous region and has a reputation as one of the most traditional areas in Colombia. Two villages in Nariño, with somewhat different climates and subcultures, were selected for the present study.

Nazate

Nazate is situated in a high valley that borders the Cumbal volcano; it consists of about 60 households. Most of the people of Nazate have Indian blood and Indian surnames, but a mixed Indian-Spanish culture(although the only language spoken today in Nazate is Spanish.) Only a few "white" people (really of mixed Indian-Spanish blood but with Spanish surnames) live in the village; they generally are large landowners. Relations between the whites and the Indians are rather strained because of a feud about 30 years ago over possession of communal lands. The main crops grown are potatoes, wheat, and barley. The larger farmers are primarily cattle breeders.

Most of the houses are constructed of *adobe* with straw roofs and dirt floors.

None of the homes has a latrine, electricity, or running water. There are no active programs of Acción Comunal, the extension service, or U.S. Peace Corps in Nazate, although they do exist in nearby villages.

La Cañada

La Cañada is located on the northern edge of the state of Nariño. The River Mayo forms the northern border of the village, which nearly adjoins the town of San Pablo. A road runs the length of the *vereda* and ends in San Pablo. There are about 65 households in the community.

The size of landholdings is extremely small; only a few farms are more than one hectare (2.47 acres). In fact, the standard unit of land measure is the *plaza* (one-tenth of a hectare). The larger farmers raise coffee, whereas the smaller operators mainly grow corn, bananas, yucca, and anise.

The extension service does not operate in the village, but there is an office in nearby San Pablo. Extension personnel feel that the people of La Cañada are not eager to help themselves through community development efforts. Two members of the U.S. Peace Corps installed electricity in about 80 percent of the homes in the village in 1961, but they did not undertake further work because of a lack of community cooperation.

Many of the villagers are physically and mentally degenerate. Much intermarriage has occurred among the families, resulting in many deaf, dumb, and physically deformed persons. Although syphilis is widespread, most villagers never visit the medical doctor in San Pablo.

THE TYPICAL RESPONDENT

Although there are important differences in the characteristics of the respondents from village to village, the reader may find it useful to think of the "typical peasant" in terms of a composite of all of our villagers. He possesses about two years of low-quality formal education, in fact, only about 30 percent of the informants were able to read a simple sentence (when asked to do so during the research interviews), and are considered functionally literate. Print mass media exposure is suprisingly high in terms of this relatively low level of literacy; about 40 percent of the respondents report exposure to a newpaper at least one a week[4] and about 16 percent have access to a magazine at least once a month. Radio reaches approximately 55 percent each week, about half saw a film in the past year, and perhaps 10 percent viewed television in the past 12 months. Thus, sizeable proportions of the village household heads use the five mass media channels of communication, and those who are not so exposed likely have neighbors and friends who are.

Both agricultural and home innovations have penetrated to the six villages, although less so in La Cañada, where only 8 percent of the farmers use chemi-

---

[4] Some illiterates have exposure to newspapers and magazines as a result of someone else (often their children) reading to them (Chapter 4).

Table 17-2. Results of Personal Interviewing in the Six Columbian Villages

Results of Personal Interviewing	Támesis	Pueblo Viejo	San Rafael	Cuatro Esquinas	Nazate	La Cañada	Total
1. Residents in the village not eligible for interview[a]	53	16	16	5	12	6	108
2. Eligible respondents from whom completed interviews were not obtained	0	10	9	11	4	0	34
a. Could not be contacted after several call-backs	0	6	4	8	0	0	18
b. Refused to be interviewed	0	4	5	0	1	0	10
c. Schedules discarded due to incomplete data	0	0	0	3	3	0	6
3. Completed interviews	47	67	36	57	41	54	302
Total	100	93	61	73	57	60	444
Percentage of completed interviews from those eligible	100	87	80	84	91	100	90

[a] These household heads were not eligible for interview either because they were employed only in non-farm work, or because they worked only as farm laborers, and hence were not involved in making farm innovation decisions.

cal fertilizer, as opposed to about 85 percent in the other five villages. None of the La Cañada residents had adopted a weed sprayer at the time of our data-gathering, but approximately 75 percent of the farmers in the other five villages of study were using this innovation. Reasons for the lower rate of adoption of agricultural and home technology in certain of the six villages include the presence and degree of activity of planned change programs such as the extension service, Peace Corps, and the community development agency. In Nazate and La Cañada the village norms are relatively traditional, and both extension service and Peace Corps workers who have tried to introduce innovations have met apathy and resistance, and so they abandoned their efforts.

RESULTS OF PERSONAL INTERVIEWING

In the present inquiry an attempt was made to obtain a personal interview with the head of each farm household in five of the villages and with a sample of farm household heads in Támesis. Table 17–2 shows that interviews were completed with 90 percent of those eligible, a total of 302 respondents. Most of the data analysis in the present book, however, is based upon that supplied by the 255 informants in Pueblo Viejo, San Rafael, Cuatro Esquinas, Nazate, and La Cañada.

REFERENCES

Abegglen, James C., 1958, *The Japanese Factory*. New York: Free Press.

Abell, Helen C., 1965, *Farm Radio Forum Project-Ghana*, 1964–65. Ottawa: Government of Canada, External Aid Office, Mimeo Report.

Abrahamson, Mark, 1965, "Cosmopolitanism, Dependence-Identification and Geographical Mobility," *Administration Science Quarterly*, 10:98–106.

ACPO, 1965, *What Are the Objectives of Acción Cultural Popular?* Bogotá: ACPO Department of Sociology.

Adams, Don, 1960, "The Monkey and the Fish: Cultural Pitfalls of an Educational Adviser," *International Development Review*, 2:22–24,

Agee, James, and Walker Evans, 1939, *Let Us Now Praise Famous Men*. Boston: Houghton Mifflin.

Allahabad Agricultural Institute, 1957, *Extension Evaluation*, Allahabad, India: Allahabad Agricultural Institute.

Allport, G. W., 1954, "The Historical Background of Modern Social Psychology," in Gardner A. Lindzey, ed., *Handbook of Social Psychology*. Cambridge, Mass.: Addison-Wesley.

Almond, Gabriel A., and James Coleman, 1960, *The Politics of the Developing Areas*. Princeton, N.J.: Princeton University Press.

————, and Sidney Verba, 1963, *The Civic Culture*. Princeton, N.J.: Princeton University Press.

Andrews, John, 1963, "*N* Ach: Factors in Stability and Change," Unpublished paper, Harvard University Center for Research in Personality.

Arensberg, Conrad M., and Arthur H. Niehoff, 1964, *Introducing Social Change*. Chicago: Aldine.

Ascroft, Joseph R., 1966a, "Reconceptualizing Functional Literacy: Toward a More Sensitive Measure of Literacy," Unpublished paper, Michigan State University.

Ascroft, Joseph R., 1966b, *A Factor Analytic Investigation of Modernization Among Kenya Villagers*, M. A. thesis, Michigan State University.

Atkinson, Brooks, 1937, *Walden and Other Writings of Henry David Thoreau*. New York: Random House.

Ayrout, Henry H., 1963, *The Egyptian Peasant*. Boston: Beacon.

Bailey, F. G., 1966, "The Peasant View of the Bad Life," *Journal of the British Association for the Advancement of Science*, 23:399–409.

Banfield, Edward C., 1958, *The Moral Basis of a Backward Society*. New York: Free Press.

Banks, Arthur S., and Robert Textor, 1963, *A Cross Polity Survey*. Cambridge, Mass.: MIT Press.

Barnett, Homer G., 1941, "Personal Conflicts and Cultural Change," *Social Forces*, 20:160–171.

Barnett, Homer G., 1953, *Innovation: The Basis of Cultural Change*. New York: McGraw-Hill.

Barzini, Luigi, 1964, *The Italians*. New York: Bantam.

389

Beal, George H., and Donald N. Sibley, 1966, "Adoption of Agricutural Technology Among the Indians of Guatemala," Paper presented at the Rural Sociological Society, Miami Beach, Fla.

Bebermeyer, James P., and Everett M. Rogers, 1966, *Mass Media and Interpersonal Communication in National Development*, Michigan State University, Department of Communication, AID Diffusion Project Working Paper 16.

Becker, Howard, 1957, "Current Sacred-Secular Theory and Its Development," in Howard Becker and Alvin Boskoff, eds., *Modern Sociological Theory in Continuity and Change*. New York: Holt, Rinehart and Winston.

Bell, Graham B., and Harry E. Hall, 1954, "The Relationship between Leadership and Empathy," *Journal of Abnormal Psychology*, 49:156–157.

Belshaw, Cyril S., 1965, *Traditional Exchange and Modern Markets*. Englewood Cliffs, N.J.: Prentice-Hall.

Bennett, John, 1966, "Further Remarks on Foster's 'Image of Limited Good'," *American Anthropologist*, 68:206–210.

Bennis, Warren G., and other, 1962, *The Planning of Change: Readings in the Applied Behavioral Sciences*. New York: Holt, Rinehart and Winston, Inc.

Bequiraj, Mehmet, 1966, *Peasantry in Revolution*. Ithaca, N.Y.: Cornell University Center for International Studies, Cornell Research Papers in International Studies 5.

Berelson, Bernard, and Ronald Freedman, 1964, "A Study in Fertility Control," *Scientific American*, 210:29–37.

Berlo, David K., 1960, *The Process of Communication: An Introduction to Theory and Practice*. New York: Holt, Rinehart and Winston.

Bisbee, Eleanor, 1951, *The New Turks: Pioneers of the Republic*, 1020–1950. Phildelphia: University of Pennsylvania Press.

Black, C. E., 1966, *The Dynamics of Modernization: A Study in Comparative History*. New York: Harper & Row.

Bonilla, Elssy, 1964, *La Predición de la Adopcíon de Hortalizas en Tres Comunidades Colombianas*, Licenciatura Thesis, Bogotá: Universidad Nacional de Colombia, Facultad de Sociología.

Bonilla de Ramos, Elssy, 1966, *Fatalism and Modernization in Colombia*, M.A. thesis, Michigan State University.

Bonilla, Frank, and José A. Silva Michelena, 1967, *A Strategy for Research on Social Policy*. Cambridge, Mass., MIT Press.

Bose, Santi Priya, 1962, "Peasant Values and Innovation in India," *American Journal of Sociology*, 67:552–560.

———, 1967, "Social Interaction in an Indian Village," *Sociologia Ruralis*, 7:156–175.

Bostian, Lloyd R., and Fernando C. Oliveira, 1965, "Relationships of Literacy and Education to Communication and to Social and Economic Conditions on Small Farms in Two Municipios of Southern Brazil," Paper presented at the Rural Sociological Society, Chicago.

Bowden, Leonard W., 1965, *Diffusion of the Decision to Irrigate: Simulation of the Spread of a New Resource Management Practice in the Colorado Northern High Plains*, University of Chicago, Department of Geography, Research Paper 97.

Bradburn, Norman M., 1960, *The Managerial Role in Turkey: A Psychological Study*, Ph.D. thesis, Harvard University.

———, and David E. Berlew, 1961, "Need for Achievement and English Industrial Growth," *Economic Development and Cultural Change*, 10:8–20.

Briones, Guillermo, and F. B. Waisanen, 1966, "Educational Aspirations, Modernization and Urban Integration," Paper presented at the American Sociological Association, Miami Beach, Fla.

Brown, Lawrence A., 1966, *Models for Spatial Diffusion Simulation*, Ph.D. thesis, Northwestern University.

Brunner, Edmund deS., 1942, "Gemeinschaft and Gesellschaft in Rural Communities," *Rural Sociology*, 7:75–77.

Bunge, William, 1962, *Theoretical Geography*. Lund, Sweden,: Gleerup.

Burnet, Mary, 1965, *Abc of Literacy*. Paris: UNESCO.

Burris, R., 1958, *The Effect of Counseling on Achievement Motivation*, Ph.D. thesis, Indiana University.

Canfield, A. A., 1951, "Sten Scale: A Modified C-Scale," *Educational and Psychological Measurement*, 11:295–297.

Cantril, Hadley, 1963, "A Study of Aspirations," *Scientific American*, 208:3–7.

Caplow, Theodore, and Kurt Finsterbusch, 1964, "Development Rank: A New Method of Rating National Development," Unpublished paper, Columbia University, Bureau of Applied Social Research.

Carlsson, Gosta, 1965, "Time and Continuity in Mass Attitude Change: The Case of Voting," *Public Opinion Quarterly*, 29:1–15.

Carothers J. O., 1959, "Culture, Psychiatry, and the Written Word," *Psychiatry*, 22:307–20.

Carstairs, G. Morris, 1958, *The Twice Born: A Study of a Community of High Caste Hindus*. Bloomington, Ind.: University of Indiana Press.

Carter, Roy E., Jr., and Orlando Sepulveda, 1964, "Some Patterns of Mass Media Use in Santiago de Chile," *Journalism Quarterly*, 41:216–224.

Cassirer, Henry R., 1959, "Audience Participation, New Style." *Public Opinion Quarterly*, 23:529–536.

Chattopadhyay, S. N., and Udai Pareek, 1967, "Prediction of Multi-Practice Adoption Behavior from Some Psychological Variables," *Rural Sociology*, 32:324–333.

Chou, Teresa Kang Mei, 1966, *Homophily in Interaction Patterns in the Diffusion of Innovations in Colombian Villages*, M.A. Thesis, Michigan State University.

Chu, Goodwin C., 1966, "When Television Comes to a Traditional Village," Paper presented at the Pacific Chapter of the American Association for Public Opinion Research, San Francisco.

———, 1967, "Media Use and Deferred Gratification in Eonomic Development," Paper presented at the Association for Education in Journalism, Boulder, Colo.

Clark, James, and Nan Lin, 1965, "Computer Simulation in the Social Sciences," Unpublished paper, Michigan State University, Department of Communication.

Coch, Lester, and John R. F. French, 1948, "Overcoming Resistance to Change," in Eleanor E. Maccoby and others, eds., *Readings in Social Psychology*. New York: Holt, Rinehart and Winston, Inc.

Cohn, Bernard S., 1959, "Changing Traditions of a Low-Caste," in Milton Singer, ed., *Traditional India: Structure and Change*. Philadelphia: American Folklore Society.

Coleman, James, 1958, "Relational Analysis: The Study of Social Organizations with Survey Methods," *Human Organization*, 16:28–36.

——— 1962, "Analysis of Social Structures and Simulation of Social Processes with Electronic Computers," in Harold Guetzkow, ed., *Simulation in Social Science: Reading*. Englewood Cliffs, N. J.: Prentice-Hall.

———, and others, 1957, "The Diffusion of an Innovation Among Physicians," *Sociometry*, 20:253–270.

Cortes, Juan B., 1961, "The Achievement Motive in the Spanish Economy between the 13th and 18th Centuries," *Economic Development and Cultural Change*, 9:144–163.

Coutu, Walter, 1951, "Role-Playing vs. Role-Taking: An Appeal for Clarification," *American Sociological Review*, 16:180–187.

Crutchfield, Richard S., 1963, "Independent Thought in a Conformist World," in S. Farber and R. Wilson eds., *Conflict and Creativity*. New York: McGraw-Hill.

Cutright, Phillips, 1963, "National Political Development: Measurement and Analysis," *American Sociological Review*, 28:153–164.

Dahl, Robert A., 1961, *Who Governs? Democracy and Power in an American City*. New Haven, Conn.: Yale University Press.

Dart, Frances E., 1963, "The Rub of Cultures," *Foreign Affairs*, 41:360–371.

Davies, James C., 1962, "Toward a Theory of Revolution," *American Sociological Review*, 27:5–19.

Davis, James A., 1961, "Locals and Cosmopolitans in American Graduate Schools," *International Journal of Comparative Society*, 2:212–223.

Davison, W. Phillips, 1965, *International Political Communication*. New York: Praeger.

Dean, Dwight G., 1960, "Alienation and Political Apathy," *Social Forces*, 38:185–189.

De Jesus, Carolina Maria, 1963, *Child of the Dark*. New York: Signet.

De Young, John E., and Chester L. Hunt, 1964, "Communication Channels and Functional Literacy in the Philippino Barrio," in Socorro C. Espiritu and Chester L. Hunt, eds., *Social Foundations of Community Development*. Manilla: Garcia; and *Journal of Asian Studies*, 22:67–77, 1952.

Deutschmann, Paul J., 1962, "A Machine Simulation of Information Diffusion in a Small Community," Unpublished paper, San Jose, Costa Rica, Programa Interamericano de Informacíon Popular.

———, 1963, "The Mass Media in an Underdeveloped Village," *Journalism Quarterly*, 40:27–35.

———, and Orlando Fals Borda, 1962a, *Communication and Adoption Patterns in an Andean Village*, San Jose, Programs Interamericano de Informacíon Poplar, Mimeo Report.

———, and Orlando Fals Borda, 1962b, *La Communicacíon de las Ideas entre los Compesinos Colombianos*, Bogotá, Universidad Nacional de Colombia, Facultad de Sociología, Monografias Sociologias 14.

———, and A. Eugene Havens, 1964, "Discontinuances: A Relatively Uninvestigated Aspect of Diffusion," Unpublished paper, University of Wisconsin, Department of Rural Sociology.

———, and John T. McNelly, 1964, "A Factor Analysis of Characteristics of Latin American Countries," *American Behavioral Scientist*, 8:25–29.

Dobriner, William M., 1958, *The Suburban Community*. New York: Putnam.

Dodd, Stuart C., 1934, *A Controlled Experiment on Rural Hygiene in Syria*. New York: Oxford.

Donohew, Lewis, 1967, "Communication and Readiness for Change in Appalachia," *Journalism Quarterly*, 44:679–687.

———, and B. K. Singh, 1967, "Poverty 'Types' and Their Sources of Information about New Practices," Paper presented at the Association for Education in Journalism, Boulder, Colo.

Doob, Leonard W., 1961, *Communication in Africa*. New Haven, Conn.: Yale University Press.

———, 1964a, *Patriotism and Nationalism: Their Psychological Foundations*. New Haven, Conn.: Yale University Press.

———, 1964b, "Eidetic Images Among the Ibos," *Ethnology*, 3:357–363.

———, 1965a, "Exploring Eidetic Imagery Among the Kamba of Central Kenya," *Journal of Social Psychology*, 67:3–22.

———, 1965b, *Attitude Scale Items Suggested for Studies of Modernization*, New Haven, Conn.: Yale University, Department of Psychology.

———, 1966, "Eidetic Imagery: A Cross-Cultural Will-O'-the-Wisp?" *Journal of Psychology*, 63:13–34.

Dube, S. C., 1958, *India's Changing Villages: Human Factors in Community Development*. Ithaca, N.Y.: Cornell University Press.

———, 1967, "A Note on Communication in Economic Development," in Daniel Lerner and Wilbur Schramm, eds., *Communication and Change in the Developing Countries*. Honolulu: East-West Center Press.

Dumazedier, Joffre, 1956, *Television and Rural Adult Education*. Paris: UNESCO.

Durkheim, Emile, 1962, *Suicide*, trans. by John Spaulding and George Simpson. London: Routledge.

Dye, Thomas R., "The Local-Cosmopolitan Dimension and the Study of Urban Politics," *Social Forces*, 41:239–246.

Dymond, Rosalind F., 1949, "A Scale for the Measurement of Empathic Ability," *Journal of Consulting Psychology*, 13:127–133.

Eaton, Joseph W., 1952, "Controlled Acculturation: A Survival Technique of Hutterites," *American Sociological Review*, 17:331–340.

Eister, Allan Wardell, 1962, "Critical Factors in the Modernization Process in West Pakistan," *Yearbook of the American Philosophical Society*, 362–365.

Elder, Glen H., 1965, "Role Relations, Sociocultural Environments, and Autocratic Family Ideology," *Sociometry*, 28:173–196.

Erasmus, Charles J., 1961, *Man Takes Control*. Minneapolis: University of Minnesota Press.

Erlich, D., and others, 1957, "Postdecision Exposure to Relevant Information," *Journal of Abnormal and Social Psychology*, 54:98–102.

Etzioni, Amitai, and Eva Etzioni, 1964, *Social Change: Sources, Patterns, and Consequences*. New York: Basic Books.

Fals Borda, Orlando, 1955, *Peasant Society in the Colombian Andes: A Sociological Study of Saucío*. Gainesville, Fla.: University of Florida Press.

———, 1960, *The Theory and Reality of Socio-Cultural Change in Colombia*. Bogotá: Universidad Nacional de Colombia, Monografia Sociología 2.

Farace, R., Vincent 1965, "Mass Communication, Political Participation and Other National Characteristics: A Factor Analytic Investigation," Paper presented at the Association for Education in Journalism, Lincoln, Neb.

———, 1966, "Mass Communication and National Development: Some Insights from Aggregate Analysis," in *Mass Communication and the Development of Nations*. Michigan State University, International Communication Institute.

———, and others 1967, *An Exploration of Factors Underlying the Economic, Modernization, and Communication Characteristics of Puerto Rican Farmers*, Michigan State University, Department of Communication Research Report 4.

Felicino, Gloria D., 1964, "Limits of Western Social Research Methods in the Philippines: The Need for Innovation," Paper presented at the International Development Institute, East-West Center, Honolulu.

Festinger, Leon, 1964, "Behavioral Support for Opinion Change," *Public Opinion Quarterly*, 28:404–418.

Firth, Raymond, 1956, *Elements of Social Organization*. London: Watts.

Fliegel, Frederick C., 1966, "Literacy and Exposure to Instrumental Information Among Farmers in Southern Brazil," *Rural Sociology*, 31:15–28.

——— and others 1967, *Innovation in India: The Success or Failure of Agricultural Development Programs in 108 Indian Villages*, Michigan State University, Department of Communication, Diffusion of Innovations Research Report 9.

Foley, Donald L., 1952, *Neighbors or Urbanites?* Rochester, N.Y.: University of Rochester, Studies of Metropolitan Rochester 2.

Ford, Thomas R., 1966, "Value Orientations of a Culture of Poverty: The Southern Appalachian Case," Paper presented at the American Home Economics Association Workship with Low-Income Families.

Ford Foundation Agricultural Production Team, 1959, *Report on India's Food Crisis and Steps to Meet It.* Delhi: Government of India.

Ford Foundation Mass Communication Study Team, 1963, *Report of the Mass Communication Study Team Sponsored by The Ford Foundation.* New Delhi: Indian Ministry of Information and Broadcasting.

Foster, George M., 1962, *Traditional Cultures and the Impact of Technological Change.* New York: Harper & Row.

———, 1965a, "Cultural Responses to Expressions of Envy in Tzintzuntzan," *Southwestern Journal of Anthropology,* 21:24–35.

———, 1965b, "Peasant Society and the Image of Limited Good." *American Anthropologist,* 67:293–315.

———, 1966, "Foster's Reply to Kaplan, Saler, and Bennett," *American Anthropologist,* 68:210–214.

———, 1967, *Tzintzuntzan: Mexican Peasants in a Changing World.* Boston: Little, Brown.

Fraser, T. M., 1961, "Achievement Motivation as a Factor in Rural Development: A Report on Research in Western Orissa," Unpublished paper, Haverford College.

Freed, Stanley A., 1957, "Suggested Type Societies in Acculturation Studies," *American Anthropologist,* 59:55–68.

Freeman, H. G., and G. G. Kassenbaum, 1956, "The Illiterate in American Society: Some General Hypotheses," *Social Forces,* 34:371–375.

Frey, Frederick W., 1964, "The Mass Media and the Peasant," Paper presented at the Association for Education in Journalism, Austin, Tex.

———, 1966, *The Mass Media and Rural Development in Turkey,* Cambridge, Massachusetts Institute of Technology, Center for International Studies, Rural Development Research Report 3.

Friedmann, Frederick G., 1960, *The Hoe and the Book: An Italian Experiment in Community Development.* Ithaca, N.Y.: Cornell University Press.

Galbraith, John Kenneth, 1962, *Economic Development in Perspective.* Cambridge, Mass.: Harvard University Press.

Gans, Herbert J., 1962, *The Urban Villagers: Group and Class in the Life of Italian-Americans.* New York: Free Press.

Gardner John W., 1964, *Self-Renewal: The Individual and the Innovative Society.* New York: Harper & Row.

Giffin, Kim, and Larry Ehrlich, 1963, "The Attitudinal Effects of a Group Discussion on a Proposed Change in Company Policy," *Speech Monographs,* 30: 377–379.

Glaser, Barney G., 1963, "The Local-Cosmopolitan Scientist," *American Journal of Sociology,* 69:249–259.

———, and Anselm L. Straus, 1967, *The Discovery of Grounded Theory: Strategies for Qualitative Research.* Chicago: Aldine.

Goldberg, Louis G., and others, 1965, "Local-Cosmopolitan: Unidimensional or Multidimensional," *American Journal of Sociology,* 70:704–410.

Golden, Hilda Hertz, 1955, "Literacy and Social Change in Underdeveloped Countries," *Rural Sociology,* 20:1–7.

Goldsen, Rose K., and Max Ralis, 1957, *Factors Related to Acceptance of Innovations in Bang Chan, Thailand,* Ithaca, N.Y. Cornell University, Department of Far Eastern Studies Data Paper 25.

Gompertz, Kenneth, 1960, "The Relation of Empathy to Effective Communication," *Journalism Quarterly,* 37:533–546.

Gould, Peter, 1964, "A Note on Research into the Diffusion of Development," *Journal of Modern African Studies,* 2:123–125.

Gouldner, Alvin W., 1957, "Cosmopolites and Locals: Toward an Analysis of Latent Social Roles," *Administrative Science Quarterly,* 2:281–306.

Gover, Robert, 1961, *One Hundred Dollar Misunderstanding.* New York: Ballentine.

Gray, William S., 1956, *The Teaching of Reading and Writing: An International Survey.* Paris: UNESCO.

Greenberg, Bradley S., and Edwin B. Parker, eds., 1965, *The Kennedy Assassination and the American Public: Social Communication in Crises.* Stanford, Calif.: Stanford University Press.

Gregg, Phillip M., and Arthur S. Banks, 1965, "Dimensions of Political Systems: Factor Analysis of a Cross-Polity Survey," *American Political Science Review,* 59:602–614.

Gross, Neal, 1948, "Cultural Variables in Rural Communities," *American Journal of Sociology,* 53:344–350.

Gullahorn, John T., and Jeanne E. Gullahorn, 1965, "Some Computer Applications in Social Science," *American Sociological Review,* 30: 353–365.

Guka-Thakurta, P., 1966, "Electronics as a Means of Mass Communication in India," *Gazette,* 12:317–323.

Gurr, Ted, 1967, *The Genesis of Civil Violence.* Princeton, N.J.: Princeton University, Center for International Affairs.

Guzman, German, and others, 1962, *La Violencia en Colombia.* Volume 1, Bogotá: Ediciones Tercer Mundo.

———, and others, 1964, *La Violencia en Colombia,* Volume II. Bogotá: Ediciones Tercer Mundo.

Hagen, Everett E., 1961, "Psychology's Role in Economic Development," *Science,* 134:1608–1609.

———, 1962, *On the Theory of Social Change: How Economic Growth Begins.* Howewood, Ill.: Dorsey Press.

Hägerstrand, Torsten, 1952, *The Propagation of Innovation Waves.* Lund, Sweden, Royal University of Lund, Lund Studies in Geography.

———, 1965a, "Quantitative Techniques for Analysis of the Spread of Information and Technology," in C. Arnold Anderson and Mary Jane Bowman, eds., *Education and Development.* Chicago: Aldine.

———, 1965b, "A Monte Carlo Approach to Diffusion," *European Journal of Sociology,* 6:43–66.

Hapgood, David, 1965, *Africa: From Independence to Tomorrow.* New York: Atheneum.

Hamuy, Eduardo, and others, 1958, *El Primer Satelite Artificial: Sus Efectos en la Opinion Publica.* Santiago, Chile, Instituto de Sociología.

Hare, A. Paul, 1961, "Computer Simulation of Interaction in Small Groups," *Behavioral Science,* 6:261–265.

Havens, A. Eugene, 1960, "Measuring the Localite-Cosmopolite Dimensions," Paper presented at the Rural Sociological Society, University Park, Pa.

———, 1963, "El Cambio en la Technología Agricola de Subachoque," in *Factors Sociales que Inciden en el Desarrollo Economico de la Hoya del Rio Subachoque.* Bogotá, Facultad de Sociología, Universidad Nacional de Colombia.

Hayes, Samuel P. Jr., 1966, *Evaluating Development Projects.* Paris: UNESCO.

Heberle, Rudolph, 1941, "The Application of Fundamental Concepts in Rural Community Studies," *Rural Sociology,* 6:203–215.

Hendry, James B., 1964, *The Small World of Khanh Haw.* Chicago: Aldine.

Herzog, William A., Jr., 1967a, *The Effect of Literacy Training on Modernization Variables,* Ph.D. thesis, Michigan State University.

———, 1967b, "Mass Media Credibility, Exposure, and Modernization in Rural Brazil," Paper presented at the Association for Education in Journalism, Boulder, Colo.

Hickey, Gerald Cannon, 1964, *Village in Vietnam.* New Haven, Conn.: Yale University Press.

Hillery, George A. Jr., 1961, "The Folk Village: A Comparative Analysis," *Rural Sociology*, 26:337–353.

Hiniker, Paul, 1965, *Chinese Attitudinal Reactions to Forced Compliance: A Cross-Cultural Experiment in the Theory of Cognitive Dissonance*, Massachusetts Institute of Technology, Center for International Studies, Monograph C/65-18.

———, 1966, "The Mass Media and Study Groups in Communist China," in *Mass Communication and the Development of Nations*, Michigan State University, International Communication Institute.

Homans, George C. 1961, *Social Behavior: Its Elementary Forms*. London: Routledge.

Hopper, David, 1957, *The Economic Organization in the Village of North Central India*, Ph.D. thesis, Ithica, N.Y., Cornell University.

Hubbell, Charles H., 1965, "An Input-Output Approach to Clique Identification," *Sociometry*, 28:377–399.

Hunt, Charles L., 1957, "Cultural Barriers to Point Four," in Lyle W. Shannon, ed., *Underdeveloped Areas: A Body of Readings and Research*. New York: Harper & Row.

Hursh, Gerald D., ed., (in process), *Survey Research Methods in Developing Nations*. Michigan State University, Department of Communication.

Hyman, Herbert H., and others, 1967, *Inducing Social Change in Developing Communities: An International Survey of Expert Advice*. Geneva: United Nations Institute for Social Development.

Hyman, Martin D., 1966, "Determining the Effects of Status Inconsistency," *Public Opinion Quarterly*, 30:120–129.

Ingersoll, Jasper, 1966, "Fatalism in Asia: Ole Myths and New Realities, Introduction," *Anthropology Quarterly*, 39:143–147.

Inkeles, Alex, 1967a, "Forward," in Howard Schuman, *Economic Development and Individual Change: A Social-Psychological Study of the Comilla Experiment in Pakistan*. Cambridge, Mass.: Harvard University, Occasional Papers in International Affairs 15.

———, 1967b, "Becoming Modern," Paper presented at Michigan State University.

Jacobs, Milton, and others, 1964, *The Study of Communication in Thailand with Emphasis on Word-of-Mouth Communication*. Washington, D.C.: American University, Special Operations Research Office Mimeo Report.

———, and others, 1966, "A Study of Key Communicators in Urban Thailand," *Social Forces*, 45:192–199.

Jacobson, Eugene, 1966, "International Development of Social Science Research Resources," *Background*, 10:150–162.

Jain, Navin C., 1965, *The Relation of Information Sources Use to the Farm Practice Adoption and Farmers' Characteristics in Waterloo County*, M.A. Thesis, Guelph, Canada: University of Guelph.

James, William, 1923, *Psychology: Briefer Course*. New York: Holt, Rinehart and Winston, Inc.

Junghare, Y. N., 1962, "Factors Influencing the Adoption of Farm Practices," *Indian Journal of Social Work*, 23:291–296.

Kagan, Jerome, 1959, "The Stability of TAT Fantasy and Stimulus Ambiguity," *Journal of Consulting Psychology*, 23:266–271.

Kahl, Joseph A., 1962, "Urbanizacão e Mundancas Ocupacionais no Brazil" (Urbanization and Occupational Change in Brazil), *America Latina*, 4:21–30.

———, 1968, *The Measurement of Modernism: A Study of Values in Brazil and Mexico*. Austin: University of Texas.

Kaplan, David, and Benson Saler, 1966, "Foster's 'Image of Limited Good': An Example of Anthropological Explanation," *American Anthropologist*, 68:202–206.

Karlsson, Georg, 1958, *Social Mechanisms: Studies in Sociological Theory*. Uppsala, Sweden: Almquist and Wilksells; and New York: Free Press.

Karpat, Kemel H.,1960, "Social Effects of Farm Mechanization in Turkish Villages," *Social Research*, 27:83–103.

Katz, Elihu, 1957, "The Two-Step Flow of Communication: An Up-to-Date Report on an Hypothesis," *Public Opinion Quarterly*, 21:61–78.

———, and Paul F. Lazarsfeld, 1955, *Personal Influence: The Part Played by People in the Flow of Mass Communications*. New York: Free Press.

Katz, Robert L., 1963, *Empathy: Its Nature and Uses*. New York: Free Press.

Keith, Robert F., 1966, *Communication Behavior and Change Orientation of Foreign Change Agents in Technical Training Programs*, M.A. Thesis, Michigan State University.

———, and others, 1966a, "Mass Media Exposure and Modernization Among Villagers in Three Developing Countries: Towards Cross-Cultural Generalizations," Paper presented at the Association for Education in Journalism, Iowa City, Iowa.

———, and others, 1966b, "Mass Media Exposure and Modernization Among Villagers in Three Developing Countries: Towards Cross-Cultural Generalizations," in *Mass Communication and the Development of Nations*, Michigan State University, International Communication Institute.

Kendall, P. L., and K. Wolf, 1949, "The Analysis of Deviant Cases," in Paul F. Lazarsfeld and Frank Stanton, eds., *Communications Research, 1948–1949*. New York: Harper & Row.

Kennedy, John G., 1966, " 'Peasant Society and the Image of Limited Good': A Critique," *American Anthropologist*, 68:1212–1225.

Klapper, Joseph T., 1960, *The Effects of Mass Communication*. New York; Free Press.

Klineberg, Otto, 1966, *The Human Dimension in International Relations*. New York: Holt, Rinehart and Winston, Inc.

Kluckhohn, Florence R., and Fred L. Strodtbeck, 1961, *Variations in Value Orientations*. New York: Harper & Row.

Kolb, David A., 1963, "Achievement Motivation Training for Underachieving High School Boys," Unpublished paper, Cambridge, Mass., Harvard University.

Kroeber, A. L., 1948, *Anthropology*. New York: Harcourt.

Kuo, Jeanne, 1968, *Predictors of Innovativeness as a Modernization Variable: An Exploratory Investigation Across Cultures*, M. A. thesis, Michigan State University.

Lane, Robert E., 1966, "The Decline of Politics and Ideology in a Knowledgeable Society," *American Sociological Review*, 31:649–662.

Lazarsfeld, Paul F., and Robert K. Merton, 1964, "Friendship as Social Process: A Substantive and Methodological Analysis," in Monroe Berger and others eds., *Freedom and Control in Modern Society*. New York: Octogon.

———, and others, 1944, *The People's Choice*. New York: Duell, Sloan, and Pearce; Meredith Press.

Lee, Alfred McClung, 1965, "Preface," in J. A. Ponsioen, *The Analysis of Social Change Reconsidered: A Sociological Study*. The Hague: Mouton.

Lenski, Gerhard E., 1954, "Status Crystallization: A Non-Vertical Dimension of Social Status," *American Sociological Review*, 19:405–413.

Lerner, Daniel, 1953, "A Scale Pattern of Opinion Correlates: Communication Networks, Media Exposure, and Concomitant Responses," *Sociometry*, 16:266–271.

———, 1958, *The Passing of Traditional Society: Modernizing the Middle East*. New York: Free Press.

———, 1963, "Toward a Communication Theory of Modernization," in Lucien W. Pye, ed., *Communications and Political Development*. Princeton, N.J. Princeton University Press.

———, 1964a, "Literacy and Initiative in Village Development," in MIT Center for International Studies, *Rural Development Research Report*, Cambridge, Mass.: MIT-CIS Mimeo Report.

————, 1964b, "Basic Problems in the Contemporary Transformation of Traditional Societies," in William T. DeBary and A. T. Embree, eds., *Approaches to Asian Civilizations*. New York: Colombia University Press.

————, 1965, "Enlightenment and Communication," Paper presented at the Symposium on Comparative Theories of Social Change, Ann Arbor, Mich.: Foundation for Research on Human Behavior.

————, 1967a, "Communication and the Prospects of Innovative Development," in Daniel Lerner and Wilbur Schramm, eds., *Communication and Change in the Developing Countries*. Honolulu: East-West Center Press.

————, 1967b, "International Cooperation and Communication in National Development," in Daniel Lerner and Wilbur Schramm, eds., *Communication and Change in the Developing Countries*. Honolulu: East-West Center Press.

————, and David Riesman, 1955, "Self and Society: Reflections on Some Turks in Transition," *Explorations*, 5:67–80.

Leslie, Charles M., 1960, *Now We Are Civilized: A Study of the World View of the Zapotec Indians of Agitta, Oaxaca*. Detroit: Wayne State University Press.

Levi, Carlo, 1947, *Christ Stopped at Eboli*. New York: Farrar, Straus.

Levine, Jacob, and John Butler, 1952, "Lecture vs. Group Decision in Changing Behavior," *Journal of Applied Psychology*, 36:29–33.

LeVine, Robert A., 1966, *Dreams and Deeds: Achievement Motivation in Nigeria*. Chicago: University of Chicago Press.

Lewin, Kurt, 1958, "Group Decision and Social Change," in Eleanor E. Maccoby and others, eds., *Readings in Social Psychology*. New York: Holt, Rinehart, and Winston, Inc.

Lewis, Oscar, 1951, *Life in a Mexican Village: Tepoztlan Re-Studied*. Urbana, Ill.: University of Illinois Press.

————, 1960a, "Some of My Best Friends Are Peasants," *Human Organization*, 19:180–183.

————, 1960b, *Tepoztlan: Village in Mexico*. New York: Holt, Rinehart and Winston. Inc.

————, 1961, *The Children of Sanchez: Autobiography of a Mexican Family*. New York: Random House.

————, 1962, *Five Families: Mexican Case Studies in the Culture of Poverty*. New York: Wiley.

————, 1964a, *Pedro Martinez: A Mexican Peasant and His Family*. New York: Random House.

————, 1964b, "The Culture of Poverty," in John J. TePaske and Sydney Nettleton Fisher, eds., *Explosive Forces in Latin America*. Columbus, Ohio: The Ohio State University Press.

Lindzey, Gardner, 1961, *Projective Techniques and Cross-Cultural Research*. New York: Appleton-Century-Crofts.

————, and Shirley H. Heinemann, 1955, "Thematic Apperception Test: Individual and Group Administration," *Journal of Personality*, 23:34–55.

Lippitt, Ronald, and others, 1958, *Dynamics of Planned Change*. New York: Harcourt, Brace.

Lipps, Theodor, 1909, *Leitfaden der Psychologie*. Leipzig: Engelmann.

Lipset, Seymour Martin, 1960, *Political Man: The Social Bases of Politics*. New York: Doubleday.

Loomis, Charles P., 1967, "In Praise of Conflict and Its Resolution," *American Sociological Review*, 32:875–890.

Lopreato, Joseph, 1962, "Interpersonal Relations in Peasant Society: The Peasant's View," *Human Organization*, 21:21–24.

Louis, Roger, and Joseph Rovan, 1955, *Television and Tele-Clubs in Rural Communities: An Experiment in France*. Paris: UNESCO, Reports and Papers on Mass Communication 16.

Machiavelli, Niccolo, 1961, *The Prince*. Baltimore, Penquin.

MacLean, Malcolm S. Jr., and others, 1959, "Mass Media Behavior of Locals and Cosmopolitans," Paper presented at the Association for Education in Journalism.

McClelland, David C., 1961, *The Achieving Society*. Princeton, N.J.: Van Nostrand.

———, 1963a, "National Character and Economic Growth in Turkey and Iran," in Lucien W. Pye, ed., *Communications and Political Development*. Princeton, N.J.: Princeton University Press.

———, 1963b, "The Achievement Motive in Economic Growth," in Bert F. Hoselitz and Wilbert E. Moore, eds., *Industrialization and Society*. Paris: UNESCO.

———, 1964a, "Changing Values for Progress," Unpublished paper, Harvard University.

———, 1964b, "Toward a Theory of Motive Acquisition," Unpublished paper, Harvard University.

———, 1964c, "The Achievement Motive in Economic Growth," in David E. Novack and Robert Lehachman, eds., *Development and Society: The Dynamics of Economic Change*. New York: St. Martin's.

———, and others, 1953, *The Achievement Motive*. New York: Appleton-Century-Crofts.

———, and others, 1958, "The Effect of the Need for Achievement on Thematic Apperception," in J. W. Atkinson, ed., *Motives in Fantasy, Action and Society*. Princeton, N.J.: Van Nostrand.

McCrone, Donald J., and Charles F. Cnudde, 1967, "Toward a Communication Theory of Democratic Political Development: A Causal Model," *American Political Science Review*, 61:72–79.

McLeod, Jack M., and others, 1967, "Mass Media Exposure and Political Knowledge in Quito, Ecuador," Paper presented at the Association for Education in Journalism, Boulder, Colo.

McLuhan, Marshall, 1962, *The Gutenberg Galaxy*. Toronto: University of Toronto Press.

———, 1964, *Understanding Media: The Extensions of Man*. New York: McGraw-Hill.

McNelly, John T., 1966, "Mass Communication and the Climate for Modernization in Latin America," *Journal of Inter-American Studies*, 8:345–357.

McNemar, Quinn, 1962, *Psychological Statistics*. New York: Wiley.

McQuitty, Louis L., 1957, "Elementary Linkage Analysis for Isolating Orthogonal and Oblique Types and Typal Relevancies," *Educational and Psychological Measurement*, 17:207–229.

Madigan, Frances C., 1962, "Predicting Receptivity to Community Development Innovations," *Current Anthropology*, 3:207–208.

Malinowski, Bronislaw, 1948, *Magic, Science and Religion and Other Essays*. Boston: Beacon.

Mandelbaum, David G., 1963, "Foward," in William H. Wiser and Charlotte Viall Wiser, *Behind Mud Walls, 1930–1960*. Berkeley, Calif.: University of California Press.

Marco Surveys, Ltd., 1965, *A Baseline Survey of Factors Affecting Agricultural Development in Three Areas of Kenya*. Nairobi; Kenya Ministry of Labour and Social Services.

Marsh, Robert M., 1953, *Marginal Projectivity and Communication Behavior in Modern Syria*, M.A. thesis, Columbia University.

Martin, Ferrer S., 1951, *Muestra Piloto de las Escuelas Radiofonicas Rurales*. Bogotá: Acción Cultural Popular, Escuelas Radiofonicas de Sutatenza.

Marx, Karl, and Frederick Engels, 1933, *Selected Works*, Volume 1. New York: International Publishers.

Mason, Robert G., 1964, "The Use of Information Sources in the Process of Adoption," *Rural Sociology*, 29:40–52.

Mead, George H., 1934, *Mind, Self and Society*. Chicago: University of Chicago Press.

Mead, Margaret, 1955, *Cultural Patterns and Technical Change*. New York: Mentor.

———, 1964, *Continuities in Cultural Evolution*. New Haven, Conn.: Yale University Press.

Mendez, Alfredo D., and Frederick B. Waisanen, 1964, "Some Correlates of Functional Literacy," Paper presented at the Ninth Congress of the Inter-American Society of Psychologists, Miami Beach, Fla.

Menefee, Selden, and Audrey Menefee, 1965, "An Experiment in Communications in Four Indian Villages," *Indian Journal of Social Research*, 6:148–158.

———, and Audrey Menefee, 1967, "A Country Weekly Proves Itself in India," *Journalism Quarterly*, 44:114–117.

Menzel, Herbert, 1957, "Public and Private Conformity Under Different Conditions of Acceptance in the Group," *Journal of Abnormal and Social Psychology*, 55:398–402.

Merei, Ferenc, 1949, "Group Leadership and Institutionalization," *Human Relations*, 2:23–39.

Merton, Robert K., 1957, *Social Theory and Social Structure*. New York: Free Press.

Meyren, Delbert T., 1962, "The Rural Communications Media as a Determinant of the Diffusion of Information about Improved Farming Practices in Mexico," Paper presented at the Rural Sociological Society, Washington, D.C.

Miller, Gerald R., 1966, *Speech Communications: A Behavioral Approach*. Indianapolis: Bobbs-Merrill.

Mills, C. Wright, 1959, *The Sociological Imagination*. New York: Grove.

Milne, A. A., 1926, *Winnie-The Pooh*. New York: Dutton.

Miner, Horace, 1953, "The Folk-Urban Continuum," *American Sociological Review*, 17:529–437

Misra, B. D., 1967, "Correlates of Males' Attitudes Toward Family Planning," in Donald J. Bogue, ed., *Sociological Contributions to Family Planning Research*, University of Chicago, Community and Family Study Center.

MIT Center for International Studies, 1964, *Rural Development Research Report: Preliminary Report*, Cambridge, Mass.: MIT, CIS.

Mitchell, James V. Jr., 1961, "Analysis of the Factorial Dimensions of the Achievement Motivation Construct," *Journal of Educational Psychology*, 52:179–181.

Mitchell, Robert E., 1964, "Methodological Notes on a Theory of Status Crystallization," *Public Opinion Quarterly*, 28:315–325.

Morrison, Denton E., 1962, *A Conceptual and Empirical Study in Measurement Validity*, Ph.D. thesis, Madison, University of Wisconsin.

———, 1964, "Achievement Motivation of Farm Operators: A Measurement Study," *Rural Sociology*, 29:367–384.

Mosher, Arthur T., 1966, *Getting Agriculture Moving: Essentials for Development and Modernization*. New York: Praeger.

Moss, Louis, 1955, "The Evaluation of Fundamental Education," *International Social Science Bulletin*, 7:398–417.

Moulik, T. K., and others, 1966, "Predictive Values of Some Factors of Adoption of Nitrogenous Fertilizers by North Indian Farmers," *Rural Sociology*, 31:467–447.

Neal, Arthur G., and Solomon Rettig, 1963, "Dimensions of Alienation Among Manual and Non-Manual Workers," *American Sociological Review*, 28:599–608.

———, and Melvin Seeman, 1964, "Organizations and Powerlessness: A Test of the Mediation Hypotheses," *American Sociological Review*, 29:216–226.

Neill, Ralph E., 1963, *Achievement Motivation Among Ohio Farmers*, M.S. thesis, Columbus, Ohio: The Ohio State University.

———, and Everett M. Rogers, 1963, *Measuring Achievement Motivation Among Farmers*, Columbus, Ohio Agricultural Experiment Station, Departmental Bulletin Series AE 346.

Neurath, Paul M., 1960, *Radio Farm Forums in India*. Delhi: Government of India Press.

———, 1962, "Radio Farm Forum as a Tool of Change in Indian Villages," *Economic Development and Cultural Change*, 10:275–283.

Newcomb, Theodore M., 1953, "An Approach to the Study of Communicative Acts," *Psychological Review*, 60: 393–404.

Nicol, John, and others, 1954, *Canada's Farm Radio Forum*. Paris: UNESCO.

Niehoff, Arthur, 1964, "Theravada Buddhism: A Vehicle for Technical Change," *Human Organization*, 23:108–112.

———, 1966a, *A Casebook of Social Change*. Chicago: Aldine.

———, 1966b, "Discussion of Fatalism in Asia: Old Myths and New Realities," *Anthropology Quarterly*, 29: 244–253.

———, 1967, "Intra-Group Communication and Induced Change," Unpublished paper, Alexandria, Virginia, HUMRRO.

———, and J. Charvel Anderson, 1965, "Peasant Fatalism and Socio-Economic Innovation," *Human Organization*, 25:273–283.

Norbeck, Edward, 1965, *Changing Japan*. New York: Holt, Rinehart and Winston, Inc.

Olsen, James, 1965, "Instructional Materials for Functionally Illiterate Adults," *Adult Leadership*, 13:275–305.

Park, Robert E., 1928, "Human Migration and the Marginal Man," *American Journal of Sociology*, 33:881–893.

Parsons, Talcott, 1961, "Some Considerations on the Theory of Social Change," *Rural Sociology*, 26:219–239.

Passin, Herbert, and John W. Bennett, 1943, "Changing Agricultural Magic in Southern Illinois: A Systematic Analysis of Folk-Urban Transition," *Social Forces*, 22:98–106.

Paul, Benjamin D., 1955, *Health, Culture and Community: Case Studies of Public Reactions to Health Programs*. New York: Russell Sage.

Pelto, Pertti J., 1960, "Innovation in an Individualistic Society," Paper presented at the American Anthropological Association.

Phillips, Herbert P., 1965, *Thai Peasant Personality: The Patterning of Interpersonal Behavior in the Village of Bang Chan*. Berkeley, Calif.: University of California Press.

Pierce, Joe E., 1964, *Life in a Turkish Village*. New York: Holt, Rinehart and Winston, Inc.

Piker, Steven, 1966, "The Image of Limited Good: Comments on an Exercise in Description and Interpretation," *American Anthropologist*, 68:1201–1211.

Pitts, Forrest R., 1964, "Introductory Remarks at the Working Conference on Spatial Simulation Systems," University of Pittsburgh.

Planning Research and Action Institute, 1962, *The Dehati Radio Goshthi Programme: An Evaluation of Its Impact and Organization*. Lucknow, India: Planning Research and Action Institute.

———, 1966, *Report on Family Planning Communication Action Research Project*. Lucknow, India: Planning Research and Action Institute.

Pool, Ithiel de Sola, 1963, "The Mass Media and Politics in the Modernization Process," in Lucian W. Pye, ed., *Communications and Political Development*. Princeton, N.J.: Princeton University Press.

———, 1966, "The Necessity for Social Scientists Doing Research for Governments," *Background*, 10:111–122.

————, 1967, "The Mass Media and Politics in the Modernization Process," in Daniel Lerner and Wilbur Schramm, eds., *Communication and Change in the Developing Countries*. Honolulu: East-West Center Press.

————, and Robert Abelson, 1961, "The Simulmatics Project," *Public Opinion Quarterly*, 25:167–183.

————, and others, 1964, *Candidates, Issues, and Strategies: A Computer Simulation of the 1960 Presidential Election*. Cambridge, Mass.: MIT Press.

Portocarrero, Cesar A., 1966, *Empathy and Modernization in Colombia*, M.A. thesis, Michigan State University.

Powdermaker, Hortense, 1962, *Copper Town: Changing Africa*. New York: Harper & Row.

President's Science Advisory Committee, 1967, *The World Food Problem*, Volume 1, Washington, D.C.: U.S. Government Printing Office.

Priess, Jack J., 1954, *Functions of Relevant Power and Authority Groups in the Evaluation of County Agent Performance*, Ph.D. thesis, Michigan State University.

Pye, Lucien W., 1963, *Communications and Political Development*. Princeton, N.J.: Princeton University Press.

Radke, Marian, and Dana Klisurich, 1947, "Experiments in Changing Food Habits," *Journal of American Dietetics Association*, 23:430–409.

Rahim, S. A., 1961, *Diffusion and Adoption of Agricultural Practices: A Study of Patterns of Communication, Diffusion and Adoption of Improved Agricultural Practices in a Village in East Pakistan*, Comilla, Pakistan Academy for Village Development.

————, 1966, "A Factor Analysis of Modernization Variables Among Pakistani Peasants," Unpublished paper, Michigan State University, Department of Communication.

Ramos, Eduardo, 1966, *Client-Change Agent Relationships in Three Colombian Villages*, M.A. thesis, Michigan State University.

Ramsey, Charles E., and others, 1959, "Values and the Adoption of Practices," *Rural Sociology*, 24:35–47.

Rao, Y. V. Lakshmana, 1963, *Communication and Development: A Study of Two Indian Villages*, Ph.D. thesis, University of Minnesota.

————, 1966, *Communication and Development: A Study of Two Indian Villages*. Minneapolis: University of Minnesota Press.

Redfield, Robert, 1941, *The Folk Culture of Yucatan*. Chicago: University of Chicago Press.

————, 1956, *Peasant Society and Culture*. Chicago: University of Chicago Press.

Reichel-Dolmatoff, Geraldo, and Alicia Reichel-Dolmatoff, 1961, *The People of Aritama: The Cultural Personality of a Colombian Mestizo Village*. Chicago: University of Chicago Press.

Rhoads, William G., and Anison C. Piper, 1963, *Use of Radiophonic Teaching in Fundamental Education*, Williamstown, Mass., Williams College, Roper Public Opinion Research Center.

Riesman, David, 1952, *Faces in the Crowd: Individual Studies in Character and Politics*. New Haven, Conn.: Yale University Press.

Rogers, Everett M., 1958, "A Conceptual Variable Analysis of Technological Change," *Rural Sociology*, 23:136–145.

————, 1962, *Diffusion of Innovations*. New York: Free Press.

————, 1964a, "Achievement Motivation and the Adoption of Farm Innovations in Colombia," Paper presented at the Society for Applied Anthropology, San Juan, Puerto Rico.

————, 1964b, "Comparative Study of the Process of Innovation: Information Sources in the Adoption Process for 2,4-D Weed Spray in Three Colombian Peasant Neighborhoods," Paper presented at the First Interamerican Research Symposium on the Role of Communications in Agricultural Development, Mexico City.

————, 1965a, "Attitudes, Values, and Motivations of Subsistence Farmers: Toward a Subculture of Peasantry," Paper presented at the Conference on Subsistence and Peasant Economics, University of Hawaii, East-West Center.

————, 1965b, "Mass Media Exposure and Modernization Among Colombian Peasants," *Public Opinion Quarterly*, 29:614–625.

————, 1966a, *Elementos de Cambio Social en America Latina: Difusíon de Innovaciones*. Bogatá: Ediciones Tercer Mundo and Universidad Nacional de Colombia, Facultad de Sociología, Monograficas Sociologicas 23.

————, 1966b, "Mass Media Exposure and Modernization among Colombian Peasants," in *Mass Communication and the Development of Nations*, East Lansing, Michigan State University, International Communication Institute.

————, 1968, "Motivations, Valves, and Attitudes of Subsistence Farmers: Toward a Subculture of Peasantry," in Clifton R. Wharton, Jr., ed., *Subsistence Agriculture and Economic Development*. Chicago: Aldine.

————, and George M. Beal, 1958, *Reference Group Influences in the Adoption of Agricultural Technology*, Ames, Iowa State University, Department of Economics and Sociology Mimeo Bulletin.

————, and Elssy Bonilla de Ramos, 1965, "Prediction of the Adoption of Innovations: A Progress Report," Paper presented at the Rural Sociological Society, Chicago.

————, and William Herzog, 1966, "Functional Literacy among Colombian Peasants," *Economic Development and Cultural Change*, 14:190–203.

————, and Wicky L. Meyen, 1965, "Communication Sources for 2,4-D Weed Spray Among Colombian Peasants," *Rural Sociology*, 30:213–219.

————, with Ralph E. Neill, 1966, *Achievement Motivation Among Colombian Farmers*, Michigan State University, Department of Communication, Diffusion of Innovations Research Report 5.

————, and others, 1964, "Measuring Achievement Motivation Among Colombian Farmers," Paper presented at the Ninth Congress of the Inter-American Society of Psychologists, Miami Beach, Fla.

————, with Floyd Shoemaker, 1968, *Communication of Innovations: A Cross-Cultural Approach*. New York: Free Press.

————, and Johannes C. van Es, 1964, *Opinion Leadership in Traditional and Modern Colombian Peasant Communities*, Michigan State University, Department of Communication, Diffusion of Innovations Research Report 2.

Rokeach, Milton, 1960, *The Open and Closed Mind: Investigations with the Nature of Belief Systems and Personality Systems*. New York: Basic Books.

Rosen, Bernard C., 1961, "Family Structure and Achievement Motivation," *American Sociological Review*, 26:574–585.

————, 1964, "The Achievement Syndrome and Economic Growth in Brazil," *Social Forces*, 43:341–354.

Rostow, Walter W., 1961, *The Stages of Economic Growth*. New York: Cambridge.

————, 1964, *View from the Seventh Floor*. New York: Harper & Row.

Ryan, Bryce, and Neal C. Gross, 1943, "The Diffusion of Hybrid Seed Corn in Two Iowa Communities," *Rural Sociology*, 8:15–24.

Sangree, Walter H., 1952, *Mel Hyblacum: A Study of the People of Middletown of Sicilian Extraction*, M.A. thesis, Wesleyan University.

Sariola, Sakari, 1965, "Fatalism and Anomie: Components of Rural-Urban Differences," *Kansas Journal of Sociology*, 1:188–196.

Sawhney, Man Mohan, 1966, "Farm Practice Adoption and the Use of Information Sources and Media in a Rural Community in India," Paper presented at the Rural Sociological Society, Miami Beach, Fla.

Schatzman, Leonard, and Anselm Strauss, 1955, "Social Class and Modes of Communication," *American Journal of Sociology*, 60:329–338.

Schneider, Louis, and Svenne Lysgaard, 1953, "The Deferred Gratification Pattern: A Preliminary Study," *American Sociological Review*, 18:142–149.

Schnore, Leo F., 1961, "The Statistical Measurement of Urbanization and Economic Development," *Land Economics*, 37:229–245.

Schramm, Wilbur, 1963, "Communication Development and the Development Process," in Lucien W. Pye, ed., *Communications and Political Development*, Princeton, N.J.: Princeton University Press.

———, 1964, *Mass Media and National Development*, Stanford, Calif.: Stanford University Press.

———, and others, 1967a, *The New Media: Memo to Educational Planners*. Paris: UNESCO.

———, and others, 1967b, *New Educational Media in Action: Case Studies for Planners*, Volume 1. Paris: UNESCO.

Schultz, Theodore W., 1964, *Transforming Traditional Agriculture*. New Haven, Conn.: Yale University Press.

Schuman, Howard, and others 1967, "Social Psychological Effects and Noneffects of Literacy in a New Nation," *Economic Development and Cultural Change*, 16:1–14.

Seeman, Melvin, 1959, "On the Meaning of Alienation," *American Sociological Review*, 24:783–791

Sen, Lalit K., 1962, *Social Dimensions of Modernization in Four Indian Villages*, Ph.D. thesis, Madison, Wis.: University of Wisconsin,

———, and Prodipto Roy, 1966, *Awareness of Community Development in Village India*, Hyderabad, India, National Institute of Community Development.

Shanin, Teodor, 1966, "The Peasantry as a Political Factor," *Sociological Review*, 14:5–27.

Shibutani, Tamotsu, 1966, *Improvised News: A Sociological Study of Rumor*. Indianapolis: Bobbs, Merrill.

Simpson, Dick, 1964, "The Congruence of the Political, Social and Economic Aspects of Development," *International Development Review*, 6:21–25.

Smith, Dick Horton, and Alex Inkeles, 1966, "The OM Scale: A Comparative Socio-Psychological Measure of Individual Modernity," *Sociometry*, 29:353–377.

Smith, Henry Clay, 1966, *Sensitivity to People*. New York: McGraw-Hill.

Smith, T. Lynn, 1956, "Values Held by People in Latin America Which Affect Technical Cooperation," *Rural Sociology*, 21:68–75.

Sonquist, John A., and James N. Morgan, 1964, *The Detection of Interaction Effects: A Report on a Computer Program for the Selection of Optional Combinations of Explanatory Variables*, University of Michigan, Survey Research Center Monograph 35.

Spain, David Howard, 1962, *The Culture of Poverty in a West Virginia Coal Camp*, M.A. thesis, Ohio State University.

Spector, Paul, and others, 1963, *Communication and Motivation in Community Development: An Experiment*. Washington, D.C., Institute for International Services.

Spicer, Edward H., ed., 1952, *Human Problems in Technological Change*. New York: Russell Sage.

Srinivas, M. N., 1952, *Religion and Society Among the Coorgs of South India*. New York: Oxford.

———, 1962, *Caste in Modern India and other Essays*. Bombay: Asia Publishing House.

———, 1966, *Social Change in Modern India*. Berkley, Calif: University of California Press.

Stanfield, J. David, (1968), *Trust and National Development*, Ph.D. thesis, Michigan State University.

————, and others, 1965, "Computer Simulation of Innovation Diffusion: An Illustration from a Latin American Village," Paper presented at the American Sociological Association and the Rural Sociological Society, Chicago.

Stewart, Don, and Thomas Hoult, 1959, "A Social-Psychological Theory of the Authoritarian Personality," *American Journal of Sociology*, 65:274–279.

Stickley, S. Thomas, 1964, *Socio-Economic Correlates of Levels of Living Among Farmers in Three Colombian Neighborhoods*, M.S. thesis, The Ohio State University.

————, and others, 1967, *Levels of Living Among Farmers in Three Colombian Neighborhoods*, Columbus, Ohio State University, Department of Agricultural Economics and Rural Sociology, Mimeo Bulletin AE 414.

Stirling, Paul, 1965, *Turkish Village*. London: Weidenfeld and Nicolsen.

Stonequist, Everett V., 1937, *The Marginal Man: A Study in Personality and Culture Conflict*. New York: Scribner.

Strassman, Paul, 1964, "The Industrialist," in John J. Johnson, ed., *Continuity and Change in Latin America*. Stanford, Calif.: Stanford University Press.

Strunk, Orlo, 1957, "Empathy: A Review of Theory and Research," *Psychological Newsletter*, 9:47–57.

Stuckert, Robert P., 1958, "A Configurational Approach to Prediction," *Sociometry*, 21:225–237.

Stycos, J. Mayone, 1952, "Patterns of Communication in a Rural Greek Village," *Public Opinion Quarterly*, 16:59–70.

Subcommittee on International Organizations and Movements of the U.S. House of Representatives, 1967, *Modern Communications and Foreign Policy*. Washington, D.C.: U.S. Government Printing Office, Report 5.

Tannous, Afif I., 1956, "Technical Exchange and Cultural Values: Case of the Middle East," *Rural Sociology*, 21:76–79.

Tarde, Gabriel, 1903, *The Laws of Imitation*, New York: Holt, Rinehart and Winston.

Tax, Sol, (1963), *Penny Capitalism*, Chicago, University of Chicago Press.

Taylor, Charles L., 1967, "Communications Development and Political Stability," Paper presented at the Association for Education in Journalism, Boulder, Colo.

Teune, Henry, 1966, "Advantages and Problems of International Collaboration in Social Science Research," *Background*, 10:177–192.

Thomas, W. I., and Florian Znaniecki, 1918, *The Polish Peasant in Europe and America*. Chicago: University of Chicago Press.

Thompson, W. E., and J. E. Horton, 1960, "Political Alienation as a Force in Political Action," *Social Forces*, 38:190–195.

Thurstone, L. L., 1947, *Multiple Factor Analysis: A Development and Expansion of the Vectors of the Mind*. Chicago, University of Chicago Press.

Tiedemann, Clifford E., and Carlton S. Van Doren, 1964, *The Diffusion of Hybrid Seed Corn in Iowa: A Spatial Simulation Model*, Michigan State University, Institute for Community Development and Services, Technical Bulletin B-44.

Toennies, Ferdinand, 1967, *Community and Society*, trans. by Charles P. Loomis. East Lansing: Michigan State University Press.

Tolstoy, Leo, 1962, *Fables and Fairy Tales*. New York (Reprinted from Second Reader, 1872).

Torres, Camilio, and Berta Corredor, 1961, *Las Escuelas Radiofonicas de Sutatenza*, Colombia, Bogotá, Oficina Internacional de Investigaciones Sociales de FERES.

Troldahl, Verling C., and Frederic A. Powell, 1965, "A Short-Form Dogmatism Scale for Use in Field Studies," *Social Forces*, 44:211–214.

Tumin, Melvin, M., and Arnold S. Feldman, 1956, "Status, Perspective and Achievement: Education and Social Class Structure in Puerto Rico," *American Sociological Review*, 21:464–472.

Uleman, James S., 1966, "*N* Influence, A New Power-Related Motive: Development and Validation of a TAT Measure," Paper presented at the Midwestern Psychological Association.

UNESCO, 1961, *Mass Media in the Developing Countries: A UNESCO Report to the United Nations.* Paris.

United Nations Economic and Social Council, 1963, *World Campaign for Universal Literacy.* New York: United Nations Economic and Social Council Document E/3771.

USDA, 1964, *The World Food Budget, 1970.* Washington, D.C.: USDA Foreign Agricultural Economic Report 19.

Useem, John, and others, 1963, "Men in the Middle of the Third Culture," *Human Organization,* 22:169–179.

Van Es, Johannes C., 1964, *Opinion Leadership in Colombian Veredas with Different Norms on Social Change,* M.S. Thesis, The Ohio State University.

Wagley, Charles, 1964, "The Peasant," in John J. Johnson, ed., *Continuity and Change in Latin America.* Stanford, Calif.: Stanford University Press.

Waisanen, F. B., and Jerome T. Durlak, 1966, "Mass Media Use, Information Source Evaluation and Perceptions of Self and Nation," Paper presented at the American Sociological Association, Miami Beach. Fla.

Warden, Sandra Ardah, 1964, *The Local-Cosmopolitan Dimension of Individual Value Orientation: A Study,* M.A. Thesis, Michigan State Universiy.

Webb, Eugene J., and others, 1966, *Unobtrusive Measures: Nonreactive Research in the Social Sciences.* Skokie, Ill.: Rand McNally.

Weber, Max, 1930, *The Protestant Ethic and the Spirit of Capitalism.* New York: Scribner.

Westley, Bruce H., and Malcolm S. MacLean, Jr. 1957, "A Conceptual Model for Communication Research," *Journalism Quarterly,* 34:31–38.

Wharton, Clifton R., Jr., 1963, "The Economic Meaning of 'Subsistence'," *Malayan Economic Review,* 8:46–58.

Whiting, Gordon C., 1967a, *Empathy, Mass Media, and Modernization: A Study of Rural Brazil,* Ph.D. thesis, Michigan State University.

———, 1967b, *Empathy, Mass Media, and Modernization in Rural Brazil,* East Lansing, Michigan State University, Department of Communication, Diffusion of Innovations Technical Report 1.

———, 1967, *Innovation in Brazil: Success and Failure of Agricultural Programs in 76 Minas Gerais Communities,* Michigan State University, Department of Communication, Diffusion of Innovations Research Report 7.

Whittenbarger, Robert, and Eugenio Maffei, 1966, "Innovativeness and Related Factors in a Rural Colombian Community," Paper presented at the Rural Sociological Society, Miami Beach.

Wiser, William H., and Charlotte Viall Wiser, 1963, *Behind Mud Walls, 1930–1960.* Berkeley, Calif.: University of California Press.

Wish, John J., 1967, *Diffusion of Food Marketing Innovations in Puerto Rico,* Ph.D. thesis, East Lansing, Michigan State University.

Wolf, Eric R., 1955, "Types of Latin American Peasantry: A Preliminary Discussion," *American Anthropologist,* 57:452–471.

———, 1956, "Aspects of Group Relations in a Complex Society: Mexico," *American Anthropologist,* 58:1065–1078.

Wolff, Kurt H., 1950, *The Sociology of Georg Simmel.* New York: Free Press.

Wolpert, Julian, 1967, "A Regional Simulation Model of Information Diffusion," *Public Opinion Quarterly,* 30:597–608.

Wright, Peter C., 1965, *An Evaluation of Plan Jutiapa, A Pilot Literacy Program,* University of South Florida, Mimeo Report.

————, and others, 1967, *The Impact of a Literacy Program in a Guatemalan Ladino Peasant Community*, University of South Florida, College of Education, Mimeo report.

Yadav, Dharam P., 1967, *A Comparative Analysis of Communication Structure and Innovation Diffusion in Two Indian Villages*, Ph.D. thesis, Michigan State University.

Young, Frank W., and Ruth C. Young, 1962, "The Sequence and Direction of Community Growth: A Cross-Cultural Generalization," *Rural Sociology*, 27:374–386.

Yuill, Robert S., 1964, *A Simulation Study of Barrier Effects in Spatial Diffusion Problems*, Northwestern University, Department of Geography, Technical Report 1.

Zetterberg, Hans L., 1965, *On Theory and Verification in Sociology*. Totowa, N.J.: Bedminister Press.

NAME INDEX

Abegglen, James C., 254
Abell, Helen C., 135
Abelson, Robert, 347
Abrahamson, Mark, 158
ACPO, 78
Adams, Don, 169
Aesop, 35
Agee, James, 68
Allahabad Agricultural Institute, 181
Allport, G. W., 197
Almond, Gabriel A., 69, 378
Anderson, J. Charvel, 55, 277, 278, 279, 289, 301
Andrews, John, 252
Arensberg, Conrad M., 277, 313, 314
Ascroft, Joseph R., 65, 75, 77, 316, 325, 329, 331, 333
Atkinson, Brooks, 169
Ayrout, Henry H., 36

Bailey, F. G., 20, 27, 29
Banfield, Edward C., 27, 32, 35
Banks, Arthur S., 69, 322
Barnett, Homer G., 128, 313
Barzini, Luigi, 30
Beal, George H., 130, 131, 211, 302
Bebermeyer, James P., 99, 134
Becker, Howard, 9, 148
Bell, Graham B., 213
Belshaw, Cyril S., 20
Bennett, John, 28
Bennis, Warren G., 169
Bequiraj, Mehmet, 37
Berelson, Bernard, 374
Berlew, David E., 246
Berlo, David K., 49, 196
Bisbee, Eleanor, 150
Black, C. E., 3, 15
Bonilla de Ramos, Elssy, 64, 273, 280, 289, 308, 309
Bonilla, Frank, 41
Bose, Santi P., 39, 235
Bostian, Lloyd R., 77
Bowden, Leonard W., 348
Bradburn, Norman M., 246, 254
Briones, Guillermo, 78, 79, 115
Brown, Lawrence A., 348

Browning, Robert, 11
Brunner, Edmund deS., 148
Bunge, William, 347
Burnet, Mary, 69, 71
Burris, R., 247
Butler, John, 143

Canfield, A. A., 103
Cantril, Hadley, 225, 379
Caplow, Theodore, 9, 69
Carlsson, Gosta, 43
Carothers, J. O., 71, 72
Carstairs, G. Morris, 27, 32, 33
Carter, Roy E., Jr., 102, 103
Cassier, Henry R., 136, 137
Chattopadhyay, S. N., 303
Chou, Theresa Kang Mei, 64, 181, 219, 236
Chu, Goodwin C., 35, 110, 111, 115, 122, 377
Clark, James, 343
Cnudde, Charles, 45, 341
Coch, Lester, 143
Cohen, Bernard S., 16
Coleman, James, 69, 193, 236, 347, 358
Corredor, Berta, 78
Cortes, Juan B., 246
Coutu, Walter, 196
Crutchfield, Richard S., 364
Cutright, Phillips, 8, 9, 69

Dahl, Robert A., 188
Dalton, George, 189
Dart, Frances E., 191
Davies, James C., 12, 158
Davis, James A., 158
Davison, W. Phillips, 97, 111
De Jesus, C. M., 26
Dean, Dwight G., 378
Deutschmann, Paul J., 5, 6, 29, 56, 69, 81, 84, 87, 97, 102, 103, 104, 105, 109, 111, 129, 159, 173, 294, 302, 316, 318, 319, 320, 322, 324, 327, 348, 349, 357
DeYoung, John F., 74, 76
Dobriner, William M., 158, 159
Dodd, Stuart C., 372
Donohew, Lewis, 39, 150, 323, 325, 329, 331, 333, 341

409

SUBJECT INDEX

Acceptance, 273, 277
Achievement motivation, 2, 50, 54, 55, 66, 171, 177, 242–272.
  age, 269
  among peasants, 243–244
  antecedents, 248, 253–257, 262
  aspirations, 248, 256, 257, 263, 266, 269
  birth order, 248, 254, 255, 262, 263, 266
  change agent contact, 178, 180, 248, 256, 263, 266, 269
  consequences, 248, 257–261, 262, 268, 270
  cosmopoliteness, 151, 154, 157, 161, 162 163, 165, 168, 248, 263, 264, 265, 266, 269
  cross-cultural consistency of findings, 267–272
  definition, 34, 54, 243, 265
  education, 79, 248, 256, 257, 263, 264, 265, 266
  empathy, 204, 207, 211–212, 214, 248, 256, 257, 262, 263, 264, 265, 266, 267, 269
  farm production, 248, 259, 260–261, 263, 266, 270
  farm size, 248, 258–260, 262, 263, 266, 270
  fatalism, 256–257, 266, 283, 285, 287, 288, 289, 290
  father absence, 266
  innovativeness, 248, 258, 259, 263, 266, 270, 292, 297, 298, 299, 315
  land tenure, 248, 259, 260, 263, 266
  level of living, 248, 259, 261, 263, 266, 270
  literacy, 85, 86, 87, 248, 256, 257, 262, 263, 264, 265, 266, 269
  mass media exposure, 102, 111, 112, 119, 121, 248, 256, 263, 264, 265, 266, 269
  measures of, 54, 245, 249, 250, 251, 267
  modernization, 247–249, 256–258, 316, 330
  needed research, 271–272
  occupational, 54
  opinion leadership, 227, 228, 240
  in other cultures, 267
  patriarchalism, 248

  political knowledgeability, 256, 263, 266, 269
  social status, 248, 259, 261, 262, 263, 265, 266
Adopter categories, 295–296, 314–315
  characteristics of, 297–300
  early adopters, 132, 295, 296, 297, 298, 314
  early majority, 132, 295, 296, 297, 298, 314
  innovators, 132, 133, 188, 291, 295, 296, 297, 298, 314, 315
  laggards, 295, 296, 297, 298, 314, 315
  late majority, 132, 295, 296, 297, 298, 314
  nonadopters, 132
Adopter categorization, 294–296
Adoption, 5, 56, 86, 144, 170, 277
Age, 237
  achievement motivation, 269
  as an intervening variable, 206, 207, 208, 210, 211, 212, 214
  change agent, 177
  empathy, 206, 207, 208, 210
  innovativeness, 302, 303
  mass media exposure, 101, 102, 107, 119, 120
  opinion leadership, 227–229
Aggregate level of analysis, 81
Aggregate research, 319–323
  criticism of, 322–323
  on development, 319–323
Alliance for Progress, 13
Animation, 231
Antecedent variables, 49, 50, 51, 52, 59, 66
  definition, 49
Apathy, 274, 275, 279, 289
Arbitrary time-order, 59, 60, 66
Aspiration, 12, 36, 50, 54, 55, 66, 115, 171, 177
  achievement motivation, 248, 255, 256, 257, 263, 266, 269
  change agent contact, 180
  cosmopoliteness, 151, 156, 161, 162, 163, 165, 168
  definition, 33
  educational, 54, 79
  empathy, 204, 207, 213, 214, 215

415

Heterogeneity, 145
Heterophily, 182, 202, 233, 234, 235, 236, 237, 241, 364
  heterophily gap, 182
  in data gathering, 364
  technical competence, 237
Homogeneity, 144, 233
Homophily, 177, 178, 181–183, 193, 198, 211, 233–238, 241, 349
  as a barrier to communication, 235–236
  in change agent-client relationship, 181–183
  communication flow, 233–238
  definition, 181, 233
  determinants of, 237
  in dyads, 236
  in traditional and modern villages, 237, 238
Homophily index, 238
Horizontal empathy, 201
Hostility toward government authority, 25, 29, 30, 40
Hypotheses, 46–48, 366
  empirical, 47, 48, 67
  middle range, 47
  theoretic, 46, 47, 48, 67
"Hypodermic needle" model of mass communication, 126, 221

Illiteracy, 68
  functionally illiterate, 68
Illiterates, 71, 72, 75, 78, 84, 104, 105, 116, 139, 282
  in media forums, 142
Immanent change, 5, 6, 7, 17
  definition, 5
Inconspicuous consumption, 34–35
Indebtedness
  change agent contact, 178
  innovativeness, 307
Independent variables, 58
Individual as unit of analysis, 81
Individualism, 30, 157
Induction, 47, 67
Industrialization, 10, 321, 377
Inference theory, 196
Influence, 169, 221
  definition, 170
Informal leadership, 220
Information flow, 223
Information-seeking, 156, 168, 181
  innovativeness, 303
Information spread, 126, 135
Innovation decision process, 128, 129, 132, 145, 193
  awareness stage, 128, 131, 132, 170, 222
  communication channel usage, 129, 132, 133
  influence of change agent, 169, 170

interest stage, 132, 218
persuasion stage, 128, 132, 222
trial stage, 128, 131, 132
Innovation diffusion patterns, 240
Innovations, 15, 50, 52, 61, 64, 86, 135, 140, 171, 191, 202, 222, 277, 347, 348, 350
  saliency, 222
Innovative leadership orientation, 328, 332, 333, 334, 338, 340
  change agent contact, 332, 333
  formal participation, 332, 333
  innovativeness, 332, 333
  opinion leadership, 332, 333
Innovativeness, 2, 50, 52, 55, 56, 64, 66, 69, 115, 177, 237, 238, 290–315
  achievement motivation, 248, 258, 259, 263, 266, 270, 292, 297, 298, 299, 315
  age, 302, 303
  agricultural, 56, 85, 294, 304–305
  aspirations, 292, 297, 298, 299, 315
  change agent contact, 176, 177, 178, 179, 180, 193, 292, 297, 298, 299, 302, 303, 315
  consequences of, 314
  cosmopolite channel use, 133
  cosmopoliteness, 151, 157, 161, 162, 163, 165, 168, 292, 297, 298, 299, 302, 303, 306, 307, 308, 315
  debt, 306, 307
  definition, 56, 85, 294, 304–305
  differences in predicting home and agricultural, 306–307, 315
  economic factors, 312–313
  education, 79, 302, 303, 307
  empathy, 204, 207, 211, 214, 215, 218, 292, 297, 298, 299, 304, 305, 308, 315
  farm production, 305
  farm size, 297, 298, 299, 302, 303, 304, 305, 306, 307, 310, 315
  fatalism, 275, 276, 283, 284, 287, 288, 289, 290, 303
  formal participation, 302
  home, 56, 85, 294, 306–307, 329, 330
  knowledgeability, 302, 303, 306
  lack of, 25, 31–32
  level of living, 302
  literacy, 85, 86, 92, 113, 292, 297, 298, 299, 306, 315
  mass media exposure, 102, 109, 110, 111, 114, 116, 119, 121, 292, 297, 298, 299, 302, 308, 315
  magazine exposure, 305
  measuring, 294
  modernization, 291–292, 316, 324, 325, 329, 330, 332, 333, 339
  needed research, 312–314, 315
  opinion leadership, 227, 228, 229–231, 232, 240, 292, 297, 298, 299, 303, 304, 305, 306, 310